WORSHIP
SEEKING
UNDERSTANDING

WORSHIP
SEEKING
UNDERSTANDING

windows into christian practice

John D. Witvliet

 Baker Academic

A Division of Baker Book House Co
Grand Rapids, Michigan 49516

© 2003 by John D. Witvliet

Published by Baker Academic
a division of Baker Book House Company
P.O. Box 6287, Grand Rapids, MI 49516-6287
www.bakeracademic.com

Printed in the United States of America

Library of Congress Cataloging-in-Publication Data
Witvliet, John D.
     Worship seeking understanding : windows into Christian practice / John D.
     Witvliet.
        p. cm.
     Includes bibliographical references and index.
     ISBN 0-8010-2623-7 (pbk.)
     1. Worship. I. Title.
BV10.3.W58 2003
264—dc21   2002043795

Contents

15   How Common Worship Forms Us for Our Encounter
      with Death   291

       Other Worship-Related Writings by John D. Witvliet   309
       Index   311

Acknowledgments

My first thanks are owed to my chief liturgical mentors, my parents, John L. and Betty Witvliet. My dad, from the pulpit, and my mom, from the pew next to me, taught me much about the beauty and power of Christian worship. If this volume bears any fruit for God's kingdom, it is because they faithfully planted and watered the seeds of my young faith.

I am grateful to worshiping communities that have nourished and sustained our family at very different points along the way. In some congregations, such as the South Bend Christian Reformed Church (South Bend, Indiana), Neland Avenue Christian Reformed Church (Grand Rapids, Michigan), First Jenison Christian Reformed Church (Jenison, Michigan), I have had the privilege of leading worship and its music. I am grateful for the opportunities these congregations provided and for all I learned from many individual members. We owe particular thanks for the remarkable hospitality, encouragement, and support of the South Bend congregation during our graduate school years. Each week for the past several years, we have been grateful for the ministry in Word, sacrament, and acts of justice of the Church of the Servant Christian Reformed Church (Grand Rapids, Michigan). The opportunity to worship each week in this congregation has provided more spiritual nourishment than I can express.

I am very grateful to many colleagues at Calvin College and Calvin Theological Seminary for their collegial support and contributions to these essays, including those involved with the chapel program: Dale Cooper, Cindy de Jong, Steve Garber, Cherith Fee Nordling, Robert Nordling, Neal Plantinga, Ron Rienstra, and Sue Rozeboom; musical colleagues: Judy Czanko, David Fuentes, John Hamersma, Linda Hoisington, Merle Mustert, Joel Navarro, Charsie Sawyer, Pearl Shangkuan,

7

Calvin Stapert, and Dale Topp; and Worship Institute co-laborers: Joyce Borger, Emily Brink, Emily Cooper, Norma de Waal Malefyt, Kent De Young, Betty Grit, Cindy Holtrop, Ed Seely, Kathy Smith, Lisa Vander Molen, Howard Vanderwell, and Kristen Verhulst. Cindy Holtrop and Emily Cooper were particularly close collaborators during the completion of most of these essays.

I could easily list dozens of faculty members at Calvin College and Calvin Theological Seminary as indirect contributors to this volume. I am grateful to the following for specific conversations that directly informed essays presented here: Claudia Beversluis, John Bolt, Harry Boonstra, Carl Bosma, James Bratt, John Cooper, Robert De Vries, Rebecca De Young, David Diephouse, Charles Farhadian, Ronald Feenstra, Susan Felch, Duane Kelderman, Arie Leder, Henry Luttikhuizen, Karin Maag, Richard Muller, Ronald Nydam, Neal Plantinga, Debra Rienstra, David Rylaarsdam, Quentin Schultze, Howard Slenk, Laura Smit, Pieter Tuit, and Calvin Van Reken. I am very grateful for the strong administrative support of Robert Berkhof, Gaylen Byker, Joel Carpenter, Janel Curry-Roper, Henry De Vries, Steve Evans, Shirley Hoogstra, and Tom McWhertor to the work of both the chapel program and the Calvin Institute of Christian Worship, as well as of seminary administrators Gary Bekker, James De Jong, Henry De Moor, Duane Kelderman, and Neal Plantinga.

I also want to express heartfelt gratitude to Lilly Endowment Inc. and staff members Chris Coble, Craig Dykstra, and John Wimmer and to the Luce Foundation and program officer Michael Gilligan. Although this book is not a direct result of grant-funded programs or research, the relationships made possible by grants from these organizations have been enormously enriching and instructive.

I am very appreciative for the wisdom of several friends, colleagues, mentors, and collaborators in congregations, colleges, seminaries, and publishing companies in so many places. As I skimmed these essays again, so many individuals came to mind: Alison Adam, Anton Armstrong, Craig Barnes, Dorothy Bass, Robert Batastini, Tom Beaudoin, Carol Bechtel, Jeremy Begbie, John Bell, Roy Berkenbosch, Eleanor Bernstein, Barbara Boertje, Sandra Bowden, Horace Clarence Boyer, Paul Bradshaw, John Bright, Doug Brouwer, Wayne Brouwer, Timothy Brown, Philip Butin, Ron Byars, Jim Caccamo, Constance Cherry, Paul Colloton, Melva Costen, Jonathan Crutchfield, Carl Daw, Marva Dawn, Lisa De Boer, Paul Detterman, Michael Driscoll, Arlo Duba, Bill Dyrness, Randall Engle, Patricia Evans, Margot Fassler, Alfred Fedak, John Ferguson, Ted Gibboney, Justo Gonzalez, Fred Graham, Michael Hamilton, Sam Hamstra, Nathan Hatch, C. Michael Hawn, Margo Houts, Mary S. Hulst, Martin Jean, Robert Johnson, Todd Johnson, Trygve Johnson, James F. Kay, Helen Kemp, Barry Krammes, Charlotte

Kroeker, Robin Leaver, Jorge Lockward, Thomas G. Long, George Marsden, Martin Marty, Nathan Mitchell, Martha Moore-Keish, Sally Morgenthaler, Richard Mouw, John Paarlberg, Alvin Plantinga, Bert Polman, Jon Pott, Robb Redman, Jack Roeda, Anthony Ruff, Lester Ruth, Don Saliers, Greg Scheer, John Schuurman, Tom Schwanda, Joachim Segger, Bryan Spinks, Carl Stam, James Steel, John Sutton, Martin Tel, Karen Westerfield Tucker, Annetta Vander Lugt, Leonard Vander Zee, Leanne Van Dyk, John Van Engen, Amy Van Gunst, Lukas Vischer, Grant Wacker, Geoffrey Wainwright, Karen Ward, Robert Webber, Paul Westermeyer, James F. White, John Wilson, Nicholas Wolterstorff, Rodney Wynkoop, and Randall Zachman. Wisdom from each of them is scattered throughout the book.

I am grateful for the interest of Baker Academic in publishing these essays and, in particular, to editors Robert N. Hosack and Melinda Van Engen for their assistance in the publication process.

I offer particular thanks to several student research assistants who contributed to aspects of these essays, including Joyce Borger, Michael Borgert, Carrie Titcombe, and David Vroege. I owe a special word of thanks to Joyce Borger for extraordinary efforts to track down elusive citations and for her very perceptive comments on nearly every essay included here.

Most significantly, I offer loving thanks to my wife, Charlotte, for so many gifts in all aspects of life. She has both directly and indirectly honed many of the ideas presented here. Her patience and persistence made our graduate school years—during which most of these essays were begun—more of an adventure than a burden. Far more than that, our marriage has brought, in times of both grief and happiness, a deep and abiding solidarity and joy that leaves me with unspeakable gratitude.

Each previously published essay is printed with permission of the original publisher, with minor adaptations.

Chapter 1, "The Former Prophets and the Practice of Christian Worship," was published in *Calvin Theological Journal* 37 (2002): 82–94. This paper was developed for a conference on the Former Prophets held at Calvin Theological Seminary in the summer of 2000. I am grateful to Prof. Arie Leder for the invitation to participate in this event and for his helpful comments on this paper.

Chapter 2, "Praise and Lament in the Psalms and in Liturgical Prayer," was published in a simplified three-part version as "A Time to Weep (I): Liturgical Lament in Times of Crisis," *Reformed Worship* 44 (June 1997): 22–26; "A Time to Weep (II): Lament in Advent Worship," *Reformed Worship* 45 (September 1997): 22–25; "A Time to Weep (III): Lament in Lenten Worship," *Reformed Worship* 46 (December 1997):

11–13. This paper was originally delivered at a conference on praise and lament in the Christian life held at Calvin Theological Seminary in 1996. I am grateful to Prof. Carl Bosma for his encouragement to study these themes already in 1992, for his invitation to deliver this paper, and for his subsequent comments on this essay.

Chapter 3, "Covenant Theology in Ecumenical Discussions of the Lord's Supper," was published in *Worship* 71, no. 2 (March 1997): 98–123. I am grateful to Prof. Regis Duffy of the University of Notre Dame for his hospitality and encouragement. Our conversations about Calvin's eucharistic theology led to this study.

Chapter 4, "Theological Models for the Relationship between Liturgy and Culture," was published in *Liturgy Digest* 3, no. 2 (summer 1996): 5–46. I am grateful for the invitation of journal editor Nathan Mitchell to address this topic. My assignment was to introduce a wide variety of readers, especially those involved in the University of Notre Dame's Center for Pastoral Liturgy, to the range of scholarly approaches to questions of worship and culture.

Chapter 5, "Images and Themes in John Calvin's Theology of Liturgy," was published in *The Legacy of John Calvin: Calvin Studies Society Papers 1999*, ed. David Foxgrover (Grand Rapids: Calvin Studies Society, 2000), 130–52. I am grateful to the Calvin Studies Society for the invitation to address this topic, to Ward Holder for his thoughtful response to the paper, and to Randall Zachman for early conversations about several themes in this paper.

Chapter 6, "Baptism as a Sacrament of Reconciliation in the Thought of John Calvin," was published in *Studia Liturgica* 27, no. 2 (1997): 152–65. This paper was first presented in a doctoral seminar on the history of rites of reconciliation taught by Prof. Michael Driscoll at the University of Notre Dame. I am grateful to him for his encouragement and critique.

Chapter 7, "The Americanization of Reformed Worship," was published as "What Has America Contributed to Reformed Worship?" *Reformed Liturgy & Music* 30, no. 3 (1996): 103–11. I am grateful to editor Dennis Hughes for the invitation to address this topic and for early conversations with George Marsden and Nathan Hatch about the scope of and approach to the topic.

Chapter 8 was previously unpublished. I am grateful to Prof. James F. White of the University of Notre Dame for his insights at several points in the development of this paper and to Lester Ruth for his insights into worship practices in nineteenth-century America.

Chapter 9, "The Spirituality of the Psalter in Calvin's Geneva," was published in *Calvin Theological Journal* 32 (1997): 273–97. It was presented as an invited lecture to the Calvin Studies Society at their 1995 meeting. Since its first appearance, this essay has also been reprinted two other times: in *Calvin Studies Society Papers, 1995, 1997*, ed. David Foxgrover (Grand Rapids: Calvin Studies Society/CRC Product Services, 1998), 93–117; and in the Japanese publication *Musica Ecclesiae Reformatae* 3 (2000): 25–63.

Chapter 10, "Soul Food for the People of God," was published in *Liturgical Ministry* 10 (spring 2001): 101–10. It was first delivered at a national worship conference sponsored by the Evangelical Lutheran Church in America. Since its first appearance, this essay has been reprinted as "We Are What We Sing," *Reformed Worship* 60 (June 2001): 4–9; and "Soul Food for the People of God: Ritual Song, Spiritual Nourishment, and the Communal Worship of God," in *Lifting Up Jesus Christ: Yesterday, Today, and Forever. Proceedings of the Worship 2000 Jubilee*, ed. Robert Buckley Farlee (Minneapolis: Augsburg Fortress, 2001), 85–97.

Chapter 11, "The Blessing and Bane of the North American Evangelical Megachurch," was published in *IAH Bulletin* (*Internationalen Arbeitsgemeinschaft für Hymnologie*) 26 (July 1998): 133–56. This paper was delivered at the Joint International Conference of the Hymn Society in the United States and Canada, the Hymn Society of Ireland and Great Britain, and the International Society of Hymnological Research held at York, England. It was a particularly challenging and instructive task to introduce conference participants to the music of North American megachurches in the shadows of York Minster. I am grateful for the encouragement of Carl P. Daw Jr., executive director of the Hymn Society in the United States and Canada, for all his work to promote excellent hymnody in North America. Since its first appearance, this essay has been reprinted in *The Hymn* 50 (January 1999): 6–12; *Jahrbuch für Liturgik und Hymnologie* 37 (Göttingen: Vandenhoeck & Ruprecht, 1998), 196–213; and *The American Organist* 34, no. 5 (May 2000): 50–56.

Chapter 12, "Making Good Choices in an Era of Liturgical Change," was published in *Reformation and Revival* 9, no. 2 (spring 2000): 15–28. Some of this material was originally developed for a spring 1999 article in *Christian Courier* and further developed for a public lecture at Regent College in Vancouver, British Columbia, in the spring of 2000.

Chapter 13, "Planning and Leading Worship as a Pastoral Task," was published in *Reformed Worship* 49 (September 1998): 30–33. It was first presented at the opening session of the 1998 Calvin Symposium on Worship and the Arts. I am grateful to editor Emily R. Brink for her encouragement and support.

Chapter 14, "Celebrating the Christian Passover in Easter Worship," was published in *The Banner* (25 March 2002): 16–18. I am grateful to editor John Suk for the invitation to address this topic for *The Banner*'s annual Easter issue.

Chapter 15, "How Common Worship Forms Us for Our Encounter with Death," was written for a colloquium sponsored by the Valparaiso Center for the Education and Formation of People in Faith led by Dorothy Bass and Thomas G. Long. I am especially grateful to each of them and other seminar participants for collegial support and for their comments on earlier drafts of this paper.

Introduction

Worship Seeking Understanding

Before you is a collection of fifteen essays on the practice of Christian worship. At first glance, this may seem like an unlikely collection. As you drop in at various points along the way, you may find references to both aesthetic theory and popular music, both metrical psalm singing and enthusiastic revivalism, both sacramental theology and funerals. You may discover some paragraphs that aptly describe your church on a Sunday morning and others that seem so far afield that you may wonder if they have anything to do with your Sunday churchgoing. These juxtapositions are exactly the point of this collection, for these essays, taken together, attempt to build bridges in three directions at the same time: between theory and practice, between one worship-related discipline and another, and between one Christian tradition and another. As challenging as building these bridges might be, I am convinced that the most fruitful avenue to worship renewal involves all three.

Bridging Theory and Practice

Anselm, one of the most profound medieval theologians, gave us the phrase that underlies this book's title: *fides quaerens intellectum* ("faith seeking understanding"). This single phrase both calls theology to be grounded in faith and pushes faith toward deeper theological reflection. Correspondingly, it critiques both theology that functions as merely an intellectual exercise and faith that refuses intellectual engagement. Anselm calls us to an ever growing faith that dares to probe the deep mysteries of the gospel we proclaim.

This collection of essays is motivated by Anselm's agenda. My goal is not to explain away the experience of worship or dissect and kill it by esoteric scholarly analysis but rather to honor and cherish it by asking the questions worship itself prompts. Each of these essays arises quite naturally from the experience of worship, from questions that arise either implicitly or explicitly for all kinds of Christian worship leaders and worshipers: What exactly are we doing in worship and why? How can we account for worship's power? How does Scripture inform our worship? What historical resources can inform our approach to present challenges and controversies? How can worship be a source for pastoral ministry in a hurting and suffering world? What do our worship practices imply about the kind of God we worship?

Each of these essays is an occasional essay, written in response to an invitation to address an audience about a particular topic. In each case, the invitation was generated by a group of Christian worshipers asking questions about their practice of worship. In each case, my approach to these questions is framed in terms of questions I have found myself asking. Though I cannot attest to the level of wisdom found here, my sense is that this kind of mutual question asking within the body of Christ may be one of the best ways that we share wisdom and gain new understanding. I have certainly learned a great deal from the occasions that gave birth to these essays.

At the same time that these essays probe questions that arise out of worship, they also address some uneasiness with worship as it is practiced in many congregations. They attempt not only to understand worship but also to nourish and deepen it. To borrow from an image used later in the book, often our worship consists of thin gruel, even while the Christian Scriptures and tradition offer us rich consommé. My deepest hope is that this work will not only articulate questions about worship but will also enrich the practice of worship in congregations today. Part of this practical enrichment (which I have begun to address in other places) needs to happen through practical advice for worship planners and leaders. But part of that can happen through renewed reflection on the history, theology, and practice of worship in many times and places. That is the part these essays are designed to provide.

Of course, the deepest experiences of worship are fundamentally inexhaustible. There is no comprehensive theory or set of categories or questions that analyzes or comprehends worship entirely. For this reason, in some ways, a collection of limited, illustrative essays is even more suitable to the topic than a single exhaustive treatise. Consider these essays as provisional studies, like sketches in an artist's sketchbook. They are windows into several practices. If they succeed, perhaps they will serve to invite readers to enter the rooms into which they give a view.

On the one hand, this book represents a luxury—in both senses of the word. First, such academic study of worship is not a necessity for Christians to worship well. I do not want to give the impression that one must read all the kinds of books mentioned here in order to be a thoughtful Christian worshiper. Praise God that we do not need to understand the intricacies of worship in order to worship! That rather Gnostic notion is not my intent at all. I am also painfully aware that the vast majority of Christian communities worldwide do not have the resources to make possible this kind of practice-based academic study. At the same time, just as knowledge of the rules of football, basketball, baseball, or hockey contributes immeasurably to our enjoyment of the game, so too, an understanding of the biblical roots, theological implications, and historical patterns of worship can immeasurably deepen our faith and practice of worship. This book is also a luxury in the sense that it has afforded me an opportunity to explore such extravagant and deeply rewarding resources. What an amazing privilege it is to open up the treasure chest of Scripture and to probe both the riches and the idiosyncrasies of the Christian tradition! The academic life is a luxury indeed, in part because of all the marvelous companions, both dead and alive, we find along the way.

On the other hand, the kind of sustained reflection that this book represents is becoming more and more of a necessity in our time. Periods of significant liturgical change—and ours is certainly that—call those of us in leadership positions to reflect carefully on our place in history and culture. We desperately need new ways to frame and understand our persistent little worship wars. Unfortunately, some of the most significant paradigmatic changes in worship in our time have come with little awareness that Scripture or history has much to teach us. My own instincts tell me that when we become too glibly optimistic or too sourly pessimistic about a given worship reform proposal, we often are in danger of losing our spiritual equilibrium. Our optimistic prescriptions are often blind to the idiosyncrasies of our culture. Our pessimistic assessments often forget that the church is not ours but Christ's. Perhaps this book in a small way can help us recover our sense of equilibrium as we sort out the wheat from the chaff in recent efforts at worship renewal.

This book, then, spans a bridge between theory and practice. These essays represent the scholarly side of my work. However, most of my time, like that of many of my colleagues in worship-related disciplines, is spent negotiating the challenges of the practice of worship, answering questions such as "How do we help congregations that are dividing over debates about worship style?" "What kind of habits should our church be cultivating in the area of worship?" "Why is the church so opposed to visual arts?" and "How can we help children participate in worship more fully?" I cannot stress enough how important these practical questions are. I also must add that this book will not answer them directly. The goal of this book is rather to sketch some broad parameters so we can finally gain a vantage point from which to think about these questions profitably.

Bridging Disciplinary Conversations

The second purpose of the book is to encourage interdisciplinary discussions about the practice of worship. The more I work in the area of worship, the more I am convinced that we need to ask several different questions about worship at the same time. Musicians, missionaries, historians, artists, and pastors all come to the topic of worship with particular concerns and goals. In my work on a busy college and seminary campus, and in an office that works with many congregations, publishers, and denominations, I am constantly surprised by the existence of so many well-developed but largely independent conversations about worship practices. The summer season, for example, offers a dizzying array of conferences on preaching, seeker-driven worship, organ music, choral music, technology, liturgical history, and visual arts—and each of these in many denominations and ethnic and cultural subgroups. Many people who devote their entire lives to the practice of leading or studying worship never have the opportunity to cross the boundaries of these conversations or even to learn of their existence.

This book, then, attempts to chart a few of the boundary crossings in these conversations by publishing side-by-side essays prepared for audiences of biblical scholars, liturgical historians, musicians, and lay worship leaders, among others (readers will sense this as the audience indicators in various essays shift from "those of us scholars" to "those of us musicians" to "those of us who lead worship"). Still, there are many disciplinary boundaries I have not been able to cross here. Readers will hear little from missiology, architecture, drama, communication theory, dance, aesthetics, poetics, cultural anthropology, or ritual studies. I have dabbled in a few of these areas but judge that most of these disciplines lie too far beyond my expertise. I also regret that some of my strongest areas of interest—trinitarian theology of worship, cross-cultural expressions of worship, church architecture, models of congregational leadership, and children's participation in worship—are not reflected here. These will need to wait for another day.

Nevertheless, this book contains five modest sets of studies that cluster somewhat naturally in five disciplines. *Biblical studies* in the area of worship are necessary and relatively few in number. Most Christian traditions would affirm that Scripture informs, grounds, or regulates worship in some way. Yet the connections between biblical texts and the practice of worship are not always aptly made. A text such as John 4:24 often ends up as the great Rorschach of worship studies. We quote it in favor of whatever position we are advancing. The two essays presented here—both coincidentally on the Old Testament—are designed to look beyond single texts to the broad patterns of scriptural teaching for insights about contemporary practice.

Theological studies challenge us to sense how worship both shapes and reflects the theological imagination of a given community. Worship and doctrine are inextricably intertwined. Common worship is the locus where the church's distinctive vocabulary, narratives, and rituals are developed and enacted. Liturgy, as much as any other dimension of the church's life, writes the "lived theology" of the Christian community—that is, the theological vision that most believers live by, whether or not that vision matches that of official creeds, confessions, and classic texts. The two essays involving theological study look both inward to the life of the church as a covenant community and outward to the church's relationship with culture.

Historical studies challenge us to repent of what C. S. Lewis once called "chronological snobbery." The more my students and I study liturgical history, the more penitential we are inclined to become as we realize how far short our practice often falls! The history of worship constantly challenges us to remember the remarkable and faithful lives of our many spiritual mothers and fathers. At the same time, it is tempting to use liturgical history as propaganda. Often, we go to historical texts with our minds made up about what we prefer. Then we search for precedents to bolster our case. Honest history reminds us of both heroic faithfulness and human foibles. Essays here focus on the sixteenth and nineteenth centuries, two periods that continue to exert profound influence on Protestant worship today.

Musical studies focus on one of the most inspiring and vexing aspects of worship. Many of us who devote our lives to enriching Christian worship do this because we were transformed at one or more points along the way by the Spirit-charged power of music to express our prayer and proclaim the gospel. Music, however, is a mysterious and elusive art. Augustine, for example, worried that the same transcendent beauty of music that inspired his praise might also be a huge distraction from worship's deepest purpose. This worry is only intensified in an era in which music is not only an art but also a commodity. The essays in this section are designed to describe and analyze the practice of music, both in Calvin's Geneva and in contemporary North

American evangelical megachurches, and also to prescribe new ways of thinking about our practice of music.

Pastoral studies focus on the kinds of questions that face typical pastors and worship leaders in congregations. Here the focus is not so much on heavily footnoted historical or theological arguments as it is on framing issues in ways that are instructive for conversations in local congregations. These essays describe the virtues needed for worship planners in local congregations (consider studying these essays at your next congregational worship committee meeting) and offer new ways of approaching our worship on certain occasions such as funerals or Christian year celebrations such as Easter.

While I have divided the essays into these five categories, readers will likely discover that some essays could have appeared in more than one section. Chapter 3, for example, offers a description of covenant theology that includes sections of both biblical theology and historical analysis. The study of Calvin's theology of liturgy is historical and yet aims at a constructive theological argument. The analysis of Genevan psalmody is both historical and musical. This methodological ambiguity is actually my final goal. Ultimately, I am working toward discussions that intertwine scriptural, historical, theological, and pastoral questions. When we are confronted with difficult questions in the life of the church, our goal should be to approach them with imaginations formed by each of these disciplines. This also explains why some material—including references to covenant theology, Alexis de Toqueville, and criticisms of sacramental and individualistic approaches to liturgical music—appears in more than one essay here. (Perceptive readers who discover these repetitions should win a gold medal for perseverance!)

The essays in the first four sections are rather heavily laden with footnotes. I have chosen not to trim these notes in order to provide a bibliographic roadmap for further study, primarily because of the interest of several students.

Bridging Christian Traditions

I also dare to hope that this book contributes to new understanding in different parts of the body of Christ. For much of the past century, worship renewal has been one of the richest fruits of various ecumenical conversations and movements. Personally, I will never forget the joy of studying worship with Baptist, Lutheran, Anglican, Methodist, Presbyterian, Roman Catholic, and Orthodox students under the guidance of Roman Catholic, Orthodox, Methodist, and Anglican professors at the University of Notre Dame, or teaching Pentecostal, Lutheran, Methodist, Reformed, Presbyterian, Congregational, nondenominational, and Roman Catholic students in various courses, conferences, and seminars.

These experiences make me eager to engage a wide ecumenical audience. These essays were first presented—either in oral or written form—to Baptist, Roman Catholic, Episcopal, Presbyterian, Lutheran, and independent evangelical audiences. For example, chapter 3, on covenantal eucharistic theology, was first prepared for a largely Roman Catholic audience and cites a number of Roman Catholic historians and theologians. In this area, as in so many others, our most profitable ecumenical work arises when we work together to recover central scriptural images and themes. I am grateful for each opportunity to learn from and speak to other parts of the body of Christ.

Ecumenical conversations need not, however, soften the unique accent that we all speak as representatives of particular Christian traditions. I write out of the Reformed/Presbyterian tradition. I am a member of the Christian Reformed Church, a small denomination with roots in the Dutch Reformed tradition. I cherish the Reformed tradition and every day grow in appreciation for its strengths and awareness of its limitations. The number of references to Calvin and covenant theology in this volume will leave little doubt about my interest in traditional Reformed theology—though at some points this work attempts to approach these topics in new ways. Overall, I hope that my contribution is judged to be simultaneously orthodox, catholic, evangelical, and confessionally Reformed.

If I had one specific hope for the reception of this work, it would be to encourage deeper reflection on worship among both the Reformed/Presbyterian and more broadly evangelical communities—two of the under-represented parts of the body of Christ at any meeting of the North American Academy of Liturgy. I have thoroughly enjoyed teaching primarily evangelical students at Tyndale Seminary, Northern Baptist Seminary, and Regent College and primarily Reformed students at Calvin College and Calvin Theological Seminary. I am heartened by the serious interest that many of them have in pursuing advanced liturgical studies.

Finally, I want to clearly assert that worship renewal can never be engineered by any scholar, book, institute, or movement. Worship renewal is a gift of God's Spirit, which blows freely throughout time and space. To borrow from my colleague, perhaps, by God's grace, courses and conferences and institutes and even books such as this one can help us raise our little sails so that we are ready to catch the wind of God's Spirit and sail with joy the course set before us. I offer this book with the prayer that God may choose to use it to that effect.

Biblical Studies

1

The Former Prophets
and the Practice
of Christian Worship

Although the Former Prophets[1] contain extended descriptions of exemplary and nonexemplary liturgical events, noteworthy examples of specific liturgical acts (sermons, canticles, and prayers), and descriptions of the work of liturgical leaders (Levites, prophets, priests, judges, and musicians), relatively little work has probed how these books might either function in our worship services today or help us to better understand and articulate the deep meaning and purpose of worship. For the most part, contemporary worship specialists are busy sorting out recent innovations in worship practices. When liturgical theologians probe the connections between the Bible and worship, the Former Prophets are not the first place they look. Biblical theologians, busy honing skills in one form of criticism or another, often have limited time to draw out the implications of their work for the practices of the Christian community—and then only rarely for the practice of worship.

There are, of course, extremely helpful and encyclopedic descriptions of the worship and liturgical practices of ancient Israel, including classic works by Hans Joachim Kraus, H. H. Rowley, Roland de

1. Although they do not belong to the Former Prophets, at times I will refer to Chronicles, Ezra, Nehemiah, and Esther.

Vaux, and a more recent survey by Patrick D. Miller.[2] These works are complemented by focused, highly detailed, comparative historical studies of aspects of worship treated in the Former Prophets.[3] Most of these works are confined to straightforward historical description and, occasionally, historical speculation. Alongside these are a number of outstanding works of form, source, and literary criticism that treat texts with explicitly liturgical themes and implications.[4] These works helpfully amass voluminous canonical and extracanonical sources and provide historical and rhetorical resources for more savvy handling of a given text. Yet few, if any, of these books attempt to address the link between these ancient sources and either our understanding or our practice of worship today.

Still, some biblical theologians have probed connections between Old Testament narratives and either contemporary Christian thought or practice. Walter Brueggemann's *Israel's Praise* and Samuel E. Balentine's *The Torah's Vision of Worship* come to mind, among others.[5] Rarely, however, is any of this work dedicated to the Former Prophets, a mostly neglected part of the Old Testament.

Similarly, an exhaustive study of liturgical scholarship reveals little, if any, work on the Former Prophets. The top one hundred books on

2. A. S. Herbert, *Worship in Ancient Israel* (Richmond: John Knox, 1959); William Brown, *The Tabernacle: Its Priests and Services* (Peabody, Mass.: Hendrickson, 1996); Alfred Edersheim, *The Temple: Its Ministry and Services* (Peabody, Mass.: Hendrickson, 1994); Menahem Haran, *Temples and Temple Service in Ancient Israel* (Winona Lake, Ind.: Eisenbrauns, 1985); Roland de Vaux, *Ancient Israel: Its Life and Institutions* (Grand Rapids: Eerdmans, 1997); Patrick D. Miller, *The Religion of Ancient Israel* (Louisville: Westminister John Knox, 2000); B. A. Levine, *In the Presence of the Lord: A Study of Cult and Some Cultic Terms in Ancient Israel*, Studies in Judaism in Late Antiquity, vol. 5 (Leiden: Brill, 1974); G. A. Anderson, *Sacrifices and Offerings in Ancient Israel: Studies in Their Social and Political Importance* (Atlanta: Scholars Press, 1987); H. H. Rowley, *Worship in Ancient Israel: Its Forms and Meaning* (London: SPCK, 1967); Hans Joachim Kraus, *Worship in Israel: A Cultic History of the Old Testament* (Richmond: John Knox, 1966). The discussion of the Former Prophets as part of the Deuteronomistic history includes study of the liturgical, but in the restricted sense that the Deuteronomist is interested in deviation from the normative liturgy as prescribed by law. See Martin Noth, *The Deuteronomistic History*, Journal for the Study of the Old Testament Supplement Series 15 (Sheffield, U.K.: JSOT Press, 1981), 92.

3. John W. Kleinig, *The Lord's Song: The Basis, Function, and Significance of Choral Music in Chronicles* (Sheffield, U.K.: JSOT Press, 1993).

4. Saul M. Olyan, *Rites and Rank: Hierarchy in Biblical Representations of Cult* (Princeton, N.J.: Princeton University Press, 2000).

5. Walter Brueggemann, *Israel's Praise: Doxology against Idolatry and Ideology* (Philadelphia: Fortress, 1988); idem, *The Psalms and the Life of Faith*, ed. Patrick Miller (Minneapolis: Fortress, 1995); Robert Davidson, *Wisdom and Worship* (Philadelphia: Trinity Press International, 1990); Samuel E. Balentine, *The Torah's Vision of Worship* (Minneapolis: Fortress, 1999); Stephen Breck Reid, ed., *Psalms and Practice: Worship, Virtue, and Authority* (Collegeville, Minn.: Liturgical Press, 2001); Andrew E. Hill, *Enter*

the history, theology, and practice of Christian worship cite two paragraphs in the first-century church order *Didache* roughly one hundred times more frequently than any text in the hundreds of pages of the Former Prophets. There are a number of studies of ancient and recent lectionaries that investigate why certain texts are or are not included in official lectionaries, although here also only modest attention is given to texts from the Former Prophets.[6]

In sum, drawing connections between the Former Prophets and the practice of worship is largely uncharted territory. This modest chapter is designed to begin to make these connections. It outlines three broad themes that arise directly out of the pages of the Former Prophets and that have immediate significance for both the theology and the practice of Christian worship.

Worship as a Spiritual Barometer

First, the Former Prophets demonstrate the significance of liturgical action as a barometer of corporate spiritual health. Liturgical events (including at minimum all circumcision, sacrifice, Passover, and covenant-renewal rites) punctuate the Former Prophets at regular intervals. Nearly every one is presented as exemplary or nonexemplary of faithful response to the covenant Overlord. As diverse as the writers of these texts might be, none of them describes liturgical events neutrally.

On the good side, every time there is a revival or sign of spiritual health in Israel, out come the liturgists—even in the books that lack the liturgical orientation of Chronicles. After crossing the Jordan, Israel submits to a second circumcision and celebrates the Passover (Joshua 5). A few chapters later, after the Achan and Ai debacle, the people renew the covenant in accordance with God's instructions (Joshua 8; cf. Deut. 27:4, 12). In the Samuel narratives, spiritual health is affirmed in the life of Hannah and her temple prayers (1 Samuel 1); in Samuel's liturgical service, both as a boy (1 Samuel 2) and a mature

---

His Courts with Praise! Old Testament Worship for the New Testament Church (Grand Rapids: Baker, 1993); and David Peterson, *Engaging with God: A Biblical Theology of Worship* (Grand Rapids: Eerdmans, 1992). For a discussion of the leadership of the priesthood that occasionally addresses matters from the Former Prophets, see Rodney R. Hutton, "The Priest: Charisma by the Book," in *Charisma and Authority in Israelite Society* (Minneapolis: Fortress, 1994), 138–71.

6. See, for example, Fritz West, *Scripture and Memory: The Ecumenical Hermeneutic of the Three-Year Lectionaries* (Collegeville, Minn.: Liturgical Press, 1997); William Skudlarek, *The Word in Worship: Preaching in a Liturgical Context* (Nashville: Abingdon, 1981); Normand Bonneau, *The Sunday Lectionary: Ritual Word, Paschal Shape* (Collegeville, Minn.: Liturgical Press, 1998); and Peter C. Bower, ed., *Handbook for the Revised Common Lectionary* (Louisville: John Knox, 1996).

leader (as in the anointing of David in 1 Samuel 16); and in the prayers of David (2 Samuel 1, 22, 23). In the Kings sequence, the spiritual high points are marked by renewed liturgical activity: the consecration of the temple (1 Kings 5–8) and its subsequent restoration by Joash (2 Kings 12) and Josiah (2 Kings 23), as well as the purging of liturgical impurity, such as Jehu's massacre of Baal worshipers (2 Kings 10). Ezra features the rebuilding of the altar and the temple (chap. 3) and a liturgical confession of sin (chaps. 9–10). Nehemiah opens with a prayer (chap. 1) and culminates with a covenant-renewal liturgy (chaps. 8–10) and the dedication of the wall of Jerusalem (chap. 12). Esther culminates in the celebration of Purim, a feast in commemoration of the deliverance from Haman's plot to destroy the Jews.

On the bad side, nearly every time there is a spiritual, political, or moral decline, liturgical activity suffers. Judges 2:10–19 describes Israel's worship of other gods throughout the generations; Judges 17 reveals the entrepreneurial religion that characterized the days when Israel had no king. Samuel opens with references to an insensitive and abusive priesthood (1 Samuel 2:12–26 [a comparison of Eli's sons with Samuel]), features Saul's disobedience to God's explicit commands about sacrifice (1 Samuel 13), and describes Saul's superstition when consulting a medium (1 Samuel 28). Several texts chart the hypocrisy of worshiping both Yahweh and other gods (e.g., 1 Kings 18:21; 2 Kings 12:3). The Former Prophets thus provide repeated examples of the entire catalog of liturgical sins: disobedience, idolatry, superstition, and hypocrisy.[7]

In sum, when Israel is faithless, its worship is degenerate. When Israel is faithful, that faithfulness is expressed in corporate prayer and praise before God's face. Of course, it may be a mere truism to assert that liturgy is one reliable (though not exclusive or completely sufficient) barometer of spiritual health. It is a foundational insight into the nature of life before God. It is also perhaps nowhere more clearly seen in Scripture than in the Former Prophets, who insist that Israel was driven from God's presence, in part, for its Canaanite revisioning of covenant worship (2 Kings 17:7–20; 2 Kings 23:26–27 in connection with 2 Kings 21:1–18).

Covenant Renewal as a Primary Image for Christian Worship

Second, the Former Prophets describe liturgical events that stand in broad continuity with Christian liturgy. Of course, the vast majority of Israel's liturgical practices are not a part of Christian practice. Animal

---

7. See chapter 5, "Images and Themes in John Calvin's Theology of Liturgy," where I explore Calvin's nuanced understanding of this catalog of liturgical sins.

sacrifices are not common in today's worship—to the profound satisfaction of most church architects and janitors. The design of the temple is not a blueprint for current Christian worship spaces (though it is instructive for the categories and criteria that guide our thinking about liturgical space).[8] Today's musical styles often bear little resemblance to ancient practice. The exception to the overwhelming pattern of discontinuity is the liturgy of covenant renewal,[9] a primary image or metaphor for Christian worship. The Former Prophets provide nearly all the accounts we have of covenant-renewal ceremonies. In fact, the liturgical renewal of the covenant runs like a *Leitmotif* right through the Former Prophets and other historical narratives (Joshua 8, 24; 2 Kings 23; 2 Chronicles 15, 34–35; Nehemiah 9–10; see also Deut. 31:10–13).

The significance of this liturgical act is grounded in the relative importance and centrality of covenant language in describing the divine-human relationship in the Old Testament. Despite the temptation for some Christian traditions to overstate its significance, the covenant is a central biblical image or metaphor for describing the relationship that God has established with Israel.[10] Brevard S. Childs concludes, "Regardless of the age and circumstances lying behind the Deuteronomic covenant formulation, its theology became the normative expression of God's relation to Israel and served as a major theological category for unifying the entire collection comprising the Hebrew scriptures."[11] George Mendenhall and Gary Herion, in their *Anchor Bible Dictionary* article, simply declare, "'Covenant' in the Bible is the major metaphor used to describe the relation between God and Israel (the people of God)."[12]

8. See Arie C. Leder, "Christian Worship in Consecrated Space and Time," *Calvin Theological Journal* 32 (1997): 253–72.

9. See Michael W. Duggan, *The Covenant Renewal in Ezra-Nehemiah (Neh. 7:72b–10:40): An Exegetical, Literary, and Theological Study* (Atlanta: Society of Biblical Literature, 2001).

10. Earlier studies that emphasize the centrality of covenant include Walter Eichrodt, *Theology of the Old Testament*, vol. 1 (London: SCM; Philadelphia: Westminster, 1961–67), 13–14; John Barton Payne, *The Theology of the Older Testament* (Grand Rapids: Zondervan, 1962); G. Ernest Wright, *The Old Testament and Theology* (New York: Harper & Row, 1969); and John Bright, *Covenant and Promise: The Prophetic Understanding of the Future in Pre-Exilic Israel* (Philadelphia: Westminster, 1976). For criticism and discussion, see John H. Hayes and Frederick Prussner, *Old Testament Theology: Its History and Development* (Atlanta: John Knox, 1985), 183–84, 257–59; Brevard S. Childs, *Biblical Theology of the Old and New Testaments* (Minneapolis: Fortress, 1992), 413–38; and John H. Stek, "'Covenant' Overload in Reformed Theology," *Calvin Theological Journal* 29 (1994): 12–41.

11. Childs, *Biblical Theology of the Old and New Testaments*, 419.

12. George E. Mendenhall and Gary A. Herion, "Covenant," in *The Anchor Bible Dictionary*, vol. 1 (New York: Doubleday, 1992), 1179. See also "Covenant and Canon as Context," which is part 2 of Brueggemann, *The Psalms and the Life of Faith*, 135–216.

In ancient Near Eastern culture, the covenant relationship was established and reaffirmed through ritual liturgical action, a ritual matrix described most thoroughly by Klaus Baltzer.[13] In the Old Testament, the people gathered when God established a covenant (Exodus 19–24), and Moses instructed them to gather every seven years so that all Israel, including the alien, might "listen and learn to fear the LORD your God and follow carefully all the words of this law. Their children, who do not know this law, must hear it and learn to fear the LORD your God" (Deut. 31:12–13). Once in the land, Israel gathered to reaffirm that covenant (e.g., Joshua 8, 24); after the exile, the people gathered under the direction of the priests to renew the covenant they had threatened with insistent faithlessness (Nehemiah 8–10, esp. 9:5–38).

Further, the Psalms frequently describe worship as an act of making vows to the Lord (e.g., "From you comes my praise in the great congregation; my vows I will pay before those who fear him" [Ps. 22:25 NRSV; see also 56:12; 66:13; 116:14])—language that clearly evokes the promise-based language of covenant life. Just as in the covenant of marriage a bride and groom speak their covenant vows in a public ritual to establish their relationship or a husband and wife reaffirm those promises in a public renewal of their marriage vows, so too the people of Israel gather in God's presence to reaffirm the covenant God established with them.[14]

Of all the covenant-renewal narratives, Joshua 24:1–27 has some of the most beautiful rhetoric and theological redolence.[15] This particular narrative emphasizes several aspects of Israel's covenant liturgy that stand in continuity with Christian practice: The assembly gathers self-consciously *coram Deo*, before the face of God, for a corporate action, with no mention of those who dissented or did not feel like making the vow (v. 1). The current covenantal vows are set in the context of the narrative of God's saving activity (vv. 2–13). Human speech is received by the gathered community as divine discourse (note the attribution of divine discourse in vv. 2–13).[16] A vow of fidelity to God is a resounding no against all false gods (vv. 14–15). The assembly is gath-

13. Klaus Baltzer, *The Covenant Formulary in Old Testament, Jewish, and Early Christian Writings*, trans. David Green (Philadelphia: Fortress, 1971). See also Paul Kalluveettil, *Declaration and Covenant: A Comprehensive Review of Covenant Formulae from the Old Testament and the Ancient Near East* (Rome: Biblical Institute Press, 1982).

14. Of course, the covenant between God and Israel is depicted as a covenant not between equals but between a Suzerain and a vassal.

15. William T. Koopmans, *Joshua 24 as Poetic Narrative* (Sheffield, U.K.: JSOT Press, 1990).

16. This is a paradigmatic scriptural example of the type of divine discourse analyzed extensively in Nicholas Wolterstorff, *Divine Discourse: Philosophical Reflections on the Claim That God Speaks* (Cambridge: Cambridge University Press, 1995).

ered not for the purpose of learning or even prayer but for making a vow to serve God (vv. 16–24).

The covenant language does not end with the advent of the New Testament age. Rather, Scripture challenges us to see that in Christ, God has extended a new covenant promise to the church (Jer. 31:31–34; 2 Cor. 3:6; Hebrews 8–9). Recall all the places in which marriage is a metaphor or image to describe the church's relationship with God (Isa. 62:5; Jer. 2:2; Hosea 3:1; Rev. 19:7; 21:2, 9).

Just as the old covenant had liturgical renewal ceremonies, so too the new covenant is renewed through public celebrations of fidelity and commitment. The Lord's Supper is the paradigmatic and highest form of this liturgical renewal. Each of the New Testament accounts of the institution of the Lord's Supper explains its meaning in terms of covenant imagery. The Lukan and Pauline accounts speak of "the new covenant in my blood" (Luke 22:20; 1 Cor. 11:25), while the Matthean and Markan accounts refer to "my blood of the covenant" (Matt. 26:28; Mark 14:24).

In each epoch of church history, at least some key theologians and preachers have highlighted this theme. In the early church, John Chrysostom preached sermons that helped his congregation understand the Lord's Supper as new covenant renewal.[17] Klaus Baltzer, for example, in his analysis of the so-called Clementine liturgy in *Apostolic Constitutions VIII*, concluded that structurally it "can be termed a 'Christian covenant renewal.'"[18] Much later, the covenant image became a central theme for seventeenth-century Anglicans and Puritans.[19] As late as 1743, French Reformed pastor Jean-Frédéric Ostervald could argue that "it may be understood, that Sacraments were initiated, that they may be public pledges, and seals of the divine covenant, both on God's part, and on ours. For by them God offers, and confirms his grace to us, and we testify, and bind over our faith and obedience unto him."[20] In the past decade, the covenant image has been central in some ecumenical discussions of the eucharist. Calling the eucharist the "meal of the New Covenant," *Baptism, Eucharist,*

17. Chrysostom's homily no. 82 on the Gospel of Matthew in Daniel Sheerin, *The Eucharist: Message of the Fathers of the Church* (Wilmington, Del.: Michael Glazier Books, 1986). See also Chrysostom's homily no. 27 on 1 Corinthians.

18. Baltzer, *Covenant Formulary*, 171. Interestingly, the baptismal rite in the Apostolic Constitutions VII refers to baptism as a "seal of the covenant," language that would become central in many Reformation catechisms and confessional statements.

19. Kenneth Stevenson, *Covenant of Grace Renewed: A Vision of the Eucharist in the Seventeenth Century* (London: Darton, Longman, and Todd, 1994). See also James B. Torrance, "Covenant or Contract? A Study of the Theological Background of Worship in Seventeenth Century Scotland," *Scottish Journal of Theology* 23 (1970): 51–76.

20. Jean-Frédéric Ostervald, *A Compendium of Christian Theology* (London: SPCK, 1743), 343–44.

and Ministry contends that in the eucharist, "united to our Lord and in communion with all the saints and martyrs, we are renewed in the covenant sealed by the blood of Christ." The document explicitly links this understanding to the Old Testament context: "Christians see the eucharist prefigured in the Passover memorial of Israel's deliverance from the land of bondage and in the meal of the Covenant on Mount Sinai (Exodus 24)."[21]

Just as the people of Israel gathered together to renew their covenant with God (i.e., Josh. 24:1–27), so we Christians gather to renew the new covenant God has made with us in Christ. Christian worship is like a covenant-renewal service in which the gathered reaffirm the vows made with God in Christ. Guided by a liturgy, in a worship service, we renew the promises we made (and often failed to keep) to God, and we hear again the promises God has made (and kept!) in Christ. One legitimate, nourishing, robust, vital reason for assembling today is nothing less than the renewal of the new covenant we have with God in Christ.

The pastoral question we face is whether most people experience worship this way or whether, in contrast, they really experience it as a meeting of a religious social club, or an educational forum, or a form of entertainment. Because these other kinds of events are common in our culture, we are bound to take our expectations for them with us into worship. In contrast, worshipers need to be challenged to see the worship event as a deeply participational, relational event in which we are active listeners, speakers, promise receivers, and promise givers.

Retracing the Time Line of Divine Action in Corporate Worship

Third, the Former Prophets provide robust examples of a paradigmatic liturgical action of Jewish and Christian worship—that of memorializing past divine action. "Tell of all his wonderful acts" is more than a simple textual refrain in David's canticle (1 Chron. 16:9b); it is the fundamental practice of liturgy. Thus, Deborah's canticle in Judges 5 is a bardlike tale of divine action in the experience of the community. It seems to modern readers more like a story than a prayer or a hymn of praise. Similarly, the sermon in the Joshua 24 covenant-renewal ceremony (vv. 2–13) provides a detailed description of past covenant fidelity as the ground or basis for a future-oriented covenant promise. Further, the extended covenant-renewal prayer in Nehemiah 9 (vv. 9–31) traces the whole sweep of divine action from creation to the Red Sea deliverance to the up-and-down history of Israel's life in the Promised Land.

21. *Baptism, Eucharist, and Ministry* (Geneva: World Council of Churches, 1982), Eucharist, sections I.1 and II.B.11.

Each of these three examples (one a song, one a sermon, one a prayer) provides a highly stylized account of vast segments of God's history with Israel. Each of these liturgical actions places the worshiper before a great redemptive time line extending back through God's dealings with the people and ahead into an unknown but covenantal future. Shorter or fragmentary historical recitation is a part of nearly every other canticle, prayer, and oration recorded in the Former Prophets.[22] In addition, these textual accounts are complemented by other memorializing acts, such as the twelve stones at Gilgal (Joshua 4).

It is these texts from the Former Prophets, along with complementary historical psalms, that have grounded an essential Christian conviction about liturgy, which has received particular emphasis in the Reformed tradition. Nearly every major work on the meaning and purpose of liturgy written by a prominent Reformed theologian has emphasized the memorializing function of liturgy, the way it recounts divine action in the past in ways that anticipate divine action in the future. J.-J. von Allmen insisted that "liturgy connects the Church with the history of salvation. . . . It unites the Church of all places and times around the permanently decisive *magnalia Dei.*"[23] John Burkhart posits that "true worship celebrates the most definite God of the covenant in Moses and Jesus, the God of Abraham, Isaac, and Jacob; of Sarah, Rebekah, and Rachel; and of countless others. Fundamentally, worship is the celebrative response to what God has done, is doing, and promises to do."[24] E. H. Van Olst contends that in liturgy "people come together to celebrate the mighty acts of God . . . the basic structure of the saving acts of God [in which] the remembrance of Israel as well as the liturgical celebration of the church is rooted."[25] Nicholas Wolterstorff concurs: "A striking feature of the Christian liturgy is that it is focused not just on God's nature but on God's actions; and more specifically, on actions which took place in historical

22. See also 1 Sam. 12:6–25. Outside the Former Prophets see Deut. 26:5–9; Acts 7:2–53; 13:16–40. These accounts usually begin with a reference to Abraham and end with events at the time of the audience being addressed. Often these rehearsals of redemptive history include what might be called a homiletical turning point, a point at which the speaker urges the gathered to respond in light of the rehearsed history; see Josh. 24:14; 1 Sam. 12:16; Neh. 9:32. Stephen's and Paul's rehearsals do not similarly call for a response, but the following narrative depicts a response: Acts 7:54–58; 13:42–48. For an in-depth study of the covenant renewal in 1 Samuel 12, see J. Robert Vannoy, *Covenant Renewal at Gilgal: A Study of 1 Samuel 11:14–12:25* (Cherry Hill, N.J.: Mack Publishing Company, 1978).

23. J.-J. von Allmen, *Preaching and Congregation* (Richmond: John Knox, 1962), 36.

24. John E. Burkhart, *Worship* (Philadelphia: Westminster, 1982), 17, and also 31–33.

25. E. H. Van Olst, *The Bible and Liturgy* (Grand Rapids: Eerdmans, 1991), viii, 6.

time."[26] Hughes Oliphant Old simply concludes: "That God acts in history is fundamental to our theology; that we rejoice in these mighty acts is fundamental to our worship."[27] The rehearsal of God's actions in history is commonly accepted as a fundamental component of Christian liturgy.

This history-oriented approach to liturgy can be cast in boldest relief by contrasting it with some alternatives. First, such memorializing worship contrasts with ahistorical mystical introspection.[28] The preface to the 1993 *Book of Common Worship* explains:

> An important characteristic of worship in the Reformed tradition is that it centers on God rather than ourselves and our feelings. Our attention is drawn to the majesty and glory of the triune God, who created all things and by whose power all things are sustained, who was revealed in Jesus Christ raised from the dead to rule over all things, and who is at

26. Nicholas Wolterstorff, "The Remembrance of Things (Not) Past: Philosophical Reflections on Christian Liturgy," in *Christian Philosophy*, ed. Thomas P. Flint (Notre Dame: University of Notre Dame Press, 1990), 128. Wolterstorff suggests that the absence of commemoration-memorializing in Christian liturgy likely signals the influence of "immediately experiential, or abstractly theological or ethical, approaches to God" (142). He points out that Immanuel Kant believed both that God could not act in history and that traditional liturgy would fade away because it was so bound up with remembrance of God acting in history.

27. Hughes Oliphant Old, *Leading in Prayer: A Workbook for Worship* (Grand Rapids: Eerdmans, 1995), 237. This point is also made in Elmer Arndt, *The Font and the Table* (Richmond: John Knox, 1967), 17, 20, 27; Craig Douglas Erickson, *Participating in Worship: History, Theory, Practice* (Louisville: Westminster John Knox, 1989), 54–56; Duncan Forrester, J. Ian H. McDonald, and Gian Tellini, *Encounter with God* (Edinburgh: T & T Clark, 1996), 199; John Frame, *Worship in Spirit and Truth* (Phillipsburg, N.J.: Presbyterian and Reformed, 1996), 4–5, 79, 125–26; Eugene Heideman, *Reformed Bishops and Catholic Elders* (Grand Rapids: Eerdmans, 1970), 47–48; and Hughes Oliphant Old, *Guides to the Reformed Tradition: Worship That Is Reformed according to Scripture* (Atlanta: John Knox, 1984), 29–31, 41, 111, 136–40.

28. The following criticism of mysticism is directed specifically against ahistorical forms of mysticism that seek an experience of God apart from historical time and often posit a God beyond the divine economy. Commenting on mysticism in the interpretation of Paul, Lewis Smedes argues that "oriental mysticism could not tolerate dependence on specific historical events or concrete historical personalities. The one thing people need is to escape the concrete things of history and to be immersed into the divine life. . . . Mysticism and history were incompatible as foundations of religion" (*Union with Christ: A Biblical View of New Life in Christ* [Grand Rapids: Eerdmans, 1983], 28). Donald Bloesch distinguishes ahistorical mysticism from acts of meditation that are "centered on the works and acts of God not only in creation but also and preeminently in Jesus Christ" (*The Struggle of Prayer* [San Francisco: Harper & Row, 1980], 21). In the same vein, G. C. Berkouwer once noted that "mysticism is at home in spatial concepts, whereas revelation pertains to the temporal" (*The Return of Christ*, trans. James Van Oosterom [Grand Rapids: Eerdmans, 1972], 29).

work as the giver of life in and among us by the power of the Holy Spirit.[29]

This point is echoed in the work of John Beardslee, who argues that "worship is the worship of God, and not the celebration of our feelings about nature and common experience." Similarly, Duncan Forrester, J. Ian H. McDonald, and Gian Tellini contend that when worship is concerned only "with inward, subjective, individual and ultimately incommunicable truths," then it "is in danger of losing its *raison d'être* as a result of the extreme subjectivizing of faith."[30] The point of liturgical celebration is not merely to cultivate a common religious sentiment but to rehearse God's actions in history.

This orientation to divine actions in history is central to many recent works in theology proper. In several of these, arguments by theologians for an economically oriented approach to the doctrine of God are frequently accompanied by arguments for an economically oriented approach to the worship of God. Donald Bloesch, for example, links mysticism with an attempt "to transcend the Trinity by positing a 'God above God,' an infinite abyss that lies beyond personality and diversity," which he identifies as "incontestably other than the God of Abraham, Isaac, and Jacob."[31] Both in seeking knowledge of God and

29. *The Book of Common Worship* (Louisville: Westminster John Knox, 1993), 8. Note the prominent relative clauses in this passage that identify God as an agent of historical actions. Likewise, in his work on the Lord's Supper, von Allmen argues that "the Christian Supper offers those who participate in it, not the experience of being in communion with a myth, but participation in historical events" (*The Lord's Supper*, trans. W. Fletcher Fleet [Richmond: John Knox, 1969], 23).

30. John Beardslee, "Some Implications for Worship in Traditional Reformed Doctrine," *Reformed Review* 30 (1977): 212; and Forrester et al., *Encounter with God*, 222–23. Similarly, Thomas Torrance laments recent developments in Protestant worship in which "it becomes detached from the liturgical frame grounded in the great dramatic events of salvation history, and slips into self-expressionism and subjectivism" ("The Spiritual Relevance of Angels," in *Alive to God: Studies in Spirituality*, ed. J. I. Packer and Loren Wilkinson [Downers Grove, Ill.: InterVarsity, 1992], 131).

31. Bloesch, *Struggle of Prayer*, 21, 27; and idem, *God, the Almighty: Power, Wisdom, Holiness, Love* (Downers Grove, Ill.: InterVarsity, 1995), 60, 176, 192, 231–34. This is not to say that contemplative prayer has no place in Christian worship but that contemplation is focused on historical events. Thus, Jürgen Moltmann argues that "Christian meditation and contemplation are . . . at their very heart *meditatio crucis*," i.e., meditations on a historical event (*The Trinity and the Kingdom: The Doctrine of God*, trans. Margaret Kohl [New York: Harper & Row, 1981], 8). Similarly, James Torrance contrasts "contemplation of the Ideal, abstracted from all particulars," and contemplation "of the trinitarian mystery of the Person of Christ in loving communion with him in all the historical particularity of his incarnation, death, resurrection, and continuing, mediatorial ministry," contemplation which is "intensely particular, personal, and historical, not a flight from the world but a sharing in his concern for the world" ("Contemplating the Trinitarian Mystery of Christ," in *Alive to God*, 151).

in worshiping God, Christians properly attend to God by means of rehearsing God's actions in history.

Second, as the celebration of particular historical events, Christian liturgy is not merely a celebration of nature and natural cycles. Adrio König places great emphasis on the fact that ancient Israel changed its calendar of feasts from one "linked with nature, into one which was tied to history" and thus transformed what had been celebrations of natural cycles into celebrations of historical events. König argues that this shift in liturgical practice corresponded to the theological commitment to conceive of God based on God's action in history.[32] Christians have inherited this historically oriented pattern of liturgy. König argues that this is the fitting approach to the Christian God, the God of Jesus Christ. Christian worship is rooted in history. It is offered to the God who is conceived and named as an agent involved in particular historical events.

In Christian liturgy, the act of remembrance by a recital of God's specific deeds is nowhere clearer than in the emerging eucharistic prayers of the second and third centuries. In Justin Martyr's description of the eucharist, we are told that "the president . . . sends up prayers and thanksgivings to the best of his ability."[33] In all probability, the desired charism was that of the ability to recite adequately the full range of God's deeds in history. Soon, in formalized and prescribed liturgical texts, the eucharistic prayer of thanksgiving con-

---

32. Adrio König, *Here Am I* (Grand Rapids: Eerdmans, 1982), 124, also 171. A similar point is made by E. H. Van Olst: "The most important feasts in the Bible began as nature festivals. . . . The striking thing about these festivals is that they have been historicized—that is, they have received their content and meaning from the history of redemption" (*Bible and Liturgy*, 28, see also 15–20, 38–46). Hughes Oliphant Old uses the same point to critique some practices associated with the Christian year: "The recent efforts to bring back the celebration of the old liturgical calendar has suspicious similarities to a revival of the nature religions, natural theology, a cyclical interpretation of life, and the resurgence of the religions of fortune and fertility. One does penance in Advent when winter sets in and one rejoices at Easter when the flowers reappear in the spring. It is all quite natural, but this fascination with liturgical seasons sometimes seems not much more than a revival of Canaanitism" (*Guides to the Reformed Tradition*, 161). Similarly, K. H. Bartels concludes that "all the church's worship is and always has been historical, verbal, and personal rather than nature-oriented, mystical or dramatic. This is true of the preaching of the word, which aims to give outward expression to something which has happened in the past. . . . This same applies also to the Lord's Supper" ("Remember," in *The New International Dictionary of New Testament Theology*, ed. Colin Brown [Grand Rapids: Zondervan, 1978], 3:246). A similar point is made in Forrester et al., *Encounter with God*, 222.

33. Justin Martyr, *First Apology*, trans. Edward Rochie Hardy, Library of Christian Classics, vol. 1, Early Christian Fathers (Philadelphia: Westminster, 1953), 287. See Allan Bouley, O.S.B., *From Freedom to Formula: The Evolution of the Eucharistic Prayer from Oral Improvisation to Written Texts* (Washington, D.C.: The Catholic University of Music Press, 1981).

sisted largely of an extended *anamnesis* of God's deeds. The most famous of all these prayers, the so-called prayer of Hippolytus, reads as follows:

Then the deacons shall present the offering to the bishop, and he, laying his hands on it with all the presbyters, shall give thanks, saying:

"The Lord be with you."
And all shall say: "and with your spirit."
"Up with your hearts."
"We have them with the Lord."
"Let us give thanks to the Lord."
"It is fitting and right."
And then he shall continue thus:
"We render thanks to you, O God, through your beloved child Jesus Christ,
whom in the last times you sent to us
    as saviour and redeemer and angel of your will
who is your inseparable Word, through whom you made all things,
and in whom you were well pleased.
You sent him from heaven into the Virgin's womb;
and conceived in the womb,
he was made flesh and was manifested as your Son,
being born of the Holy Spirit and the Virgin.
Fulfilling your will and gaining for you a holy people,
he stretched out his hands when he should suffer,
that he might release from suffering those who have believed in you.
And when he was betrayed to voluntary suffering
that he might destroy death, and break the bonds of the devil and
    tread down hell, and shine upon the righteous, and fix a term, and
    manifest the resurrection,
he took bread and gave thanks to you, saying
    'Take, eat; this is my body, which shall be broken for you.' Likewise also the cup, saying, 'This is my blood, which is shed for you; when you do this, you make my remembrance.'

"Remembering therefore his death and resurrection, we offer to you the bread and the cup, giving you thanks because you have held us worthy to stand before you and minister to you. And we ask that you would send your Holy Spirit upon the offering of your holy Church; that, gathering it into one, you would grant to all who partake of the holy things to partake of the fullness of the Holy Spirit for the strengthening of faith in truth, that we may praise and glorify you through your child Jesus Christ, through whom be glory and honor to you, with the holy Spirit, in your holy Church, both now and to the ages of ages. Amen."[34]

34. Geoffrey J. Cuming, *Apostolic Tradition: A Text for Students* (Bramcote, Notts.: Grove Books, 1976), 10–11.

The longest portion of the prayer, following the opening greeting and preceding the words of institution, is nothing more than a recital of God's deeds in Christ. This prayer has become the foundation for a good deal of modern liturgical reform.[35]

Of course, this is only one memorializing liturgical practice. The Christian year, rightly understood, is a narrative journey along a time line of God's action in history, especially God's history in Jesus Christ. Not only eucharistic but also baptismal prayers recount the whole history of God's saving action "from believing Noah" right down to the present day. Scores of narrative hymns mirror the historical Psalms in recounting vast sweeps of history.[36] In each of these ways, Christian liturgy recounts the history of God's action in the world and anticipates similar action in the future.

In fact, one criterion to apply to worship in any congregation, regardless of the liturgical style it embraces, is that of historical remembrance and proclamation: Does worship proclaim the whole sweep of divine activity past, present, and future? Does worship induct participants into a cosmology in which God is at work faithfully in continuity with past divine action? Does worship convey a sense of hope for the future grounded in God's faithful action in the past?

For comfortable North American worshipers and worship leaders today, the great temptation is to slip into expressions of petition, thanksgiving, and proclamation that are nearly exclusively focused on the present moment. Perhaps this is an inevitable result of lives and churches that are content with the status quo. Our songs, prayers, and sermons emphasize God's immediate goodness and even the vitality of our intimate experience of God. For us to experience the riches of fully biblical worship, our prayer, praise, and proclamation should be carried out as if we stand before a cosmic time line of God's actions, fully aware of divine faithfulness from the creation of the world to its full re-creation in Christ. It is this vast and specific awareness that grounds our hope when days are difficult and that leads us beyond the immediate concerns of our little egocentric worlds.

In sum, these three themes—liturgical integrity, covenant renewal, and historical recitation—are fundamental both to the world of the Former Prophets and to the practice of Christian worship today. These themes demonstrate the value of developing a biblical understanding of worship on the basis not only of favorite, isolated texts but

35. See Frank C. Senn, *New Eucharistic Prayers: An Ecumenical Study of Their Development and Structure* (Mahwah, N.J.: Paulist Press, 1987).

36. The recovery of a full *anamnesis* in the baptismal and eucharist prayers has been a central feature in recent liturgical reform. See, for example, *The Book of Common Worship*, 39, 42–43, 69–70, 410.

also the whole sweep of scriptural teaching. They only scratch the surface of how the rich and varied narratives in the Former Prophets can inform our understanding and practice of worship. They also invite further work on the large project of connecting scriptural teaching with present liturgical practice.

2

Praise and Lament
in the Psalms
and in Liturgical Prayer

Recent studies of the canonical Psalms have generated a number of memorable metaphors for grasping the power of psalmic prayer. Walter Brueggemann, after Paul Ricoeur, speaks of the spiritual struggle to maintain equilibrium, a struggle worked out through the sequence of orientation, disorientation, and reorientation.[1] John Goldingay, in response, describes the life of prayer as an ever repeating cycle, or spiral, of praise and prayer, prayer and praise.[2] These approaches to the *function* of psalms in the life of faith echo deeper *structures* in the texts of the canonical Psalms themselves. Hence, N. H. Ridderbos, a generation ago, perceived a "golden cycle" of praise and prayer in the Psalms,[3] while Claus Westermann identified the "two poles of praise and lament"[4] around which the Psalms are constructed.

---

1. Walter Brueggemann, "Psalms and the Life of Faith: A Suggested Typology of Function," in *The Psalms and the Life of Faith*, ed. Patrick D. Miller (Minneapolis: Fortress, 1995). See also his *Message of the Psalms: A Theological Commentary* (Minneapolis: Augsburg, 1984).

2. John Goldingay, "The Dynamic Cycle of Praise and Prayer in the Psalms," *Journal for the Study of the Old Testament* 20 (1981): 85–90. Brueggemann specifically avoids the image of a cycle. See "Psalms and the Life of Faith," 8 n. 16.

3. N. H. Ridderbos, *De Psalmen: Opnieuw uit de Grondtekst Vertaald en Verklaard,* vol. 2, Psalm 42–60, in *Korte Verklaring der Heilige Schrift* (Kampen: Kok, 1973), 159. This reference was pointed out to me by Carl J. Bosma.

4. Claus Westermann, *The Living Psalms,* trans. J. R. Porter (Grand Rapids: Eerdmans, 1984), 10.

What these metaphors and analytical grids have in common, I would argue, are four essential insights. First, there is a startling *diversity* of affect and experience in the life of prayer. Religious experience in the Judeo-Christian tradition is as multiform as life itself. Second, the life of faith involves *movement* from lament to praise and back again that evidences the magnetic pull of tenacious faith, on the one hand, and a candid grappling with the problems of this world, on the other.[5] Third, these varied religious affections *counterbalance* each other this side of the eschaton. Lament and praise are incomplete without the other, lest praise, particularly general or descriptive praise, be misunderstood as smug satisfaction or lament be understood as a denial or refusal of grace.[6] Fourth, at some deep level, these diverse expressions *cohere*. Praise and lament do not tear each other apart. However anguished the tension between Psalm 88 and 150, they coexist in the Hebrew Psalter and in the life of prayer. They both can be mapped on the metaphoric fields these scholars have described.

As both Brueggemann and Patrick D. Miller, among others, have argued, these metaphors and structures are instructive for the life of prayer today. In Miller's words, the movement from lament to praise and praise to lament depicts "the very structure of faith in relation to God."[7] This chapter arises out of the conviction that these insights have specific implications for the life of the church as it is expressed in public worship. The thesis is twofold: First, our public worship must constantly seek to broaden its affective range, to express what Nicholas Wolterstorff has described for a number of years now as the trumpets of joy, the ashes of repentance, and the tears of lament.[8] Second, we must be far more intentional about how we achieve this, learning from the Psalms themselves how to sound our laments and praises with poise and passion.[9] Indeed, the fruit of careful scholarly

5. This movement is helpfully described by James Luther Mays as follows: "The prayers for help, the songs of praise for help, and the songs of trust reflect a movement from helplessness through salvation to gratitude and to the life of trust based on the experience of salvation. . . . The movement is the basic pattern of the Christian's relation to God through Christ" (*The Lord Reigns: A Theological Handbook to the Psalms* [Louisville: Westminster John Knox, 1994], 42).

6. See Gordon Lathrop, *Holy Things: A Liturgical Theology* (Minneapolis: Fortress, 1993), 57, 164.

7. Patrick D. Miller Jr., *They Cried to the Lord: The Form and Theology of Biblical Prayer* (Minneapolis: Fortresss, 1994), 55.

8. Nicholas Wolterstorff, "Trumpets, Ashes, Tears," *Reformed Journal* 36 (February 1986): 17–22. Brueggemann identifies the extensive spectrum of covenantal prayer in the Old Testament that "runs the gamut from serenity to anger" and then suggests that "faithful prayer requires keeping the entire range operational" ("Prayer as an Act of Daring Dance: Four Biblical Examples," in *Psalms and the Life of Faith*, 147).

9. My thesis is informed in part by Brueggemann's *Israel's Praise: Doxology against Idolatry and Ideology* (Philadelphia: Fortress, 1992), 7.

study of biblical praise and lament lies in part in its liturgical applications.[10] I will address these by commenting on three structures that shape Christian worship—the ad hoc structuring of prayer in times of crisis, the regularized structure of the Christian year, and the typical structure of Lord's Day worship—with particular attention to the possibilities for liturgical lament.

Lament in Times of Crisis

Let's begin with a difficult situation. What happens on Sunday morning in public worship after a young child in your congregation is taken deathly ill? Or when an adolescent's extended battle with an eating disorder threatens to rip apart a young family? Or when an otherwise upstanding member of the community is shown to be an unrepentant perpetrator of domestic abuse? Or when nearly two hundred people die in an Oklahoma City bomb blast? Or when the entire world is shocked by the terror of 9/11? Or when a barrage of suicide bombs threaten to undo peace in the Middle East? That is, what happens in public worship when conventional songs of praise would be nothing more than a bright facade?

These moments are pastorally crucial,[11] and they occur in the life of many congregations with astonishing regularity. These moments are more critical for pastoral spiritual formation than a full docket of church education programs. And how we handle them may say more about the gospel we proclaim than a year's worth of sermons.

As far as public worship is concerned, I suppose all would agree that it is best not to remain untouched by such situations. There are always stories such as the one James White is fond of recalling, of a certain Anglican rector who, after the onslaught of a decimating flood,

10. Liturgical lament has received a fair amount of attention lately, including Michael Downey, "Worship between the Holocausts," *Theology Today* 43 (1986): 75–87; J. Frank Henderson, *Liturgies of Lament* (Chicago: Liturgy Training Publications, 1994); Marcia Sachs Littell, ed., *Liturgies on the Holocaust: An Interfaith Anthology* (Lewiston, N.Y. and Queenston, Ont.: The Edwin Mellon Press, 1986); Don E. Saliers, "Lamenting and Confessing: Truthful Prayer," in *Worship as Theology: Foretaste of Divine Glory* (Nashville: Abingdon, 1994); Lester Meyer, "A Lack of Laments in the Church's Use of the Psalter," *Lutheran Quarterly* 7 (1993): 67–78; David N. Power, "When Worship Is to Lament," in *Worship, Culture, and Theology* (Washington, D.C.: Pastoral Press, 1990); idem, "Worship after the Holocaust," *Worship* 59 (1985): 447–55; Gail Ramshaw, "The Place of Lament within Praise: Theses for Discussion," *Worship* 61 (1987): 317–22; and Nicholas Wolterstorff, "Liturgy, Justice, and Tears," *Worship* 62 (1988): 386–403.

11. And they are crucial for liturgical leaders, although not always recognized as such. As Brueggemann comments, "The one-sided liturgical renewal of today has, in effect, driven the hurtful side of experience either into obscure corners of faith practice or completely out of Christian worship into various forms of psychotherapy and growth groups" ("From Hurt to Joy, from Death to Life," in *Psalms and the Life of Faith*, 68).

prayed the prayer book as always without alteration. The collect of the day read: "Water your earth, O Lord, in due season." No, these situations require our sensitive and honest attention. Injustices must be identified. Enemies must be named. Solidarity with the suffering and, above all, deep and soul-searching faith must be expressed.

But what exactly are we to do in such situations?[12] How can we express our anger, fear, and bewilderment? At the risk of sounding naive, let me suggest that we take the Psalms themselves as our model. When faced with an utter loss of words and an oversupply of volatile emotions, we best rely not on our own stuttering speech but on the reliable and profoundly relevant laments of the Hebrew Scriptures. This strategy capitalizes on the most salient features of the Psalter. As Sigmund Mowinckel has argued, the Psalms of lament were likely composed ad hoc, for occasional festivals or times of crisis.[13] As Brueggemann has observed, the Psalms arise out of "situations of regression," out of the "extremities of life and faith,"[14] the same context as contemporary communities in distress. And as Miller has pointed out, the language of the Psalms is open and metaphorical, well suited for application to other times and places.[15] Although their language is occasional, the Psalms are not so specific that they cannot be used as liturgy (not just as Scripture) today. For all these reasons, the Psalms themselves can well become our mentors for liturgical praise and lament. The diversity, movement, balance, and coherence of full-orbed liturgical prayer is nurtured best by the canonical Psalms.

By suggesting the use of biblical laments in crisis situations, I do not mean to suggest that we should merely pick out memorable phrases or metaphors from particular texts. For too long we have been content to single out a favorite or convenient versicle or, perhaps worse, to assemble what Hughes Oliphant Old has described as "collages of dismembered psalm verses" for liturgical use, while totally ignoring the structures and contexts by which these verses gain mean-

12. See also the particular liturgies for the long-term seriously ill, for persons suffering from addiction and substance abuse, for victims of crime, survivors of abuse, and other occasions for lament in Frank Henderson, *Liturgies of Lament* (Chicago: Liturgy Training Publications, 1994). See also Robert E. Webber, *The Ministries of Christian Worship*, The Complete Library of Christian Worship, vol. 7 (Nashville: StarSong, 1994), 273–85. There is a long line of volumes that contain prayers and liturgical texts written for particular occasions and periods of suffering and lament. Among them is a volume by a notable Reformed liturgist: Eugene Bersier, *Prayers in Time of War*, ed. Hugh Martin (London: SCM, 1939).

13. Sigmund Mowinckel, *The Psalms in Israel's Worship*, trans. D. R. Ap-Thomas, vol. 1 (Oxford: Oxford University Press, 1962), 193.

14. Brueggemann, "Psalms and the Life of Faith: A Suggested Typology of Function," in *Psalms and the Life of Faith*, 7.

15. Miller, *Interpreting the Psalms*, 8, 21–26.

ing.[16] Voluminous scholarly study of biblical prayer in the past two generations has focused on how the content and meaning of individual psalms arise from basic structures or patterns of prayer and, more specifically, how individual psalms improvise within a given structure. I am suggesting that in public worship we work within the basic forms we have learned to discern, and then, like a jazz soloist who embellishes a common musical theme, we improvise in the context of our particular tragedy.

Thus, most basically, we learn how to *structure* our lament from the structure of the biblical laments themselves. Our lament begins with *invocation,* a startling confession that even in crisis we approach a personal and accessible God.[17] In lament, we do not recoil from the tension that this presents, a tension that Miller has described concerning Psalm 22 as "an almost unbearable sense of contradiction between the roaring cry of dereliction and the address that repeatedly insists that the silent, forsaking, distant God is 'my God.'"[18] Then our lament freely addresses this personal God through the picturesque gallery of images used in direct address in the Psalms. We pray to Yahweh, the rock, the fortress, the hiding place, the bird with encompassing wings. These metaphors are not just theological constructs but means of directly addressing the deity. And as we pray them, these metaphors shape and reshape how we conceive of this God. They hone our image of God with the very tools that God gave us.

Our prayer continues with bold *lament.* We bring theodicy right into the sanctuary. We learn from the Psalms the value of direct discourse. Our pale subjunctives and indirect speech ("We would want to ask you why this might be happening") is transformed to bold and honest address ("How long, O LORD? Will you forget me forever?"). Such honesty in its own way comforts the bereaved and expresses solidarity with the wronged. Their questions and protestations are not illegitimate in the life of prayer, for prayer may well feature question marks alongside exclamation points. Honest worship expresses genuine doubt as well as assurance.[19] The Psalms teach us that doubt can

16. Hughes Oliphant Old, *Leading in Prayer: A Workbook for Worship* (Grand Rapids: Eerdmans, 1995), 55–76.

17. Samuel Balentine, *Prayer in the Hebrew Bible: The Drama of Divine-Human Dialogue* (Minneapolis: Fortress, 1993), 265.

18. Patrick D. Miller Jr., *They Cried to the Lord: The Form and Theology of Biblical Prayer* (Minneapolis: Fortress, 1994), 59.

19. See Robert Davidson, *Wisdom and Worship* (Philadelphia: Trinity Press International, 1990), 118–31; and this comment by Paul Ferris Jr.: "The Hebrews, like their Semitic cousins and their Sumerian predecessors, demonstrate what to the Western mind is a remarkable proclivity to complain to their deity and consider it in some sense a part of worship" (*The Genre of Communal Lament in the Bible and the Ancient Near East* [Atlanta: Scholars Press, 1992], 166).

be expressed as an act of faith, that prayer may include not just pleas for God's help but even complaints to God concerning injustice and ever present evil.[20] We also learn from the Psalms that biblical lament comes in many forms. Some lament is directed toward the enemy; some is directed toward God. Some is individual and isolated; some is communal and comprehensive. Lament is a response to the full range of problems in the human condition. The Psalms specifically name isolation, shame, despair, danger, physical impairment, and death as cause for lament.[21] Each has its own logic and metaphorical correlates, which in turn provide us with a rich storehouse of language to enrich our prayers.

Then our prayer continues with specific *petition:* Heal us, free us, save us. We express, with Westermann, that "lamentation has no meaning in and of itself"[22] but leads *necessarily* to petition. Noticing with Miller that petitions in the Psalms correspond with the laments they follow, we learn to search for specific petitions that are fitting to our lament.[23] In fact, our lament, our petition, and our eventual praise of God fit together like hand and glove. The very attributes for which we praise God are those we invoke in times of need.

Finally, our prayer ends with *expressions of hope,* confidence, and trust, however muted by the present situation. Lament is eschatological prayer. It always looks to the future. It may not be possible to sing praise in times of crisis. Yet praise is anticipated, even as the community yearns for the resolution of the crisis. Praise is the fully expected outcome of even crisis and despair.

Thus, form criticism of lament identifies and instructs us in a model for liturgical prayer in times of crisis. If nothing else, liturgical leaders would do well to reflect on the stunning and artful ways in which psalmic prayers adapt this structure, with a mind to providing the same sort of imagination and resourcefulness in public

20. Craig C. Broyles has argued that "upon closer examination of the lament category we have discerned two distinct forms of appeal: the psalms of 'plea,' which affirm the praise of God, and the psalms of 'complaint,' which charge God with failing certain traditions normally expressed as praise. In the former subcategory, praise appears as a motif in its own right; in the latter, praise is presented as that which the lament denies" (*The Conflict of Faith and Experience in the Psalms: A Form-Critical and Theological Study,* Journal for the Study of the Old Testament Supplement Series 52 [Sheffield, U.K.: Sheffield Academic Press, 1989], 221). See also the critique in Miller, *They Cried to the Lord,* 68–70, 382 n. 60; Joseph Blenkinsopp, "Can We Pray the Cursing Psalms?" in *A Sketchbook of Biblical Theology* (New York: Herder & Herder, 1968), 83–87; and Gerrit S. Dawson, "Praying the Difficult Psalms," *Weavings* 6 (1991): 28–35.

21. See Ferris, *Genre of Communal Lament,* 116–20.

22. Claus Westermann, *Praise and Lament in the Psalms* (Atlanta: John Knox, 1981), 266.

23. Miller, *They Cried to the Lord,* 99–101.

prayer today. Both carefully written and extemporaneous prayers can rely on this very structure as a prototype or guide. All of us—whether experienced worship leaders or novices—would benefit from rehearsing in our private studies the practice of formulating prayer according to biblical models. In sum, most basically, the Psalms provide us with a structure to guide us as we lead God's people in liturgical prayer.

An even more direct strategy is to pray the Psalms themselves. Take a specific psalm of *disorientation*, with its extreme and specific language, with its passionate plea and lament against God, and allow it to shape communal prayer.[24] Choose a psalm because it is "a genuine and sensitive match between expression and experience."[25] Choose Psalm 69 for a crisis of shame, Psalm 51 for a crisis of guilt, Psalm 38 or Psalm 41 for medical crises, Psalm 88 for times of utter despair, Psalm 71 for the afflictions of old age, and Psalm 143 for occasions of oppression or victimization. Then bring it to life with imagination and passion.

We might choose to simply pray the psalm as it is, without embellishment, with a deliberate pace that allows the worshiping community to enter into the pathos of the text. Or we might improvise on the psalm text, speaking the words of the psalm, followed by our own very specific application. Consider the following example of a congregation lamenting a case of domestic abuse. The text alternates between Psalm 13 (NRSV), *an individual lament,* and a pointed prayer written for the specific occasion.[26]

> *How long, O LORD? Will you forget me forever?*
> *How long will you hide your face from me?*
> *How long must I bear pain in my soul,*
> *and have sorrow in my heart all day long?*
> *How long shall my enemy be exalted over me?*

> Lord, our Lord,
> we feel forgotten.
> This abuse rips apart our faith.

24. I propose this in respectful disagreement with Westermann, who suggests that "on account of their fundamentally different background, such psalms can no longer be the prayer of a Christian congregation" (*Living Psalms,* 23).

25. Brueggemann, "Psalms and the Life of Faith," 27. Among the psalms that are appropriate for such situations are Psalms 13, 59, 64, 102, 142, and 143. These psalms feature direct and urgent speech that is appropriate to a situation of crisis, without extensive historical references that might complicate their use as prayers today.

26. In the context of the liturgy, the words of the psalm and the words of the prayer that improvise on the psalm should be distinguished, perhaps by having each led by a different leader, by printing one and not the other, or by some other means.

The victim, our sister ____, is alone in despair.
How long must this persist?

Consider and answer me, O Lord my God!
    Give light to my eyes, or I will sleep the sleep of death,
and my enemy will say, "I have prevailed";
    my foes will rejoice because I am shaken.

The perpetrator of this abuse is winning!
Please, Lord, stop him!
We cannot bear to see this fool—
the enemy of our sister and of us—
believe he is successful.

But I trusted in your steadfast love;
    my heart shall rejoice in your salvation.
I will sing to the Lord,
    because he has dealt bountifully with me.

We long to sing praise,
to have our sister begin to sense your goodness again.
For deep down, we trust in your goodness. Amen.

After such a prayer, the community is not likely to read Psalm 13 the same way ever again. Suddenly the biblical prayer has become the prayer of the community. And perhaps by God's grace, the victim will be able to sense that biblical faith, and the God to whom it is directed, is not hostile to her isolation but rather embraces her pain.

In many critical settings, this rendering of lament will be too hasty. Indeed, one problem in liturgical lament is that we arrive too quickly at the vow of praise, the happy ending, glossing over the pithy cries of lament that conceal deep and brooding affections. Though it is not a final solution, consider expanding this improvisation on a lament psalm so that it encompasses an entire service. Take a full hour to pray through a given psalm of lament such as Psalm 13.

In so doing, we have begun the process of prayer on the occasion of crisis. But this is only the beginning. Here our scholarly sources, with their heuristic metaphorical grids, are particularly helpful, pointing out a lacuna in most liturgical prayer. Their call for balance, move-ment, and coherence in prayer challenges us to measure our liturgical prayer against psalmic prayer. The prayers of the Psalms enter fully into lament but then move, as faith demands, toward declarative praise. What about our liturgical prayer? Even if we are sensitive enough as worship leaders to acknowledge crisis, how often do we seek to lead worshipers over time through disorientation to reorienta-tion? Often, we must acknowledge, we leave worshipers "behind" in lament, hastening during subsequent days and weeks to return quickly to normalcy, to descriptive (general) praise and songs of well-being. Or, conversely, we are content to linger in lament with them, praying week after week concerning a given crisis with a sense of despair that fails to sense the magnetic pull of eschatological hope. Liturgical prayer in times of crisis is not complete with the expression of lament. The lament is but one step on a long journey back toward declarative (Psalm 30) and descriptive praise (Psalm 103). Thoughtful worship leaders will be eager to lead a congregation slowly but surely from lament to praise over time, all with a specific moment of crisis in mind, for specific lament can and should only be practiced in a congregation with room for specific praise and thanksgiving at occasions of "reorientation." If we are to lament with startling specificity, we also need to give praise with startling specificity, with declarative hymns of praise that name specific gifts of God to the worshiping community.[27]

Psalms 13, 30, and 146, taken together, express the full range of the cycle of psalmic prayer. Psalm 13's concluding vow of praise (v. 6) pivots right into Psalm 30's opening *proclamation* of praise (v. 1). And Psalm 30's thanksgiving for specific divine intervention leads right into Psalm 146's language of all-encompassing praise. This pairing suggests creative ways to structure liturgical prayer. Consider three possibilities: First, if we have used Psalm 13 with reference to a specific crisis, then we might look for the pastorally appropriate time (perhaps it will be only days or weeks but perhaps months or years later) to pray Psalm 30 as the flipside of Psalm 13 and then finally Psalm 146 in the same way, improvising on its structure and phraseology. Second, when praying Psalm 30 and then Psalm 146, explicitly recall Psalm 13 as the prayer of the original occasion of crisis. This is the key to offering praise with full integrity. Third, mirror this structure for liturgical prayer in liturgical preaching. Consider a sermon series, perhaps titled—after Calvin—"Anatomy of the Soul," that begins with Psalm 13 and moves to Psalm 30 and then to 146, encompassing disorientation and reorientation, lament and praise.[28] In so doing, consider the goal of such preaching not to solve the problem of evil but rather to lead worshipers more deeply into these biblical prayers.[29]

27. This is one reason why the Christian community needs qualified composers. Writing occasional music for times of lament or praise is perhaps the most fitting correlate to psalms of declarative praise.

28. Another interesting approach to a series of sermons on the Psalms might begin with Brueggemann's study, "Bounded by Obedience and Praise: The Psalms as Canon," in *Psalms and the Life of Faith,* 189–213, and feature sermons on Psalms 1, 25, 73, 103, and 150, per his canonical exegesis.

29. Of course, this cycle of Psalms can run in two directions, for a congregation's prayer of well-being, its prayer of Psalm 146, is not complete this side of the eschaton.

All of this is not to say that every biblical lament is equally suitable as a model, nor that this is the only way to lament. Yet this strategy of structuring our liturgical prayer after particular biblical texts and combinations of texts has several advantages. First, it provides ample warrant for saying such strident things to God. This reduces the need to provide a long and windy justification for doing so in the context of the liturgy. It gives us permission to do what our religious culture might not permit us to do otherwise. Similar liturgical advice was perhaps best expressed by Richard Baxter more than three centuries ago: "The safest way of composing a Stinted Liturgie, is to take it all, or as much as may be, for words as well as matter, out of Holy Scripture." Why? Because "all are satisfied of the infallible truth of Scripture, and the fitness of its expressions, that are not like to be satisfied by man's."[30]

Second, this practice provides a plumb line to test our pastoral instincts. Brueggemann, following Peter Berger and others, has observed that structured language serves both to enhance and to limit our experience of despair.[31] In the case of a grieving family, for example, the church can help them by providing language to acknowledge and even to enhance their feeling of helplessness. At the same time, such language provides a limit for that experience. To those who suffer, biblically shaped liturgical laments convey three important and interwoven themes: Their suffering is real, it is not the last word, and it is spiritually significant—all without a theological treatise on the subject.

Third, it provides a strong structure out of which can arise genuinely spontaneous prayer. We free church Protestants should cherish our tradition of free, extemporaneous prayer.[32] Yet what we consider to be entirely spontaneous prayers are often nothing more than long sequences of euchological cliché. Without structure, we forfeit the possibility of genuine spontaneity—something every jazz soloist knows. The Psalms teach us the value of spontaneous prayer. Many psalms clearly arise out of immediate experience and reflect unre-

---

Thoughtful worship leaders will also then be eager to help a worshiping community sense when it must complement its descriptive praise with lament, if not for itself then in solidarity with others. For a congregation that assumes that all is right with the world, the cycle of prayer—or a sermon series on the Psalms—might need to begin with a different point in the cycle, from Psalm 146 to the shock of Psalm 13 and then only Psalm 30. Such a congregation could be reminded that the horrors presented daily on the national news ought to be an insistent call to public prayer, a vital part of an in-the-world spirituality.

30. Richard Baxter, *Five Disputations of Church Government and Worship* (London: n.p., 1659), 378.

31. Brueggemann, "The Formfulness of Grief," in *Psalms and the Life of Faith*, 86.

32. Here I agree with Hughes Oliphant Old, *Leading in Prayer: A Workbook for Worship* (Grand Rapids: Eerdmans, 1995), 5.

strained expression of guilt, fear, or anger.[33] Yet they also teach us the value of form. Many of the most immediate and personal of the Psalms clearly rely on tried and true phrases and structures of speech.[34] Improvising on fitting psalms is one of the simplest ways of judiciously balancing freedom and form.

Fourth, this strategy of structuring liturgical prayer in times of crisis according to the movement from lament to declarative praise to descriptive praise lends integrity to our praise. Brueggemann has spoken about the ambivalence of descriptive praise, calling for a hermeneutic of suspicion to question whether these songs of well-being are really smooth cover-ups for wishing to maintain the status quo, for ignoring the cries of the poor. But if they are sung *subsequent to* and in full awareness of God's help in time of crisis, they take on a new and powerful integrity.[35] In so doing, our praise powerfully unites themes of redemption and creation. The experience of restoration becomes not an end in itself but a means by which we are able to perceive more clearly the cosmic creative work of God in creation and re-creation.

Fifth, this strategy provides a way for individuals caught up in isolated and lonely struggles with tragedy or injustice to find a voice in a community of worshipers. Lament is often so deeply personal.[36] How can an entire community ever hope to empathize with the isolation and individuality of the victim? Perhaps finally it cannot. Yet praying the Psalms in this way may allow, again by God's grace, a particular victim or sufferer to sense an unacknowledged solidarity with women and men of faith who have prayed these canonical prayers through centuries of pain and violence. This is one distinct advantage of the purposeful use of ancient prayers. Relatedly, the "I" psalms reflect the notion of corporate personality that is key to Israel's identity. Their first person singular subjects acknowledge the individual worshiper before God. Yet their expression of broad national sentiments suggest that they are not merely isolated soliloquies.[37] Praying the Psalms may give even modern worshipers in individualistic societies a sense of participating in the corporate personality of the body of Christ.

33. Westermann, *Living Psalms*, 15, 14.

34. Brueggemann: "In the use of form, the community does a specific task, that is rehabilitation of a member from a chaotic experience to a structure experience in this particular life-world" ("Formfulness of Grief," 96).

35. See Goldingay, "Dynamic Cycle of Praise and Prayer in the Psalms," 86.

36. See J. Christiaan Beker, *Suffering and Hope: The Biblical Vision and the Human Predicament* (Grand Rapids: Eerdmans, 1987), 3, 122.

37. Martin Ravdal Hauge, *Between Sheol and Temple: Motif Structure and Function in the I-Psalms*, Journal for the Study of the Old Testament Supplement Series 178 (Sheffield, U.K.: Sheffield Academic Press, 1995).

Sixth, this strategy allows these biblical texts to shape us in an immediate and direct way. In such prayer, these texts burrow into our bones, as it were, and become part of our spiritual identity. Significantly, it is not just the prayers of the Psalms in general nor a theology of lament in general that forms us. Instead, particular texts, with particular twists on otherwise stereotypical ways of praying, form us in faith.[38] This strategy gives worshipers, especially suffering worshipers, biblical landmarks to anchor personal prayer and worship. It gives us a place to put a bookmark in our Bibles. It gives us texts to recall at family reunions and anniversary commemorations. This is a tangible gift that thoughtful liturgy can provide for victim and congregation alike in times of crisis.

Lament in the Christian Year

But not every Sunday is an occasion of crisis. Many worship services are planned and led in the routine of life.[39] How do praise and lament function in liturgical routine?

The answer is found, I believe, in the two large structures that shape public worship in countless congregations, for well-balanced liturgy, like praise and lament in the Psalms, has its own poles, or cycles, or sense of equilibrium. The points of correspondence or analogy between the Psalm cycles and these cycles have much to teach us.

Consider first of all the large pattern of the Christian year. Every year, time and time again, we journey from the eschatological lament of Advent to the profound adoration of the incarnate Christ at Christmas and Epiphany, from the baptismal soul-searching of Lent to the unbridled praise of Easter morning. This yearly journey provides ready-made moments to give voice to the cries and acclamations of people at every point in the journey of faith.[40] Indeed, one of the richest benefits of a well-celebrated Christian year is that it provides not

38. The concern for discerning the particularities of individual texts has been central to the work of Westermann, among others. See *Praise and Lament in the Psalms*, 166. My intent is to suggest that this be realized in the context of public worship.

39. Though in some congregations almost every worship service will be marked by a vigorous sense of disorientation or reorientation.

40. Congregations who do not follow the Christian year should nevertheless provide occasions for both thanksgiving and lament. Here the Puritan practice of days of thanksgiving and days of humiliation (or fast days) provide an instructive historical study. See Charles E. Hambrick-Stowe, *The Practice of Piety: Puritan Devotional Disciplines in Seventeenth-Century New England* (Chapel Hill: University of North Carolina Press, 1982); and Leigh E. Schmidt, "Time, Celebration, and the Christian Year in Eighteenth-Century Evangelicalism," in *Evangelicalism: Comparative Studies of Popular Protestantism in North America, the British Isles, and Beyond, 1700–1990*, ed. Mark A. Noll, David W. Bebbington, and George A. Rawlyk (New York: Oxford University Press, 1994), 90–109.

only a balanced diet of biblical readings and theological themes but also a balanced diet of the Christian affections in the life of prayer.

Good Friday

Out of the entire cycle of the Christian year, I would like to consider two particular celebrations with redolent possibilities for lament.[41] First, consider Good Friday. Preparing liturgy for Good Friday is one of the most challenging pastoral and theological exercises imaginable. In fact, the ability to plan and lead Good Friday liturgy with theological insight and pastoral sensitivity would make a fine exit requirement for seminary M.Div. students. Do we celebrate the Lord's Supper or not? Do we rejoice or do we weep? How do we, on this day, proclaim Christ crucified *and* risen? For many, it is such an odd day. We feel as though we need to be sad, but we are not sure why.

Generally, liturgical strategies for the day run in two directions. One strategy is that of historical reconstruction: We dramatize the passion, rehearse the seven last words, and plan three-hour services in darkness. One congregation even rigged a way to rip the curtain that hung in its chancel at the ninth hour. This strategy follows a pattern described by the Spanish nun Egeria, who visited Jerusalem in the late fourth century and described in detail a pattern of worship that retraced Jesus' passion step by step, hour by hour.[42] This strategy, which liturgists call "historicization," has much to commend it.[43] At its best, this strategy roots our worship in the historical events of Jesus' life and becomes *anamnesis,* remembrance, in its deepest Hebraic sense. Yet it is also incomplete. By itself, this remembrance does not celebrate the staggering metaphysical significance of the cross nor its profound meaning for the life of prayer. For that we need something more.

41. Every season in the Christian year presents its own redolent possibilities for expressing different aspects of lament and praise. Space permits an examination of only these two events.

42. Egeria's colorful description of Good Friday worship reads as follows: "Friday . . . at midday they go before the Cross—whether it is rain or fine, for the place is out of doors—into the very spacious and beautiful courtyard between the Cross and the Anastasis, and there is not even room to open a door, the place is so crammed with people. . . . The whole time between midday and three o'clock is taken up with readings. They are all about the things Jesus suffered. . . . It is impressive to see the way all the people are moved by these readings, and how they mourn. You could hardly believe how every single one of them weeps during the three hours, old and young alike, because of the manner in which the Lord suffered for them" (John Wilkinson, *Egeria's Travels* [London: SPCK, 1971], 137–38).

43. A classic study of this is Robert Taft, "Historicism Revisited," in *Liturgical Time,* ed. Wiebe Vos and Geoffrey Wainwright, *Studia Liturgica* 14 (1982): 97–109, reprinted in Robert Taft, *Beyond East and West: Problems in Liturgical Understanding* (Washington, D.C.: Pastoral Press, 1984), 15–30.

A second liturgical strategy for Good Friday might be called, somewhat crassly, performing a funeral for Jesus. This type of service mimics a funeral in every way possible: We sing dirges, speak eulogies, and offer prayers that bemoan the sad fate of the prophet from Nazareth. In short, although we might sense the ambiguity of the moment, we do what it takes to leave church feeling sad. This strategy may well lead to what J. Christiaan Beker has described as "passion mysticism, a meditation on the wounds of Christ, or . . . a spiritual absorption into the sufferings of Christ," which he finds alien to Pauline theology.[44] It is reflected in Roman Catholic piety by the cult of the sacred heart and in Protestant piety by gospel hymns that center exclusively on the blood of Jesus. By themselves, these expressions too are incomplete, for Good Friday is more than merely a day of death. It is a day that transforms death. On Good Friday, we learn that our journey to death was shared by the very Son of God.

So consider another strategy, perhaps an addition to the first and a transformation of the second. This strategy considers Good Friday the *locus classicus* for lament, a day for prayer in solidarity with the cries of the world—indeed, in solidarity with the suffering and dying Lord himself. Here we can learn a lesson from some early liturgists. For centuries prior to the Reformation, Good Friday was the occasion for the longest and most intense intercessory prayer of the entire year.[45] When the medieval Roman Church pared down the Mass by trimming the general intercessory prayer, early liturgists (probably quite conservative ones) stepped in to preserve that lengthy prayer for use on this one day of the year.[46] Their instincts have much to teach us.

Part of what we celebrate on Good Friday (and the word *celebrate* is crucial) is that Christ has completely identified with us in suffering, even to death (Isa. 53:12; Heb. 4:14–16). On Good Friday we hear

44. J. Christiaan Beker, *The Triumph of God*, trans. Loren T. Stuckenbruck (Minneapolis: Fortress, 1990), 88.

45. See G. G. Willis, "The Solemn Prayers of Good Friday," in *Essays in Early Roman Liturgy* (London: SPCK, 1964), 1–48; Louis Duchesne, *Christian Worship: Its Origin and Evolution, a Study of the Latin Liturgy Up to the Time of Charlemagne*, trans. M. L. McClure (New York: E. & J. B. Young, 1903), 172–73; and Louis van Tongeren, "A Sign of Resurrection on Good Friday: The Role of the People in the Good Friday Liturgy until c. 1000 A.D. and the Meaning of the Cross," in *Omnes Circumadstantes: Contributions towards a History of the Role of the People in the Liturgy*, ed. Charles Caspers and Marc Schneiders (Kampen: Kok, 1990), 101–19.

46. For a modern equivalent to this solemn prayer of intercession, see *The Book of Common Worship* (Louisville: Westminster John Knox, 1993), 283–87; and *The Book of Common Prayer* (New York: Church Hymnal Corporation, 1979), 277–80. For the use of lamentations in tenebrae for Holy Week, see *The Book of Occasional Services*, 2d ed. (New York: Church Hymnal Corporation, 1988), 72ff.; and Hoyt L. Hickman et al., *Handbook of the Christian Year* (Nashville: Abingdon, 1986), 177–89.

again Christ pray the lament of Psalm 22 and suddenly remember how wondrous it is that we have an intercessor who is able to sympathize with our weakness (Heb. 4:14–16; 5:7–9). On Good Friday we hear Jesus pray for his enemies, redefining how lament functions in a life of faith.[47] On Good Friday we recall the words of Paul that confer mysterious significance on the suffering of those who are united with Christ in death (2 Cor. 1:5; 4:10; Phil. 3:10; Col. 1:24; 1 Peter 4:12–16). On Good Friday especially we sense the complete identification of Christ with us, the basis for an all-important vicarious humanity of Christ by which our prayer and worship are made possible.[48] What better time than this to practice a spiritual discipline of lament in solidarity with those who suffer, including Jesus himself?

In part, Good Friday lament can be practiced through the use of the full traditional intercessory prayer for Good Friday, described above. Or perhaps this is the day when Psalm 88, the darkest of all the Psalms, can be used liturgically. Better yet, consider using Psalm 22 to structure Good Friday liturgical prayer, the very psalm spoken by Jesus on the cross. Begin Good Friday intercessions with Psalm 22:1–21, followed by extemporaneous prayers of intercession and lament. Then conclude the prayers with verses 22–31, a decisive song of hope that anticipates Easter praise.[49] Concerning the Psalms of lament, Dietrich Bonhoeffer once observed that "no individual can repeat the lamentation Psalms out of his own experience; it is the distress of the entire Christian community at all times, as only Jesus Christ has experienced it entirely alone, which is here unfolded."[50] This liturgical suggestion for Good Friday takes Bonhoeffer's words seriously. It challenges us to move toward lament in full awareness of the christological anchor to the life of prayer. If lament is new to your congregation's liturgical life, then begin with lament on Good Friday.

Advent

Second, consider Advent, the season of anticipation and hope. Despite both the overwhelming influence of the shopping mall on Advent spirituality and the persistent temptation to conflate Advent with Christmas, the intent and genius of Advent is first of all to cultivate eschatological hope.

---

47. Miller, *They Cried to the Lord*, 309.
48. James B. Torrance, "The Vicarious Humanity of Christ," in *The Incarnation*, ed. Thomas F. Torrance (Edinburgh: Handsel Press, 1981), 127–47.
49. See Westermann, *Living Psalms*, 298.
50. Dietrich Bonhoeffer, *Psalms: The Prayer Book of the Bible*, trans. James H. Burtness (Minneapolis: Augsburg, 1970), 47.

Eschatology, of course, is one of the main themes of twentieth-century theology. Holocausts and world wars invite apocalyptic and eschatological thinking. One fruit of this interest is new appreciation for the ways in which prayer and worship are eschatological acts. Hans Joachim Kraus[51] and Brueggemann, among others, have emphasized this aspect of Old Testament prayer. Beker has echoed this emphasis in New Testament theology. Both J.-J. von Allmen, the late Swiss Reformed liturgical theologian, and Don Saliers have applied an eschatological framework directly to the church's liturgy.[52] As Saliers summarizes: "All petitions and intercessions are part of an eschatological dimension of all praise and thanksgiving. . . . The very act of prayer as petition or intercession for the whole world is an implicit prayer that the kingdom or final rule of God may come to the whole world."[53]

Now, we know the importance of eschatology *theologically*. The question is whether we can realize this eschatological vision *liturgically*. Can eschatology, particularly eschatological lament, shape spirituality in the midst of the Christian community? And can it do so even when the use of six-syllable words is not permitted?

Here our leadership of liturgical prayer is crucial. By praying eschatologically and by pointing out to worshipers how and why we are doing it, we cultivate, however slowly, an eschatological spirituality. Consider two strategies for Advent. First, use psalms that express eschatological lament and longing. Psalm 80 is a traditional psalm for Advent. Its refrain is the paradigmatic Advent prayer: "Restore us, O God; make your face shine upon us, that we may be saved." And its prominent use of the vine/vineyard metaphor figures prominently in later christological and eschatological prayer texts.[54] The meaning of Advent is best realized when we sense the analogy between Israel's hope and our own: We, like Israel, yearn for the coming of the Messiah, the full arrival of the kingdom. By the liturgical use of this psalm and others like it, we identify ourselves with Israel in a tangible, liturgical way.

Second, we must pray with an eye to the future so as to express and arouse intense hope and yearning. This happens in two ways. It happens through expressions of hope that arise out of situations of de-

51. Kraus, *Theology of the Psalms*, 102. For a fascinating study of the messianic and eschatological understanding of the Greek Psalter, see Joachim Schaper, *Eschatology in the Greek Psalter* (Tübingen: J. C. B. Mohr [Paul Seibeck], 1995).

52. J.-J. von Allmen, *Worship: Its Theology and Practice* (New York: Oxford University Press, 1968).

53. Don E. Saliers, "Liturgy Teaching Us to Pray: Christian Liturgy and Grateful Lives of Prayer," in *Liturgy and Spirituality in Context: Perspectives on Prayer and Culture*, ed. Eleanor Bernstein (Collegeville, Minn.: Liturgical Press, 1990).

54. See, for example, the prayer of thanksgiving in the *Didache*.

spair, praying, "O come, O come, Immanuel" in full awareness that "captive Israel mourns in lowly exile here."[55] This is the prayer of *eschatological petition*. It also happens when prayer names acts of justice, integrity, and shalom as signs of the coming kingdom and presents them as signs of the kingdom of God in this world. This might be called *eschatological praise*.

While explicitly eschatological petition and praise need not be limited to Advent, Advent is a time for calling attention to the future orientation of both petition and praise. Imagine the following concise introduction to an Advent intercessory prayer: "Today in prayer, we give thanks for the birth of a new child to the Smiths, we ask for healing for Jill, for Larry, for Michelle. Especially today, in Advent, our prayer is oriented to the future. Because we believe in the Advent gospel, our prayers today feature two key words (and children, I challenge you to listen for them)—the words are *hope* and *promise*." To complement this liturgical practice, consider asking junior high students to write out Advent prayers entirely in the future tense, publishing in church newsletters explicitly eschatological laments for use in personal and family worship, or agreeing to begin every church-sponsored Advent and Christmas celebration with the quiet singing of "O Come, O Come, Immanuel." No doubt these suggestions will be variously applied in different communities. But the point remains the same: Advent must teach us to pray, even to lament, with our faces turned toward the future.

These moments in the Christian year, just like individual psalms, take on new significance when seen against the backdrop of the whole cycle of biblical prayer. Individual celebrations in the Christian year, like individual prayers in the Psalms, need to be interpreted and understood in a larger context. They are part of a cycle of prayer that runs from praise to lament to thanksgiving and back again. Just as passionate lament in the Psalter has the effect of unleashing declarative praise after times of crisis, so too serious and sturdy lament and intercessions on Good Friday and during Advent have the effect of immeasurably deepening our Christmas and Easter praise. Just as descriptive psalmic praise dislodged from lament invites a hermeneutic of suspicion, so too Christmas and Easter praise can become suspiciously saccharine without the journey through Lent and Advent. It is well-accepted spiritual advice that the best way to prepare oneself for ecstatic and unbounded praise on Easter is to enter fully into the pathos of Good Friday. The same is true for Christmas and Advent—and

55. This language is borrowed from the classic Advent prayers, the "O-Antiphons," which underlie the hymn "O Come, O Come, Immanuel." For a modern version of the prayers, see *The Book of Common Worship*, 166–67.

for lament and praise. Praying only part of the cycle, whether in the Christian year or in the Psalms, is a mark of tepid spirituality.

Lament in Weekly Worship

The Christian year is one large structure that nurtures the full range of affections in liturgical prayer, but it is not the only structure that shapes our worship. Consider also the classical pattern of Lord's Day worship. Taken as a whole, Sunday morning liturgy, just like the Psalter, has a range of affect and movement. In the course of well-celebrated Sunday worship, we praise, lament, give thanks, and intercede. Telescoped to its bare essentials, we gather with thanks, come before God in humble submission, offer unbridled praise, hear the Word with thanksgiving, respond with confession, offer intercession, share the meal of our participation in the works of God in Christ, and leave with dedication and promise. Within this pattern are expressions of plea and praise, disorientation and reorientation, that must be noticed and enlarged.

The Opening of Worship

Again, we will examine two key moments in this structure for worship. We begin right at the beginning. As with any event, the opening moments of worship accomplish a great deal: They establish who leads and who follows and the general ethos, mood, and purpose of the event. To use Ricouer's and Brueggemann's language, they establish whether the event arises out of "orientation" or "disorientation." Does worship begin with a statement of well-being or an acknowledgment of suffering? With praise or plea?

No doubt the *Sitz im Leben* ("particular context") of the worshiping community answers these questions quite naturally. Communities that gather in posh North American suburbs and those that gather in a war-torn Bosnian enclave inevitably begin worship in very different ways. The purpose and significance of the gathering is determined by the immediate social context of the community. But should the context be all-determinative? Should posh suburban churches merely repeat their songs of orientation?

Here we can learn a lesson from the shape of classic Christian liturgies, Eastern and Western, for both Eastern and Western liturgy, in most of their classic forms, begin with two paradigmatic liturgical prayers: *kyrie eleison* and *gloria in excelsis Deo*, lament and praise, disorientation and reorientation.

The *kyrie* is truly a lament (though it has been remade as a confession of sin in some liturgical structures). It is a plea for mercy. Later in the medieval period, *kyrie* was improvised, with extended tropes that elaborated and even localized this most simple cry for help. The *gloria*, we might say a bit anachronistically, is a blending of declarative and descriptive praise. As descriptive praise, it brings together the familiar verbs by which we praise God. As declarative praise, it links them with concrete events in history.

This juxtaposition at the opening of worship is significant for both pastoral and theological reasons. Theologically, it maintains the eschatological tension of the "already" and "not yet" as worship begins and helps avoid the twin temptations of triumphalism and despair. Similarly, it helps worshipers avoid simply repeating general descriptive praise of God, unleashed from a sense of God's particular creative and redemptive acts in human history. Pastorally, the presence of these two prayers at the outset provides a point of entry for worshipers at different points in the life of faith. Every Sunday morning gathering includes people of praise and people of lament—people whose silence and pain crave release and people whose joy seeks resonance in community.[56] Whether mournful or joyous, whether exhausted or invigorated, all worshipers find a point of contact somewhere in the spectrum between *kyrie* and *gloria*.

How do we do this today? What are some liturgical resources for those for whom *kyrie* and *gloria* are a foreign liturgical tongue? Consider three specific suggestions. The first is structural: Maintain both lament and praise in the typical pattern for the opening of Sunday worship. Whether, like the classic Eastern and Western liturgies, we use *kyrie eleison* and *gloria in excelsis;* whether, like Calvin's *Form of Prayers,* we begin with prayers of humble penitence and continue with psalms of praise; or whether we begin with quiet informal gathering songs of humility and then join in solemn processional hymns of praise, this juxtaposition at once anchors worship in both the real world and in the coming kingdom.

The second suggestion is rhetorical. In leading worship, in giving transitions and introductions to acts of worship, make every attempt to identify with both "disoriented" and "oriented" worshipers. Perhaps the greatest enemy of this today is the ritual of the weekly witticism with which worship often begins. In leading worship, we often borrow patterns of speech from self-help seminars and late-night television comedians. We feel compelled to begin with references to the weather or with a dandy quip to incite a cheap laugh. The penchant for informality, what Cornelius Plantinga Jr. has called a "rhetorical downshift" in our liturgical leadership, often thwarts the possibility that the

---

56. The vital link between worship and pastoral care is explained in William H. Willimon, *Worship as Pastoral Care* (Nashville: Abingdon, 1979).

opening of worship will identify with a worshiper's deepest hopes and fears.[57]

The third suggestion concerns the texts we place on the congregation's lips at the outset of worship. The required balance of lament and praise commends the use of selected psalms themselves,[58] as is prescribed, for example, in the 1955 liturgy of the French Reformed Church.[59] Especially useful are declarative hymns of praise that bring together an immediate sense of total dependence on God, the distinct memory of occasions of grief and lament, and an awareness of God's recent intervention. Choose a specific declarative psalm, introduce it with a specific reference to an event in the life of the community, and then sing it passionately.

Prayers of Intercession

In addition to the opening of worship, a crucial liturgical moment for lament is the prayer of intercession that, in classical Christian liturgy, follows and responds to the proclamation of the Word.[60] At first thought, this prayer may seem like anything but lament. Prayers of intercession typically ask for a great deal—for healing, for wisdom, for material blessings, for spiritual growth, and the like—but they do not seem to express lament. This, I contend, is a distortion of the prayers of intercession. Both in the New Testament and in the subsequent history of Christian worship, prayers of intercession are fundamentally prayers for others, prayers in solidarity with those

57. Cornelius Plantinga Jr., *Fashions in Folly: Sin and Character in the 90s* (Grand Rapids: Calvin Theological Seminary, 1993), 8.

58. Churches in the free church tradition have complete flexibility to choose these and other psalms for the opening of worship. Yet churches with fixed liturgical texts often have similar freedom in the choice of opening or processional canticles or hymns, for which a metrical setting of these psalms might be appropriate.

59. *Liturgie de l'Eglise Réformée de France.* See *Recueil de textes liturgiques* (Tournon: Eglise Réformée de France, 1985).

60. See James F. White, *Introduction to Christian Worship*, rev. ed. (Nashville: Abingdon, 1990), who observes that "the chief problem with the pastoral prayer is that it often tries to do everything and often ends by doing nothing" (162). The eighteenth-century Reformed pastor and liturgist, Jean-Frédéric Ostervald, gives helpful pastoral advice on this point: "It has been our object to embrace in this service all the acts of divine worship. These are to confess our sins, to adore God, to praise him, to render him thanks, to consecrate ourselves to him, to call upon him, and to read his word. All these acts . . . have not been comprehended in a single prayer; but are set forth separately and distinctly, that all, even the most simple, may understand what they are doing, whilst engaged in public worship; that they may comprehend in what this worship consists, and that they may be able to distinguish its several parts" (preface to the Liturgy of Neuchatel, *Verbum Caro*, vol. 9, no. 34 [1955], 69–81). For more on the prayers of intercession, see Old, *Leading in Prayer*, 175–224; and C. John Weborg, *Leadership Handbooks of Practical Theology*, vol. 1, *Word and Worship*, ed. James D. Berkley (Grand Rapids: Baker, 1992), 157–65.

who suffer. They enact the basic *for-another* posture of prayer that follows from a theology of the cross, according to the twin claims of Miller ("The prayer for the suffering of others is the paradigm of faithful prayer")[61] and Beker ("Solidarity is no longer a debatable option but rather an inescapable reality").[62] In the midst of the worshiping community, which gathers with the assurance of Christ's presence, the paradigmatic prayer is not only "How long, O LORD? Will you forget *me* forever?" but also "How long, O LORD? Will you forget *them* forever?"

This insight suggests several ways in which our practice of intercessory prayer can be sharpened. First, it challenges us to affirm Karl Barth's assertion that the intercessory prayer of the church should be "as wide in scope as possible."[63] We might take as our mentor the bishop Fructuousus of Tarragone (d. 259), who entered his death saying, "I am bound to remember the whole Catholic Church from sunrise to sunset."[64] Again, history has much to teach us about how this can be achieved. Classical Eastern and Western liturgical texts featured a regular pattern for intercessions that required liturgical leaders to pray each week for a wide range of concerns: the local church, the worldwide church, political leaders, the oppressed, the sick, and so on.[65] Every week, public intercessions covered the entire list, no matter how long the service had gone on. Such patterns, widely available today, need not be straightjackets that limit our prayers but rather models that challenge us to grow in praying for others. This aspect of weekly worship is no place to cut corners.

Second, this insight challenges us to integrate fully our liturgical prayer and our life in this world. Westermann claimed that "we can only describe and understand the psalms as originating from worship when worship is seen as the unifying center of the nation's common life. . . . Prayer in public worship would lose its force without these experiences outside the sanctuary: such prayer is only given life by the movement inwards from outside and back again into daily life."[66] Each time we read a newspaper or watch the evening news, we are preparing for liturgical prayer. Likewise, each time we join in liturgi-

---

61. Miller, *They Cried to the Lord*, 324.

62. Beker, *Suffering and Hope*, 20.

63. Karl Barth, *Selected Prayers*, trans. Keith R. Crim (Richmond: John Knox, 1965), 6–7.

64. Josef A. Jungmann, *The Mass of the Roman Rite: Its Origins and Developments*, vol. 2, trans. Francis A. Brunner (New York: Benziger Bros., 1959), 154.

65. For a modern reflection of these historical patterns, see *The Book of Common Worship*, 99–124.

66. Westermann, *Living Psalms*, 7.

cal prayer, we are preparing to read the newspaper and watch the evening news. My suggestion is that we nurture an "intercessory spirituality" that seeks to turn every dimension of our lives in the world into a topic for liturgical prayer. Consider introducing intercessory prayer by a simple, unadorned reading of headlines from weekly newspapers to focus attention on the priestly role of the church for the world, as in the following example of an intercessory prayer for two worship leaders:

[Introduction]: Our prayers will be divided into three sections:
    prayers for national and international concerns,
    prayers for local community needs,
    and prayers for personal, individual brokenness.
To make our prayers concrete, each prayer will be preceded by a
    list of newspaper headlines from the past week.

1. We pray now for the brokenness of our nation and world.
Dateline, September 1995
    • Serbs, Croats Resume Fighting in Croatia
    • South Africa Death Toll Rises to 25 in Attacks
    • Agents Discover Fake Visa Ring
    • Two More Arrested in Tourist's Death

2. God of power, God of mercy,
We lament before you the brokenness of our world,
    a world of war
    of disease
    of mistrust
    of violence.
We claim your promise to be with us.
In your power, heal our world, we pray. [silent prayers]

1. We pray now for the brokenness of our local community.
Dateline, September 1995
    • Vandals Break in at Local School
    • Charges Dropped in Prostitution Case
    • One Hospitalized, Another Arrested in Stabbing

2. Our gracious God,
Our community, too, is broken.
    The institutions that hold us together often seem to be breaking.
    The comfort of our lives is often disturbed by fear.
We claim your promise to be with us.
In your power, heal our community, we pray. [silent prayers]

1. We pray now for individual, personal needs and brokenness.
Dateline, September 1995
   • Loneliness America's Greatest Killer
   • Two More Press Claims of Sex Discrimination
   • Numbers of Abused Children Up This Year
   • Worker Dissatisfaction High at Local Plant

2. Loving God,
So many lives are broken and filled with pain,
   haunted with memories of failure, guilt, abuse,
   stuck in ruts of boredom and loneliness,
   searching for meaning and happiness.
We pray for your comforting presence, for your power to heal and
   forgive. Work powerfully in our world, we pray. [silent prayers]
Through Jesus Christ our Lord, Amen.

1. [Assurance] Jesus said: Come to me—all you who labor and are
   heavily burdened—and I will give you rest. Take my yoke upon
   you and learn from me, for I am gentle and lowly in heart and
   you will find rest for your souls.

2. Friends in Christ,
Jesus died for us and rose again in victory. His words are sure. In
   him, we find life and rest for our souls.

In addition to this suggestion, consider the following:

   • Include within intercessory prayers hymns and songs that specif-
     ically lament reasons for which creation groans: environmental
     abuse, natural disaster, warfare, domestic abuse, and others.[67]
   • Give particular attention to concerns and problems identified
     earlier in the reading and preaching of the Word. (The immediate
     consequence of some sermons is most naturally lament—and not
     just because they are bad sermons.)
   • Include in the prayers of the people each week one prayer from
     Christians who live in a different country.[68]
   • Include in intercessory prayers specific references to the voca-
     tions of two or three members of the congregation and the par-
     ticular dilemmas they face, moving systematically to include
     each member of the local church community over time.

67. See, for example, the memorable texts of "A Congregational Lament" and "The
City Is Alive, O God," in *Psalter Hymnal* (Grand Rapids: CRC Publications, 1987).
68. See, for example, the prayers printed in *With All God's People: The New Ecumenical Prayer Cycle* (Geneva: WCC Publications, 1989).

In short, invest energy in making the prayers of the people one of the "highlights" of weekly Sunday worship.

One of the great benefits of enriching intercessory prayer following the service of the Word is the effect this has on the celebration of the Lord's Supper. Again, the metaphor of a cycle or a spiral is helpful. At the Lord's Supper, we pray the Great Prayer of Thanksgiving, which is like an epic poem that recites God's deeds in history. Just as in the psalm cycle, in which the most poignant acclamations of thanksgiving erupt out of psalms of lament, so too eucharistic thanksgiving takes on deeper meaning when it follows intense prayers of intercession and lament. Experienced presiders may even take liberty to extend the recital of God's deeds in the eucharistic prayer to name specific gifts of God to the local community that correspond to the prayers of intercession just offered. And while this may sound like only an abstract liturgical point for only liturgical connoisseurs, I am convinced that it is pastorally true: Deeply meaningful intercessory prayers change everything about how worship is perceived.

In sum, well-celebrated Christian worship shares the same characteristics as the Psalter. It expresses a *range* of affections. It leads the community in a *movement* into deeper praise and lament, pulled along by both the daily joys and sufferings of worshipers and the startlingly good news of the gospel. It refuses to deny the tension between praise and lament by simply giving up on one or the other. It also refuses to be pulled apart by this tension. In part, such worship is possible with careful attention to the structures that shape Christian worship, structures that resemble or are analogous to the structures Brueggemann, Goldingay, and others have described in the Psalms. The occasional structures of lament and praise in times of crisis and the cyclic structures that shape our yearly and weekly worship are the primary means by which the prayers of orientation, disorientation, and reorientation are expressed. At their best, these structures at once enrich, correct, and balance the corporate prayer life of the church.

In conclusion, we must affirm that the liturgical application of these important lessons from biblical prayer cannot be overemphasized. Liturgy, as Brueggemann has pointed out, is world-making speech. It is a crucial aspect of spiritual formation. It trains us in the deep grammar of faith, hope, and prayer. This lesson is especially important today. The primary influence on liturgy today is the clarion call for relevance to postmodern, media-soaked people. Our liturgical strategizing nowadays begins with market analysis. Leaving the task of assessing the merits of this approach for another day, we can acknowledge that market surveys tell us what we long have guessed. We are ministering in a broken world. Even in North American suburbia, all is not well. And whether you are a baby boomer or a buster, there is nothing as relevant as showing up at church on Sunday morning and joining a congregation that is willing to name precisely and intercede passionately for the very problems that drove you there in the first place. Tellingly, advocates of both so-called traditional and contemporary forms of worship have recently prescribed that churches take more seriously their role as priests in shaping both prayers of lament and praise.[69] The simultaneous call for intentionality in our liturgical prayer by both liturgical reformers and biblical scholars signals an important opportunity for the church today. May God's Spirit bless conversations among them so that the church may be formed in an ever more deeply biblical faith.

---

69. See, for example, Sally Morgenthaler, *Worship Evangelism: Inviting Unbelievers into the Presence of God* (Grand Rapids: Zondervan, 1995), 112–13; and Saliers, *Worship as Theology*, 118–25.

Theological Studies

3

Covenant Theology
in Ecumenical Discussions
of the Lord's Supper

Recent contributions to eucharistic theology have proceeded largely by explicating and extending the varied scriptural images and motifs associated with the dominical feast. The meaning of the eucharist is described in *Baptism, Eucharist, and Ministry,* for example, by means of the familiar five images of thanksgiving to the Father, *anamnesis* (remembrance) of Christ, invocation of the Spirit, communion of the faithful, and meal of the kingdom.[1] While these images have been expanded and shaped along theological lines, as their trinitarian form suggests, their roots are invariably scriptural. In an ecumenical context, this method has the distinct advantage of proceeding from a common (scriptural) starting point, with the added result of bringing biblical and liturgical theologians into the same conversation.

1. *Baptism, Eucharist, and Ministry* (Geneva: World Council of Churches, 1982), hereafter referred to as BEM. This document represents a remarkable achievement in articulating dimensions of sacramental theology that are held by Christians of most traditions and denominations. Theologizing about the eucharist by means of explicating images in this fashion may have been pioneered by Yngve Brilioth, whose *Eucharistic Faith and Practice; Evangelical and Catholic* (London: SPCK, 1930) discusses the following: joyful thanksgiving, commemoration, communion, sacrifice, and presence. More recent examples of this method include James F. White, *Sacraments as God's Self-Giving* (Nashville: Abingdon, 1983), which describes seven biblical themes as the basis for eucharistic theology; and Horton Davies, *Bread of Life and Cup of Joy: Newer Ecumenical Perspectives on the Eucharist* (Grand Rapids: Eerdmans, 1993), which describes eight.

Another advantage of this approach is its preference for metaphor over more rigid and abstract categories and questions. Traditional issues, such as the persistent dispute over the mode of Christ's presence, are still discussed but only in light of the more encompassing and, dare we say, more fundamental biblical concepts of thanksgiving, commemoration, kingdom meal, and communion. Some of these metaphors take on a life of their own, generating an extended vocabulary and application. The metaphor of sacrifice, for example, has generated a constellation of related terms: altar, anaphora, offertory, priest, and oblation.[2] Additionally, some images or metaphors function as interpretive frameworks or hermeneutical keys by which other concepts are understood. BEM, for example, proposes to view the concept of eucharistic sacrifice in terms of *anamnesis*.[3] Thus, we come to understand and reconfigure our sacramental theology by emphasizing one or more scriptural images for the eucharist and by interpreting some in light of others.

Tucked away in several ecumenical discussions and in the catalog of images in BEM is the image of covenant. Calling the eucharist the "meal of the New Covenant," BEM contends that in the eucharist, "united to our Lord and in communion with all the saints and martyrs, we are renewed in the covenant sealed by the blood of Christ."[4] Recalling the words of institution that refer to the "blood of the covenant," this image taps a rich vein of biblical narratives, poetry, and liturgical activity that provides a fascinating window into biblical theology and, I will argue, holds rich potential for theology today. Nevertheless, the image of covenant has been largely ignored by many recent contributions to sacramental theology. It is not cataloged, for example, in Horton Davies's review of recent contributions to sacramental theology. It is given only a few pages of attention in the works of David Power, William Crockett, Hans Bernhard Meyer, Xavier Léon-Dufour, and Herbert Vorgrimler, to mention only a few contributions to the field.[5] Thus, it is not surprising that John Reumann con-

2. Gordon Lathrop, *Holy Things: A Liturgical Theology* (Minneapolis: Fortress, 1993), 139–40.

3. BEM, section on Eucharist, Commentary, par. 8 (p. 11).

4. BEM, section on Eucharist, section I, par. 1 (p. 10) and section II, part B, par. 11 (p. 12).

5. David Power, *The Eucharistic Mystery* (New York: Crossroad, 1993), 53–54; William R. Crockett, *Eucharist: Symbol of Transformation* (New York: Pueblo, 1989), 17–20; Hans Bernhard Meyer, *Eucharistie: Geschichte, Theologie, Pastoral* (Regensburg: Verlag Friedrich Pustet, 1989), 82; Xavier Léon-Dufour, *Sharing the Eucharistic Bread: The Witness of the New Testament*, trans. Matthew J. O'Connell (New York: Paulist Press, 1987), 141–53; and Herbert Vorgrimler, *Sacramental Theology*, trans. Linda M. Maloney (Collegeville, Minn.: Liturgical Press, 1992), 21, 140–41. Of the five, the treatment by Léon-Dufour is the most complete. The covenant motif is relatively more prom-

tends that "the covenant aspect of the Christian Sacrament is a topic not yet exhausted in modern analysis."[6]

This discussion intends to remedy this gap by exploring the implications of the biblical image of covenant for the understanding of and meaningful participation in the Lord's Supper. Toward this end, this chapter analyzes the biblical texts that present the covenant image, observes briefly some historical attempts at reconstructing a covenantal understanding and practice of the eucharist, and argues that covenant theology offers manifold possibilities for future theologizing about the meaning of eucharistic participation.[7]

Covenant in Scripture

Perhaps surprisingly, each of the New Testament accounts of the Lord's Supper refers to the concept of covenant. The Lukan and Pauline accounts speak of "the new covenant in my blood" (Luke 22:20; 1 Cor. 11:25), hearkening to the famous prophecy of Jeremiah concerning the "new covenant" that the Lord would make with the people of Israel (Jer. 31:31).[8] The Matthean and Markan accounts, in one of the more significant departures from the earlier Lukan/Pauline tradition, record Jesus speaking of "my blood of the covenant" (Matt. 26:28; Mark 14:24), recalling both the covenant ratification rite described in Exodus 24, which also had its "blood of the covenant" (Exod. 24:8), and a messianic prophecy (Zech. 9:11). These accounts signal how significant the notion of covenant was for the understanding of the eucharist in the early church. Together they point to a previously existing tradition of thinking along covenantal lines.

More specifically, the Lukan and Pauline accounts link the New Testament ritual meal with an Old Testament promise. Here is a fundamental point of discontinuity between Old and New Testament ex-

---

inent in Eduard Schweizer's all-too-brief monograph *The Lord's Supper according to the New Testament*, trans. James M. Davis (Philadelphia: Fortress, 1967). Laurance Hull Stookey, in *Eucharist: Christ's Feast with the Church* (Nashville: Abingdon, 1993), features "covenant" as a primary matrix for the eucharist, although the scope of this project does not allow for extended treatment. A few older works feature the covenant theme prominently. See Scott McCormick, *The Lord's Supper* (Philadelphia: Westminster, 1966), 59–72; and G. D. Yarnold, *The Bread Which We Break* (London: Oxford University Press, 1960), 21–25.

6. John Reumann, *The Supper of the Lord: The New Testament, Ecumenical Dialogues, and Faith and Order on Eucharist* (Philadelphia: Fortress, 1985), 40.

7. For more on this theme, see chapter 1, "The Former Prophets and the Practice of Christian Worship."

8. The Lukan text does present some vexing textual issues. Verses 19b–20 do not appear in all the earliest manuscripts. See Alasdair I. C. Heron, *Table and Tradition: Toward an Ecumenical Understanding of the Eucharist* (Philadelphia: Westminster, 1993), 5–6.

perience: What had been only a promise of a new covenant is now fulfilled in Christ and signed in drinking of the cup. In addition to obvious verbal parallels to Jeremiah 31, Johannes Betz suggests that the
identification of the new covenant with the person of Christ evokes
the Servant Songs of Isaiah (Isaiah 42, 49, 50, 52–53).[9] Relying on
Betz, Alasdair Heron suggests:

> The covenant is thus personified in the person here addressed to God:
> he is not merely a sign of the covenant, or a means by which it will be
> made, but rather is himself the bond of alliance between God and the
> people, the pledge of God's faithfulness. Against this background, the
> most likely meaning of Jesus' saying, "This is the new covenant in my
> blood," is something like, "This is the covenant which I myself am, and
> which I shall seal by my own death."[10]

Calling the cup "the new covenant in my blood" makes what was promised to be present and, more specifically, personified in Christ himself.

In contrast, the Matthean and Markan accounts typologically link
two ritual actions: the Old Testament covenant ratification (Exodus
24) and the New Testament eucharist.[11] In Hebrews, as in the institution narratives, Christ's blood functions in the new covenant as the
sprinkled blood functioned in the old one (cf. Heb. 9:19–21). Exodus
24:1–11 records two ceremonies, a blood rite and a meal rite, that
confirm Israel's promise to live in the covenant established by God
through his redemption in the Red Sea and his gift of covenant ordinances on Sinai.[12] Blood from the ritually sacrificed animals and identified as "the blood of the covenant" was sprinkled on the gathered
community. Then the elders of Israel beheld the presence of God and
ate and drank in the presence of God. Like this ratification ritual, the
New Testament narrative highlights the significance of a covenant "in
blood," and although the New Testament account speaks not of sprin-
kling blood but of drinking the cup, this action efficiently evokes the
significance of both Exodus 24 rites of covenant ratification: It is at

9. The identification of the covenant with the Servant himself (Isa. 42:6) is an especially telling parallel, as is the presence of two phrases of Isaiah 53:12 in the institution
narrative: "poured out" and "the sins of many."

10. Heron, *Table and Tradition*, 13. A further connection can be made with the
prophecy of Ezekiel (cf. Ezekiel 36). See Léon-Dufour, *Sharing the Eucharistic Bread*,
150.

11. This typological application is observed by BEM: "Christians see the eucharist
prefigured in the Passover memorial of Israel's deliverance from the land of bondage and
in the meal of the Covenant on Mount Sinai (Exod. 24)" (Eucharist, section I, par. 1).

12. See Philippe Rouillard, "From Human Meal to Christian Eucharist," in *Living
Bread, Saving Cup*, ed. R. Kevin Seasoltz (Collegeville, Minn.: Liturgical Press, 1982),
138–39.

once a blood rite and a rite of table fellowship.[13] Of special significance in the Matthean/Markan tradition is the clear emphasis on the
blood of Jesus, which points to the sacrificial nature of Christ's death.
The significance of Christ's blood as a sacrificial offering is revealed
more poignantly by the writer of Hebrews (9:11–18). Significantly, the
argument in Hebrews is made on the basis of the same typology as the
institution narrative intimates: Christ's blood functions in the new
covenant as the sprinkled blood functioned in the old one (cf. esp.
Heb. 9:19–21).

The New Testament, therefore, presents two textual traditions for
the institution narrative, with two subtly different renderings of the
covenant motif. The way in which the meanings suggested by these
two passages fit together is a matter of some debate. Joachim Jeremias concluded simply that "both formulations signify substantially
the same thing," of which a common text might be "This (wine) (is)
my blood (shed for the concluding) of the covenant."[14] William
Crockett, however, reflecting a larger consensus of scholarly opinion,
concludes that "the two versions of the cup saying present two different Old Testament backgrounds for understanding the redemptive
significance of Jesus' death."[15] As G. R. Beasley-Murray concludes,
"Mark's language, reflecting Exodus 24, reflects the terms of the cult,
while that of Luke and Paul, reflecting Jeremiah 31, is fundamentally
eschatological."[16]

What is certain is that all these covenant references, in both Old
and New Testaments, point to the integral connection between covenant and the forgiveness of sins. The blood described in Exodus 24,
for example, has long been understood as a symbol of the atonement.[17] The promise of the new covenant in Jeremiah 31 specifically
elucidates that "I will forgive their wickedness and will remember
their sins no more" (31:34). The Servant Song tradition of Isaiah
freely speaks of how the servant "bore the sin of many" (53:12). And
the institution narratives themselves make the connection clear: "my
blood of the covenant, which is poured out for many *for the forgiveness
of sins*" (Matt. 26:28). Thus, the covenant motif in the institution narrative is most fundamentally a soteriological claim.

13. See Léon-Dufour, *Sharing the Eucharistic Bread,* 143.
14. Joachim Jeremias, *The Eucharistic Words of Jesus,* trans. Norman Perrin (New
York: Charles Scribner's Sons, 1966), 169.
15. Crockett, *Eucharist,* 20.
16. G. R. Beasley-Murray, *Jesus and the Kingdom of God* (Grand Rapids: Eerdmans,
1986), 265.
17. This point is well established by Pesch's study of the Targum commentaries on
the passage. See R. Pesch, *Das Abendmahl und Jesu Todesverständnis* (Freiburg: Herder,
1978).

The importance of the covenant motif, revealed in the covenant references in the institution narrative, is also underscored by the links between the Lord's Supper and the Old Testament Passover. These links are described most influentially by Jeremias.[18] Although the past generation of exegetical studies has witnessed a good deal of debate about the precise dating of the Last Supper in relation to the pascal meal, Max Thurian reflects the general consensus of the scholarly community in concluding that the "eucharist can not be understood unless it is placed in the atmosphere of the liturgical meal which the Jews celebrated, and still celebrate, each year at Passover."[19] The Passover celebrated God's deliverance of Israel from Egypt, the very basis for the covenant relationship between God and Israel. The identification of Jesus as the paschal lamb (1 Cor. 5:7) suggests that Jesus himself is the basis for the new covenant relationship.[20] At the very least, these paschal references substantiate the tendency of the first Christians to understand Christ in terms of a previously existing theological matrix. The old symbols and categories of paschal lamb and covenant still carried meaning, however much they were transformed by the person of Christ.

But what does all this mean? How and why is the covenant reference in the presentation of the Lord's Supper significant? The connection between covenant and forgiveness of sins, which has already been observed, is undoubtedly part of the answer. But a more complete answer depends on further analysis of what meanings were evoked by the covenant reference in the context of the Last Supper. And as the presence of covenant language at so many key points in the history of Israel attests, there was no lack of potential for evoking profound meanings.[21] In fact, the notion of a covenant was one of the primary means by which the people of Israel understood their relationship with God.

On the basis of this very intuition, the notion of covenant came to

18. Jeremias, *Eucharistic Words of Jesus*, 41–62. Jeremias's conclusions are supported by the contemporaneous work of Notker Füglister, *Die Heilsbedeutung des Pascha* (München: Kösen-Verlag, 1963).

19. Max Thurian, "The Eucharistic Memorial, Sacrifice of Praise and Supplication," in *Ecumenical Perspectives on Baptism, Eucharist, and Ministry* (Geneva: World Council of Churches, 1983), 91. See Heron, *Table and Tradition*, for a summary of the relevant evidence for assessing whether the Last Supper was a Passover meal (17–33).

20. The role of the covenant motif is not, however, *primarily* established on the basis of this paschal imagery, for it may well be that this Passover connection cannot account for every theological theme tapped in the institution narratives, including the phrase "blood of the covenant." As Heron suggests, "Nor does Jewish thought at that time appear to have made any very close connexion between the blood of the Passover lamb and the 'blood of the covenant'" (*Table and Tradition*, 9).

21. Significant Old Testament covenants include the covenant with Noah (Gen. 9:8–17), Abraham (Gen. 15:9–21; 17), Phinehas (Num. 25:10–31), and David (2 Sam. 7:5–16), as well as the Sinai covenant (Exodus 19–24) and the new covenant (Jeremiah 31).

be a much discussed topic in twentieth-century attempts to recon-struct the theology of the people of Israel. Although studies from the 1960s that saw covenant as the unifying thread in the theology of Israel have been criticized for taking covenant language too seriously and too simplistically,[22] the most recent attempts to articulate the theological substructure of the Hebrew Scriptures have again returned to cove-nant as a central motif. As Brevard Childs concludes, "Regardless of the age and circumstances lying behind the Deuteronomic covenant formulation, its theology became the normative expression of God's re-lation to Israel and served as a major theological category for unifying the entire collection comprising the Hebrew scriptures."[23] And George Mendenhall and Gary Herion, in their *Anchor Bible Dictionary* article, simply declare, "'Covenant' in the Bible is the major metaphor used to describe the relation between God and Israel (the people of God)."[24] As these analyses suggest, the single notion of covenant implies much more than a soteriological strategy; it implies, rather, a full-orbed theo-logical system. In fact, this single metaphor has implications not only for theology proper but also for ethics, ecclesiology, and eschatology. The following five points attempt to summarize the essential compo-nents of covenant theology.

First, God is a God of action and promise. The covenant motif is one that highlights God's action in the world, God's operation in the econ-omy of salvation. The Noahic covenant pointed to God's creation of the cosmos. The Sinai covenant recalled God's deliverance of Israel from Egypt. The basis for covenant in the actions of God was ensured in the covenant formulary, which always began with a recital of God's deeds.[25]

22. And, more particularly, for conflating all Old Testament covenants into one type. For these studies, see Walter Eichrodt, *Theology of the Old Testament*, vol. 1, trans. J. A. Baker (London: SCM; Philadelphia: Westminster, 1961), 13–14; John Barton Payne, *The Theology of the Older Testament* (Grand Rapids: Zondervan, 1962); G. Ernest Wright, *The Old Testament and Theology* (New York: Harper & Row, 1969); and John Bright, *Covenant and Promise: The Prophetic Understanding of the Future in Pre-Exilic Israel* (Philadelphia: Westminster, 1976). For criticism and discussion, see John H. Hayes and Frederick Prussner, *Old Testament Theology: Its History and Development* (Atlanta: John Knox, 1985), 183–84, 257–59; Brevard Childs, *Biblical Theology of the Old and New Tes-taments* (Minneapolis: Fortress, 1992), 413–38; and John H. Stek, "'Covenant' Overload in Reformed Theology," *Calvin Theological Journal* 29 (1994): 12–41.

23. Childs, *Biblical Theology of the Old and New Testaments*, 419.

24. George E. Mendenhall and Gary A. Herion, "Covenant," in *The Anchor Bible Dic-tionary*, vol. 1 (New York: Doubleday, 1992), 1179. See also "Covenant and Canon as Context," which is part 2 of Walter Brueggemann, *The Psalms and the Life of Faith*, ed. Patrick D. Miller (Minneapolis: Fortress, 1995), 135–213.

25. Klaus Baltzer, *The Covenant Formulary in Old Testament, Jewish, and Early Christian Writings*, trans. David E. Green (Philadelphia: Fortress, 1971). The parallels of this covenant formulary to later Jewish and Christian forms of prayer, including eucha-ristic prayers, are significant.

But the covenant motif does not restrict its view to God's action in the past; it also observes that God is a God of promise: "I will be your God" is the constant refrain of the Old Testament covenant narratives. Thus, the theology proper implied by covenant is action and promise oriented. God's being, and even God's presence, is featured less than God's action.[26]

Second, a covenant enacts a relationship and confers an identity. Through covenant, YHWH becomes known to the nations as the God of Israel. As the writer of Hebrews expresses it, "God is not ashamed to be called their God" (11:16). As Piet Schoonenberg observes, "In both testaments, above all in the old, God is first recognized as Yahweh, the God who has bound himself up with Israel as God of the covenant and God of history."[27] Israel's identity, likewise, is that of a covenant people. This bears theological significance, for uniquely, Israel's God is one who apparently desires relationship, not separation. Therefore, a covenant worldview is one whose metaphysic is more relational than absolute,[28] for here is a God who is, in Schoonenberg's phrase, "interpersonal."

Third, in the covenant relationship, it is God who is primary. It is God who initiates relationship.[29] The covenant relationship is not one among equals. In covenant, God graciously condescends to establish a relationship with Israel. God's primacy is also reflected in the act of establishing covenant, for it is God who proposes, makes possible, and enacts covenant. Covenant ratification in Exodus 24 is possible only after the deliverance from Egypt and the giving of the law to Moses.

Fourth, a covenant relationship is completed by faithful and thankful obedience. This obedience does not establish or effect covenant relationship but is a response to it. A covenant thus involves an obligation to act in a way that is fitting to the type of relationship established. The instructions for cultic organization, the dietary laws, and the laws for community organization presented in Exodus, Leviticus, and Numbers do not by themselves establish covenant or even main-

26. God's being and presence are not to be minimized as aspects of Old Testament theology. Exodus itself is framed by narratives that feature these categories, as well as by frequent references to the "glory of the LORD" (Exodus 3, 19, 33, 40).

27. Piet Schoonenberg, S.J., *Covenant and Creation* (Notre Dame: University of Notre Dame Press, 1969), ix.

28. Ibid., 18. By this I do not mean binary, nor do I mean synthetic. This is not the worldview of Hegel, nor of Whitehead.

29. There are references in the Old Testament to *beritim* among equals (Gen. 21:27; 26:31; 31:44–54; 1 Kings 5:12; 15:19; 20:32–34; Amos 1:9). Yet in every reference to a covenant between God and the people of Israel, the covenant is established on the pattern of either unconditional ancient royal grant covenants or conditional suzerain-vassal covenants, which are not among equals.

tain it. Rather, they provide a means by which Israel can respond fittingly to actions of God on their behalf.

Some covenants between God and Israel attributed a greater significance to Israel's faithful obedience of covenant regulations. Both the second covenant with Abraham (Genesis 17) and the Sinai covenant most properly resemble conditional suzerain-vassal covenants of the ancient Near East. Such a covenant can be broken by either party, leaving the other party free from covenant obligation. The implication that Israel was bound to God only so far as Israel's obedience maintained the covenant has led some to question the continued use of the concept of covenant in Christian theology. Herbert Vorgrimler, for example, argues:

> Old Testament research has shown that in the final redaction of Deuteronomy the notion that God is related to his people Israel by means of a kind of contract between lord and vassal was abandoned: YHWH is a faithful God whose indescribable fidelity is not connected with human fulfillment of a contract. The concept of covenant has a juristic coloring and does not, of itself, include the ideas of love and graciousness.[30]

Yet not all covenants between God and Israel are of this type. The Noahic covenant, for example, is unconditional: God will never destroy the world again, regardless of the activity of the human race (Gen. 9:8–17). Other unconditional covenants include the Davidic covenant (2 Sam. 7:5–16) and the new covenant (Jer. 31:31–34), the two covenants, importantly, that sound with messianic overtones.

Fifth, a covenant is sealed by ritual ratification. The common pattern for covenant ratification has been described most thoroughly by Klaus Baltzer.[31] Several elements are common to the ratification ritual: an account of a history of any previous relationship between covenant partners, a summary of the intended future relationship, further details about that relationship, an invocation of gods to witness the covenant, and a pronouncement of curse and blessing. Accompanying such a covenant statement may be a ritual meal (Gen. 31:54; Exodus 24).[32] The covenant is also frequently ritually renewed in a pattern resembling covenant ratification (Exodus 34; Deut. 31:9–13; Joshua 24; 2 Kings 23; 2 Chronicles 15; Ezra 9–10; Nehemiah 9–10).

30. Vorgrimler, *Sacramental Theology*, 21 n. 5. Vorgrimler does not give the source for his analysis of Deuteronomy.

31. Klaus Baltzer, *The Covenant Formulary: In Old Testament, Jewish, and Early Christian Writings*, trans. David E. Green (Philadelphia: Fortress, 1971). See also Paul Kalluveettil, *Declaration and Covenant: A Comprehensive Review of Covenant Formulae from the Old Testament and the Ancient Near East* (Rome: Biblical Institute Press, 1982).

32. Gillian Feeley-Harnick, *The Lord's Table: Eucharist and Passover in Early Christianity* (Philadelphia: University of Pennsylvania Press, 1981).

These five characteristics, then, are common to the long tradition of covenant theology that reappears throughout the Old Testament. At times, the notion of covenant is clearly in the background; at other times, it serves as a primary literary and theological motif that anchors an entire book, such as Deuteronomy. But in each case, common meanings are evoked: Israel is reminded that it serves a God of promise and action, a God who initiates relationship, a God who invites thankful obedience and condescends to provide an opportunity for ritual affirmation of covenant love.

The covenant metaphor is certainly not as prominent in the New Testament as in the Old. Yet the references in the institution narratives mentioned above are supported by others that indicate precisely how this traditional motif might function in light of the coming of Christ.[33] Markus Barth, for example, goes so far as to say that "all references to *remembrance, blood of the covenant poured out* (for forgiveness of sin), *new covenant*, as well as the phrases *for you* and *for many*, carry the connotations they bear in Israel's Bible and worship."[34] Similarly, Mendenhall and Herion suggest that "the entire [New Testament] tradition points to some very important *substantive* connections with the type of suzerainty treaty exhibited in the Sinai covenant."[35] And W. G. Kümmel describes Jesus' ministry as culminating in the new eschatological covenant.[36]

One important set of these references is found in the Pauline corpus and is concentrated in Paul's letters to Corinth. In 2 Corinthians 3:6–18, for example, Paul describes ministry in the new covenant.[37] As Carol Kern Stockhausen observes, Paul's use of covenant language points to the radical discontinuity between the old and new covenants.[38] Significantly, Paul identifies the "new covenant" as a spiritual,

33. The covenant background to the New Testament has been explored by J. Reumann, "Heilsgeschichte in Luke," in *Studia Evangelica* 4, ed. F. L. Cross (Berlin: Akademie-Verlag, 1968), 86–115; and A. R. Millard, "Covenant and Communion in First Corinthians," in *Apostolic History and the Gospel*, ed. W. Ward Gasque and Ralph P. Martin (Exeter, U.K.: Paternoster, 1970), 242–48.

34. Markus Barth, *Rediscovering the Lord's Supper: Communion with Israel, with Christ, and among the Guests* (Atlanta: John Knox, 1988), 15.

35. Mendenhall and Herion, "Covenant," 1199.

36. W. G. Kümmel, *The Theology of the New Testament* (Nashville: Abingdon, 1973).

37. See Carol Kern Stockhausen, *Moses' Veil and the Glory of the New Covenant* (Rome: Pontificio Instituto Biblico, 1989); W. C. van Unnik, "La conception de la nouvelle alliance," *Recherches Biblique* V (Louvain: Desclée de Brouwer, 1960); Herman Ridderbos, *Paul: An Outline of His Theology*, trans. John Richard de Witt (Grand Rapids: Eerdmans, 1975); and N. T. Wright, *The Climax of the Covenant: Christ and Law in Pauline Theology* (Minneapolis: Fortress, 1992). Van Unnik attributes the Pauline concepts of righteousness and the mission to the Gentiles to an implicit theology of covenant in Paul. See Stockhausen, *Moses' Veil*, 44.

38. Stockhausen, *Moses' Veil*, 44.

not a written, covenant and develops this covenant reference not by explicating a particular ancient text (such as Jeremiah 31) but rather by forming what Stockhausen has called a "pool of covenant concepts."[39] Specifically, Paul sees a fundamental connection between the idea of the new covenant and that of the sending of the Spirit (2 Corinthians 3), which was likely the result of the coalescence of these concepts under the rubric of covenant prior to his time.

But by far the most significant elaboration of New Testament covenant theology is found in the letter to the Hebrews, also a crucial text in the development of eucharistic theology. The writer of Hebrews takes great pains to compare and contrast the old and new covenants. Like the old covenant, the new covenant is a covenant in blood (10:29; 12:24; 13:20). Unlike in the old covenant, the blood is that offered by the high priest himself (9:13f.; 10:12). Thus, the new covenant is mediated by Christ (8:6; 12:24) and is superior to the old (7:22). Interestingly, the writer of Hebrews neither directly refers to the eucharist nor compares the ways in which the old and new covenants were ritually ratified or renewed. What Hebrews does accomplish, however, is the elevation of the covenant motif in the New Testament canon, suggesting its vitality in the theologizing of the early church.

Finally, the covenant concept in both the Old and New Testaments is the context for the significant conjugal image applied to Christ's relationship with the church. This image was prefigured already in the Old Testament in both Hosea's portrayal of God's relationship with his people in conjugal terms and in the new covenant prophecy (Jer. 31:32). When Paul describes Christ as the spouse of the church and when the Apocalypse of John waxes eloquent about the forthcoming marriage feast of the Lamb, they are relying on a familiar image of God, who is eager to be bound in covenant with the worshiping community. The eucharistic implications of the marriage feast image are particularly significant for developing a eucharistic theology that is oriented to the eschatological reign of God. But the full implications of even this image are not discernible without its background in covenant.

In sum, the concept of covenant is a primary theological matrix that stands behind vast portions of Scripture, from the long series of Old Testament covenants right through to the theological interpretation of Jesus' ministry offered by the writer of Hebrews. And while no single image or metaphor can capture the full range of meanings carried by the Old and New Testament Scriptures, the concept of cove-

39. Stockhausen: "With the exegetical formation of the pool of covenant concepts around Jeremiah 31 (38 LXX) and its companion texts, a Christian understanding of covenant came into being. So the modern interpreter has gained historical insight into the process through which biblical theology is born. The 'covenant pool' *is* Paul's covenant theology. It is not produced by Paul's text in 2 Cor. 3:1–6; it lies behind it" (ibid., 64).

nant is remarkably adept at coalescing seemingly divergent traditions and interpretations. The careful connections drawn between covenant and eucharist thus tap into a rich stream of biblical theology.

Covenant in the History of Christianity

Given its prominence in Scripture, it is not surprising that the concept of covenant has frequently surfaced throughout the history of the church as Christians have sought to rearticulate the foundational insights of their faith. As with other themes in Christian theology, the historical use of the covenant motif has much to teach us about both its pitfalls and its prospects. Toward this end, it is helpful to distinguish three ways in which the covenant motif has functioned throughout the history of the church. Though the identification of these three is somewhat arbitrary, the differences among them are significant for sorting out the way in which this motif can most profitably be used in current ecumenical discussion.

A first use of the covenant motif restricts its reference to links between Jesus' death, our atonement, and the eucharist. Following the lead of Hebrews, this approach acknowledges the significance of understanding Jesus' death in light of the Old Testament sacrificial system without claiming anything more for the covenant metaphor. The covenant reference in the institution narratives has ensured that each generation of scriptural exegetes and preachers gives it some attention. John Chrysostom's careful expository preaching is but one example:

> But he speaks of the cause of his passion, the taking away of sins. And he calls it "blood of the new covenant," that is, of the promise of the gospel of the New Law. For he promised this also of old, and this comprises the Covenant that is in the New Law. And as the Old Covenant had sheep and calves, so this one has the Lord's blood. Hence also he shows that He is about to die, and for that reason He mentions a covenant, and He also reminds them of the former covenant, for that also was established by blood.[40]

Here is a classic example of relating the words of institution to the account of the covenant in Exodus 24 and observing their soteriological significance. It may be taken as a representative of countless others throughout the history of the church.

A second use of the covenant motif begins like the first but then goes on to suggest that the eucharist be viewed *primarily* in terms of

---

40. John Chrysostom's homily no. 82 on the Gospel of Matthew in Daniel Sheerin, *The Eucharist: Message of the Fathers of the Church* (Wilmington, Del.: Michael Glazier Books, 1986), 196. See also Chrysostom's homily no. 27 on 1 Corinthians (214).

covenant, whereby the eucharist is understood as covenant renewal. Baltzer, for example, in his analysis of the so-called Clementine liturgy in *Apostolic Constitutions VIII*, concluded that structurally it "can be termed a 'Christian covenant renewal.'"[41] Particularly significant is the addition of the phrase "this is the mystery of the new covenant," not only in reference to the cup but also in reference to the bread.[42] While this interpretation may impose upon the text an understanding that was not fully shared by the Christian community in Antioch in the fourth century, this is not the case with regard to many later generations of Christians who freely and self-consciously spoke of the eucharist as covenant renewal. As Kenneth Stevenson has chronicled, this was especially prominent among both Anglican and Puritan divines in seventeenth-century England.[43] In some cases, this insistence on covenant imagery persisted even into the Enlightenment period. As late as 1743, French Reformed pastor Jean-Frédéric Ostervald could argue that "it may be understood, that Sacraments were initiated, that they may be public pledges, and seals of the divine covenant, both on God's part, and on ours. For by them God offers, and confirms his grace to us, and we testify, and bind over our faith and obedience unto him."[44] The liturgical application of the covenant motif has not been restricted to Protestant thought, surfacing also in Roman Catholic theology. Emil Joseph Lengling, for example, has defined the liturgy of the church as "the actualization of the new covenant."[45]

While these explicit sources clearly establish the importance of the covenant motif in the history of Christian eucharistic theology, it may be that an implicit reference suggests the most fundamental connection with eucharistic theology, at least in the West. I refer here to the Latin term *sacramentum*, which became for Christians in the West the name for the genus of rituals in which the eucharist is the star species. *Sacramentum* originally referred, at least in one of its primary senses,

41. Baltzer, *Covenant Formulary*, 171. Interestingly, the baptismal rite in the *Apostolic Constitutions VII* refers to baptism as a "seal of the covenant," language that would become central in many Reformation catechisms and confessional statements.

42. The *Apostolic Constitutions* also features an early use of the phrase "seal of the covenant" in reference to baptism (*AC* 7.42). The Liturgy of St. James also features a reference to covenant, adding the phrase "the new covenant" in its *anamnesis*, a phrase that was not present in either the anaphora of *Mystagogical Catechesis* or in the Egyptian anaphora of St. Basil, from which St. James was likely redacted.

43. Kenneth Stevenson, *Covenant of Grace Renewed: A Vision of the Eucharist in the Seventeenth Century* (London: Darton, Longman, and Todd, 1994).

44. Jean-Frédéric Ostervald, *A Compendium of Christian Theology* (London: SPCK, 1743), 343–44.

45. Emil Joseph Lengling, "Liturgie/Liturgiewissenshaft," in *Neues Handbuch theologischer Grundbegriffe*, ed. P. Eicher (Munich: Kosel-Verlag, 1984–1985), 29, quoted in Vorgrimler, *Sacramental Theology*, 21.

to a soldier's oath of loyalty to the Roman Empire. Participation in a *sacramentum* meant taking an oath of loyalty. Pliny's famous letter of 112 c.e., for example, observed that the Christians gathered *se sacramento obstringere*, "to bind themselves by oath." Calling the eucharist a *sacramentum* clearly established it as an act of promise.[46] The resemblance to covenant renewal, while not explicit, is more than trivial.

The fittingness of the covenant image to the eucharist is further underscored by the striking resemblance of historic eucharistic liturgy to the covenant ratification or renewal ritual. Beginning with the recounting of God's deeds and, in particular, those deeds that enact and transform God's relationship with his people, the traditional eucharistic prayer continues by invoking God's presence in the feast and imagining the future of God's relationship with his people. This function is often embodied in the epicletic portions of the eucharistic prayer as, for example, the gathered congregation prays that they "may become one body and one spirit, and may have a portion with all the saints."[47] Thus, Christian liturgy's inheritance from Jewish patterns of prayer consists not only in a particular structure for prayer but also in a covenantal experience of faith.

A third use of the covenant motif elevates it still further, giving it primacy of place as the cornerstone of a theological system. Even as Walter Eichrodt elevated the concept of covenant as the single interpretive framework that unified his description of Old Testament theology, so this approach assigns covenant the same role in the systematization and explication of Christian theology. An early example of this approach might come from Irenaeus, who described the economy of salvation in terms of a series of four covenants, "one, prior to the deluge, under Adam; the second, that after the deluge, under Noah; the third, the giving of the law, under Moses; and the fourth, that which

46. See Mendenhall and Herion, "Covenant," 1198. This is not, of course, the full sense of the term as described by Augustine, who forever changed how this term would function in eucharistic theology. Interestingly, when Ulrich Zwingli exegeted the term *sacrament* in his *Commentary Concerning True and False Religion* (1525), he went behind Augustine, so to speak, to argue that a sacrament was primarily a pledge or a sign, the sense of Pliny's use of the term.

47. From the Egyptian anaphora of St. Basil, R. C. D. Jasper and G. J. Cuming, *Prayers of the Eucharist: Early and Reformed* (Collegeville, Minn.: Liturgical Press, 1990), 71. Almost any historic eucharistic prayer could supply a relevant text. The concluding portions of most eucharistic prayers fulfill the function of envisioning the future relationship of God and the worshiping community. We pray, especially at the Lord's Supper, in the direction of our covenantal expectations. In addition, one could argue that the pattern of covenant renewal argues for the integral connection of Word and sacrament, that as in Exodus 24, the covenant can be ratified or renewed in a fellowship meal only after the account of God's works has been recited. See Hughes Oliphant Old, *Themes and Variations for a Christian Doxology* (Grand Rapids: Eerdmans, 1992), 111–37.

renovates man, and sums up all things in itself by means of the gospel,"[48] with eucharistic bread and cup serving as "the new oblation of the new covenant."[49] Many centuries later, the covenant motif resurfaced as a significant component in the nominalism of Gabriel Biel.[50]

But the full flowering of covenant theology would have to wait for the sixteenth century and, in particular, for the Reformed branch of Protestantism. Prominent already in the sixteenth-century writings of Oecolampadius, Capito, Zwingli, Calvin, and especially Bullinger, the covenant motif reached its summit in the work of Dutch Calvinist Johannes Cocceius, whose *Summa Doctrinae de foedere et testamento Dei* (1648) featured the covenant motif as its primary interpretive framework.[51] A similar appropriation of covenant theology was made by the Puritan extension of Calvinist thought, as found in the work of William Ames and Richard Baxter. But covenantal theology was in no way restricted to the Reformed tradition, for it was featured by such wide-ranging figures as Lancelot Andrewes[52] and John Wesley. As careful a student as Geoffrey Wainwright notes the striking similarity in Wesley's and Calvin's use of covenant.[53] Likewise, covenant was an important dimension of Lutheran eucharistic theology.[54] In fact, it was the concept of covenant, *diatheke*, that sup-

48. Irenaeus, *Against Heresies*, 3.11.8, in *The Writings of Irenaeus*, vol. 1, trans. Alexander Roberts and W. H. Rambaut (Edinburgh: T & T Clark, 1869), 295.

49. Irenaeus, "Fragments from the Lost Writings of Irenaeus," no. 37, in *The Writings of Irenaeus*, vol. 2, trans. Alexander Roberts and W. H. Rambaut (Edinburgh: T & T Clark, 1869), 176.

50. Heiko Oberman, *The Harvest of Medieval Theology: Gabriel Biel and Later Medieval Nominalism* (Cambridge: Harvard University Press, 1963).

51. The most important works on this vast topic include J. Wayne Baker, *Heinrich Bullinger and the Covenant: The Other Reformed Tradition* (Athens, Ohio: Ohio University Press, 1980); Lyle Bierma, "Federal Theology in the Sixteenth Century: Two Traditions," *Westminster Theological Journal* 45 (1983): 304–21; Charles S. McCoy, *History, Humanity, and Federalism in the Theology and Ethics of Johannes Cocceius* (Philadelphia: Center for the Study of Federalism, Temple University, 1980); Charles S. McCoy and J. Wayne Baker, *Fountainhead of Federalism: Heinrich Bullinger and the Covenantal Tradition* (Louisville: Westminster John Knox, 1985); David N. J. Poole, *The History of the Covenant Concept from the Bible to Johannes Cloppenburg "De Foedere Dei"* (San Francisco: Mellen Research University Press, 1992); Stephen Strehle, *Calvinism, Federalism, and Scholasticism: A Study of the Reformed Doctrine of the Covenant* (New York: Peter Lang, 1988); Jon Von Rohr, *The Covenant of Grace in Puritan Thought* (Atlanta: Scholars Press, 1986); and David A. Weir, *The Origins of the Federal Theology in Sixteenth-Century Reformation Thought* (Oxford: Clarendon Press, 1990).

52. Stevenson, *Covenant of Grace Renewed*, 52.

53. Geoffrey Wainwright, *Geoffrey Wainwright on Wesley and Calvin: Sources for Theology, Liturgy, and Spirituality* (Melbourne: Uniting Church Press, 1987), 36. See Old, *Themes and Variations*, 129.

54. See, for example, Martin Chemnitz, *The Lord's Supper = De Coena Domini*, trans. J. A. O. Preus (St. Louis: Concordia, 1979), 115f.

ported Luther's unflinching argument against the notion of the eucharistic sacrifice.[55]

In the twentieth century, the covenant image was featured prominently in the writings of both Roman Catholic and Protestant systematic theologians, to say nothing of the thousands of pages written on the subject by biblical theologians. Not surprisingly, covenant was featured prominently in the writings of Karl Barth, particularly in his treatment of baptism.[56] More recently, it has been used as a central motif in the writings of Hendrikus Berkhof, as well as by Roman Catholic theologians as diverse as Donald Keefe, Piet Schoonenberg, and J.-M. R. Tillard.[57] Given this wealth of material, it is all the more surprising that it has not surfaced more in ecumenical discussions of the eucharist.

It is this final category that provides the careful observer with a red flag or two about the use of the covenant motif. Briefly stated, an over-reliance on covenant language can result and has resulted in a number of indiscretions. First, per Vorgrimler's criticism, covenant language can degenerate into contractual theology.[58] That is, the human response to God's institution of a covenant relationship can be taken too seriously. Moral rectitude can be taken as a prerequisite rather than a by-product of participation in the community of faith. Just as a modern marriage is belittled by a prenuptial contract, so a covenant relationship can degenerate into a moral contract. Second, the covenant motif can be unduly elevated, causing other more prominent biblical images to be disregarded. One writer has spoken recently of "covenant

55. Luther understood *diatheke* not primarily as covenant in the broad relational sense described earlier but rather in the narrower sense of promise or testament. Luther's understanding pitted "sacrifice," an offering from the church to God, against "testament," a gift from God to the church; for him it was a choice of one or the other, and "sacrifice" was the wrong one. As Luther observed, "It is impossible for a thing to be a sacrifice and a testament at the same time" (quoted in Vilmos Vajta, *Luther on Worship* [Philadelphia: Muhlenberg Press, 1958], 38–46). This meant that the Mass ought to be understood primarily in terms of the promise of God, where the Words of Institution could just as well be called words of promise (41).

56. See Arthur C. Cochrane, "Karl Barth's Doctrine of the Covenant," in *A Covenant Challenge to Our Broken World*, ed. Allen O. Miller (Atlanta: Darby, 1982), 156–64, reprinted in Donald K. McKim, ed., *Major Themes in the Reformed Tradition* (Grand Rapids: Eerdmans, 1992), 108–16.

57. Hendrikus Berkhof, *Christian Faith: An Introduction to the Study of the Faith*, trans. Sierd Woudstra (Grand Rapids: Eerdmans, 1979); Donald J. Keefe, S.J., *Covenantal Theology: The Eucharistic Order of History* (Lanham, Md.: University Press of America, 1991); Schoonenberg, *Covenant and Creation*; and J.-M. R. Tillard, *L'eucharistie: Pâque de L'Église* (Paris: Les Éditions Du Cerf, 1964).

58. James B. Torrance, "Covenant or Contract? A Study of the Theological Background of Worship in Seventeenth Century Scotland," *Scottish Journal of Theology* 23 (1970): 51–76.

overload in Reformed theology," arguing that the New Testament concept of the kingdom of God should be featured more prominently than covenant, reflecting a balance more in tune with the New Testament itself.[59] This warning is especially important in eucharistic theology, where the convergence and interplay among biblical images is precisely the source of so many promising developments in ecumenical discussion. Third and finally, the covenant motif cannot be separated from the narrative and historical specificity of the biblical covenants.[60] Although the concept of covenant can be construed in the abstract, it is not this abstraction that ought to be operative in theology but rather the rootedness of covenant in the history of Israel. Lifting the Mosaic covenant, for example, from its context of God's emancipation of Israel from Egypt empties it of its potential to speak to soteriological issues and distorts its contribution to theology proper.

Prospects for Contemporary Eucharistic Theology

Given these warnings, how ought this covenant motif function today? What role should it be assigned in contemporary eucharistic theology? The following paragraphs suggest four possible uses for this rich biblical concept. Although related, they are not necessarily interdependent. That is, the covenant metaphor is a possible but not a necessary context in which any of the following issues might be discussed.

First, the covenant motif is potentially helpful for nuancing the debate concerning the persistent problem of eucharistic presence. It is consequential that this debate has always returned to the strikingly simple words of Jesus, "This is my body. This is my blood." But is this what the New Testament records? Matthew and Mark record "This is my body" but then later continue, "This is my blood of the covenant" (Matt. 26:26, 28; Mark 14:22, 24). Luke and Paul record "This is my body" but then later continue, "This cup is the new covenant in my blood" (Luke 22:19–20; 1 Cor. 11:24–25). So while all four accounts of the institution narrative say without equivocation that "this is my body," in every case their reference to the cup is not simply "this is my blood" but one that links the cup to the covenant motif. However one feels about the traditional dispute over the substance of Christ in the eucharistic elements, this interpretive framework cannot be ignored.

59. Stek, "'Covenant' Overload in Reformed Theology," 12–41.
60. Stek notes, for example, that in the Reformed tradition, the organizing principle of covenant "came to have . . . a probative force of [its] own, even when at times these constructs strained and constrained the biblical data to their limits and beyond" (ibid., 16).

But what might this imply? Let me suggest that it means that what is rendered present to the eucharistic community is not only the person of Christ but also the new reality that has been brought into being through Christ. When Christ extends his cup to us, it is not only himself that is given but also the full promise of all that the new covenant implies. The eucharist, then, is not only a moment for presence but a moment of action. In this gesture, God acts, signing and sealing the promise of the new covenant in Christ's blood. God's people, in turn, respond in faith and hope, claiming their participation in this new covenant.

This does not minimize the significance of the presence of Christ for the worshiping community, for the covenant motif itself recalls a meal eaten in the presence of God (Exodus 24). What is significant, then, is not the subversion of the notion of presence but a transformation of it. This experience of the presence of God in Christ may be taken not as a final stasis, or resting point, for which God's people yearn. Just as in Exodus, where the meal in the presence of God precipitated a relationship that was lived out over the many ensuing years of Israel's history, so too our participation in Christ's blood of the covenant points to promises that will guide the living out of a covenant relationship. The benefit of God's presence, then, is better reflected in eucharistic worship and subsequent acts of justice than it ever could be in extended periods of adoration of the sacrament without such acts.

Second, the covenant image points to the binding together of Christians with their God in eucharist. The eucharist is both communion and *koinonia* in their deepest sense. Just as the elders of Israel ate in the presence of God at the ratification of the covenant (Exodus 24), so too our participation in the eucharist is a sign of union with Christ. In the covenantal language of *St. Patrick's Breastplate*, eucharistic participation is an act whereby "I bind unto myself today the strong name of Trinity." The intimacy of the relationship is implied by the act of eating and drinking, by which we take into ourselves the very substance that signifies our relationship.

Further, the covenant motif provides yet one more reminder that the eucharist is essentially a corporate event, for in covenant bond, worshipers are linked both with God and one another. In the words of Herman Ridderbos:

> As in the making of the covenant at Sinai the shedding of blood was of foundational significance (Exod. 24:8), so the new relationship between God and his people, promised in prophecy, rests on the sacrifice of Christ in which the church receives a share in the Supper. In the Supper, therefore, the foundations of the church are laid bare. The Supper is no

personal affair between the individual believer and Christ. It is the covenantal meal, the congregational meal *par excellence*.[61]

Just as the Sinai covenant was given to a people, so too the new
covenant in Christ's blood is given to those who drink of the cup. Just
as that community rendered its post-Sinai worship, so too we join in
corporate celebration of the new covenant. God's covenanting activity
is never restricted to an individual. Even when God established a covenant with one person, as with Noah, the implications of the covenant
extended far beyond that individual. In the Noahic covenant, God's
promise never to destroy the world procures benefits for all of humanity and, indeed, for all of creation. The notion of covenant does not allow for an individualistic understanding of the Christian faith.

Third, covenant provides the context for understanding links between eucharist and eschatology. For the people of Israel, the promise
of the future was expressed in covenantal terms (Jeremiah 31), with
all hope dependent on God's initiative, even in the face of wanton un-
faithfulness on the part of God's people. Thus, it is not surprising that
Jürgen Moltmann considers covenant theology "the start of a new eschatological way of thinking." For Moltmann, this theological matrix
calls "to life the feeling for history,"[62] serving as a constant reference
to the works of God throughout the history of salvation and as a sure
basis for future promise. In part, this is due to the inherent connection between covenant and promise, as Alasdair Heron observes: "The
note of promise associated with the covenant also reminds us again of
the fact that the eucharist does not only have to do with what *has
been*, but also with what *will be*. The covenant leads on into the future:
'I will be your God and you will be my people.' . . . The covenant is the
promise of the coming kingdom."[63]

This same link of eucharist to eschatology is made exegetically by
Ernst Käsemann, who argued that "the new *diatheke* [covenant] is
nothing other than the form of the *basileia tou theou* [kingdom of
God] which Christ has introduced as an already present reality." Given
this association, it is the cup that grants "participation in this dispensation of divine rule in that it grants participation in the death of
Jesus on which the dispensation is founded."[64] The exegetical case for
the linking of covenant and kingdom is made on the basis of passages

61. Ridderbos, *Paul*, 423.
62. Jürgen Moltmann, *A Theology of Hope*, trans. James W. Leitch (New York:
Harper & Row, 1967), 70.
63. Heron, *Table and Tradition*, 32.
64. Ernst Käsemann, "Anliegen und Eigenart des paulinischen Abendmahls," in *Ex-
egetische Versuche und Besinnungen* I, 28–31, quoted in Wainwright, *Eucharist and Eschatology*, 42.

such as Luke 22:29 that carefully echo the Old Testament covenant formula.[65]

In addition, as has already been established, covenant theology is an important theological foundation for understanding the provocative eschatological texts concerning the feast to come in the kingdom of heaven. When Revelation 19 depicts the triumphant marriage feast of the Lamb, it is building on the well-established conjugal image for Christ and the church (Matt. 25:1–10; Eph. 5:25–32), which in turn rests on covenant theology. Even more striking is John's description of the New Jerusalem, which he offers in terms of the Old Testament covenant refrain: "They will be his people, and God himself will be with them and be their God" (Rev. 21:3). Here is perhaps the best case for the continued use of the covenant metaphor, for even in the seemingly impossible task of envisioning the future reign of God, one of the fundamental biblical images used is that of covenant. This reference serves as a fitting *inclusio* to the canon of Scripture, which began with a God who was present to his creatures in the Garden and who, even after their disobedience, sought to restore a relationship on covenantal terms, first with Noah and then with Abram, Moses, and David.

Fourth and finally, covenant theology provides a starting point for discussing the ethical implications of the eucharist. The twentieth-century liturgical movement is justly famous for a renewed appreciation for the relationship between liturgy and ethics.[66] Like the prophet Amos of old, modern prophetic voices, such as Virgil Michel and the liberationists, have called for the church to renew not only its liturgical celebration but also its commitment to the poor. The ethical implications of participation in the eucharist have often been expressed using the language of covenant. As Cipriano Vagaggini suggested, "Among all Christian acts, the Mass is par excellence the new covenant, the new alliance, in the blood of Christ. Whoever participates in the Mass, especially in communion, accepts this covenant and makes

65. The Hebrew formula for the making of a covenant was rendered in the Septuagint as *diatheken diatithemai*. The reference to conferring the kingdom in Luke 22 uses the same verb *diatithemai*.

66. See, for example, James L. Empereur and Christopher Kiesling, *The Liturgy That Does Justice* (Collegeville, Minn.: Glazier/Liturgical Press, 1989); Kathleen Hughes and Mark R. Francis, *Living No Longer for Ourselves: Liturgy and Justice in the Nineties* (Collegeville, Minn.: Liturgical Press, 1991); Daniel F. Polish and Eugene J. Fisher, *Liturgical Foundations of Social Policy in the Catholic and Jewish Traditions* (Notre Dame: University of Notre Dame Press, 1983); Mark Searle, *Liturgy and Social Justice* (Collegeville, Minn.: Liturgical Press, 1980); William H. Willimon, *The Service of God: Christian Work and Worship* (Nashville: Abingdon, 1983); and two theme issues on the subject: *Reformed Liturgy and Music* 19 (1985); and *Journal of Religious Ethics* 7, no. 2 (fall 1979): 139–248.

it solemnly his own. And a covenant involves obligation."[67] Similarly, David Power argues:

> As a covenant people, the church lives under the pledge of God's fidelity and in the remembrance of its vow to give God praise in word and deed. This vow includes the commitment to recall the story of the passion and its promise even in times of desperation. As a covenant community the church lives out the witness to God required of it, and with the hope that the remembrance of Christ's saving passion inspires. Through drinking of the cup of which Christ drank, through sharing together in the cup of the blood poured out, the church expresses and appropriates its reality as a covenant people. Covenant as a covenant found in the two commandments of love of God and neighbor, as an eschatological wisdom that is an alternative wisdom to wisdoms of the world, shapes the community of those who take part in the sacrament.[68]

Likewise, Vorgrimler says, "The liturgy makes this covenant present, whenever it is celebrated, and thus keeps before our eyes the fact that God expects of the partners in the covenant a particular ethical standard of behavior."[69] The very notion of covenant obligation recorded especially in the Sinai covenant conveys the urgency of human obedience in light of God's gracious condescension.

Such discussion has the advantage of taking seriously Paul's moral exhortations concerning participation in the eucharist. First Corinthians 11:27–32, which, interestingly, can be viewed as a parallel to the curse or malediction formulae found in traditional *berit* (covenants), makes clear that "unworthy" participation mocks the profound significance of the eucharistic celebration. The Pauline exhortation is made in strident terms: Improper reception is nothing less than a sin "against the body and blood of the Lord" (11:27). Despite the strong language, this sense of this warning does not figure prominently in either current eucharistic debate nor in the piety of most worshiping communities. In their recovery of eucharist as thanksgiving, most recent liturgies have shunned any reference to the moral obligations that accompany reception. The absence of reference to this significant text in BEM is yet another sign of its relative nonuse by modern Christians.

In part, this is explained by its overuse in communities that took covenant language too seriously. In seventeenth-century Scotland, for example, efforts to fence the table, inspired by this very section of

---

67. Cipriano Vagaggini, *Theological Dimensions of the Liturgy*, vol. 1, trans. Leonard J. Doyle (Collegeville, Minn.: Liturgical Press, 1959), 85.

68. Power, *Eucharistic Mystery*, 298.

69. Vorgrimler, *Sacramental Theology*, 141.

1 Corinthians, were symptomatic of the degeneration of covenant into contract.[70] The danger, of course, was then and is now that such rigorous exhortation might distort the portrait of God's grace depicted by the eucharist or spook zealous Christians from partaking in the eucharist for fear of eating and drinking judgment to themselves.[71] The challenge here is nothing more or less than the church's ancient struggle with antinomianism, on the one hand, and moral rigorism, on the other. The question is how the church can hold together its firm moral convictions with an unflinching conviction concerning the free and unmerited grace of God. It is this question that covenant theology is poised to answer, for in covenant, God is the unbound initiator of the relationship we are privileged to share. God's grace deigns to order the economy of salvation and to offer this gift to the world. Yet participation in covenant also commends to us free and thankful obedience to this gracious God, in accordance with the structures with which his free will has endowed the universe.

Also relevant to this discussion is the distinction between covenants made above. When Exodus 24 is taken as the only or even the primary Old Testament covenant to which the words of institution might refer, the mandatory obligation of covenant obedience and the conditional nature of the covenant itself tempt exegetes to highlight the contractual nature of the community's relationship with God. But the unconditional structure of the new covenant, so clearly the basis of vast portions of New Testament theology, provides a basis for connecting eucharist and ethics without the trap of contractual language. In addition, new covenant ethics avoids legalism because of its eschatological character. The promise of Jeremiah 31 is that God will inscribe the law on our hearts. Disobedience and faithlessness, in this anticipated future, is inconceivable. Affirming one's participation in the new covenant by means of reception of the eucharist stands as a witness to one's sanctification and participation in this new order of reality, which is hardly juridical in content or tone.

In sum, all four institution narratives explain the significance of the eucharistic meal in terms of the time-honored Old Testament theme of covenant. Throughout the history of the church, Christians have used this concept to explain the significance not only of the economy of salvation in general but also of participation in the eucharist in particular. The image of covenant continues to provide the Christian community with resources that could nuance and even transcend traditional disputes concerning the eucharist. In part, this is due to the

---

70. Torrance, "Covenant or Contract?" 68.

71. Certainly, the Jansenists and Pietists are examples of those who have emphasized this moral rigor to their peril.

far-reaching implications of covenant theology for theology proper, ethics, eschatology, and ecclesiology. As Power has suggested, "The covenant is an image that opens up vistas of interpretation beyond a link with any specific text."[72] Further, this concept brings together and crystallizes otherwise competing and independent concepts, such as sacrifice and promise, grace and obedience. It is not by any means the only or even the most fruitful biblical image for the eucharist, but it is one that deserves to be reclaimed from those given secondary status in recent ecumenical discussions and one that warrants significant attention in future work in eucharistic theology. When John Reumann says of BEM, "Some might want 'covenant' stressed more," he is right![73]

72. Power, *Eucharistic Mystery*, 53.
73. Reumann, *The Supper of the Lord*, 152.

4

Theological Models
for the Relationship
between Liturgy and Culture

F ew liturgical topics have generated as much interest in the past
generation as the relationship between liturgy and culture. Liturgical
historians have become increasingly interested in questions of social
and cultural history in efforts to discern the nature of the inevitable
interaction between cultural forces and liturgical practices in each period of church history. Liturgical theologians have attempted to explicate the meaning of particular liturgical actions by devoting special
attention to the ways in which they are shaped by their cultural environments. And those interested in efforts at liturgical reform have become increasingly concerned with the ways in which local cultural
mores can best contribute to liturgical celebration. These cultural
concerns were highlighted most famously in the "Constitution on Sacred Liturgy": "Even in the liturgy the Church does not wish to impose
a rigid uniformity in matters which do not involve the faith or the
good of the whole community. Rather does she respect and foster the
qualities and talents of the various races and nations."[1] This agenda
has led to a large program for the inculturation of particular rites,
texts, symbols, and gestures in many liturgical traditions.

1. "Constitution on Sacred Liturgy," art. 37, in *Vatican Council II: The Conciliar and
Post Conciliar Documents*, ed. Austin Flannery, O.P. (Grand Rapids: Eerdmans, 1992),
13.

Part of the challenge in approaching this area of study and practice is the need to deal with a vast and disparate literature on the subject. The relationship between liturgy and culture is, in fact, addressed by at least the following eight discrete bodies of literature:

1. *Liturgical history.* This literature includes studies of the ways in which Christian liturgy has been shaped, intentionally or not, by cultural influences in the past. The topic of cultural influence has particularly interested students of early Christian liturgy who have long wrestled, for example, with the particular influence of Greco-Roman culture on the emerging patterns of liturgy in the West.[2]

2. *Missiology/evangelization.* This literature analyzes both liturgical practices and a given cultural milieu for the express purpose of evangelization. Often "target" cultures are analyzed to determine "points of contact" for the proclamation of the gospel and the celebration of Christian worship. This literature has been especially influential in reshaping the practice of Protestant worship in North America, as missiological concerns have called for reforming worship practices to conform with cultural patterns of communication.[3]

3. *Cultural anthropology.* This literature attempts to study the cultural dynamics of a given community, most often by someone from the outside. This literature is sometimes used by church communities to develop theories of inculturation or models for cross-cultural evangelization.[4]

4. *Cultural criticism.* This literature attempts to articulate and either defend or critique salient aspects of a given culture. It is often written from within a given cultural environment.[5]

5. *Contextual theology.* This literature reflects on the ways in which culture shapes theological reflection and, more particularly, how aspects of the Christian tradition can be expressed in terms of particular cultural patterns. An overview of this literature is provided by Stephen Bevans in *Models of Contextual Theology.*

---

2. Typical studies in this area include Thomas J. Talley, "Roman Culture and Roman Liturgy," in *Rule of Prayer, Rule of Faith: Essays in Honor of Aidan Kavanagh, O.S.B.,* ed. Nathan Mitchell and John F. Baldovin, S.J. (Collegeville, Minn.: Liturgical Press, 1996), 18–31; and Pierre-Marie Gy, "The Inculturation of the Christian Liturgy in the West," *Studia Liturgica* 20 (1990): 8–18.

3. See, for example, Ed Dobson, *Starting a Seeker Service: How Traditional Churches Can Reach the Unchurched* (Grand Rapids: Zondervan, 1993); and George R. Hunsberger and Craig Van Gelder, *The Church between Gospel and Culture: The Emerging Mission in North America* (Grand Rapids: Eerdmans, 1996).

4. For this literature, see the bibliography in *Liturgy Digest* 2, no. 2 (1994).

5. For a list of typical works, see note 38 below.

6. (*Theological*) *social ethics.* This literature attempts to describe how Christianity bears upon culture as a whole and how the Christian community can best interact with particular social, political, and cultural patterns and practices. The most cited work in this field is H. Richard Niebuhr's *Christ and Culture.*
7. *Ritual studies.* This literature studies the dynamic of ritual (including liturgical) action, with particular attention to the ways in which significant meaning is expressed and reflected in and through culturally specific ritual action.[6]
8. *Liturgical inculturation.* This literature involves the specific attempts of liturgists to develop both theories and models for adapting or "inculturating" particular rites, symbols, and gestures.[7]

This list is certainly not exhaustive; moreover, some of these areas of study cannot be neatly divided from others. But this list is sufficient to demonstrate the complexity of study in this area. Liturgists have a great deal of experience in some of these fields and very little in others. The success of future efforts toward liturgical inculturation may well depend on the willingness of liturgists to engage a broad cross section of this literature while being well aware of the working assumptions and stated purposes of each discipline.

One important distinction to make at the outset of any discussion of liturgy and culture is the difference between analysis of one's own cultural milieu and analysis of another cultural context. The areas of scholarly inquiry described above tend to divide along this distinction. Cultural anthropology and evangelization often (though not always) concern the analysis of another cultural environment, while the processes of local liturgical inculturation and cultural criticism often (but not always) are approached from within a cultural environment.

This distinction is mirrored by the nature of the role and presence of the Christian church within a particular cultural environment. Some efforts at inculturation occur within cultures in which the church is already established. These efforts find support from a church already largely inculturated. In contrast, some moves toward cultural engagement consist of missionary enterprises aimed at establishing Christian churches in new cultural contexts, such as early Jesuit missionary efforts with Native Americans or current efforts to evangelize various third world countries.

6. For guides to this literature, see the bibliographies in *Liturgy Digest* 1, no. 1 (1993), and 2, no. 2 (1994).
7. Typical examples of this work include S. Anita Stauffer, ed., *Worship and Culture in Dialogue* (Geneva: Lutheran World Federation, 1994); and Anscar Chupungco, *Liturgical Inculturation: Sacramentals, Religiosity, and Catechesis* (Collegeville, Minn.: Liturgical Press, 1992).

These two strands of cultural involvement are rarely considered together. The former is typically the domain of social ethicists, the latter
the domain of missionaries and missiologists. But what is significant
for the discussion of liturgical inculturation is the striking similarity
between these two tasks, for each requires an assessment and evaluation of the cultural context, the articulation of a posture for relating to
that culture, and the development of strategies with which to engage
it. In each of these efforts, Christian churches are addressing an aspect of human culture and are doing so in a self-consciously Christian
way. Liturgists considering cultural issues must learn from the insights of both social ethicists and missiologists, from both cultural analysts and cultural anthropologists, from both "internal" cultural critiques and "external" cultural analyses.

This chapter begins with two sections that correspond to these two
concerns. The first examines various approaches to cultural questions
by Christians living within a particular cultural environment. This section is based on a review and analysis of H. Richard Niebuhr's influential *Christ and Culture*. The second section examines efforts to probe
cross-cultural patterns of exchange, particularly in light of recent conversations about contextual theology. This section is based on a review
and analysis of Steven Bevans's *Models of Contextual Theology*. Finally,
a third section explores common themes in recent writings concerning liturgical inculturation in light of this preceding analysis.

Models of Christ and Culture: The Legacy of H. Richard Niebuhr

The most influential book of the twentieth century on the relationship between the Christian faith and culture is almost certainly
H. Richard Niebuhr's *Christ and Culture*.[8] Niebuhr's classic volume is
an attempt to come to terms with the myriad ways Christians have
chosen to interact with culture and their subsequent attempts to justify
their actions theologically. The book presents a streamlined typology of
five typical approaches Christians take in regard to cultural issues.

Niebuhr's book is actually one of a small genre of volumes that has
attempted to analyze the ways in which Christians have interacted
with culture. Antedating Niebuhr's work is the analysis offered by German scholar Ernst Troeltsch.[9] Since the publication of *Christ and Cul-*

8. H. Richard Niebuhr, *Christ and Culture* (New York: Harper & Row, 1951).
9. Ernst Troeltsch, *The Social Teaching of the Christian Churches*, trans. Olive Wyon,
2 vols. (New York: Macmillan, 1931). Niebuhr acknowledges his dependence on
Troeltsch (*Christ and Culture*, xii). Troeltsch's threefold typology consisted of three christological images and their attendant ecclesiological ramifications. His three types were
(1) Christ as Lord—an emphasis of sectarian, morally rigorous communities; (2) Christ
as Redeemer—an emphasis of sacramental, established churches; and (3) Christ as
Spirit—an emphasis of mystical Christianity.

ture, a number of works have attempted to redraw the lines of analysis in slightly different ways.[10] But Niebuhr's book certainly remains the most influential and widely read of these studies. Niebuhr's influence has also extended to Christian liturgists. Works by John Fenwick and Bryan Spinks, Kathleen Hughes, S. Anita Stauffer, Geoffrey Wainwright, Paul Westermeyer, and James F. White, among others, have all prominently featured Niebuhr's typology.[11] These examples are no doubt multiplied by countless other references in informal dialogs at professional conferences, church assemblies, and the like. In fact, Niebuhr's typology may be among the most often used bits of twentieth-century theological jargon.

The problem with such pervasive use and influence, of this or any popular work, is that the work's ideas can quickly be divorced from the author's own stated purpose or the genius of the original analysis. Even liturgical decisions can be hastily categorized as "of culture" or "against culture," without a sense for what Niebuhr intended these labels to mean. The aim of the next paragraphs is simply to hear Niebuhr in his own words, to reform our perception of his "types" on the basis of the original text. The following paragraphs present a quick tour of *Christ and Culture,* with specific reference to some of Niebuhr's most famous passages. Brief comments and analysis follow this basic explication.[12]

10. See, for example, Robert Webber, *The Church in the World: Opposition, Tension, or Transformation?* (Grand Rapids: Zondervan, 1986); John H. Yoder, "A People in the World: Theological Interpretation," in *The Concept of the Believer's Church,* ed. James Leo Garrett Jr. (Scottdale, Pa.: Herald Press, 1969), 250–83; Charles H. Kraft, "The Church in Culture—A Dynamic Equivalence Model," in *Down to Earth: Studies in Christianity and Culture,* ed. John R. W. Stott and Robert Coote (Grand Rapids: Eerdmans, 1980), 211–30; George R. Saunders, *Culture and Christianity: The Dialectics of Transformation* (New York: Greenwood Press, 1988); Marvin K. Myers, *Christianity Confronts Culture* (Grand Rapids: Zondervan, 1987); and Arnold van Ruler, "Christ Taking Form in the World: The Relation between Church and Culture," in *Calvinist Trinitarianism and Theocentric Politics: Essays toward a Public Theology,* trans. John Bolt (Lewiston, N.Y.: Edwin Mellon Press, 1989), 105–48.

11. John Fenwick and Bryan Spinks, *Worship in Transition: The Liturgical Movement in the Twentieth Century* (New York: Continuum Books, 1995), 165–66; S. Anita Stauffer, "Christian Worship: Toward Localization and Globalization," in *Worship and Culture in Dialogue,* ed. S. Anita Stauffer (Geneva: Lutheran World Federation, 1994), 9–10; Geoffrey Wainwright, *Doxology: The Praise of God in Worship, Doctrine, and Life* (New York: Oxford University Press, 1980), 384–98; Paul Westermeyer, "The Present State of Church Music: Historical and Theological Reflections," *Word and World* 12 (summer 1992): 214–20; James F. White, "Worship and Culture: Mirror or Beacon?" *Theological Studies* 35 (1974): 288–301; and Kathleen Hughes, "Liturgical Year: Conflict and Challenge," in *The Church Gives Thanks and Remembers,* ed. Lawrence J. Johnson (Collegeville, Minn.: Liturgical Press, 1984), 69–86. Hughes uses Niebuhr's typology to examine the relationship between the civil and the Christian year.

12. Page references are included in parentheses within the text.

Christ and Culture Revisited

Niebuhr identifies the subject of his famous book as "the double wrestle of the church with its Lord and with the cultural society with which it lives in symbiosis" (xi). As this summary and the title of the book itself suggest, Niebuhr's analysis is set between the "two poles" of Christ and culture (11) or, to put it another way, within a Christ-culture dialectic. By "Christ," Niebuhr presumably means the whole of the gospel message as encompassed by cult, conduct, and creed. He acknowledges the sheer diversity of the ways in which "Christ" is interpreted (12) but still acknowledges a "fundamental unity which is supplied by the fact that the Jesus Christ to whom men are related in such different ways is a definite character and person whose teachings, actions, and sufferings are of one piece" (12). By "culture," Niebuhr means "that total process of human activity" that "comprises language, habits, ideas, beliefs, customs, social organization, inherited artifacts, technical processes, and values" (32). It is in the broad sense of these terms that Niebuhr's analysis is cast.

Niebuhr begins by noting the pervasiveness of the Christ-culture question. In an important programmatic sentence, Niebuhr observes that "repeated struggles of Christians with this problem have yielded no single Christian answer, but only a series of typical answers which together, for faith, represent phases of the strategy of the militant church in the world" (2). It is these typical answers or approaches that Niebuhr seeks to illuminate. He does so according to a typology that, "though historically inadequate, has the advantage of calling to attention the continuity and significance of the great *motifs* that appear and reappear in the long wrestling of Christians with their enduring problem [of Christ and culture]" (44). The rest of the book treats each of the five types in turn, devoting a full chapter to describing the inner logic and some prominent historical examples of each.

Christ against Culture

Niebuhr's first type—Christ against culture—"uncompromisingly affirms the sole authority of Christ over the Christian and resolutely rejects culture's claims to loyalty" (45). This position emphasizes the "two themes of love and faith in Jesus Christ" but concurrently contends that "the counterpart of loyalty to Christ and the brothers is the rejection of cultural society" (47). In this view, "that world appears as a realm under the power of evil . . . into which the citizens of the kingdom of light must not enter" (48). The key to the Christian life from this point of view is the "new and separated community" (49). Recalling the language of the *Didache,* this form of Christianity distinguishes sharply between the "two ways" of good and evil (50): "The line was sharply drawn between the new people and the old society, between obedience to the law of Christ and simple lawlessness" (51). For Tertullian, a prime example of this type, "the conflict of the believer is not with nature but with culture, for it is in culture that sin chiefly resides" (52, also 78), a position carried to a further extreme by Leo Tolstoy (60). Representatives of this movement share a "common acknowledgment of the sole authority of Jesus Christ and the common rejection of the prevailing culture. Whether that culture calls itself Christian or not is of no importance, for to these men it is always pagan and corrupt" (64–65).

Niebuhr expresses great appreciation for this position, especially for the sincere and single-minded efforts of many representatives of this type (66). He also acknowledges that "the movement of withdrawal and renunciation is a necessary element in every Christian life," in that "the relation of the authority of Jesus Christ to the authority of culture is such that every Christian must often feel himself claimed by the Lord to reject the world" (68).

Yet he offers a sturdy critique of this position as well. For one, culture, as Niebuhr points out, is inevitable: All persons and communities are influenced by their cultural environment. Christ's call comes to inculturated persons (69); "hence the radical Christians are always making use of the culture, or parts of the culture, which ostensibly they reject" (69, also 73). They must use cultural forms and patterns of communication to address culture at large in the very act of confessing Christ as Lord (70). Second, Niebuhr contends that "the tendency in exclusive Christianity is to confine the commandments of loyalty to Christ, or love of God and neighbor, to the fellowship of Christians" (71). This is often accompanied by a decided denigration of the powers of human reason, especially in contrast with the givens of revelation (76). Most profoundly, this position raises the knotty theological problem of the "relation of Jesus Christ to the Creator of nature and Governor of history as well as to the Spirit immanent in creation and in the Christian community" (80–81). Niebuhr states the problem this way: "Their rejection of culture is easily combined with a suspicion of nature and nature's God; their reliance on Christ is often converted into a reliance on the Spirit immanent in him and the believer; ultimately they are tempted to divide the world into the material realm governed by a principle opposed to Christ and a spiritual realm guided by the spiritual God" (81).

Christ of Culture

Niebuhr's second type—Christ of culture—is accepted by those who "feel no great tension between church and world, the social laws and Gospel, the workings of divine grace and human effort, the ethics of salvation and the ethics of social conservation or progress. On the one hand they interpret culture through Christ, regarding those elements in it as most important which are most accordant with his work and person; on the other hand they understand Christ through culture, selecting from his teaching and action as well as from the Christian doctrine about him such points as seem to agree with what is best in civilization" (83). Generally, representatives of this type "understand the transcendent realm as continuous in time or character with the present life" (84). In this perspective, cultural life is the outworking of the gospel.

This type is well represented by the Gnostics, who sought "to reconcile the gospel with the science and philosophy of their time" (86). In both the Gnostics and Abelard, whom Niebuhr singles out as a medieval representative of this type, "what is offered here is kindly and liberal guidance for good people who want to do right" (90). In its most influential form, that of "cultural Protestantism," this type advanced the notion that "the human situation is fundamentally characterized by man's conflict with nature [not God]. Man the moral being, the intellectual spirit, confronts impersonal forces" (101). In this view, "it is almost inevitable that Jesus Christ should be approached and understood as a great leader of the spiritual, cultural cause, of man's struggle to subdue nature, and of his aspirations to transcend it" (101). Here, Jesus Christ is less a Lord to be obeyed and more an example to be followed.

Niebuhr has some commendation for this type. He notes that representatives of this type have greatly extended the influence of the Christian gospel (103), particularly among the culturally elite (104). Further, Niebuhr acknowledges that this view highlights the ways in which Jesus himself was radically embedded in the culture of his time (105), as well as Jesus' many calls for this-worldly justice and healing (106). Niebuhr also points out that many critiques of cultural Christianity are not offered by those who *oppose* the equation of culture and Christianity but rather by those who disagree about *which* culture to christen (102).

Yet Niebuhr's primary thrust is to critique this type. He notes the propensity for this type to "distort the figure of the New Testament Jesus" by endlessly remaking Jesus in the image of a given culture through steady streams of apocryphal gospels (109). (Think only of the many quests for the historical Jesus that have arisen out of liberal Protestant theology.) Such efforts lead to the common charge that "loyalty to contemporary culture has so far qualified the loyalty to Christ that he has been abandoned in favor of an idol called by his name" (110). Other negative tendencies Niebuhr identifies include a general depreciation for revelation (110–11) and for divine grace in favor of "self-reliant humanism" (113).

After analyzing these two extreme positions, Niebuhr describes three moderating positions or hybrids. These moderating positions share several theological positions. First, they agree that "the fundamental issue does not lie between Christ and the world . . . but between God and man" (117). (Hence, Christ and culture cannot simply be set up as opposite dialectical poles.) Second, each confesses that "Jesus Christ is the Son of God," inseparably united to the "Father Almighty who created heaven and earth"; thus, "Christ and the world [creation] cannot be simply opposed to each other" (117). Also, each mediating group believes that obedience to Christ "must be rendered in the concrete, actual life of natural, cultural [humanity]" (118), an obedience now stymied by the presence of sin (118). Yet despite agreement on these matters, widespread differences in theology and practice led Niebuhr to distinguish three moderate positions: the "synthesists, dualists, and conversionists" (120).

Christ above Culture

The synthetic—or Christ above culture—position "affirms both Christ and culture" in a way that admits that "the Christ who requires . . . loyalty is greater and more complex in character than the easier reconciliations envisage" (121). What distinguishes this position from the other mediating positions is the way in which the synthesist "analyzes the nature of the duality in Christian life, and combines in a single structure of thought and conduct the distinctly different elements" (122). This structure begins by affirming, or synthesizing, what is held in common by Christians and non-Christians, an example being Clement's simultaneous reliance on Christian and non-Christian sources in the development of his ethics (125). This approach continues by suggesting that Christ can offer a way to exceed the possibilities of a given cultural milieu; hence, Christ "above" culture. Thomas Aquinas, whom Niebuhr identifies as "probably the greatest of all the synthesists in Christian history" (128), "in his system of thought . . . combined without confusing philosophy and theology, state and church, civic and Christian virtues, natural and divine laws, Christ and culture" (130); that is, "he combined into one system of divine demands and promises the requirements cultural reason discerned and those which Jesus uttered, the hopes based on the purpose in things as known by the cultivated mind and those grounded on the birth, life, death, and resurrection of Christ" (130–31). Aquinas's system combined natural theology and revealed theology in a way that redefined the Christ-culture relationship. For Aquinas, according to Niebuhr, "Culture discerns the rules for culture, because culture is the work of God-given reason in God-given nature. Yet there is another law besides the law rational men discover and apply. The divine law revealed by God through His prophets and above all through His Son is partly coincident with the natural law, and partly transcends it as the law of man's supernatural life" (135). Thus, all knowledge begins with the natural reason, which is then extended and completed by the "higher" authority of the gospel.

Niebuhr's evaluation of the Christ above culture position begins on a positive note. He observes that this position advocates an integrity or unity between natural and revealed truth that appeals to all (142), that it upholds common civil virtues and just social institutions in common society that provide an "intelligible basis" for cooperative efforts between Christians and others (143), while still maintaining that "the gospel promises and requires more than the rational knowledge" (144).

Yet Niebuhr also points out potential problems: "The effort to bring Christ and culture, God's work and man's, the temporal and eternal, law and grace, into one system of thought and practice tends, perhaps inevitably, to the absolutizing of what is relative, the reduction of the infinite to a finite form, and the materialization of the dynamic" (145). That is, this view is tempted to equate a given culture's perspective, and the synthesis that results, with ultimate truth. All synthesis between faith and reason, Niebuhr argues, is "provisional and symbolic" (145), "since it consists of fragmentary, historical, and hence of relative [that is, culture-bound] formulations of the law of creation" (145). The temptation for those who accept a given synthesis is to "become more concerned about the defense of the culture synthesized with the gospel than about the gospel itself" (146). Also likely is "the institutionalization of Christ and gospel," bound up as they are with a particular cultural point of view (146).

Christ and Culture in Paradox

A second mediating position—Christ and culture in paradox—begins with a strong sense of conflict, the conflict between God and humanity, "between the righteousness of God and the righteousness of self" (150). The "fundamental situation" is that "grace is in God and sin is in [humanity]" (151). This fundamental opposition or dialectic parallels the opposition of law and grace and divine wrath and mercy. These contrasting extremes characterize the approach of the "dualists" (149).

This sense of conflict sets the dualists in contrast with the synthesists, for "the dualist Christians differ considerably from the synthesists in their understanding of both the extent and thoroughness of human depravity" (152). While the synthesist is optimistic about the ability of natural reason to discern truth, the dualist is pessimistic concerning anything except the grace of God. Yet unlike adherents of the Christ against culture position, the dualist knows that cultural influence is inevitable, "that God indeed sustains him in it and by it" (156). It is for this reason that the dualist speaks in paradoxes: The dualist is "standing on the side of man in the encounter with God, yet seeks to interpret the Word of God which he has heard coming from the other side. . . . He is under the law, and yet not under the law but grace; he is sinner, and yet righteous; he believes, as doubter; he has assurance of salvation, yet walks along the knife-edge of insecurity" (156–57).

The clearest representative of this type for Niebuhr is Martin Luther. According to Niebuhr, Luther "makes sharp distinctions between the temporal and spiritual life, or between what is external and internal, between body and soul, between the reign of Christ and the world of human works or culture" (171). In Luther's famous words, "There are two kingdoms, one the kingdom of God, the other the kingdom of the world. . . . God's kingdom is a kingdom of grace and mercy . . . but the kingdom of the world is a kingdom of wrath and severity" (171). Life in this world is filled with the tension between the pulls of each. There is tension between the "spirit," which motivates cultural activity, and the "technique," which one employs in that activity (177). Thus, "living between time and eternity, between wrath and mercy, between culture and Christ, the true Lutheran finds life both tragic and joyful" (178).

Niebuhr's assessment as always begins on a positive note. He notes that this type honestly reflects Christian experience, that it "mirrors the actual struggles of the Christian who lives 'between the times'" (185). Also, this model "takes into account the dynamic character of God, man, grace, and sin" (185). The Christ-culture interaction and tension is worked out in the real world of real decisions by real people. It cannot be neatly or statistically contained.

These virtues are, however, matched by some vices, for "dualism tends to lead Christians into antinomianism and into cultural conservatism" (187). Antinomianism comes about as the "relativization of all the laws of society," which is promoted "through the doctrine that all are comprehended under sin" (187). Cultural conservatism results because Christians such as Paul and Luther seem to be "deeply concerned to bring change into only one of the great cultural institutions and set of habits of their times—the religious" (188). As Niebuhr sees it, "Conservatism is a logical consequence of the tendency to think of law, state, and other institutions as restraining forces, dykes against sin, preventers of anarchy, rather than as positive agencies" for social reform (188). This position, in contrast to the final type, contends that "in all temporal work in culture men are dealing only with the transitory and dying" (189).

Christ the Transformer of Culture

Niebuhr's final position—Christ the transformer of culture—has much in common with the other mediating positions, especially the dualist position, yet it is distinguished from the dualist position by its "more positive and hopeful attitude toward culture" (191). This attitude is preserved by three theological claims: first, that creation was completely good and that the redemption of Christ works toward re-creation, not a new creation (191–92); second, that the fall into sin was pervasive but not comprehensive, such that "the problem of culture is therefore the problem of its conversion, not of its replacement by a new creation" (194); and finally, that God is intimately involved in history, interacting with humanity in the present to bring about more fully the reign of God (194–96). Based on these three assumptions, the Christian attitude toward culture is that of conversion. Culture itself is and should be constantly "converting" more fully according to the gospel in order to more fully embody the reign of God.

Niebuhr cites Augustine as one of the classic representatives of this type. Niebuhr admits that Augustine is claimed by proponents of every type, with some reason (207), but argues that the main thrust of his thought, particularly his views of creation, fall, and regeneration (208, 209–15), place him in this fifth category: "Christ is the transformer for Augustine in the sense that he redirects, reinvigorates, and regenerates that life of man, expressed in all human works, which in present actuality is the perverted and corrupted exercise of a fundamentally good nature" (209). Christ renews what was originally very good in creation but was corrupted in the fall. The new creation is a re-creation, a restoration, a transformation. John Calvin, like Augustine, looked "for the present permeation of all life by the gospel" (217). This final position clearly reflects Niebuhr's own preference, a point emphasized by the lack of negative critique of this type.

Christ and Culture concludes with an "unscientific postscript" in which Niebuhr admits that his analysis is both "unconcluded and inconclusive" (230). There is, he suggests, no exclusively correct approach (231–32). Niebuhr also admits the limits of such models. They can crystallize our thinking about cultural questions, but finally the models must be put away, and life must be lived. Christian believers and Christian communities must inevitably make decisions about the approach they will take in regard to cultural questions: "The problem of Christ and culture must come to an end only in a realm beyond all study in the free decisions of individual believers and responsible communities" (233). These decisions are necessarily limited by the inevitably relative and incomplete knowledge, faith, and historical awareness that can be brought to any one decision (234–38). But in the context of community (245) and on the basis of thoughtful analysis and tenacious faith (250–56), we strive to live the gospel in particular cultural contexts.

Comment

In sum, it might be said that ever since the apostle Paul challenged Christians to be *in* but not *of* the world, Christian efforts to conceptualize the relationship between the gospel and culture have resulted in an endless search for an apt preposition. Niebuhr's accomplishment lies in his gift for identifying telltale prepositions (in, of, above, etc.) and for explicating the world of meaning that lies behind their use. The value of Niebuhr's work is certainly due in part to the trenchant character of his presentation. His memorable five categories crystallize some of the more important theological commitments of various traditions and set them on the brink of praxis, where they function to motivate and guide individual Christians and church communities.

Second, Niebuhr's work is helpful in its perceptive linkage of particular approaches to culture with particular theological claims. Christian cultural engagement is a theologically redolent task. Those who use Niebuhr's typology must do so with a full view to the theological implications of this typology. As Douglas Ottati has observed, "Readers of *Christ and Culture* regularly pay too much attention to the five types and too little attention to the theo-logic of its more detailed analysis."[13] Niebuhr reminds us that *prima facie* negative judgments about culture imply a radical view of the fall and a limited appreciation for creation. He points out that one's view of evil—whether evil is understood to consist of the cleavage between God and humanity or between humanity and nature—shapes one's outlook on culture. He observes that attitudes toward culture often mirror Christology. Particular emphases in our understanding of Christ—such as emphases on Christ as lawgiver, cosmic ruler, social reformer, or redeemer—inevitably shape the ways in which Christians interact with culture. Christology, anthropology, ecclesiology—in fact, nearly the entire range of theological inquiry—have implications for such interaction. These interrelationships require careful attention for all thoughtful efforts at inculturation.

But despite these positive contributions, Niebuhr's work has hardly escaped critique. Even recent works continue to peck away at Niebuhr's approach, arguing with his historical analysis, his division of types, or the idea of constructing a typology in the first place.

---

13. Douglas F. Ottati, "Culture and Culture: H. Richard Niebuhr," *American Presbyterians* 66 (winter 1988): 325.

One line of critique has called attention to the fact that Niebuhr's typology simply enshrined his own version of Christianity (Christ the transformer of culture) as the preferred option. This has had the effect, so the critiques charge, of giving cultural engagement a blanket approval without calling for discernment of the particular strengths or weaknesses of a given cultural practice. This is the line of thought pursued, for example, by Stanley Hauerwas and William Willimon in their much read *Resident Aliens:*

> [Niebuhr's] call to Christians to accept "culture" (where is this mono- lithic "culture" Niebuhr describes?) and politics in the name of the unity of God's creating and redeeming activity had the effect of endorsing a Constantinian social strategy. "Culture" became a blanket term to un- derwrite Christian involvement with the world without providing any discriminating modes for discerning how Christians should see the good or the bad in "culture."[14]

Hauerwas and Willimon advocate cultural engagement that is rooted in a strong sense of Christian identity as a community of faith. They see Niebuhr's language of "transformation" as leading ultimately to the ex- treme Christ of culture position, with all its attendant weaknesses.

A second line of critique charges that Niebuhr's categories are sim- plistic.[15] As this line of critique runs, any one culture and the Chris- tian message are too nuanced, rich, and complex to admit any mono- lithic strategy. To be fair, Niebuhr frames his analysis with careful caveats, admitting that his types could be multiplied nearly infi- nitely (231), that the types are not mutually exclusive, and that they are somewhat artificial (43). Still, the point is well-taken. At a given time and place, Christians may need to be participating vigorously in some forms of cultural life, seeking to transform others, and avoiding still others. Likewise, culture itself exerts influence on several levels of meaning, fragmented as it is into a variety of subcultures. Of great danger are blanket statements about either culture as a whole or the nature of Christian cultural engagement within a culture. As William

14. Stanley Hauerwas and William Willimon, *Resident Aliens* (Nashville: Abingdon, 1989), 40.
15. Among recent works on Niebuhr are D. Kevin McNeir, "Searching for the Trans- formed Non-Conformist: A Comparative Analysis of the Ethical Reflections of H. Richard Niebuhr and James M. Gustafson," *Koinonia* 3 (1991): 131–49; James R. Cochrane, "Christ and Culture: Now and Then," *Journal of Theology for Southern Africa* 71 (1990): 3–17; Jack Schwandt, "Niebuhr's Christ and Culture: A Re-examination," *Word and World* 10 (1990): 368–73; Brian J. Walsh, "The Transformation of Culture: A Review," *Conrad Grebel Review* 7 (1989): 253–67; and Charles W. Schriven, *The Transformation of Culture: Christian Social Ethics after H. Richard Niebuhr* (Scottdale, Pa.: Herald Press, 1988).

Dyrness points out, Niebuhr's five categories must be seen "not as fixed options, but as emphases that are more or less appropriate according to the circumstances."[16]

The Liturgical "Use" of Niebuhr's Categories

For our purposes, what is important is what Niebuhr's categories offer for considering the relationship between liturgy and culture. One way in which liturgists have used Niebuhr's categories is to align certain liturgical movements and practices with his five types. Thus, Geoffrey Wainwright, for example, sees monastic prayer, Reformed protests to the Mass, and *glossalalia* in Pentecostal worship as fitting the Christ *against* culture type; the liturgical reforms of Charlemagne and alignment of Anglican worship with the state in England are possible analogs to Christ *of* culture; and the liturgical use of cultural art, including everything from medieval sculpture to jazz, represents Christ *above* culture.[17]

A complicating factor in the appropriation of Niebuhr's categories is that liturgy itself often plays an ambiguous role in the way in which a given community participates in the Christ-culture relationship. In a largely forgotten passage early in *Christ and Culture*, Niebuhr specifically contends that the "enduring problem" with which he is concerned is "*not* essentially the problem of Christianity and civilization" (11), for the important reason that "Christianity, whether defined as church, creed, ethics, or movement of thought [or, we might add, liturgy], *itself moves between the poles of Christ and culture*" (11, emphasis added). That is, while a given community may, because of a particular theological orientation, tend toward one of Niebuhr's five types, the liturgy of that community may not be the best place to observe that particular type at work.

In fact, the relationship between liturgy and a given community's engagement with culture may be quite ambiguous. The relationship between Christian worship and the Christianity-culture encounter has varied greatly from tradition to tradition, even from parish to parish. Roughly four broad approaches can be discerned. The following brief analysis presents these four approaches, these four ways in which liturgy may be involved in the way a given community interacts with its cultural context.

A first type occurs when liturgical expression lies largely outside the Christianity-culture dialectic. In this case, worship is an oasis from Christian cultural engagement. Worship is the hour when the church

16. William A. Dyrness, "Beyond Niebuhr: The Gospel and Culture," *Reformed Journal* 38, no. 2 (February 1988): 11–13.
17. Wainwright, *Doxology*, 388–98.

meets together, collects its thoughts from its fray with the world. External culture may be the object of many prayers spoken in worship, but external culture is treated as an unwanted guest. The particular cultural forms used in the liturgy itself are those of a vigorously defended ecclesial subculture of texts, music, art forms, and rhetoric. Worship may have the sense of being otherworldly, of being an oasis from the world or a prefigurement of heaven. Some might conclude that Tridentine Catholicism, traditional Orthodox liturgy, or the liturgy rendered in immigrant Protestant communities roughly corresponds to this type. These communities are typically made up of people who are active in cultural involvement outside the church. But the church itself attempts to preserve an enclave or subculture that is defended as protection against the onslaught of "external" cultural influences.

A second type lies on the opposite end of the spectrum and views Christian liturgy as a—if not *the*—means by which world engagement takes place. In this approach, worship is used as a means of either preaching a given sociopolitical vision or of actually confronting proponents of a dominant local culture. In its most extreme form, this approach limits cultural engagement to what may occur in liturgy. Examples of this type abound. Early nineteenth-century revivals and sermons preached by social gospel adherents of the early twentieth century, while different in almost every respect, were both world engaging. In our own time, this approach is championed by proponents of the Church Growth movement, largely a twentieth-century descendent of nineteenth-century revivalism.[18]

A third approach, like the second, values liturgy for its role in the process of cultural engagement. But unlike the second, it sees the role of liturgy as being indirect. Liturgy itself does not engage culture or accomplish mission. Rather, it attempts to prepare Christians to engage in those tasks outside the liturgy and prays for the efforts of Christians as they leave worship and enter the world. Meanwhile, it maintains an independent integrity, having its own unique purposes, methods, and modes of participation.

Proponents of this approach include many of the central Roman Catholic figures in the so-called liturgical movement. As Mark Searle has observed:

> For Guéanger in France in the aftermath of the French revolution, for Pius X in the aftermath of the *Risorgimento,* for our own Virgel Michel in the midst of the Great Depression, for Romano Guardini in Nazi Germany, the whole motivation of the liturgical movement was *countercul-*

18. James F. White, *Protestant Worship: Traditions in Transition* (Louisville: Westminster John Knox, 1989), 171ff.; and Frank C. Senn, "'Worship Alive': An Analysis and Critique of 'Alternative Worship Services,'" *Worship* 69 (1995): 194–224.

tural. . . . The goal of the proposed reforms was to rescue the liturgy from the accommodations to individualism, emotionalism, and worldliness that had already occurred.[19]

Liturgy had its own purpose and goal, for which it needed to be rescued. Liturgy, in turn, is the basis for cultural renewal. In the words of Virgil Michel, "The liturgy is the indispensable basis of Christian social regeneration,"[20] and again, liturgy is "the fruitful source of a wider social growth in Christ, of the penetration of all human contacts and activities with the Spirit of Christ."[21] Liturgy here does not function as a social gospel sermon or a seeker service; it is not the primary means for cultural engagement. Rather, by maintaining an independent integrity, it stands apart from culture, forms Christians who engage culture, and, in so doing, wields its cultural influence. Again in the words of Searle, "Celebrating the liturgy should train us to recognize justice and injustice when we see it. It serves as a basis for social criticism by giving us a criterion by which to evaluate the events and structures of the world."[22]

A fourth approach, like the third, attempts to negotiate between the extremes of the first and second examples. Unlike the third, it views liturgy as a (but not *the*) means for direct cultural engagement. This approach views liturgy as one of a number of arenas for cultural engagement, paralleling Christian efforts in education, politics, business, science, and so on. It sees liturgy as an opportunity to model an honest and balanced form of cultural engagement that is open to use a variety of cultural forms, but only for its own ends and only with rigorous self-consciousness. This approach acknowledges both that worship is not primarily an activity for engagement with the world and that participants—whether Christians or prospective Christians—are inculturated human beings whose lives are irrevocably shaped by the culture in which they live. An example of this fourth type are the liturgical reforms promoted by the nineteenth-century Danish bishop Nikolai Grundtvig. Grundtvig was deeply concerned about the relation-

19. Mark Searle, "Culture," in *Liturgy: Active Participation in the Divine Life*, Federation of Diocesan Liturgical Commissions (Collegeville, Minn.: Liturgical Press, 1990), 34–35.

20. Quoted in Kathleen Hughes, *How Firm a Foundation: Voices of the Early Liturgical Movement* (Chicago: Liturgy Training Publications, 1990), 189.

21. Virgil Michel, "Nine Years After," *Orate Fratres* 10, no. 1 (1935–36): 6, quoted in Mark R. Francis, "Liturgical Inculturation in the United States and the Call to Justice," in *Living No Longer for Ourselves: Liturgy and Justice for the Nineties*, ed. Kathleen Hughes and Mark R. Francis (Collegeville, Minn.: Liturgical Press, 1991), 84. See also R. William Franklin and Joseph M. Shaw, *The Case for Christian Humanism* (Grand Rapids: Eerdmans, 1991), 97ff.

22. Mark Searle, "Serving the Lord with Justice," in *Liturgy and Social Justice*, ed. Mark Searle (Collegeville, Minn.: Liturgical Press, 1980), 29.

ship between the church and culture and mobilized Christians to combat Danish expansionist political policy and to controvert the de-humanizing effects of industrialism by revitalizing Danish folklife. He was also a liturgical pioneer, restoring weekly eucharist and reinvigorating Danish church music. Grundtvig's particular liturgical strategy, interestingly, sought to make the liturgy one of many means of cultural engagement. The folk art that he encouraged was brought into the worship space; the hymns he wrote placed social concerns in the context of doxology; the liturgies he planned claimed public attention and witnessed to the Christian commitment to engage local culture.[23]

As these four approaches suggest, the way liturgy figures into Niebuhr's analysis is difficult to discern. It is extremely difficult to simply categorize certain liturgical acts or approaches as being "of culture" or "against culture." Niebuhr's analysis, helpful as it is, is incomplete for students of liturgy and culture. Fortunately, other scholarly conversations have much to add to Neibuhr's approach.

Models for Contextual Theology

One such conversation is offered in the field roughly defined by the term "contextual theology." This field is particularly concerned with how cultural contexts shape theology.[24] Liturgists are well aware of frequent calls over the past generation for the inculturation of liturgy. The move toward liturgical inculturation has been paralleled by theological inculturation. The development of numerous local and cultural theologies has much to teach us.

23. See Franklin and Hall, *Case for Christian Humanism,* 155–61; and A. M. Allchin, "Grundtvig: An English Appreciation," *Worship* 58 (1984): 420–33.

24. Among the primary theoretical works in this field are K. C. Abraham, ed., *Third World Theologies: Commonalities and Divergences* (Maryknoll, N.Y.: Orbis, 1990); Harvie Conn, *Eternal Word and Changing Worlds: Theology, Anthropology, and Mission in Trialogue* (Grand Rapids: Zondervan, 1984); Charles H. Kraft, *Christianity in Culture: A Study in Dynamic Biblical Theologizing in Cross-Cultural Perspective* (Maryknoll, N.Y.: Orbis, 1979); Bruce C. E. Fleming, *Contextualization of Theology: An Evangelical Assessment* (Pasadena: William Carey Library, 1980); Dean S. Gilliland, *The Word among Us: Contextualizing Theology for Mission Today* (Dallas: Word, 1989); V. Samuel and C. Sugden, eds., *Sharing Jesus in the Two Thirds World* (Grand Rapids: Eerdmans, 1983); Robert J. Schreiter, *Constructing Local Theologies* (Maryknoll, N.Y.: Orbis, 1985); Aylward Shorter, *Toward a Theology of Inculturation* (Maryknoll, N.Y.: Orbis, 1988); Wilfred Cantwell Smith, *Towards a World Theology: Faith and the Comparative History of Religion* (Philadelphia: Westminster, 1981); David J. Hesselgrave and Edward Rommen, *Contextualization: Meanings, Methods, and Models* (Grand Rapids: Baker, 1989); Bruce J. Nicholls, *Contextualization: A Theology of Gospel and Culture* (Downers Grove, Ill.: InterVarsity, 1979); R. Daniel Shaw, *Transculturation: The Cultural Factor in Translation and Other Communication Tasks* (Pasadena: William Carey Library, 1988); and Max L. Stackhouse, *Apologia: Contextualization, Globalization, and Mission in Theological Education* (Grand Rapids: Eerdmans, 1988).

One of the more helpful tour guides to the diverse literature on contextual theology is Stephen B. Bevans's *Models of Contextual Theology*.[25] Bevans defines contextual theology as "a way of doing theology in which one takes into account: the spirit and message of the gospel; the tradition of the Christian people; the culture in which one is theologizing; and social change in that culture" (1). He argues that contextual theology is inevitable and necessary due to the simple fact that "our context influences our understanding of God and the expression of our faith" (2). In addition, "there has never been a genuine theology that was articulated in an ivory tower with no reference to or dependence on the events, the thought forms, or the culture of its particular place and time" (4). Bevans presents five approaches to contextual theology, five ways of conceiving of the relationship between the theological tradition of the Christian gospel and a given cultural environment. He insists that these are not mutually exclusive models and may in fact be complementary at different stages of contextualization.[26] The following paragraphs summarize these five models with a view to their implications for liturgical theology and practice.

Translation Model

Bevans's first type of theological inculturation is called the translation model. The chief goal of this model is to translate "the Christian message into ever-changing and always particular contexts" (30). The goal, therefore, is to find a "dynamic or functional equivalent" for a given idea in various cultural contexts, much like the dynamic equivalence principle used by various Bible translation committees (32). This model is unique in "its insistence on the message of the gospel as an unchanging message" (30). Local cultural structures are then considered "convenient vehicles for this essential, unchanging deposit of truth" (31). This method presupposes that the essential message of Christianity is supracultural and can be separated from a given culturally bound mode of expression. It insists "that there is 'something' that must be 'put into' other terms. There is always something from the outside that must be made to fit inside; there is always something 'given' that must be 'received'" (33). Thus, the first step in contextual theology is "to strip [theology] of its cultural wrappings—the cultural husk—in order to find the gospel kernel" (33); then one can "rewrap" the message in a new cultural context. This model, more than others,

25. Stephen B. Bevans, *Models of Contextual Theology* (Maryknoll, N.Y.: Orbis, 1992). Another helpful typology is included in Hesselgrave and Rommen, *Contextualization*.

26. As such, future study may well compare how these models complement stages in liturgical inculturation as outlined in David N. Power, "Liturgy and Culture Revisited," *Worship* 69 (1995): 236–38.

"takes seriously the message of Christianity as recorded in the scriptures and handed down in tradition" (35). In sum, "the primary concern of the translation model is the preservation of Christian identity while attempting to take culture, social change, and history seriously" (47). Bevans cites David J. Hesselgrave and John Paul II as proponents of this type (37–46).

Anthropological Model

Bevans's second model is an anthropological model in which the primary concern is "the establishment or preservation of cultural identity by a person of Christian faith" (47). This model emphasizes the cultural context of the receiver and eschews most efforts to call that context into question by the Christian gospel. It emphasizes inculturated human experience within a given culture as a source for theology: It seeks to discern "the web of human relationships and meanings that make up human culture, and in which God is present, offering life, healing, and wholeness" (48). The "guiding insight" of this model is that "human nature, and therefore human culture, is good, holy, and valuable" (49). God's revelation is not assumed to be supracultural but rather is to be found "within the values, relational patterns, and concerns of a culture" (49). Thus, the practitioner of this model "looks for God's revelation and self-manifestation within the values, relational patterns, and concerns of a culture" (49): "By applying the techniques of anthropology and sociology, therefore, the practitioner of the anthropological model attempts to listen to a particular culture in order to hear within its complex structure the very Word of God" (51). This model "would insist that, while the acceptance of Christianity might challenge a particular culture, it would not radically change it" (49–50). This model has the benefit of taking culture seriously. Yet as Bevans points out, it can also lead to a certain cultural romanticism that uncritically accepts everything in a local cultural context as good (53), as well as a proclivity to downplay the value of intercultural exchange (53). Robert E. Hood and Vincent Donovan are Bevans's examples of this type (54–62).

Praxis Model

Bevans's third model is called a praxis model. In this model, social change serves as a basis for theology. This model flows from the insight that "the highest level of knowing is intelligent and responsible doing" (66). Action does not flow from knowledge but is epistemologically prior to any knowledge. This model is based on the maxim that "we know best . . . when our reason is coupled with and challenged by our action" (65), an insight derived from the thought of Karl Marx and appropriated by liberation theologians. This model understands revelation "as the presence of God in history—in the events of every-day life, in social and economic structures, in situations of oppression" (68). This presence "is one of beckoning and invitation, calling men and women of faith to locate God and cooperate with God in God's work of healing, reconciling, liberating" (68). Theology emerges out of a continuous cycle of "committed action" and "reflection" on the action, the cultural situation, the Bible, and the Christian tradition (69). This emphasis on action means that faith and theology are always rooted in the daily lives and concrete circumstances of Christians (71), in contrast to isolated academic speculation. Douglas John Hall and a group of Asian feminist theologians serve as Bevans's examples of this type (72–80).

Synthetic Model

The fourth model—the synthetic model—is a middle-of-the-road model that does not focus exclusively on a given message, cultural framework, or mode of action but rather seeks to learn from all three. It is a both/and model that "takes pains to keep the integrity of the traditional message, while acknowledging the importance of taking culture and social change seriously" (82). It looks for a synthesis "between one's own cultural point of view and the points of view of others" instead of constantly focusing attention on the particularities of a given contextualized theology. It works with elements that are unique to given cultures, as well as those perceived to be common among all cultures, and strives for both "uniqueness" and "complementarity" (83). It assumes that genuine cross-cultural communication and cross-fertilization are not only possible but advantageous and that "every culture can borrow and learn from every other culture and still remain unique" (83). In fact, "only when cultures are in dialogue" can "we have true human growth" (84). The process of inculturation or contextualization for this model consists of the constant juggling and eventual synthesis of every possible source of information, from cultural analysis to theological reflection to cross-cultural dialog. Bevans presents the work of Kosuke Koyama and José De Mesa as examples of this type (88–96).

Transcendental Model

Bevans's fifth and final model is a transcendental model, the primary task of which is "attending to the affective and cognitive operations in the self-transcending subject" (97). The focus in this model is not so much on the product of theology as it is on the theologian who produces it. Good theology arises from a person who "operates as an authentic, converted subject" (97). This model, developed along the lines of Karl Rahner and Bernard Lonergan, operates within a neo-

Kantian framework in which the interior world of the human person is given primary emphasis.[27] Reflection on subjectivity is the starting point for theology. If the subjectivity of the theologian has been "converted" or redirected by an encounter with the gospel, then his or her theology will emerge as authentic and relevant. In this view, "theology is conceived as the process of 'bringing to speech' who I am as a person of faith who is, in every possible respect, a product of a historical, geographical, social and cultural environment" (98). When this is accomplished, other persons from the same cultural environment may well identify with similar experiences or perhaps be led to see the world in a new way and hence be "converted." Thus, "one begins to theologize contextually not by focusing on the essence of the gospel message or of tradition as such, nor even by trying to thematize or analyze culture or expressions of culture in language. Rather, the starting point is transcendental, concerned with one's own religious experience . . . [which is] determined at every turn by one's context" (98). Thus, "the development of a truly contextual theology takes place as a person wrestles with his or her own faith and shares that faith with others with the same cultural parameters" (100). Contextual theology is not "translated" into a given cultural context by someone from the outside but rather is expressed by someone from within a culture who has been converted by the gospel. Bevans suggests that the work of Sallie McFague and Justo L. González are examples of this type (102–10).

Throughout his analysis, Bevans refers to several liturgical questions. He recounts his own experience of leading an Advent liturgy after which he was confronted by a disgruntled worshiper from India. This worshiper found the pervasive image of the sun difficult to appropriate because of his cultural environment, where the sun is an experience not of warmth and light but of exhaustion, illness, and oppressiveness (xiii). Bevans observes the problem of the need to import eucharistic wine to the Philippines (5) and the problem of water baptism in the Masai culture of Africa, where pouring water over a woman's head is a cultural ritual of cursing (6). As these examples function in his analysis, it becomes clear that contextual theology and liturgical inculturation are necessarily intertwined.[28]

Bevans's analysis provides a basis for careful scrutiny of hidden assumptions about the nature of liturgy and its relationship to its cultural environment. In fact, each model raises questions about the na-

27. Further work could helpfully bring together Rahner's understanding of worship and this model for contextual theology. See Michael Skelley, *The Liturgy of the World: Karl Rahner's Theology of Worship* (Collegeville, Minn.: Liturgical Press, 1991), esp. chap. 4.

28. See also Schreiter, *Constructing Local Theologies*, 117–21.

ture of both liturgy and liturgical inculturation. Is the liturgy a given that must be "translated" into various cultural contexts and environments (translation model)? Does liturgical inculturation begin with extant Christian liturgy or with the particular religious rituals of a given culture (anthropological model)? Does liturgical inculturation proceed by analysis and subsequent reform or by reform and subsequent analysis (praxis model); that is, is the committee appointed before or after efforts at liturgical inculturation? Should liturgy strive for increasing synthesis of cultural forms as a reflection of cultural diversity throughout the world (synthesis model), or should it strive to accent cultural particularity in any given environment? Or is authentic liturgical experience only that which is expressed by a converted subject (transcendental model) whose reflections from within a given cultural point of view produce liturgical reform?[29]

Also of interest is the relationship between Bevans's analysis and Niebuhr's typology. In many ways, Bevans and Niebuhr are working on very different projects. Niebuhr is concerned with the ways in which Christians participate in given cultural institutions, while Bevans is primarily concerned with methods for doing theology. Niebuhr describes a broad spectrum that includes both flight from culture and accommodation to culture, while Bevans's five models all presuppose significant attempts at cultural engagement.

Yet there is also much that these works have in common. For one, they share an interest in linking particular theological commitments with certain approaches to cultural engagement. (In fact, the value of Bevans's analysis lies in part in its role as a supplement to Niebuhr's with an attention to recent theological movements.) In so doing, both books challenge readers to wrestle with what exactly the Christian faith is: Is the gospel a way of thinking, a way of acting, or a way of responding to a given cultural environment? Together, Niebuhr's and Bevans's typologies reveal common patterns of thought across paradigms. Bevans's synthetic model is much like Neibuhr's Christ above culture type, while Bevans's anthropological model resembles Niebuhr's Christ of culture type. Both are eager to describe how particular theological views of creation and incarnation shape one's view of culture.

Second, both books attempt to give fair voice to a genuine plurality of approaches within the Christian tradition. This plurality is also reflected in the history of the relationship between liturgy and culture,

29. Concerning this question, see David N. Power, "Liturgy and Culture," in *Worship: Culture and Theology* (Washington, D.C.: Pastoral Press, 1990), who argues that "inculturation cannot be artificially induced but needs to flow from the personal faith of people, expressed within the symbols and institutions of their own particular culture" (68).

though scholarly reflection on liturgy and culture has not yet produced a typology for this relationship. Even in recent years, liturgical inculturation has included a wide variety of expressions, ranging from Anglican liturgies in India to evangelical seeker services in North America, from the Roman Catholic rites in Zaire to Pentecostal celebrations in South America. These various liturgical forms represent vastly different notions of what constitutes Christian worship in its relationship with culture. Further scholarly reflection could helpfully proceed by charting this diversity in much the same way as Niebuhr and Bevans have done.[30]

Theological Models and Liturgical Inculturation

As this all-too-brief analysis suggests, the various approaches to cultural engagement and contextual theology outlined by Niebuhr and Bevans provide a stimulating vantage point from which to address the relationship between liturgy and culture. This very question is the subject of a bevy of recent works, providing ample evidence that cultural questions remain at the center of liturgical reflection. Although the literature on liturgical inculturation is very diverse, several common themes emerge across studies. The following seven basic descriptive theses attempt to identify and summarize these common themes.[31] These theses are described here with reference to some of the recent work in liturgical inculturation and in terms of the models outlined by Niebuhr and Bevans.

Thesis 1: All liturgical action is culturally conditioned. No circumspect attempt at liturgical reform, liturgical inculturation, or cultural critique can glibly assume that liturgy is not shaped by its cultural environment. All liturgical participants are products of a particular culture, with its patterns of communication and symbolization. Liturgical traditions are themselves products of earlier cultural contexts. Often this is most noticeable in the liturgical use of nonverbal communication (gestures, movement, dance), in extemporaneous speech (the style, rhetoric, and pace of homilies and spoken introductions), in the environment for worship (including color, symbol, and spatial parameters), and music (including rhythm, harmony, the degree of improvisation, and other stylistic features). It is impossible for any ecclesial community, any church authority, or any liturgical reform to escape the influence of culture, as Niebuhr pointed out in his critique

30. One attempt at this project is the typology proposed in M. Francis Mannion, "Culture, Liturgy and," in *The New Dictionary of Sacramental Worship*, ed. Peter Fink (Collegeville, Minn.: Liturgical Press, 1990), 310–12.
31. This is not by any means a comprehensive or exhaustive review. Readers are encouraged to follow up on this analysis by referring to the sources identified in the notes.

of the Christ against culture type. As Mark Searle concluded, "So natural . . . and so inevitable is this process [of inculturation] that the issue confronted by Church authorities has usually been not whether enculturation should be undertaken but whether it should be approved or stopped."[32]

This basic observation seriously questions the way in which liturgy and culture are conceptualized in relation to each other, for liturgy and culture do not relate to each other like two boxers in a heavyweight fight. They are not two entities in mutual opposition. Rather, one is the context, the milieu, in which the other comes to life: Culture is liturgy's habitat. The key question is not whether a particular culture shapes liturgy but how. This suggests that the process of liturgical inculturation need not begin by seeking to invent a new rite or a new style of music but rather by expressing the countless implicit ways in which a given liturgical tradition is already a product of culture. Bevans's transcendental model advocates the self-conscious expression of one's own experience, the thematization of otherwise implicit ways of perceiving the world. Although different theological communities might quibble about the prescriptive force of such expressions, nearly every tradition would agree that this descriptive exercise is useful and helpful. Liturgical inculturation best begins with an accurate description of existing cultural influences on liturgical celebration.

Thesis 2: The relationship between liturgy and culture is theologically framed by the biblical-theological categories of creation and incarnation. Inculturation is both possible and necessary because of the twin claims that "in the beginning God created the heavens and the earth" and that "the Word became flesh and lived among us." Both Niebuhr's analysis and Bevans's analysis refer again and again to these theological foundations. Both argue that cultural engagement both reflects and shapes the ways in which communities embody commitments to these fundamental theological principles.

Creation provides the ontological basis and the conceptual framework for Christian cultural engagement. If creation is highly valued and understood as providing the basis for human cultural activity, then Christian cultural engagement will likewise be highly valued and seen as containing great potential for good. If creation is devalued or subordinated to redemption in a larger theological scheme, then any serious form of cultural engagement will undoubtedly be viewed skeptically. Indeed, a strong sense of God's creation reinforces the understanding that estrangement, alienation, and sin are not an inherent part of human cultural endeavor but rather a parasite that weakens

32. Searle, "Culture," 28.

and distorts legitimate cultural expressions of faith.[33] The concept of "culture," as well as any particular culture, need not be depreciated *prima facie*. Relatedly, a strong sense of God's creating activity also points to the vast scope and plurality of cultural possibilities for the fulfillment of creation. As Geoffrey Wainwright asserts, "There are certain areas of the liturgy in which stylistic and formal pluralism can easily be seen as a welcome manifestation of the abundant variety of humanity at the level of creation."[34] The sheer diversity of the created order points to countless unrealized possibilities for the life of the church in the world.

Incarnation provides the model or paradigm for the church's involvement with culture. The gospel accounts present Jesus' life as a simultaneous full *participation in* and *critique of* culture. The incarnation provides a metaphor for the life of the church in the world. The terminology for addressing liturgy and culture, in fact, closely parallels theological interpretations of the incarnation (the term "in-culturation" bears a metaphorical resemblance to "in-carnation").[35] The church, as the body of Christ in the world, mirrors this christological pattern. It is constituted not as a timeless, bodiless idea but rather as an embodied, concrete, worldly reality. The church is a full participant in culture, a cultural agent that both reflects and shapes a local cultural environment. As such, the church need not shy away from critical engagement with every aspect of a local cultural environment. At the same time, it must not be reticent to question and critique cultural practices that devalue creation, that restrict a sense of God's redeeming activity in the world, and that deny eschatological hope.

Thesis 3: Liturgical inculturation requires theologically informed cultural criticism of one's own cultural context. As Hugh Montefiore has observed, it is "comparatively easy to ask awkward questions about the suitability of another culture as the vehicle for communicating the Gospel; but it is very difficult to ask them about one's own."[36] Yet this is precisely what liturgists are called to do. All liturgical communities function in the context of a complex and multifaceted cultural milieu. Along with careful study of liturgical theology and history, liturgists are challenged to study and observe the main lines of cultural context

33. See Cornelius Plantinga Jr., *Not the Way It's Supposed to Be: A Breviary on Sin* (Grand Rapids: Eerdmans, 1995), for a masterful explication of this Augustinian theme.

34. Wainwright, *Doxology,* 362.

35. Then also there is John Pobee's suggestion of the term *skenosis* (tenting or indwelling), which bears obvious resemblance to the metaphorical world of John 1. See John S. Pobee, "The Skenosis of Christian Worship in Africa," *Studia Liturgica* 14 (1980/1981): 37–52.

36. Hugh Montefiore, *The Gospel and Contemporary Culture* (London: Mowbray, 1992), 1.

in which they live and work.[37] Fortunately, liturgists have many mentors and fellow workers in this task, given the huge industry that has grown up in our time around the description and criticism of culture. Cultural pundits, advertising strategies, and sociological studies all teach us about the defining characteristics of life in the twenty-first century.[38] Other serious studies have much to teach about the relationship between religious expression and the life of the church and particular features of North American culture.[39]

Such cultural criticism, while necessary reading for liturgists, is also often problematic, especially in creating the persistent temptation to oversimplify "liturgical diagnoses" in light of contemporary culture. Materialism, subjectivism, and individualism are surely marks of Western culture, but they cannot be taken as single overarching categories to explain every cultural movement or to denigrate every attempt at inculturation within the Western world. Recent social and anthropological theory has moved away from a vision of a given culture as a unified whole, now distinguishing structural and improvisational dimensions at work in any given cultural setting. Margaret Ar-

37. For a helpful overview of the theoretical approaches to cultural criticism, see Robert Wuthnow, James Davidson Hunter, Albert Bergesen, and Edith Kurzweil, *Cultural Analysis: The Work of Peter L. Berger, Mary Douglas, Michel Foucault, and Jürgen Habermas* (Boston: Routledge and Kegan Paul, 1984).

38. Among the vast bibliography of sources of this type, some of the most prominent works include Robert Bellah, *Habits of the Heart: Individualism and Commitment in American Life* (Berkeley: University of California Press, 1985); Allan Bloom, *The Closing of the American Mind* (New York: Simon & Schuster, 1987); Steven Connor, *Postmodernist Culture* (Cambridge, Mass.: Basil Blackwood, 1989); Peter F. Drucker, *The New Realities* (New York: Harper & Row, 1989); Christopher Lasch, *The Culture of Narcissism: American Life in an Age of Diminishing Expectation* (New York: W. W. Norton, 1979); idem, *The True and Only Heaven: Progress and Its Critics* (New York: W. W. Norton, 1991); idem, *The Minimal Self: Psychic Survival in Troubled Times* (New York: W. W. Norton, 1984); Neil Postman, *Amusing Ourselves to Death: Public Discourse in an Age of Show Business* (New York: Penguin Books, 1985); Richard Fox and T. J. Lears, eds., *The Culture of Consumption* (New York: Pantheon Books, 1983); Michael Kammen, *Mystic Chords of Memory: The Transformation of Tradition in American Culture* (New York: Knopf, 1991); Joshua Meyrowitz, *No Sense of Place: The Impact of Electronic Media on Social Behavior* (New York: Oxford University Press, 1985); Gregor Goethals, *The Electronic Golden Calf: Images, Religion, and the Making of Meaning* (Cambridge, Mass.: Cowley Publications, 1990); and idem, *The TV Ritual: Worship at the Video Altar* (Boston: Beacon, 1981).

39. Reginald Bibby, *Fragmented Gods: The Poverty and Potential of Religion in Canada* (Toronto: Irwin, 1987); Wade Clark Roof, *A Generation of Seekers: The Spiritual Journeys of the Baby Boom Generation* (San Francisco: Harper, 1993); Wade Clark Roof and William McKinney, *American Mainline Religion: Its Changing Shape and Future* (New Brunswick, N.J.: Rutgers University Press, 1987); Robert Wuthnow, *The Struggle for America's Soul: Evangelicals, Liberals, and Secularism* (Grand Rapids: Eerdmans, 1989); and idem, *Christianity in the Twenty-First Century* (New York: Oxford University Press, 1993).

cher even speaks of the "myth of cultural integration."[40] This is helpful caution for those who use popular works of cultural criticism to defend or critique a given liturgical practice.

Relatedly, any given descriptive adjective of culture will likely contain seeds of both promise and warning. Take, for example, a recent exchange concerning the "subjectivism" of North American culture and its implications for liturgical practice. In his analysis, M. Francis Mannion concludes that it will lead to a "bitter harvest" in which worship degenerates into "therapy," becomes disengaged from its role in social transformation, and—along with Scripture and the church itself—becomes a slave to inner realities and personal dispositions.[41] In contrast, Michael Aune considers this assessment "needlessly inflammatory" and proposes that precisely this sort of subjectivism may lead us to realize new potential for appropriating the objective meaning of liturgical action.[42] Here the same cultural trait is used in very different ways. There is likely both good and bad in many of the single-word characterizations of contemporary North American culture (i.e., anti-intellectual, postmodern, imagistic, etc.). The goal for all thoughtful liturgists is not simply to arrive at an apt description of culture but rather to discern how particular cultural traits both enhance and obscure the nature and purpose of liturgy, and how liturgical reform can capitalize on the unrealized potential of contemporary cultural traits. Such judicious appropriation of cultural criticism is significant for every model in either Niebuhr's or Bevans's typology. No intentional synthesis, transformation, accommodation, or opposition to particular cultural characteristics is possible without first carefully discerning the inner dynamics and processes of a given cultural environment.

Thesis 4: The extremes of either complete identification with or rejection of a given culture are to be avoided at all costs. Identification with culture, among other things, threatens the meaning of Christian symbols. In the words of Langdon Gilkey, "Religious symbols that lose a special judgment and a special promise over against culture also lose

40. Margaret S. Archer, *Culture and Agency: The Place of Culture in Social Theory* (Cambridge: Cambridge University Press, 1988), 1–21. See also Anthony Giddens, *Central Problems and Social Theory* (Berkeley: University of California Press, 1979); and Giles Gunn, *The Culture of Criticism and the Criticism of Culture* (New York: Oxford University Press, 1987).

41. M. Francis Mannion, "Liturgy and the Present Crisis of Culture," *Worship* 62 (1988): 102–7.

42. Michael B. Aune, "Worship in an Age of Subjectivism Revisited," *Worship* 65 (1991): 224–38. For two recent works that pair cultural criticism and liturgical reflection, see Marva Dawn, *Reaching Out without Dumbing Down* (Grand Rapids: Eerdmans, 1995); and Regis Duffy, *An American Emmaus: Faith and Sacrament in the American Culture* (New York: Crossroad, 1995).

their life and reality."[43] The denial of cultural elements, in contrast, fundamentally calls into question the very human-ness of liturgy itself. The largest challenge is both to remain faithful to the gospel of Jesus Christ and to be appropriately responsive to the cultural context. According to Robert Hovda:

> "Cultural adaptation" is a two-edged sword in the liturgical life of the churches. If it means that liturgy is the work of a concrete faith community in a particular time and place, and, therefore, that it cannot be celebrated except in the context and out of the stuff of that church's life and experience, it is simply a requisite of true public worship. If, however, it should become, by some jaded process in the corporate psyche of the local church, an excuse for capitulating to inimical aspects of the culture of the time and place, then it is devilish indeed. Then it becomes an excuse for avoiding the gospel call to reconcile, to liberate and unify the human family, to witness to and work for the reign of God.[44]

In sum, the twin dangers that cultural engagement seeks to avoid are "cultural capitulation," on the one hand, and "cultural irrelevancy,"[45] on the other. In every instance of cultural engagement, there must be a yes and a no, a being in but not of, a continuity and a discontinuity with accepted cultural practices.[46] Or to use Niebuhr's categories, Christ against culture or Christ of culture are unnecessary and harmful extremes that should be avoided.

Thesis 5: Liturgical action must reflect common elements in the Christian tradition through the unique expressions of a particular cultural context. There must be a judicious balance of particularization and universality. As Wainwright phrases it, "While indigenization is necessary on account of the relevance of the Christian gospel to *every* culture, a concomitant danger is that this particularization may be understood in such a way as to threaten the universal relevance of the gospel to *all* cultures."[47] Contextualization should serve to highlight, not obscure, distinctive elements of the Christian faith. In her contribution to the Study Team on Worship and Culture of the Lutheran

43. Langdon Gilkey, "Symbols, Meaning, and the Divine Presence," *Theological Studies* 35 (1974): 253. Thus, the key question involves "how the church can minister to the world without losing itself," the title of Gilkey's early but influential book on the subject (New York: Harper & Row, 1964).

44. Robert Hovda, "The Amen Corner," *Worship* 58 (1984): 251.

45. Kenneth Smits, "Liturgical Reform in a Cultural Perspective," *Worship* 50 (1976): 98.

46. Gordon Lathrop, "A Contemporary Lutheran Approach to Worship and Culture: Sorting Out the Critical Principles," in *Worship and Culture in Dialogue*, 142–46. This point also questions the uncritical adoption of Bevans's anthropological model.

47. Wainwright, *Doxology*, 366.

World Federation, S. Anita Stauffer identifies four basic dualities that define judicious liturgical inculturation. Liturgy must be both "authentic and relevant," "Lutheran [that is, oriented to a particular tradition] and catholic," "local and global," "Christocentric and anthropocentric."[48] Each of these parameters attempts to bring together universal and particular dimensions of liturgical experience.

Again, as with liturgy and culture, particularity and universality need not be conceived of as irreconcilable opposites, for particular cultural contexts are the milieu in which common ("universal") liturgical actions are given expression. In fact, the most successful attempts at liturgical inculturation may be those in which the particularities of a given culture enhance universal elements of Christian worship. Kenyan congregational processional and offertory dances and Korean participational intercessory prayers are not successful because they are quaintly "ethnic," as (condescendingly) viewed by the Western liturgical "establishment."[49] They are successful precisely because they express and deepen common Christian liturgical actions through unique cultural forms. The universal is expressed most clearly through the particular.

Thesis 6: This balance of particularization and universality requires "a mediating strategy" for liturgical inculturation. Often such strategies are summarized in a single phrase: "transforming culture," "dynamic equivalence," "creative assimilation." Among the most influential methods are the three outlined by Anscar Chupungco for use in the inculturation of Roman Catholic liturgy. The first, dynamic equivalence, attempts to replace "an element of the Roman liturgy with something in the local culture that has an equal meaning or value."[50] This method places heavy emphasis on the Roman liturgy as a standard. It brings to mind Bevans's translation model, as well as the methodology of Bible translators who work to convey the meanings of the Hebrew and Greek biblical texts in modern languages. The second is creative assimilation, in which particular cultural forms are assimilated into liturgical expression. This brings to mind Bevans's synthetic model, which looks for the utilization of any and all fitting forms of liturgical expression in a given environment. The third, organic progression, attempts to supplement the Roman liturgy with rites that grow from the existing liturgy and take shape in dialectical contact

48. Stauffer, "Christian Worship," 11–15.
49. On these examples, see R. Kevin Seasoltz, "The Dancing Church: An Appreciation," *Worship* 67 (1993): 253–61; and Myung Hyuk Kim, "Lessons from the Prayer Habits of the Church in Korea," in *Teach Us to Pray: Prayer in the Bible and the World*, ed. D. A. Carson (Grand Rapids: Baker, 1990).
50. Anscar Chupungco, *Liturgical Inculturation: Sacramentals, Religiosity, and Catechesis* (Collegeville, Minn.: Liturgical Press, 1992), 37.

with a local culture.[51] This method, which arguably corresponds to Bevans's anthropological model, calls for genuine creativity in the development of new ritual forms.

To Chupungco's three methods may be added the concept of a "broken symbol," first described by Paul Tillich and recently advocated by Gordon Lathrop. Tillich identified Jesus' relationship with inherited cultural and religious patterns in terms of the metaphor "broken myth."[52] As Lathrop describes it, "In a broken myth the terms of the myth and its power to evoke our own experience of the world remain, but the coherent language of the myth is seen as insufficient and its power to hold and create as equivocal. The myth is both true and at the same time wrong, capable of truth only by reference to a new thing, beyond its own terms."[53] Biblical meanings, according to this perspective, arise as old pre-Christian patterns of communication (narratives, rituals, etc.) are invested with new meaning, as they are juxtaposed with the person and work of Jesus Christ. Thus, proselyte baptism is transformed into Christian baptism, and pagan myths are transformed into Christian parables. This pattern becomes a model for liturgical inculturation when local cultural practices are utilized but "broken" in a process that transforms them into fitting expressions for Christian liturgy.

Thesis 7: The constituent liturgical actions of the Christian church— including proclamation of the Word, common prayer, baptism, and eucharist—are among the "universal" or common factors in the Christian tradition. In his analysis of contextual theology, Bevans specifically links a good deal of liturgical inculturation with the translation model, in which the "essential components" in rites are retained, while less essential components are adapted to local cultural contexts (30). The implication of this model is that an essential, universal entity exists that must be translated or adapted to a local cultural environment.

A similar assumption is operative in many recent discussions of liturgical inculturation. Thus, Lathrop identifies the central, nonnegotiable elements of Christianity as follows:

> The center is this: Christian assemblies gather around a washing rite now done in Jesus' name, around the Scriptures read so that the cross and resurrection which bring all people to God may be proclaimed, and around the thanksgiving over the shared bread and cup. These things are not optional, if the assembly wishes to be Christian. . . . [Cultural

51. Ibid., 47–51.
52. Paul Tillich, *Dynamics of Faith* (New York: Harper, 1957), 52–54.
53. Gordon Lathrop, *Holy Things: A Liturgical Theology* (Minneapolis: Fortress, 1993), 27.

patterns] are not welcome to obscure the gift of Christ in the Scripture read and preached, in the water used in his name, and in the thanksgiving meal.[54]

Likewise, Don Saliers raises the question of a "canon" of Christian liturgy, noting the "persisting orders or forms of Christian worship" that are common to nearly every cultural manifestation of the Christian church.[55] And Chupungco proposes to define inculturation as follows:

> Liturgical inculturation . . . may be defined as the process of inserting the texts and the rites of the liturgy into the framework of the local culture. As a result, the texts and rites assimilate the people's thought, language, value, ritual, symbolic, and artistic pattern. Liturgical inculturation is basically the assimilation by the liturgy of local cultural patterns. It means that liturgy and culture share the same pattern of thinking, speaking, and expressing themselves through rites, symbols, and artistic forms.[56]

Chupungco conceptualizes both the Roman liturgy and a given culture as two separate entities engaged in dialectic relationship. Note how his description assumes "the liturgy" as a given and on that basis calls for mutual interaction between liturgy and culture, such that "both undergo internal transformation" without "losing their identity."[57]

These three sources represent what may be described as a consensus among a wide range of liturgists that there are some nonnegotiable common aspects to Christian worship in every culture. The question raised by Neibuhr's and Bevans's work is exactly how these nonnegotiable aspects should be conceptualized. To use medieval philosophical language, is liturgy or some aspect of liturgy a part of the "essence" of Christianity that then takes on various "accidents" of particular cultural contexts? Or are common liturgical actions a part of the "kernel" of Christianity that is embedded in the "husk" of various cultural patterns?[58] Or is Christian liturgy primarily an inculturated *code* in which the supracultural gospel *message* is given expres-

---

54. Lathrop, "A Contemporary Lutheran Approach," 141, 139.

55. Don E. Saliers, *Worship as Theology* (Nashville: Abingdon, 1995), 166–70. Indeed, the "shape of the liturgy" is often implicitly acknowledged as the canon of Christian worship, as in this comment by Frank Senn: "Inculturation can take place without obscuring the catholic shape of the liturgy" (*The Witness of the Worshiping Community* [New York: Paulist Press, 1993], 108).

56. Chupungco, *Liturgical Inculturation*, 30.

57. Ibid. Chupungco is necessarily working with the givenness of the Roman Catholic liturgy. Liturgists working in traditions that do not have a prescribed or official liturgy will need to do much more than Chupungco has described.

58. Concerning this metaphor, see Schreiter, *Constructing Local Theologies;* Stackhouse, *Apologia*, 107ff.; and Bevans, *Models of Contextual Theology*, 33.

sion? Each of the metaphors raises significant questions for Christian liturgists. This is especially true in light of the general twentieth-century Western tendency to question any claims for universality. Future work in the theory of liturgical inculturation may well focus on the nature and extent of the common liturgical actions and the best metaphors to describe it.

To conclude, liturgical practice is always shaped by the converging influence of liturgical tradition, cultural context, and theological self-consciousness. Reflection on liturgical practice requires attention to each of these three elements. What is crucial for this process of reflection is that cultural, historical, and theological interests not be unduly separated. As this chapter has demonstrated, the very process of reflecting on culture is shaped by theological commitments and perspectives. An abundant diversity of approaches to cultural questions throughout the history of the church points to the sheer complexity of the relevant issues. The typological approaches of Niebuhr and Bevans provide a helpful starting point for liturgists to approach the complex possibilities of this area of reflection. Through rigorous self-assessment, discerning cultural analysis, and full awareness of the nature and purpose of liturgical action, liturgists can hope to make liturgical recommendations that both avoid the pitfalls and capitalize on the resources of particular cultural contexts.

PART

3

Historical Studies

5

Images and Themes in John Calvin's Theology of Liturgy

The conventional portrait of John Calvin's contribution to the history of Christian liturgy focuses much more on what Calvin deplored than what he preferred. The typical paragraph on Calvin in standard liturgical histories portrays Calvin as a stern and unrestrained iconoclast and an ardent opponent of popish forms. If Calvin is given two paragraphs, there may be mention of his un-Zwinglian sacramental theology and his promotion of vernacular metrical psalmody, but no more. Liturgical specialists who write a bit more about Calvin typically go on to cite his preference for weekly celebrations of the Lord's Supper and might outline and analyze Calvin's own published liturgical texts. But rarely do analysts pause to think about the theology of worship that supports his liturgical reform. And the tone of many of these treatments is, generally speaking, one of polite indulgence. So strong is this tendency that Elsie McKee can quip, "It is common knowledge that Calvin and worship are incongruous topics, and that, whatever the strengths of those who are predestined to the glory of God, they are hopeless failures when it comes to liturgy." [1]

1. Elsie Anne McKee, "Context, Contours, Contents: Towards a Description of the Classical Reformed Teaching on Worship," *Princeton Theological Seminary Bulletin* 16 (1995): 172; also printed in *Calvin Studies Society Papers, 1995, 1997*, ed. David Foxgrover (Grand Rapids: Calvin Studies Society/CRC Product Services, 1998). Studies of Calvin's theology of liturgy prior to McKee's are relatively few in number. The primary titles, presented chronologically, include J. S. Whale, "Calvin," in *Christian Worship:*

As with most caricatures, there is some truth in this portrait. There is also, however, much that this portrayal omits or skews, for in addition to his famous indictments of Rome, Calvin's writings contain a surprising—and generally unacknowledged—amount about the value, purpose, and nature of Christian liturgy.

This chapter attempts to remedy this lacuna by explicating Calvin's theology of worship or, more narrowly, his theology of liturgy (that is, his understanding of what takes place in the "stated assemblies of the church").[2] More specifically, it explores some basic themes and images in Calvin's theology of liturgy. This cannot be done comprehensively in this space. But I hope to begin and, on the basis of familiarity with many individual trees, to draw a map of the forest; that is, to sketch the conceptual cartography of Calvin's theology of liturgy.[3]

Studies in Its History and Meaning, ed. Nathaniel Micklem (London: Oxford University Press, 1936), 154–71; Bernhard Buschbeck, *Die Lehre vom Gottesdienst im Werk Johannes Calvins* (Marburg: Phillipps-Universiteit Inaug. Diss., 1968); Kilian McDonnell, O.S.B., "Calvin's Conception of Liturgy and the Future of Roman Catholic Liturgy," in *The Crisis of Liturgical Reform*, vol. 42 of *Concilium* (New York: Paulist Press, 1969), 87–97; Bruno Bürki, "Jean Calvin avait-il le sens liturgique?" in *Communio sanctorum: Mélanges offerts Jean-Jacques von Allmen* (Geneva: Labor et Fides, 1982), 157–72; Rodolphe Peter, "Calvin and Liturgy, according to the Institutes," in *John Calvin's Institutes: His Opus Magnum. Proceedings of the Second South African Congress for Calvin Research* (Potchefstroom, South Africa: Potchefstroom University for Christian Higher Education, 1986); Teunis Brienen, *De Liturgie bij Johannes Calvijn* (Kampen: de Groot Goudriaan, 1987); Pamela Moeller, "Worship in John Calvin's 1559 *Institutes* with a View to Contemporary Worship Renewal" (Ph.D. diss., Emory University, 1988); and Hughes Oliphant Old, "John Calvin and the Prophetic Criticism of Worship," in *John Calvin and the Church: A Prism of Reform*, ed. Timothy George (Louisville: Westminster John Knox, 1990).

2. This topic is broader than his theology of any particular element of worship (e.g., preaching, common prayer, baptism, etc.). This topic is narrower than worship in the broad sense of the worship Christians offer in all of life. There are numerous studies of specific elements of worship. In this category, I would include such studies as Bryan D. Spinks, "Calvin's Baptismal Theology and the Making of the Strasbourg and Genevan Baptismal Liturgies 1540 and 1542," *Scottish Journal of Theology* 48 (1995): 55–78; and B. A. Gerrish, *Grace and Gratitude: The Eucharistic Theology of John Calvin* (Minneapolis: Fortress, 1993). The best study of worship in the broad sense is McKee, "Context, Contours, Contents." These are helpful studies, yet few of them discuss the categories and topics I highlight in this chapter. I would argue that we need all three levels of analysis to grasp Calvin's thought clearly: studies of each element of liturgy, studies of liturgy as a whole, and studies of worship broadly defined.

3. I hasten to disavow any suggestion in this exposition of Calvin's thought that his contribution is singular, unique, or independent (which can be a danger of this genre of writing). The next step in this analysis will necessarily be to compare these themes with the likes of Bucer, Erasmus, Farel, Vermigli, as well as Calvin's patristic sources. Here I have in mind the kind of work so well exemplified in David C. Steinmetz, *Calvin in Context* (New York: Oxford University Press, 1995). Calvin was widely dependent on a host of sixteenth-century conversation partners, as well as several patristic sources. The danger with my approach is that it could abstract Calvin from his historical context.

At the outset, let me state two methodological premises. First, I am convinced that any study of this topic is bound to be successful only insofar as it takes into account the full range of Calvin's writings on the subject—not only the *Institutes* and liturgical texts but also the commentaries, sermons, letters, and other ecclesiastical documents of various kinds. Generally speaking, this chapter is commentary-heavy, a corrective move in response to the heavy emphasis on the *Institutes* in prior studies of Calvin's theology of liturgy.[4] Second, I am less interested in exploring Calvin's understanding of worship in itself than in exploring his understanding of the experience of the worshiper. Calvin, like his medieval forebears, did write about the theological status of the elements of worship, most significantly the elements of the Lord's Supper, but he also wrote about the dimensions of the worshiper's experience of worship. It is this theme that is highlighted in the following explication.

Calvin's Theology of Liturgical Sin

Calvin's writings on worship, particularly his commentaries, return time and time again to four primary "liturgical sins," that is, four sins that have to do with the practice of public worship.

Sin number one is disobedience. Given that Calvin's primary liturgical criterion was that liturgy should be executed according to the Word of God, it is no surprise that the first abuse he identified was that of disobedience to God's explicit commands regarding worship. Degenerate rites resulted "when every one invented something new for himself." They were rites "not based upon His Word."[5] Calvin understood many of the prophetic critiques of the worship of Israel as

4. Calvin scholarship on this topic suffers from too great a dependence on his most famous work, the *Institutes of the Christian Religion*. That is, we have been blinded to much of Calvin's imagery because people looking at Calvin's theology of liturgy generally have not read much beyond the *Institutes*. Both a major dissertation, completed at Emory University, and a major scholarly article, completed by a South African historian, have recently attempted to address Calvin's theology of worship with the limiting rubric "as seen in the *Institutes*." The *Institutes* do include many of Calvin's positive statements about liturgy, but they are often overwhelmed by his extended polemics. In the *Institutes* (and in his various treatises on the sacraments), Calvin tends to treat the sacraments as unique subjects or loci—as we might expect from him, given the tradition of seeing the sacraments as discrete topics in nearly every catechism or theological system. In the commentaries, Calvin often writes about the worship service as a whole. He writes about prayers, preaching, baptism, and the Lord's Supper as part of what causes us to be lifted up to heaven.

5. References to Calvin's writings in this chapter will include the citation of the selection from Calvin's edited works, followed by a citation of the English translation. The following abbreviations are used to identify the most frequently cited sources: OS = *Ioannis Calvini Opera Selecta*, ed. Peter Barth, Wilhelm Niesel, and Dora Scheuner, 5

injunctions against the subversion of God's explicit command for worship. His comment on Zephaniah 1:5 is typical:

> What then was it that the Prophet condemned? That they were not content with what the law simply and plainly prescribed, but that they devised for themselves various and strange modes of worship; for when men take to themselves such a liberty as this, they no longer worship the true God. . . . He shows that all kinds of worship are abominable to him whenever men depart in any measure from his pure Word. For we must hold this as the main principle—that obedience is more valued by God than all sacrifices.[6]

Significantly, the text on which he was commenting does not explicitly raise the issue of disobedience. The fact that Calvin introduced the notion of disobedience to exegete this text indicates that disobedience functioned as a "root sin" in Calvin's thought.

Sin number two is hypocrisy. Commenting on Joel 1, Calvin provided a succinct description of this sin:

> The priests did not rightly worship God; *for though their external rites were according to the command of God, yet as their hearts were polluted*, it is certain that whatever they did was repudiated by God, until, being touched with the fear of his judgement, they fled to his mercy, as the Prophet now exhorts them to do.[7]

Notice that this false worship passed the first test, the one regarding obedience to God's Word, but failed the second, the test of the heart. Calvin's emphasis, therefore, was on inner worship, the worship of the heart. Without it, external liturgy is meaningless. Calvin's commentary on Micah 6 summarizes: "Hypocrites place all holiness in external rites; but God requires what is very different; for his worship is spiritual."[8] Thus, Cain is an archetypal hypocrite as one who "wished to appease God, as one discharging a debt, by external sacrifices, without the least intention of dedicating himself to God."[9] Perhaps the classic statement on this theme is found in Calvin's commentary on Isaiah 1:11:

---

vols. (Munich: C. Kaiser, 1926–62); CO = *Ioannis Calvini Opera quae supersunt omnia*, ed. Wilhelm Baum, Edward Cunitz, and Edward Reuss, 59 vols. (Brunsvigae: A. Swetschke and Son, 1843–48); *Corpus Reformatorum*, vols. 29–87 (Brunsvigae: A. Swetschke and Son, 1843–48); *Institutes* = John Calvin, *Institutes of the Christian Religion* [1559], ed. John T. McNeill, trans. Ford Lewis Battles, Library of Christian Classics, vols. 20–21 (Philadelphia: Westminster, 1960). CO, 24:489 (Commentary on Exod. 29:38–46).

   6. CO, 44:10 (Commentary on Zeph. 1:5).

   7. CO, 42:527 (Commentary on Joel 1:13–15), italics added. Another example of this more subtle abuse was Jeroboam (see commentary on Hosea 3:2–5).

   8. CO, 23:86 (Commentary on Micah 6:6–8).

   9. CO, 23:86 (Commentary on Gen. 4:5).

> But hypocrites observe them [liturgical instructions] with the most scrupulous care, as if the whole of religion turned on this point, and think that they are the most devout of all men, when they have long and anxiously wearied themselves in observing them. And that they may be thought more devout, they likewise add something of their own, and daily contrive new inventions, and most wickedly abuse the holy ordinances of God, by not keeping in view their true object.[10]

Here especially, Calvin was less interested in the actions of worship than in the people who offer them.

Sin number three is superstition. Superstition is the failure to perceive the proper relationship between the external acts of worship and the spiritual reality of God. Thus, Calvin commented on Isaiah 66:1: "Yet, as the minds of men are prone to *superstition,* the Jews converted into *obstacles* to themselves those things which were intended to be *aids,* and *when they ought to have risen by faith to heaven, they believed that God was bound to them,* and worshiped him only in a careless manner, or rather made sport of worshiping him at their own pleasure."[11] Again, one could avoid the abuses of both disobedience and hypocrisy and still suffer from superstition. That is, one could perform rites according to Scripture and with a pure heart but with a misguided notion as to how those rites and symbols related to God. What was needed was not only obedience to God's commands and a pure heart but also right understanding, a right knowledge of the spiritual character of God. Calvin, reflecting on Genesis 33, stated, "For as *superstitious* men foolishly and wickedly *attach God to symbols,* and, as it were, *draw him down from his heavenly throne* to render him subject to their gross inventions: [in contrast] so the faithful, piously and rightly, ascend from earthly signs to heaven."[12] And in regard to Isaiah 1, he said, "[Superstition is] in the disposition of the mind, when men imitate those services which are lawful and of which God approves, but keep their *whole attention fixed on the outward form, and do not attend to their object or truth.*"[13] Note that superstition here is not pagan reliance on a wooden god. It is a sin of the mind or spirit. It is misplaced attention in regard to its object of contemplation; it is the failure to attend to the spiritual significance of a physical action. Tongue in cheek, we might call it a "liturgical attention deficit disorder." It is sin to which even orthodox Christians are prone.

Sin number four is idolatry. Calvin, like the other Reformers, was an iconoclast. He lamented what he labeled "grosser idolatry," which

10. CO, 36:38–39 (Commentary on Isa. 1:11).
11. CO, 37:437 (Commentary on Isa. 66:1), italics added. See also *Institutes* 1.4.1, 4.
12. CO, 23:454 (Commentary on Gen. 33:21), italics added.
13. CO, 36:60 (Commentary on Isa. 1:14), italics added.

occurs "when idols are worshiped openly." In this category, Calvin placed the Mass, which he believed amounted to the worship of a physical entity. But Calvin was also concerned about idolatry that emerged in a more subtle form: "The other kinds of idolatry, although more hidden, [are] abominable before God, namely, when, under the disguise of a name, men *boldly mingle whatever comes into their minds, and invent various modes of worship*."[14] Calvin's concern was for what we might call "intellectual idolatry," the mingling of ideas about God in the mind.

For Calvin, this concept was intimately linked with the knowledge of God, that large concept that is central to the structure of the *Institutes* and many significant passages throughout Calvin's corpus. In Calvin's words on Malachi 1:11, "We must bear in mind that God cannot be rightly worshiped except he is known."[15] Thus, a typical phrase from Calvin's biblical commentaries records, "So he [Paul] makes a beginning with the definition of God, so that he might prove from that how he ought to be worshiped, because the one thing depends on the other."[16] In the classic *Institutes* passage on this point, Calvin argued:

> In seeking God, miserable men do not rise above themselves as they should, but measure him by the yardstick of their own carnal stupidity, and neglect sound investigation; thus out of curiosity they fly off into empty speculations. They do not therefore apprehend God as he offers himself, but imagine him as they have fashioned him in their own presumption. When this gulf opens, in whatever direction they move their feet, they cannot but plunge headlong into ruin. Indeed, whatever they afterward attempt by way of worship or service of God, they cannot bring as tribute to him, but they are worshiping not God but a figment and a dream of their own heart.[17]

In other words, most idols—most graven images—are chiseled out not by a hammer and pick but rather by our mental faculties.

In sum, Calvin identified four particular abuses of worship: disobedience, hypocrisy, superstition, and idolatry. Though undoubtedly related, each can be clearly distinguished. Calvin used these terms in technically precise ways: Disobedience consists of ignoring God's commands for worship; hypocrisy is the separation of external from internal worship; superstition is confusion regarding the ways in which external rites relate to the presence of God; and idolatry is fixation on the wrong object of worship. Like the detailed Eskimo vocabulary for

14. CO, 40:497 (Commentary on Ezek. 20:27), italics added.
15. CO, 44:420 (Commentary on Mal. 1:11).
16. CO, 48:410 (Commentary on Acts 17:25).
17. OS, 3:41 (*Institutes* 1.4.1).

snow, Calvin's detailed vocabulary points to a nuanced understanding of the broad category of false worship. And this vocabulary—*via negativa*—provides clues to the positive, constructive comments Calvin offered at other points. It also serves as a limit to mark off the parameters of right and true worship—a fence around the playground.[18]

Metaphors and Images in Calvin's Theology of Liturgy

That is where we move next, to a playground of images, metaphors, visions, pictures, and illustrations that describe what Calvin called the "inestimable privilege of the stated assemblies of the church."

Scottish, Barthian theologian Thomas Torrance, early in his career, once argued that Calvin rejected "pictorial thinking pertaining to God."[19] Yet there is much evidence to suggest this is not correct. Although Calvin is reputed to have been an enemy of the visual arts, his prose is distinguished by the pervasive and gripping use of visual images, which he called figures or similitudes. Calvin was self-conscious about his visual rhetoric, and—as several recent studies of Calvin's rhetoric have reminded us—he extolled the virtues of such rhetorical flourishes. In his words (from one of his treatises on the Lord's Supper), "Figures are called the eyes of speech, not because they explain the matter more correctly than simple, proper language, but because they win attention by their propriety, arouse the mind by their luster, and by their lively similitude so represent what is said that it enters more effectively into the heart."[20] What follows is a survey of nine such metaphors or figures.

Spatial Metaphors

The most pervasive metaphor for Calvin is that of bidirectional movement between God and humanity: In and through the assembly, God moves down toward humanity so that humanity might rise to

18. Despite this prophetic critique, Calvin insisted on the value of liturgical action. Thus, even in his comment on the most acerbic prophetic critiques, Calvin argued, "We now see that God does not simply reject sacrifices, as far as he has enjoined them, but only condemns the abuse of them. And hence what I have already said ought to be remembered, that the Prophet here sets external rites in opposition to piety and faith, because hypocrites tear these things asunder which are, as it were, inseparable: it is an impious divorce, when anyone only obtrudes ceremonies on God, while he himself is void of piety" (CO, 42:330–31 [Commentary on Hosea 6:6–7]). For Calvin, the abuses in public liturgy must be rooted out, but not liturgy itself.

19. Thomas Torrance, "Calvin and the Knowledge of God," *Christian Century* 81 (1964): 697.

20. CO, 9:514. For recent discussion of this point, see Philip W. Butin, "John Calvin's Humanist Image of Popular Late-Medieval Piety and Its Contribution to Reformed Worship," *Calvin Theological Journal* 29 (1994): 419–31; and Serene Jones, *Calvin and the Rhetoric of Piety* (Louisville: Westminster John Knox, 1995).

God. God descends that we might ascend. This was true, Calvin believed, already for the worship Israel rendered to God under the terms of the old covenant. Concerning the liturgical actions associated with the temple and the ark of the covenant, Calvin wrote, "As [God] was not tied to one place, so the last thing He intended was to tie down His people to earthly symbols. *On the contrary He comes down to them, in order to lift them up on high to Himself. . . .* He merely uses symbols as intermediaries with which to introduce Himself in familiar ways to slow men until, step by step, they ascend to heaven."[21] In this pictorial way, Calvin described the inner dynamic of public worship, as it were, on a cosmic vertical axis.

The first movement in this dynamic sweep is always God's move toward humanity. Here we are thrust into a central and distinctive feature of Calvin's thought: God's accommodation to human capacity. In Calvin's view, God is fundamentally a being who condescends, who deigns to move down toward humanity. Such a view presupposes the great contrast Calvin drew between God's greatness and human weakness: "For God, who fills the heavens and earth, is yet said to descend to us, though he changes not his place, whenever he gives us any token of his presence; a mode of expression adopted in accommodation to our littleness."[22] This divine accommodation is accomplished in many ways: in Old Testament theophanies, in the incarnation, and in his provision of Scripture. But another instance of accommodation, not often noted in studies on this theme, is the divine provision for the liturgical life of the church.

In the old covenant, according to Calvin, God provided ceremonies by which the people of Israel could render right worship: "God [was] accommodating himself to their weaker and unripe apprehensions by the rudiments of ceremony."[23] In the new covenant, the age of the church, preaching and especially the sacraments are God's gift of accommodation to the church. For example, in his 1541 *Short Treatise on the Lord's Supper,* Calvin argued:

> For seeing we are so foolish, that we cannot receive him [Christ] with true confidence of heart, when he is presented by simple teaching and preaching, the Father, of his mercy, not at all disdaining to condescend in this matter to our infirmity, has desired to attach to his Word a visible sign, by which he represents the substance of his promises, to confirm and fortify us, and to deliver us from all doubt and uncertainty.[24]

21. CO, 48:412 (Commentary on Acts 17:24).
22. CO, 23:471 (Commentary on Gen. 35:13).
23. CO, 31:502 (Commentary on Ps. 50:14).
24. OS, 1:505 (1541 *Short Treatise on the Lord's Supper*). This area of study is an excellent example of Calvin's theology of liturgy and has been underrepresented in broader

In this way, the external rites of the church, including preaching, prayer, and sacraments, are possible because of God's gracious condescension or accommodation.

This first downward movement of worship is mirrored by the upward movement of God's people, the *sursum corda*, the lifting of one's heart. The language of ascent is a refrain that echoes throughout Calvin's corpus, echoing earlier writings by Guillaume Farel.[25] Nearly every one of Calvin's texts on public prayer, preaching, and the sacraments enjoins Christians to use these means to rise to God. Calvin's sermon on 2 Samuel 6:1–7 is a typical example:

> Thus, we must note that when God declares himself to us, we must not cling to any earthly thing, but must elevate our senses above the world, and lift ourselves up by faith to his eternal glory. In sum, God comes down to us so that then we might go up to him. That is why the sacraments are compared to the steps of a ladder. For as I have said, if we want to go there—alas, we who do not have wings—we are so small that we cannot make it. God, therefore, must come down to seek us. But when he has come down, it is not to make us dull-witted; it is not to make us imagine that he is like us. Rather, it is so that we might go up little by little, by degrees, as we climb up a ladder one rung at the time.[26]

Calvin scholarship. The classic study on this theme remains that of Ford Lewis Battles. Battles notes that the created universe and the human body are forms of accommodation, and he discusses in greater detail Scripture and the incarnation as the examples par excellence of God's accommodation. Strikingly, he devotes little attention to visual signs and liturgical acts as signs of accommodation, including only a few paragraphs on the sacraments as such ("God Was Accommodating Himself to Human Capacity," *Interpretation* 31 [1977]: 19–38). David Wright has given us some brilliant additions to the literature on divine accommodation, but again with few references to the liturgical actions of the church ("Calvin's 'Accommodation' Revisited," in *Calvin as Exegete: Papers and Responses Presented at the Ninth Colloquium on Calvin and Calvin Studies*, ed. Peter De Klerk [Grand Rapids: Calvin Studies Society, 1995], 171–90; and "Calvin's Accommodating God," in *Calvinus Sincerioris Religionis Vindex*, ed. Wilhelm H. Neuser and Brian G. Armstrong [Kirksville, Mo.: Sixteenth Century Journal Publishers, 1997], 3–19). Suzanne Selinger does observe the sacraments as a sign of accommodation, but this is only a passing reference in her work on a much larger subject (*Calvin against Himself: An Inquiry in Intellectual History* [Hamden, Conn.: Archon Books, 1984], 67). Our understanding of Calvin's concept of divine accommodation can be enriched by taking into account his understanding of public worship. For a broader study of this theme, see Stephen D. Benin, *The Footprints of God: Divine Accommodation in Jewish and Christian Thought*, SUNY Series in Judaica: Hermeneutics, Mysticism, and Religion (Albany: State University of New York Press, 1993).

25. In 1533, Farel wrote the following liturgical formula: "Therefore, lift up your hearts on high, seeking the heavenly things in heaven, where Jesus Christ is seated at the right hand of the Father; and do not fix your eyes on the visible signs which are corrupted through usage" (Hughes Oliphant Old, *The Patristic Roots of Reformed Worship* [Zurich: Theologischer Verlag, 1975], 75). See also *Institutes* 1.11.3; 2.7.1.

26. *Supplementa Calviniana*, ed. Erwin Mülhaupt, vol. 6 (Neukirchen, Kreis Moers: Neukirchener Verlag der Buchhandlung des Erziehungsvereins, 1971), Sermon on

Public worship is like a ladder. Perhaps no image crystallizes so con-
cretely this aspect of Calvin's liturgical vision.[27]

But what does ascent entail? What does it mean? And how does one
accomplish it? The key to answering these questions lies in Calvin's

2 Samuel 6:1–7. Calvin was commenting here on the ark of the covenant in Old Testament worship, but his application applies directly to the New Testament age: "The sacraments are like this, and the ark was like a sacrament—at least in principle. The people have been moved to seek God in a very tangible manner." He then went on to speak
specifically about preaching, the Lord's Supper, and baptism. In his Old Testament
commentaries, Calvin cited nearly every liturgical practice as an occasion for ascending
to heaven, including the ark of the covenant (see commentary on Isa. 56:2) and the
temple (see commentary on Isa. 66:1).

27. For other references to this ladder image, see his commentary on Gen. 3:23;
28:13; Ps. 42:1–2; Acts 17:23; and obliquely in *Institutes* 4.1.5. The pervasive imagery of
ascent and descent raises the specter of unwanted dualism in Calvin's thought—but
perhaps unnecessarily. All of this up/down imagery can quickly invite the charge that
Calvin was replicating a Neoplatonic world in which—to be maddeningly simplistic
and purposely provocative—Gothic architecture, Gregorian chant, and mystical prayer
all help the worshiper escape from earthly reality into heavenly repose. Indeed, Suzanne Selinger speaks of the fact that "historians have so often thought it necessary to
rescue him from the charge [of dualism]" (*Calvin against Himself*, 3). And probably
there are some pretty direct connections. Calvin's Platonist leanings are well known.
And then there is this ladder image, which may also indicate dependence on the influence of the long Christian tradition of spiritual writings on the ascent of the soul to
God. The image had patristic origins but was also prevalent in the sixteenth century,
perhaps most significantly in the poems of Marguerite of Navarre, with whom Calvin
corresponded. The most recent work on Marguerite is Paula Sommers, *Celestial Lad-
ders: Readings in Marguerite of Navarre's Poetry of Spiritual Ascent* (Genève: Droz, 1989).
The historical connections and inclination toward these Neoplatonic constructions are
not difficult to find.

At the same time, I suspect that the issue is more complex than might first be admitted. This is especially true if we remember that when we ascend to heaven, we find
there, according to Calvin, Jesus Christ, who, *in his humanity*, is seated at the right
hand of the Father. The presence of the human Jesus there hardly squares with a celestial, otherworldly vision of eternal repose associated with Neoplatonism.

There are also passages every once in a while in Calvin's writings that highlight the
physical materiality of liturgical action. In a description of preaching, for example,
Calvin noted that "God himself appears in our midst. . . . An inestimable treasure is
given us *in earthen vessels*" (OS, 5:8; *Institutes* 4.1.5). The same is true of the sacraments: "First of all, we ought to believe that the truth must never be separated from the
signs, though it ought to be distinguished from them. We *perceive and feel* a sign, such
as the bread which is put into our hands by the minister in the Lord's Supper; and because we ought to seek Christ in heaven, *our thoughts ought to be carried there*. By the
hand of the minister he presents to us his body, that it may be actually enjoyed by the
godly, who rise by faith to fellowship with him" (CO, 36:133 [Commentary on Isa. 6:7]).
Here, the sense of touch is important, such that the very feel of the bread aids the faithful in their contemplation of heavenly reality. I suggest, along with Philip Butin, that it
is Calvin's trinitarian language that ultimately allows him to escape the grossest errors
of dualism. Butin argues that Calvin's view is "not Neoplatonic, as if the flesh or the
world were to be avoided because they are material or tangible. Rather, the sense is

frequent use of the term "spiritual worship." For Calvin (as it was for Erasmus, among others), the ascent toward God is a purely spiritual ascent. Commenting on Psalm 95, Calvin stated, "The worshipers were to lift their eyes to heaven, and serve God in a spiritual manner."[28] The basis for this is simple: God's spiritual nature requires that worship be spiritual. So Calvin commented: "It is certain that God would never be worshiped except agreeably to His nature; from which it follows, that His true worship was always spiritual, and therefore by no means comprised in external pomp."[29] Calvin's privileged text on this point is certainly John 4:21–24, which he cited copiously throughout his commentaries, sermons, and polemical writings on liturgical matters. In his commentary on this text, Calvin noted:

> But here we must ask first, why and in what sense the worship of God may be called spiritual. To understand this we must note the antithesis between the Spirit and external figures, as between the shadow and the substance. The worship of God is said to consist in the Spirit because it is only the inward faith of the heart that produces prayer and purity of conscience and denial of ourselves, that we may be given up to obedience of God as holy sacrifices.[30]

The ascent to God that Calvin described consists of the attentive direction of the mind and heart away from external forms toward God.

This emphasis on spiritual worship introduces a second important pair of metaphors for Calvin: inward and outward, internal and external. Spiritual worship, by which we rise to God, is most fundamen-

---

Pauline. Calvin wants to stress the freedom of spiritual worship in contrast to the strictures of humanly devised and required ceremonies. Spirit stands in contrast, not to matter, but to the law, and to human attempts to please God by regulated liturgical conformity which misrepresents its object" ("Constructive Iconoclasm: Trinitarian Concern in Reformed Worship," *Studia Liturgica* 19 [1989]: 133–42). See also Philip Butin, "John Calvin's Humanist Image of Popular Late-Medieval Piety and Its Contribution to Reformed Worship," *Calvin Theological Journal* 29 (1994): 419–31.

28. CO, 32:31 (Commentary on Ps. 95:6). See also *Institutes* 1.11–13; 4.10.14; and commentary on Isa. 56:2; John 4:24; and Acts 15:9. As Alexandre Ganoczy observes, this theme was prominent in the writings of the humanists, especially Erasmus (*The Young Calvin*, trans. David Foxgrover and Wade Provo [Philadelphia: Westminster, 1987], 365 n. 106).

29. CO, 24:43 (Commentary on Exod. 25:8). See also his commentary on Isa. 66:1.

30. CO, 47:88 (Commentary on John 4:23). See also commentary on Ps. 50:14; Isa. 1:13; 11:4; and James 1:17. The language of "inward ascent of the soul" is a very Augustinian theme and is expertly surveyed in Bernard McGinn, *The Presence of God: A History of Western Christian Mysticism*, vol. 1, *The Foundations of Mysticism* (New York: Crossroad, 1991). McGinn begins his explanation of Augustine with Augustine's "account of the soul's ascension to contemplative and ecstatic experience of the divine presence" (231ff.).

tally "inside" the human person: "When they [the prophets] speak of the worship of God they describe it by outward acts, such as altars, sacrifices, washings, and such like; and indeed, the worship of God *being within the soul, there is no way in which it can be described but by outward signs,* by which men declare that they worship and adore God."[31] External worship of God is insufficient, "for it is not enough for our outward acts to be applied to God's service,"[32] and "when we have to deal with God nothing is achieved unless we begin from the inner disposition of the heart."[33]

At the same time, internal authenticity is also not sufficient. External expression is necessary. In his commentary on Genesis 12, Calvin developed a horticultural image to make his point: "The inward worship of the heart is not sufficient, unless external profession before men be added. Religion has truly its appropriate seat in the heart; but from this root, public confession afterwards arises, as its fruit."[34]

Notice how this spatial language of up/down and in/out fits with the liturgical sins discussed above. Hypocrisy is an abuse that violates the inward/outward relationship. Superstition, in contrast, violates the upward movement of worship. To summarize thus far: Calvin's theology of worship is, in part, revealed in his use of simple prepositions: up, down, in, out. God comes down, accommodating to human capacity by making provision for liturgical expression. Worshipers rise to God by offering spiritual worship, elevating their mind to God. This occurs most fundamentally within the human person and is given expression externally through tangible, public means. Notice the pervasive use of this language in his commentary on Psalm 9:11:

> It was not enough for the faithful, in those days, to depend upon the Word of God, and to engage in those ceremonial services which he required, unless, aided by *external* symbols, they *elevated* their *minds* above these, and yielded to God *spiritual* worship. God, indeed, gave real tokens of his presence in that visible sanctuary, but not for the purpose of binding the senses and thoughts of his people to earthly elements; he wished rather that these *external* symbols should serve as *ladders,* by which the faithful might *ascend* even to heaven. The design of God from the commencement in the appointment of the sacraments, and all the outward exercises of religion, was to consult the infirmity and weak capacity of his people. Accordingly, even at the present day, the true and proper use of them is, to assist us in seeking God *spiritually*

31. CO, 36:326 (Commentary on Isa. 18:7), italics added.
32. OS, 5:431 (*Institutes* 4.18.16).
33. OS, 4:73 (*Institutes* 3.3.16).
34. CO, 23:181 (Commentary on Gen. 12:7). See also his commentary on Isa. 19:18; and Dan. 6:10.

in his heavenly glory, and not to occupy our *minds* with the things of this world, or keep them fixed in the vanities of the flesh.[35]

This vivid account of up, down, in, and out is a convenient summary of the building blocks for Calvin's understanding of worship.

Sensory Metaphors

Beyond the prepositions already addressed, a second set of metaphors depicts liturgical action in terms of human sensory experience. Of these, the most pervasive are metaphors of speaking and hearing.[36] Worship is God's speech to humanity. Commenting on Jeremiah 7, Calvin argued, "The main part of true and right worship and service is to hear God speaking."[37] God's speech is realized, in part—to no one's surprise—through the preaching of the Word. Commenting on Isaiah 11:4, Calvin asserted, "When the prophet says 'by the breath of his lip,' this must not be limited to the person of Christ. For it refers to the Word which is preached by His ministers. Christ acts by them in such a manner that He wishes their mouth to be reckoned as His mouth, and their lips as His lips."[38] Yet even in visual and sacramental signs, God speaks: "Although we must maintain the distinction between the Word and the sign; yet let us know, that as soon as the sign itself meets our eyes, the Word ought to sound in our ears."[39] Thus, in worship, through word and sign, God speaks. And so do we. Prayer and praise are our speech to God, so much so that Calvin spoke of prayer as an "intimate conversation of the pious with God."[40]

Worship is also an image or mirror: "The Word, sacraments, public prayers, and other helps of this kind, cannot be neglected, without a wicked contempt of God, who manifests himself to us in these ordinances, *as in a mirror or image*."[41] This metaphorical, spiritual seeing is in some way tied to the physical, literal sight of the external forms of worship.[42] Old Testament forms were intended "so that under the

35. CO, 31:102 (Commentary on Ps. 9:11), italics added.
36. In the use of the speech metaphor, Calvin was, of course, expressing his preference for a favored Renaissance category. See William J. Bouwsma, "Calvin and the Renaissance Crisis of Knowing," *Calvin Theological Journal* 17 (1982): 204; and idem, "Calvinism as *Theologia Rhetorica*," in *Calvinism as Theologia Rhetorica*, ed. Wilhelm Wuellner (Berkeley: Center for Hermenuetical Studies in Hellenistic and Modern Culture, 1987).
37. CO, 37:693 (Commentary on Jer. 7:21).
38. CO, 36:240 (Commentary on Isa. 11:4).
39. CO, 23:240 (Commentary on Gen. 17:9).
40. OS, 4:320 (*Institutes* 3.20.16).
41. CO, 31:274 (Commentary on Ps. 27:4), italics added.
42. On this point, see T. H. L. Parker, *Calvin's Old Testament Commentaries* (Louisville: Westminster John Knox, 1986), 116–21; and Serene Jones, *Calvin and the Rhetoric*

external image the spiritual truth *might meet their eyes.*"[43] Physical sight of external forms should lead to correct spiritual perception. The same is true of sacraments: "The believer, when he sees the sacraments with his own eyes, does not halt at the *physical sight of them,* but by those steps (which I have indicated by analogy) rises up in devout contemplation to those lofty mysteries which lie hidden in the sacraments."[44] And again, a sacrament "represents God's promises as painted in a picture and sets them before our sight, portrayed graphically and in the manner of icons."[45] Like the seventh-century iconoclasts, Calvin saw the Lord's Supper as the "only true icon" of Christ.

Both physical sight and spiritual perception thus are bound up with the inward, outward, downward, upward movement of worship described earlier. Because God has descended toward humanity and provided external forms for worship, humanity can rise to God through correct internal perception of God and God's works. The mirror or image metaphor is particularly apt for the sacraments, which are experienced in part through sight: "Yet those ancient sacraments looked to the same purpose to which ours now tend: to direct and almost lead men by the hand to Christ, or rather, as images, to represent him and show him forth to be known."[46]

Calvin frequently combined metaphors of speech and sight. In the memorable Augustinian mixed metaphor, also adopted by other sixteenth-century theologians such as Peter Martyr Vermigli, the sacraments were, for Calvin, visible words: "A sacrament is nothing else than a *visible word,* or sculpture and image of that grace of God, which the words more fully illustrate."[47] Elsewhere, he called them a *vocal sign.*[48]

---

of Piety (Louisville: Westminster John Knox, 1995), 77, 102–3. On the one hand, both the seeing and the hearing, for Calvin, were metaphorical. It was ascent of the mind to heaven that he was describing in metaphorical terms. But on the other hand, Calvin retained a surprisingly literal sense of actual seeing and hearing in the act of worship. On visual sense, see his commentary on Ezek. 18:5–9.

43. CO, 24:513 (Commentary on Lev. 3:1), italics added.

44. OS, 5:262 (*Institutes* 4.14.5), italics added.

45. OS, 5:263 (*Institutes* 4.14.6). Calvin's depiction of the eucharist as the true icon of God is strikingly similar to the seventh-century iconoclast doctrine of the eucharist as the only true icon of Christ. Significantly, Calvin left the word *icon* in Greek in this passage.

46. OS, 5:278 (*Institutes* 4.14.20).

47. CO, 23:240 (Commentary on Gen. 17:9), italics added. See also his commentary on Gen. 17:9; Jer. 27:1–5; and Ezek. 2:3. The notion of sacraments as the visible word of God is thoroughly Augustinian and was common in sixteenth-century Reformation thought. See Joseph McLelland, *The Visible Words of God: An Exposition of the Sacramental Theology of Peter Martyr Vermigli* (Edinburgh: Oliver and Boyd, 1957), 128–38. Thus, sound and sight, mind and body, understanding and will are all brought to bear in the lifting of the heart of the believer to the Lord in worship.

48. See his commentary on Gen. 9:12.

Calvin's gallery of sensory images is completed by metaphors of taste or eating. Worship is also nourishment, the giving and receiving and tasting of spiritual food. This metaphor is certainly most naturally applicable to the Lord's Supper. Passage after passage of Calvin's writing on the holy meal features this metaphor prominently:

> From the physical things set forth in the Sacrament we are led by a sort of analogy to spiritual things. Thus, when bread is given as a symbol of Christ's body, we must at once grasp this comparison: as bread nourishes, sustains, and keeps the life of our body, so Christ's body is the only food to invigorate and enliven our soul. When we see wine set forth as a symbol of blood, we must reflect on the benefits which wine imparts to the body, and so realize that the same are spiritually imparted to us by Christ's blood. These benefits are to nourish, refresh, strengthen, and gladden.[49]

Yet spiritual nourishment is in no way limited to the Lord's Supper. Both the giving of the gospel and the Lord's Supper are instances of spiritual nourishment: "Daily he gives it [his body as spiritual food] when by the word of the gospel he offers it for us to partake . . . [and] when he seals such giving of himself by the sacred mystery of the Supper."[50]

The metaphor of spiritual nourishment is particularly important in order to complement and balance the mental and cognitive nature of the others. As B. A. Gerrish has observed, "Sometimes, to be sure, the spatial language appears to stand for a mental or cognitive operation: invited by the symbols, we are lifted up to heaven *oculis animisque* ('by our eyes and minds'), and this fits well with the *Sursum corda* of the liturgy. But it cannot possibly be taken to negate everything Calvin says, here and elsewhere, about feeding on the body, which is not a purely mental or cognitive operation."[51]

Note also how all three sensory images function on at least two levels, both literally and metaphorically. That is, we hear God speaking through preaching. We see and are nourished by God's grace in the Lord's Supper. But we also hear God speaking through the Supper and are fed through preaching.

Additional Images

But there is also discontinuity. As this last passage suggests, the discontinuity consists in part of the fact that in the new dispensation, the people of God followed a "spiritual manner of worshiping God." What had been a literal, physical exercise, i.e., the burning of an animal,

49. OS, 5:344–345 (*Institutes* 4.17.3).
50. OS, 5:346 (*Institutes* 4.17.5).
51. Gerrish, *Grace and Gratitude*, 175.

was now less literal and more metaphoric. In other words, it is spiritual—the same term we encountered earlier to express the human ascent to God. Calvin expressed this forcefully in his treatise *The Necessity of Reforming the Church:*

> In short, as God requires us to worship him in a spiritual manner, so we with all zeal urge men to all the spiritual sacrifices which he commends. . . . This, I say, is the sure and unerring form of divine worship, which we know that he approves, because it is the form which his Word prescribes. These are the only sacrifices of the Christian Church which have attestation from him.[52]

Further, there was discontinuity for Calvin in that Christ fulfilled the meaning and purpose of the Old Testament sacrifices once and for all. On this basis, Calvin repudiated any impression that the sacrament either repeated or effected this sacrifice anew. He was steadfastly opposed to understanding the eucharist as the self-offering of the church. He reserved the strongest polemic language to counter the sacrificial interpretation of the eucharist:

> Though the papists should shout a thousand times that the sacrifice which Christ made once for all on the cross and which they themselves make today is not different but one and the same, I shall still maintain from the apostle's own mouth that if the sacrifice of Christ availed to please God it not only put an end to other sacrifices but that it is impossible to repeat it.[53]

Worship is a sacrifice but a sacrifice of praise and not propitiation. Worshipers are priests: "For we who are defiled in ourselves, yet are priests in him, offer ourselves and our all to God, and freely enter the heavenly sanctuary that the sacrifices of prayers and praise that we bring may be acceptable and sweet-smelling before God."[54]

Along with sacrifice, covenant-making was central in Calvin's biblical theology. Calvin's exegesis of the Old Testament highlighted the significance of the various covenants between God and humanity. Calvin saw these covenants as examples of the primary bond that was made possible by God between God and humanity. The act of external worship served to ratify or enact the covenant bond between God and humanity. Thus, Old Testament sacrifices were means toward union with God as expressed in the covenant: "In like manner, the design with which sacrifices were instituted by God was to

52. CO, 6:460 (*The Necessity of Reforming the Church*).
53. CO, 55:122 (Commentary on Heb. 10:2).
54. OS, 3:481 (*Institutes* 2.15.6); see also *Institutes* 4.18.16.

bind his people more closely to himself, and to ratify and confirm his covenant."[55]

This emphasis on covenant bond was but one part of a much larger conceptual category for Calvin, that of the union of humanity with God. Calvin spoke of the service of the sanctuary as "the sacred bond of intercourse with God."[56] In the New Testament age, such union is particularly realized in the eucharist, which Calvin spoke of as "the sacrament of the Supper, by means of which our Lord leads us to communion with Jesus Christ."[57] Recalling spatial images, Calvin described the sacraments as being "like a ladder to us so that we may seek our Lord Jesus Christ, and so that we may be fully convinced that he lives in us and we are united to him."[58] Just as Old Testament worship was a bond between God and Israel, so too the worship of the Christian church serves to unite God and the worshiping church.

Next, Calvin described public worship as a school of faith: "Whenever true believers assemble together at the present day, the end which they ought to have in view is to employ themselves in the exercises of religion, to call to remembrance the benefits which they have received from God, to make progress in the knowledge of his Word, and to testify the oneness of their faith."[59] The purpose of ceremonies was to assure that the faithful were *"trained to godliness, and might make greater and greater progress in faith and in the pure worship of God."*[60] Thus, Calvin glowingly described how the worship of Israel was useful for teaching the people lessons in theology. Such lessons were offered on the subject of the atonement: "The ancient people were exercised in these ceremonies, *to teach them that God can only be appeased by the payment of a ransom"*;[61] the mediation of Christ: "Besides, it was right that they should always have before their eyes symbols, by which they would be *admonished,* that they could have no access to God but through a mediator";[62] about how one can please God: "The rite of ablution reminded the ancient people that no one can please God, except he both seek for expiation in the blood of Christ, and labour to purify himself from the pollutions of the flesh";[63] and about the judgment of God: "For when an animal was killed at the altar, all were reminded that they were

55. CO, 31:498 (Commentary on Ps. 50:4–5).
56. CO, 31:246 (Commentary on Ps. 42:1).
57. OS, 1:505 (1541 *Short Treatise on the Lord's Supper*). See also *Institutes* 4.17.33.
58. CO, 51:750 (Sermon on Eph. 5:25–27).
59. CO, 31:760 (Commentary on Ps. 81:1–3).
60. CO, 36:38 (Commentary on Isa. 1:11), italics added.
61. CO, 24:523 (Commentary on Lev. 5:6), italics added.
62. CO, 23:138 (Commentary on Gen. 8:20), italics added.
63. CO, 24:199 (Commentary on Exod. 19:10).

guilty of death."[64] Ceremonies and symbols were, in Calvin's words, useful for encouraging and stimulating faith. He frequently referred to them as "props," "stimulants," and "exercises."[65] Ceremonies and signs have value for teaching, stimulating, and assuring the believer in faith:

> But here we ought also to observe the usefulness of outward signs of repentance; for they serve as spurs to prompt us more to know and abhor sin. In this way, so far as they are spurs, they may be called *causes of repentance;* and as far as they are evidences, they may be called *effects*. They are *causes*, because the marks of our guilt, which we carry about us, excite us the more to acknowledge ourselves to be sinners and guilty; and they are effects, because, if they were not preceded by repentance, we would never be induced to perform them sincerely.[66]

Worship in public ceremonies arises out of genuine faith, to be sure, but it also causes, confirms, and stimulates it.

Finally, Calvin described worship as a testimony to the world. Calvin observed that in addition to providing tangible benefits for the life of the individual Christian believer and the community of faith, liturgical activity has a particular purpose beyond the gathered church. This purpose for the world is twofold: Christian worship both testifies to the goodness of God before the world and is an act of separation, signaling a clear delineation between the world and the worshiping community. Both themes are expressed in Calvin's analysis of Isaac's sacrifice:

> From other passages we are well aware that Moses here speaks of public worship; for inward invocation of God neither requires an altar, nor has any special choice of place; and it is certain that the saints, wherever they lived, worshiped. *But because religion ought to maintain a testimony before men,* Isaac, having erected and consecrated an altar, professes himself a worshiper of the true and only God, and *by this method separates himself from the polluted rites of heathens.*[67]

Calvin was not content with only the benefits of testimony and separation; he also wished that these acts would in turn lead others to call on

64. CO, 37:391 (Commentary on Jer. 7:21).

65. See also commentary on Gen. 8:20; 33:20; 35:7; Jer. 7:21; Dan. 9:1–3; and *Institutes* 4.1.1 and 4.10.31, where Calvin discusses the sacraments in terms of their value for edification.

66. CO, 36:374 (Commentary on Isa. 22:13), italics added.

67. CO, 23:366 (Commentary on Gen. 26:25), italics added. See also commentary on Gen. 33:20.

the Lord: "And when each recites the personal benefits which he has received, let all be animated unitedly and in a public manner to give praise to God. We give thanks publicly to God, not only that men may be witnesses of our gratitude, but also *that they may follow our example.*"[68] Christian worship, then, resulted not only in the greater union of God and his people and the edification of the church but also in a witness to the world.

In sum, Calvin painted an entire gallery of images to depict the meaning and purpose of public liturgy: Worship is like a ladder, a fruit tree, a conversation, a mirror or image, a feast, a sacrifice, a ratification of a treaty, a master teacher, a testimony. Calvin spoke about public worship with rhetoric that was imaginative and full of high expectations. Calvin's vision of sacramental worship was mystical but not magical.

Theological Framework: Trinitarian Understandings of Divine Action

These images convey the energy, force, and imagination of Calvin's view of worship. But to gain full force, they need to be set in their larger theological context. If we were to go back over all the descriptions and images of worship just outlined and were to diagram Calvin's sentences, we would find that the nominative case or subject of many of those sentences is not the gathered congregation but God. We the people warrant the dative or objective case, not the nominative.

At the heart of Calvin's vision is the notion that worship is charged with divine activity: "Wherever the faithful, who worship him purely and in due form, according to the appointment of his Word, are assembled together to engage in the solemn acts of religious worship, *he is graciously present, and presides in the midst of them.*"[69] Regarding the sacraments, Calvin argued that they "are not strictly the works of men but of God. In Baptism or the Lord's Supper we do nothing; we simply come to God to receive His grace. Baptism, from our side, is a passive work *(respectua nostri est opus passivum)*. We bring nothing to it but faith, which has all things laid up in Christ."[70] As Hughes Oliphant Old has repeatedly argued, "What Calvin has in mind is that God is active in our worship. When we worship God according to his Word, he is at work in the worship of the church. For Calvin the worship of the church is a matter of divine activity rather than human

68. CO, 31:337 (Commentary on Ps. 34:3), italics added. See also commentary on Ps. 22:22–23.
69. CO, 31:102 (Commentary on Ps. 9:11), italics added.
70. CO, 50:245 (Commentary on Gal. 5:3).

creativity."[71] Similarly, John Leith contends, "The sense of the reality of the Creator and Source of all things, the feeling of the objective presence of God, a sensitivity to the activity of God in life in general and in worship in particular, left an imprint on everything Calvin did or wrote."[72]

Calvin's theocentric view of worship is thus more fully and accurately described as a trinitarian vision. Each divine person is described as having a particular role in the inner movement or nature of worship. God the Father is agent, giver, initiator. God the Son is mediator, particularly in the office of priest. God the Spirit is prompter, enabler, and effector. In short, to use Philip Butin's phrase, worship is "trinitarian enactment," in which

> the initiatory "downward" movement of Christian worship begins in the Father's gracious and free revelation of the divine nature to the church through the Son, by means of the Spirit. In more concrete terms, this takes place in the proclamation of the Word according to scripture, by the empowerment and illumination of the Spirit. . . . The "upward" movement of human response in worship—focused around prayer and the celebration of the sacraments . . . is also fundamentally motivated by God. Human response—the "sacrifice of praise and thanksgiving"— arises from the faith that has its source in the indwelling Holy Spirit. In that Spirit, prayer, devotion, and obedience are offered to God the Father, who is the proper object of worship, through the Son Jesus Christ, who being fully divine and fully human is the mediator of the church's worship.[73]

In sum, as Calvin saw it, the weekly assembly of the church for public worship was no ordinary gathering. It was an event charged with divine activity, an arena in which the divine-human relationship was depicted and enacted. In public worship, God was not only the One to whom worship was directed but also the One who was active in the worship of the church. Through public worship—that is, through public prayers, preaching, and the celebration of baptism and the Lord's Supper—God actively worked to draw human beings into divine fellow-

71. Old, "John Calvin and the Prophetic Criticism of Worship," 234 and again, "If there is one doctrine which is at the heart of Reformed worship it is the doctrine of the Holy Spirit. It is the belief that the Holy Spirit brings the Church into being, that the Holy Spirit dwells in the Church and sanctifies the Church. Worship is the manifestation of the creation and sanctifying presence of the Holy Spirit" (*Patristic Roots of Reformed Worship*, 341).

72. John Leith, "Calvin's Doctrine of the Proclamation of the Word and Its Significance for Today," in *John Calvin and the Church*, 208.

73. Philip Butin, *Revelation, Redemption, Response: Calvin's Trinitarian Understanding of the Divine-Human Relationship* (New York: Oxford University Press, 1995), 102.

ship.[74] Only the most exalted language could convey the significance of this event. As Calvin himself expressed it, "It is an instance of the inestimable grace of God, that so far as the infirmity of our flesh will permit, we are lifted up even to God by the exercises of religion. What is the design of the preaching of the Word, the sacraments, the holy assemblies, and the whole external government of the church, but that we may be united to God?"[75]

To conclude, let us observe that these themes in Calvin's theology lead us to ask, How do our discussions of worship stack up against the measuring stick of Calvin's theology of liturgy? How many of our current discussions about worship are really theological? That is, how often do we ask whether our worship portrays and depicts the God of Abraham and the God of Jesus Christ or whether it depicts some other kind of god? How many of our discussions focus not on the mechanics of worship but on its inner meaning? How often do we actually work at aligning our efforts at worship renewal with explicit scriptural teaching? How specific are we in connecting our worship practices with biblical models, commands, warnings, and encouragement? How often do we ask whether our minds and hearts are focused on the proper relationship between our actions and our God? Have we given an account of the nature and purpose of what we are doing when we gather for liturgy? How many of us focus not on mechanics or method but on meaning? How many of our conversations move beyond what we deplore in worship to our constructive, theological vision for worship? How have we done in providing instructive images for our as-

74. The structure and logic of Calvin's theology of liturgy thus mirrors the structure and logic of other more traditionally prominent theological loci, such as the doctrine of faith. A case in point is the notion of divine agency in worship, which bears an exact correlation with Calvin's soteriological structure. Like other theological loci that attempt to relate divine and human action (e.g., the doctrine of faith, the doctrine of providence), a theology of liturgy must explain how worship is both a free act of human beings and also one that is inspired and enabled by God. If we were to ask Calvin about the main agent in worship, he would respond—as he would regarding faith—by answering "the Holy Spirit." The Holy Spirit effects the proclamation of the Word in our hearts, unites us to Christ in the Supper, and inspires our praise and prayer. The Holy Spirit makes the whole up-and-down parabola of worship work. Generally speaking, every first-rate theologian in the history of the church has approached theology of liturgy as a correlate of their larger theological system. Liturgy is an icon of life before God. For Calvin, this is true not only with respect to the doctrine of faith but also with respect to the doctrine of the knowledge of God, the doctrine of the work of Christ, and any number of other doctrines. Part of the enduring appeal of Calvin's theology of liturgy is that his position was carefully worked out in conversation with and in terms of an entire theological system. Future studies could well analyze the points of correspondence between Calvin's theology of liturgy and several of his other main theological themes.

75. CO, 31:248 (Commentary on Ps. 24:7).

semblies that "win attention by their propriety, arouse the mind by their luster . . . so that they enter effectively into the heart"? In comparison to the consommé of Calvin's rhetoric, ours is often a motley bowl of porridge.

Honest answers to these questions provide us with a large challenge. They throw us back to Calvin's own instruction and demand our common resolve to echo this advice:

> [Let us] engrave this useful lesson upon our hearts, that we should consider it the great end of our existence to be found numbered among the worshipers of God; and that we should avail ourselves of the inestimable privilege of the stated assemblies of the Church, which are necessary helps to our infirmity, and means of mutual excitement and encouragement. By these, and our common sacraments, the Lord who is one God, and who designed that we should be one in him, is training us up together in the hope of eternal life, and in the united celebration of his holy name.[76]

76. CO, 31:529 (Commentary on Ps. 52:8).

6

Baptism as a Sacrament of Reconciliation in the Thought of John Calvin

Whatever penance had become by the late Middle Ages, it began as a way to reconcile those who had once been baptized both to God and to the community of faith.[1] At its best, penance served as a pastoral strategy for taking both sin and grace seriously in the life of the Christian community. Sin needed to be named and rooted out; grace needed to be announced and celebrated. At least from the late patristic period, penance was the event where this happened. When the sixteenth-century Reformers voiced their varying degrees of opposition to penance, they did not deny the pastoral issue that penance

---

1. References to Calvin's writings in this chapter will include the citation of the selection from Calvin's edited works, followed by a citation of the English translation. The following abbreviations are used to identify the most frequently cited sources: OS = *Ioannis Calvini Opera Selecta*, ed. Peter Barth, Wilhelm Niesel, and Dora Scheuner, 5 vols. (Munich: C. Kaiser, 1926–62); CO = *Ioannis Calvini Opera quae supersunt omnia*, ed. Wilhelm Baum, Edward Cunitz, and Edward Reuss, 59 vols. (Brunsvigae: A. Swetschke and Son, 1843–48); *Corpus Reformatorum*, vols. 29–87 (Brunsvigae: A. Swetschke and Son, 1843–48); *Institutes* = John Calvin, *Institutes of the Christian Religion*, ed. John T. McNeill, trans. Ford Lewis Battles, Library of Christian Classics, vols. 20–21 (Philadelphia: Westminster, 1960); *Treatises* = John Calvin, *Theological Treatises*, trans. J. K. S. Reid, Library of Christian Classics, vol. 22 (Philadelphia: Westminster, 1954).

had once addressed. Post-baptismal sin still required an antidote, a sign of God's reconciling grace.

Among sixteenth-century Reformers, John Calvin was not atypical in his dismissal of penance as unwarranted by Scripture, prone to abuse, and injurious to the conscience and faith of the faithful. Yet repentance—the large and important theological motif connected with the practice of penance—was, for Calvin, one of the most significant and profound dimensions of the gospel. What would serve as a sign of repentance, if not penance? The answer is intimated in Calvin's extended polemic against medieval penance in his 1559 *Institutes of the Christian Religion:* "You will therefore speak most aptly if you call baptism the sacrament of penance, since it has been given to those who are intent on repentance as a confirmation of grace and a seal of assurance."[2] In another context, Calvin made the same point, decrying the papists for acting "as if baptism itself were not the sacrament of penance."[3]

This chapter seeks to explain how baptism functioned as a sign of repentance in Calvin's thought and thus came to be a sign of lifelong reconciliation in the Reformed tradition. Though this is a fairly prominent theme in Calvin's thought, it has not been treated in recent discussions of Calvin's baptismal theology, most of which either compare Calvin's view to Catholic and Lutheran views of the sacraments or discuss the issue of infant baptism in light of Calvin's opposition to the Anabaptists.[4] These studies faithfully describe many of the main contours of Calvin's theology of baptism, but they rarely describe Calvin's emphasis on baptism as a cornerstone of the Christian life. Likewise,

2. OS, 5:451–52; *Institutes* 4.19.17. Calvin cites the baptism of John "unto repentance" and Augustine's description of baptism as a "sacrament of faith and repentance" as warrants for his position. See also *Institutes* 3.4.6.

3. OS, 5:288; *Institutes* 4.15.4.

4. J. D. Benoit, "Calvin et le baptême des enfants," *Revue d'histoire et de philosophie religieuses* 17 (1937): 457–73; John E. Burkhart, "Kingdom, Church, and Baptism: The Significance of the Doctrine of the Church in the Theology of John Calvin" (Ph.D. diss., University of Southern California, 1959); Philip Walker Butin, *Revelation, Redemption, Response: Calvin's Trinitarian Understanding of the Divine-Human Relationship* (New York: Oxford University Press, 1995), 107–13; Egil Grislis, "Calvin's Doctrine of Baptism," *Church History* 31 (1962): 46–65; Jill Raitt, "Three Inter-related Principles in Calvin's Unique Doctrine of Infant Baptism," *Sixteenth-Century Journal* 11 (1980): 51–61; John W. Riggs, "Emerging Ecclesiology in Calvin's Baptismal Thought, 1536–1543," *Church History* 64 (1995): 29–43; L. G. M. Alting von Geusau, *Die Lehre von der Kindertaufe bei Calvin* (Bilthoven: Nelissen; and Mainz: Matthias-Grünewald Verlag, 1963); Bryan D. Spinks, "Calvin's Baptismal Theology and the Making of the Strasbourg and Genevan Baptismal Liturgies 1540 and 1542," *Scottish Journal of Theology* 48 (1995): 55–78; Thomas F. Torrance, "Calvins Lehre von der Taufe," *Calvin-Studien 1959*, ed. J. Moltmann (Neukirchen: Neukirchener Verlag, 1960), 95–129; and Ronald Wallace, *Calvin's Doctrine of Word and Sacrament* (Edinburgh: Oliver and Boyd, 1957).

histories of penance most often observe only Calvin's sturdy opposition to the Roman sacrament, failing to notice that Calvin's liturgical system did include baptism as a ritual sign of lifelong reconciliation.[5] This chapter is a straightforward attempt to fill these two gaps in the literature. To accomplish this, it first observes the way in which Calvin's theology of baptism was rooted in the dual doctrines of sanctification and justification, a necessary foundation for baptism to function as a sign of reconciliation. Second, it discusses the way in which Calvin articulated a vision for what might be called "baptismal piety" and, to a limited degree, called for this to be reflected in the life of the Genevan community. Finally, it reflects on the implications of these observations for liturgical renewal and for methodology in liturgical history.

Sanctification, Justification, and Calvin's Theology of Baptism

The way into Calvin's soteriology properly begins by understanding his nuanced distinction between sanctification and justification. In his extensive discussion of the way in which a Christian receives grace, Calvin—to the utter astonishment of his Lutheran counterparts—began not with a discussion of justification but rather with a cluster of terms that concern the ongoing process of the Christian life: repentance, regeneration, faith, mortification, and vivification. All of these, for Calvin, were ongoing processes through which the Holy Spirit works in the heart of the believer. Calvin defined repentance, his root metaphor for the Christian life, as "the true turning of our life to God, a turning that arises from a pure and earnest fear of him," and which

5. See, for example, Joseph Martos, *Doors to the Sacred: A Historical Introduction to Sacraments in the Catholic Church* (Tarrytown, N.Y.: Triumph Books, 1981), 301; Dorothea Sattler, *Gelebte Busse: Das menschliche Busswerk (satisfactio) im kumenischen Gespräch* (Mainz: Matthias-Grünewald Verlag, 1992), 169–76; Frank Senn, "The Confession of Sins in the Reformation Churches," in *The Fate of Confession*, ed. Mary Collins and David Power (Edinburgh: T & T Clark, 1987), 109; and Thomas N. Tentler, *Sin and Confession on the Eve of the Reformation* (Princeton: Princeton University Press, 1977), 349–63. Other histories of penance understandably omit Calvin altogether, given their exclusive orientation to the Roman Catholic Church. See James Dallen, *The Reconciling Community: The Rite of Penance* (New York: Pueblo Publishing, 1986); and Bernhard Poschmann, *Penance and the Anointing of the Sick* (New York: Herder & Herder, 1964). Notable exceptions are Kenan B. Osborne, O.F.M., *Reconciliation and Justification: The Sacrament and Its Theology* (New York: Paulist Press, 1990), 146–50; and Max Thurian, *Confession*, trans. Edwin Hudson (London: SCM, 1958), 26, who observe that Calvin sees baptism as a rite of reconciliation. See also Jean-Jacques von Allmen, "The Forgiveness of Sins as a Sacrament in the Reformed Tradition," in *Sacramental Reconciliation*, ed. Edward Schillebeeckx (New York: Herder & Herder, 1971); and Herbert Schützeichel, "Die Beichte vor dem Preister in der Sicht Calvins," *Trierer Theologische Studien* 31 (1974): 67–89.

"consists in the mortification of our flesh and of the old man, and in the vivification of the Spirit."[6] Only after this did Calvin address justification, which he defined as "the acceptance with which God receives us into his favor as righteous" and which "consists in the remission of sins and the imputation of Christ's righteousness."[7] Like many dimensions of Calvin's thought, sanctification and justification are distinguishable but inseparable. Their distinction clarifies why the Christian believer must struggle against the insidious power of sin, even after the once-for-all saving work of Jesus Christ. Their inseparability provides the believer with assurance that this very struggle is a part of God's saving action in the world. Sanctification, like justification, is an act by which God redeems creation.

With this distinction in mind, the nuance of Calvin's theology of baptism is readily discernible. As Calvin explained, baptism is a sign of *both* justification and sanctification.[8] This is amply evidenced in the exhortation included in his baptismal liturgy:

> Thus we receive a double grace and benefit from our God in baptism. . . . We have in it sure testimony that God wills to be a merciful Father to us, not imputing to us all our faults and offenses. Secondly, that he will assist us by his Holy Spirit so that we will have the power to battle against the devil, sin, and the desires of our flesh, until we have victory in this, to live in the liberty of his kingdom, which is a kingdom of justice.[9]

The same distinction is made in Calvin's Genevan Confession: "[In baptism] there is represented to us the cleansing from sin which we have in the blood of Jesus Christ, [and] the mortification of our flesh which we have by his death that we may live in him by his Spirit."[10] Calvin's view of baptism must be understood in terms of its dual reference to our justification in Christ and our growth in the Spirit following forgiveness.

This twofold reference becomes not only a theological statement about the meaning of baptism but also a blueprint for the way in

6. OS, 4:60; *Institutes* 3.3.5.

7. OS, 4:183, *Institutes* 3.11.2.

8. Ronald Wallace notes that Calvin's doctrine of baptism is developed in terms of a variety of metaphors: Calvin "sees [baptism] as a sign of the forgiveness of sins, mortification, renewal, adoption or entrance into the Church and separation from the world. He sees in it a sign of our participation in the victory of Christ over all the powers of evil" (*Calvin's Doctrine of Word and Sacrament*, 175).

9. OS, 2:32–33, translation mine. See also *Institutes* 4.15.1; 4.16.2. In this passage, "not imputing" refers to justification; the "battle against the devil, sin, and the desires of our flesh" refers to sanctification.

10. OS, 1:423; *Treatises* 30.

which baptism is to be received by the Christian believer. The significance of this point is underscored by Calvin's inclusion of it in the catechism that was used for the weekly instruction of Genevan Christians. Even Genevan children would have learned the following lesson:

> The right use of Baptism lies in faith and repentance. That is, we must first hold with a firm and hearty confidence that we, having been cleansed from all stains by the blood of Christ, are pleasing to God; then we are to feel his Spirit dwelling in us and declare this to others by our deeds, and so practice ourselves unceasingly in meditating on the mortification of the flesh and obedience to the righteousness of God.[11]

Baptized Christians must look back with confidence at God's decisive work for them in Christ but must also sense how that work continues throughout the Christian life.

> The benefit which we derive from the sacraments ought by no means to be restricted to the time when they are administered to us, as though the visible sign conveyed with itself the grace of God only at that moment when it is actually being proffered. . . . The benefit of baptism lies open to the whole course of life, because the promise which is contained in it is perpetually in force.[12]

It is precisely on this point that Calvin's theology differs from the medieval understanding that had preceded him. Undoubtedly, the theme of repentance had long been associated with baptism. The elaborate exorcisms that persisted throughout the medieval rite, which were understood as a sign of conversion or *metanoia,* are one notable example of this emphasis.[13] Nevertheless, the reconciliation signed by baptism was not always understood to apply to post-baptismal life. Although baptism signed the forgiveness of original sin and those sins committed prior to baptism, it was not generally understood to apply to post-baptismal sin—hence the need for penance. Calvin's opposition to this view was sturdy and unflinching: "The Papists are in great

11. "The Catechism of the Church of Geneva" (1545): OS, 2:135; *Treatises* 134. The relationship between baptism and justification is discussed in *Institutes* 4.15.1–4; the relationship between baptism and sanctification is discussed in *Institutes* 4.15.5–6.

12. CO, 7:720; "Articles Concerning the Sacraments," in Philip Edgumbe Hughes, *The Register of the Company of Pastors of Geneva in the Time of Calvin* (Grand Rapids: Eerdmans, 1966), 104.

13. See Hughes Oliphant Old, *The Shaping of the Reformed Baptismal Rite in the Sixteenth Century* (Grand Rapids: Eerdmans, 1992), 35. The understanding of baptism as a portrait of grace also led Reformed leaders to condemn exorcism. See Bodo Nischan, "The Exorcism Controversy and Baptism in the Late Reformation," *Sixteenth-Century Journal* 18 (1987): 31–51.

error in this matter, for they restrict baptism to the time of birth and the life that went before, as if the significance and power of it did not even extend to the time of death."[14] It was not that Calvin was facile in his acknowledgment of continuing sin. But he insisted that baptism signed God's promise to forgive both the guilt of original sin and of any sin committed after baptism:

> For so long as we live cooped up in this prison of our body, traces of sin will dwell in us; but if we faithfully hold fast to the promise given by God in baptism, they shall not dominate or rule. . . . This we must believe: we are baptized into the mortification of our flesh, which begins with our baptism and which we pursue day by day and which will, moreover, be accomplished when we pass from this life to the Lord.[15]

Baptism, quite simply, is "not destroyed by subsequent sins."[16] In yet another phrase indicating the way in which baptism replaced penance, Calvin observed, "But if penance is commended to us throughout life, the power of baptism too ought to be extended to us to the very same limits."[17]

Baptism and the Christian Life

Based on this link between baptism and both justification and sanctification, Calvin taught that baptism should serve as the foundation for the Christian life. As Hughes Oliphant Old affirms, "Of the essence of the Reformed understanding of baptism is the belief that it is a prophetic sign. It is a sign under which the whole of life is to be lived. Our baptism is always with us, constantly unfolding through the whole of life."[18] What is compelling about Calvin's treatment of this theme are the manifold ways in which he described baptism as a sign or root or anchor for the Christian life. In the single act of baptism, the Christian finds a call to Christian service, a clue to the meaning of human suffering, a basis or "fountain" from which the Christian can grow in the spiritual life, and a sign of assurance for an unsteady faith or a wounded conscience.

14. CO, 48:53; *Calvin's New Testament Commentaries: The Acts of the Apostles,* trans. John W. Fraser and W. J. G. MacDonald (Grand Rapids: Eerdmans, 1965), 1:80. Calvin is commenting here on Acts 2:38.
15. OS, 5:293; *Institutes* 4.15.11.
16. OS, 5:287; *Institutes* 4.15.3.
17. OS, 5:288; *Institutes* 4.15.4.
18. Old, *Shaping of the Reformed Baptismal Rite,* 179. Zwingli's baptismal prayer even referred to "daily discipleship" (247). Like Calvin, Luther also emphasized the baptismal character of the Christian life, though Luther did retain a modified form of penance.

The first clue that baptism served for Calvin as a sign of lifelong reconciliation was his understanding of baptism as a sign of the covenant between God and the Christian community. The covenant metaphor was prominent in early Reformed discussions of both soteriology and sacramental theology and finds its origins at least as far back as the early writings of Ulrich Zwingli.[19] Thus, it is no surprise that Calvin spoke of baptism as "'tokens' of the covenants."[20] For the Reformers, covenant theology was a useful means for construing the mutual commitment between God and his people. Thus, Calvin wrote of baptism:

> Notice that the nature of baptism is like a bond of mutual contract, for as the Lord by that symbol receives us into His household, and adds us to his people, so we put ourselves under the obligation of faithfulness to Him, and may never have any other spiritual Lord. Accordingly, as God on His part makes a covenant of grace with us, in which He promises remission of sins and new life, so on our part there is an oath to wage spiritual warfare, by which we promise allegiance to Him forever.[21]

Covenant theology is concerned primarily with agency: with what God does, with what the believer does, and how these actions are related. In baptism, God receives us and makes promises to us. The church, in turn, pledges fidelity and promises obedience. Baptism thus sets the believer on the brink of lifelong service and commitment. Christian service and godly obedience are signed by the very act of stepping forward to be baptized or presenting a child for baptism. Baptism itself is an act of God but one with undeniable implications for the life of the Christian believer. Construing baptism in covenantal terms necessarily places it at the forefront of a proper Christian spirituality, suggesting the important link between baptism and ethics.

Second, the relationship between baptism and daily piety is expressed in Calvin's description of the purpose of baptism. Baptism is administered by the church, Calvin contended, for the "arousing, nourishing, and confirming of our faith."[22] Baptism cannot be separated from its benefits, one of which (mentioned above) is that God "will assist us by his Holy Spirit so that we will have the power to battle against the devil, sin, and the desires of our flesh, until we have vic-

19. Ibid., 62.
20. OS, 5:263; *Institutes* 4.14.6.
21. CO, 49:317; *Calvin's New Testament Commentaries: The First Epistle of Paul the Apostle to the Corinthians*, trans. John W. Fraser (Grand Rapids: Eerdmans, 1960), 29. Calvin is commenting here on 1 Corinthians 1:13. See also Old, *Shaping of the Reformed Baptismal Rite*, 126ff.
22. OS, 5:295; *Institutes* 4.15.14.

tory in this, to live in the liberty of his kingdom, which is a kingdom of justice."[23] At the most basic level, this is true for the person who is baptized. Baptism is given to the baptizand for the confirmation of faith. Even infant baptism is conducted in the assurance that "infants are baptized into future repentance and faith."[24] At another level, baptism is a sign for arousing and stimulating the faith of the congregation of believers. All believers are taught and encouraged in the Christian life by perceiving the sign of baptism and thereby lifting their hearts to God.

Third, baptism is a sign of the inevitable suffering that will accompany the Christian life. Calvin advanced this point memorably in his commentary on the Synoptic Gospels. Calvin was a skilled exegete, benefiting from two generations of the humanist return to classical sources. His own exegetical work was enriched by his extensive knowledge of classical languages, including Greek and Hebrew. The link Calvin developed between baptism and suffering was, in fact, based on a clear understanding of the Greek verb *baptizo*. As Calvin explained it:

> In the word "baptism" there is an apt metaphor. For we know that in baptism believers are initiated into self-denial, into crucifying the old man, and into bearing the cross. . . . Now, whenever there is mention of baptism, let us remember that we are baptized under this condition and for this end—to fix the cross to our shoulders.[25]

Calvin knew that the verb "to baptize" literally meant to be drowned or, more freely, to be subjected to the waters of chaos. He perceived a direct link between this image and the call to self-denial and mortification that was so prominent in his discussion of sanctification. Again, this link has implications for the whole Christian life. For one, this understanding colors how the Christian should approach baptism itself: "So that men may offer themselves properly for baptism, a confession of sins is required of them, otherwise the whole action would be nothing but an empty mockery."[26] Baptism signed mortification, which in turn called for confession of sins. For another, this link affects how the Christian should approach suffering. Suffering is the liv-

23. From Calvin's 1542 baptismal liturgy: OS, 2:32, author's translation.
24. OS, 5:324; *Institutes* 4.16.20.
25. CO, 45:554; John Calvin, *Calvin's New Testament Commentaries: Harmony of the Gospels Matthew, Mark, and Luke*, trans. A. W. Morrison (Grand Rapids: Eerdmans, 1972), 2:272. Calvin is commenting here on Matthew 20:22.
26. CO, 45:115; John Calvin, *Calvin's New Testament Commentaries: Harmony of the Gospels Matthew, Mark, and Luke*, trans. A. W. Morrison (Grand Rapids: Eerdmans, 1972), 1:118. Calvin is commenting here on Matthew 3:6 and Mark 1:5. Calvin applies the passage to adults only.

ing out of one's baptism, one's union with Christ, and can be received as a means by which God works to nurture and sustain faith.

Fourth, baptism provides an anchor for Christian piety by serving as a constant source of assurance for the wounded conscience of the believer. As Ronald Wallace observes, for Calvin, the "chief practical use of Baptism is to give us the full assurance of salvation, carrying with it all the effects of renewed and confident Christian living that such an assurance inspires."[27] In Calvin's own words:

> But we must realize that at whatever time we are baptized, we are once for all washed and purged for our whole life. Therefore, as often as we fall away, we ought to recall the memory of our baptism and fortify our mind with it, that we may always be sure and confident of the forgiveness of sins.[28]

The assurance of salvation was arguably the most significant existential spiritual issue for sixteenth-century Christians. Martin Luther's battle with his own tormented conscience is only one example of the way in which sixteenth-century theology was born out of a crisis of assurance. Similarly, Calvin's treatment of election is an extended meditation on the grounds for assurance. Calvin believed that in baptism the Christian finds the sign of assurance helpful for maintaining belief in the face of doubt and guilt. In this way, Calvin attached to baptism the significance formerly given to penance. "There is no doubt," said Calvin, "that all pious folk throughout life, whenever they are troubled by a consciousness of their faults, may venture to remind themselves of their baptism, that from it they may be confirmed in assurance of that sole and perpetual cleansing which we have in Christ's blood."[29]

On this basis, the rite of baptism was, for Calvin, a fitting substitute for the rite of penance. Not only did penance lack dominical warrant, but it also failed to communicate the unmerited grace of God. It tortured the Christian conscience, Calvin believed, by requiring the perpetual naming of sins. To those who would argue that penance was warranted by the power of the keys given to the church, Calvin responded that the power of the keys "so depends upon baptism that it should by no means be severed from it." To those who would argue for the importance of the absolution, Calvin contended that "the absolution has reference to baptism."[30] Thus, three separate elements—con-

27. Wallace, *Calvin's Doctrine of Word and Sacrament*, 186.

28. OS, 5:287; *Institutes* 4.15.3. This emphasis was already present in the 1536 edition of the *Institutes*. See the discussion in John W. Riggs, "The Development of Calvin's Baptismal Theology, 1536–1560" (Ph.D. diss., University of Notre Dame, 1985), 115ff.

29. OS, 5:288; *Institutes* 4.15.4.

30. Ibid.

trition, the power of the keys, and absolution—that were once bound together within the matrix of the medieval sacrament of penance were *each* explained by Calvin in terms of baptism. Not surprisingly, then, one of Calvin's complaints about the Roman rite of penance concerned the way in which penance undermined baptismal piety. Calvin argued that penance was enacted

> as if baptism were wiped out by sin, and is not rather to be recalled to the memory of the sinner whenever he thinks of forgiveness of sins, so that from it he may gather together, take courage, and confirm his faith that he will obtain the forgiveness of sins, which has been promised him in baptism.[31]

In contrast, Calvin contended that this understanding of baptism meant that it should have a prominent place in the life of the Christian community: "The great truth . . . of our spiritual regeneration, though but once represented to us in baptism, should remain fixed in our minds through our whole life."[32]

Calvin's summons for baptismal piety was expressed in his prescriptions for the life of the Genevan church. Calvin called for the baptismal rite to become an important event in the life of the Genevan community, a time for signing the reconciling grace of God to everyone present.[33] One of the graces of the baptismal rite was that parents could "see with their very eyes the covenant of the Lord engraved upon the bodies of their children."[34] For Calvin, this sensory perception of the sacramental sign was one of its chief virtues. The sacraments, like the Word, were examples of God accommodating himself to us.[35] The importance of baptism consisted not only in the baptism itself but also in the communal witness of baptism. Private baptisms were prohibited, largely so that the ecclesial dimension of this reconciling sign would be realized. Baptism was thus a witness to the entire community of God's promise and grace. As with the Lord's Supper, one of its purposes was to attest to true

31. OS, 5:451; *Institutes* 4.19.17.

32. CO, 31:594; John Calvin, *Commentary on the Book of Psalms* (Grand Rapids: Eerdmans, 1949), 2:435. Calvin is commenting here on Ps. 63:2.

33. William Farel had insisted that attendance at baptism was important both for remembering the grace signed in one's baptism and for receiving a renewed exhortation to live the life of Christian gratitude (William Farel, *Manière et fasson*, ed. Jean-Guillaume Baum [Strasbourg: n.p., 1859], 15, cited in Old, *Shaping of the Reformed Baptismal Rite*, 161). This had also been one of Luther's stated reasons for translating the baptismal rite into the vernacular.

34. OS, 5:313; *Institutes* 4.16.9.

35. Ford Lewis Battles, "God Was Accommodating Himself to Human Capacity," *Interpretation* 31 (1977): 19–38.

religion, to allow the community to make a testimony of faith to one another.[36]

Further, Calvin called for a vigorous program of post-baptismal catechesis to rehearse the gospel promises signed and sealed in baptism. Those baptized, especially those baptized in infancy, had to be instructed in the faith. Post-baptismal catechesis was urged on the parents of all baptized children. It was built into the liturgical life of the Genevan community, with public catechetical services conducted each Sunday at midday, and preserved in the form of the numerous catechisms written to instruct children in the meaning of their baptism. The instruction that parents promised to give their children included instruction on the meaning of baptism itself.[37] Pastors, likewise, were called to catechize their parishioners lest they accomplish "an impious profanation of Baptism."[38] Thus, the reformed catechumenate was a post-baptismal (dare we say mystagogical) catechumenate, a fitting institutional counterpart to a genuinely baptismal spirituality.

Baptismal Piety and Liturgical Renewal

This brief analysis of Calvin's theology of baptism has significant implications for contemporary liturgical renewal. Calvin's reform points to the importance of the themes of reconciliation and lifelong baptismal piety in liturgical celebrations. If baptism is to serve as a cornerstone for Christian piety and proclaim the promise of reconciliation, then it must be given a prominent place in liturgical celebration. Private baptisms must be restored to their rightful place in the heart of public liturgy. When baptisms are conducted, the gathered congregation must be reminded that this act is also an invitation for all believers to recall their own baptism in thanksgiving and a challenge to live the baptismal life more fully. Certainly the growth of baptismal renewal services and the restoration of the Easter vigil in recent years are promising steps toward these ends. In these ways, the celebration of baptism becomes not an incidental but rather a foundational rite in the Christian community.[39]

36. OS, 5:277–78; *Institutes* 4.14.19. Also, in 4.15.1, Calvin writes, "Now baptism was given to us by God for these ends (which I have taught to be common to all sacraments): first, to serve our faith before him; secondly, to serve our confession before men." This point is most comprehensively treated in *Institutes* 4.15.13.

37. See Old, *Shaping of the Reformed Baptismal Rite*, 203.

38. In the "Letter to the Reader" that prefaces the Catechism of the Church of Geneva (1545): OS, 2:72; *Treatises* 89.

39. Robert Jensen states this case decisively: "If baptism is richly interpreted at a time and place and is a decisive event in the lives of those who undergo it, this both reveals and promotes a rich and sharply contoured believing community. If baptism as interpreted at a time and place is puny or speaks inappropriately to the gospel, it is

Beyond this, the language of baptism must permeate other dimensions of ecclesial life and witness. Prayers of corporate confession and statements of absolution may refer to baptism as a source of encouragement and may be conducted from the baptismal font. Preaching can regularly challenge Christians to live out the meaning of their baptism. Indeed, the Christian community should be urged to join William Willimon in thinking of preaching as "baptismal speech."[40] Funeral rites may properly begin with explicit references to baptism as a sign of dying and rising with Christ. These examples begin to suggest the ways in which the full panorama of liturgical celebrations can rehearse the good news of reconciliation signed by baptism.

This emphasis need not be limited to churches in the Reformed tradition. The lifelong implications of baptism are a universal Christian theme that remains redolent because of deeply biblical resonances. Baptism has always been fundamentally linked with forgiveness of sin (Acts 2:38; 22:16; 1 Cor. 6:11) and union or participation with Christ (Rom. 6:3; Gal. 3:27; Col. 2:11). This, in turn, implies a clear link between baptism and Christian life. Significantly, Paul's link between baptism and our participation with Christ in his death and resurrection is directed "that we might walk in newness of life" (Rom. 6:4). This theme is prominent enough to lead G. R. Beasley-Murray, for example, to speak of a "baptismal ethic" and a "baptismal pattern of doctrine and conduct."[41] Baptismal spirituality is a theme that is rooted in Scripture, common to many Christian traditions, and worthy of further emphasis in liturgical celebrations.

Implications for Method in Liturgical History

This analysis of Calvin's reform also has implications for the study of liturgical history. Liturgical history is usually told in terms of discrete rites or sacraments. There are histories of baptism, of eucharist, of ordination, and so on. Likewise, the liturgical enactment of particular theological motifs is usually described in terms of links with particular rites. Thanksgiving is typically associated with eucharist, reconciliation with penance, and so on.

These approaches, however valuable they might be as a primary

---

most likely the actuality and self-conception of the church that are antecedently puny or remote from the gospel. And when we perceive such sickness, reshaping of baptism must be and often has been a chief means to reform the church" (*Visible Words: The Interpretation and Practice of Christian Sacraments* [Philadelphia: Fortress, 1978], 151).

40. William Willimon, *Peculiar Speech: Preaching to the Baptized* (Grand Rapids: Eerdmans, 1992).

41. G. R. Beasley-Murray, *Baptism in the New Testament* (Grand Rapids: Eerdmans, 1962, 1994), 287–88.

framework for liturgical history, fail to paint a complete picture of the theological and liturgical diversity of the Christian church. More specifically, they fail to account for the redistribution of particular theological motifs in the liturgical life of some Christian communities, especially those that comprise the so-called Free Church traditions. Calvin's approach to repentance is a perfect example. In histories of penance, Calvin and the whole Reformed tradition with him typically have only a small place, if any at all. By abolishing penance in the Genevan churches, Calvin effectively wrote himself out of the history of rites of reconciliation in the West. Yet this exclusion results in an incomplete and imperfect picture of the liturgical life of the Genevan community. Although penance was indeed abolished, reconciliation was ritually celebrated, and the ongoing struggle with sin in the life of the Christian believer was acknowledged. These dimensions of Christian piety were simply located in Genevan liturgical life in a different place, in the sacrament of baptism.

This straightforward observation suggests that, in addition to studying traditional histories of rites, liturgical historians would do well to consider the ways in which a particular theme or theological motif is expressed in the full range of ritual celebrations for any given community. With respect to repentance, liturgical historians might look not only to penance but also to baptism and even to the eucharist.[42] This approach would do justice to the liturgical practice of the Reformation churches, which may have done away with penance but nevertheless emphasized reconciliation as a vital dimension of liturgical celebration.

This methodological suggestion might also be fruitfully applied to other theological motifs and to other periods of liturgical history. Just as the motif of reconciliation is typically found not only in penance but also in baptism and the eucharist, so too *eucharistia* or thanksgiving would likely be found not only in the Lord's Supper but also in baptism, reconciliation, and daily prayer. Likewise, eschatological themes might be found not only in Advent but throughout the Christian year.

Further, it may be that the supposed *locus classicus* of a given motif may in fact be where it is weakest. In some communities, for example, the Lord's Supper remains stubbornly penitential, while thanksgiving may be most prominent in the hymnody sung in conjunction with the preaching of the Word. In such an example, what is significant is not the absence of thanksgiving but rather its disjunction from the Lord's Supper.

42. See Geoffrey Wainwright, "The Eucharist as an Ecumenical Sacrament of Reconciliation and Renewal," *Studia Liturgica* 11 (1976): 1–18.

Large studies of liturgical history in terms of the relative emphasis and location of particular theological themes have yet to be attempted. But the example of repentance and baptism in Calvin's Geneva suggests that this method may provide a new and illuminating lens by which to perceive the particular insights and contributions of even formerly ignored chapters of liturgical history.

7

The Americanization
of Reformed Worship

A Democratic and Republican Christianity

In 1831, Alexis de Tocqueville made a much heralded tour of the young United States of America. The astute Frenchman, whose observations have long been a staple of American cultural history, was especially intrigued by the phenomenon of American religion: "There is," he wrote, "no country in the world where the Christian religion retains a greater influence over the souls of men than in America." Tocqueville was struck not only by the relative prominence of religion in America but also by its distinctive character. "In France," he continued, "I had almost always seen the spirit of religion and the spirit of freedom marching in opposite directions. But in America I found they were intimately united and that they reigned in common over the same country. . . . I cannot better describe it," he concluded, "than by styling it a democratic and republican religion."[1] This analysis provides a stimulating perspective for interpreting the complex history of Reformed worship in the United States.[2]

---

1. Alexis de Tocqueville, *Democracy in America*, ed. J. P. Mayer and Max Lerner (New York: Harper & Row, 1966), 268, 271–72, 265. In the same passage, Tocqueville adds, "For the Americans the ideas of Christianity and liberty are so completely mingled that it is almost impossible to get them to conceive of the one without the other" (270).

2. I offer this chapter with fear and trembling, realizing that hopelessly complex entities such as "American culture" and "Reformed tradition" defy simple analysis. The notion of "American culture" risks perpetuating what Margaret Archer calls the "myth

The force of Tocqueville's insight becomes clear in Nathan Hatch's persuasive study *The Democratization of American Christianity*. Concentrating on the influential period of the early nineteenth century, Hatch argues that the driving force in much of American Christianity is, simply, its "democratic or populist impulse."[3] Hatch's main characters are unlikely heroes, not professors at prestigious Eastern divinity schools or highly touted preachers at tall-steepled city churches but rather the backwoods itinerants, folk musicians, and lay leaders of America's heartland. Their stories demonstrate the way in which the egalitarian spirit of Jacksonian democracy shaped American Christianity and made religious virtues out of the political ideals of freedom of choice, voluntary association, and skepticism of centralized authority. As the Disciples of Christ's Alexander Campbell put it, sounding both political and spiritual overtones, American Christianity was a quest for "gospel liberty."[4]

The American version of religious populism developed in the hospitable climate of religious pluralism. American Christians, unlike many of their counterparts and forebears in Europe, could expect amicable daily contact with Christians of nearly all varieties. In New York in 1764, Dutch minister Archibald Laidlie could write, "Here we have people of all denominations except Papists."[5] Such diversity confronted Americans with something European society did not always and easily afford: a meaningful choice of religious affiliation. Though still constrained by family and ethnic associations, Americans from early on could choose their churches. To accommodate, churches were forced to acknowledge, as did the Reformed Church in America in 1793, that the church itself was "a bond of union wholly volun-

---

of cultural integration" and glossing over important regional and ethnic diversity (*Culture and Agency: The Place of Culture in Social Theory* [Cambridge: Cambridge University Press, 1988], 1–21). Any use of the term "Reformed tradition" in a brief chapter such as this is bound to ignore significant factors in the complex mosaic of Reformed churches, which involves not only diverse ethnic identities (African, English, Dutch, German, Hispanic, Huguenot, Hungarian, Scots-Irish, Korean) but also vast differences in theology and polity represented by the bewildering mix of denominations, such as CRC, OPC, PCA, PCUSA, RCA, UCC, etc.

    3. Nathan O. Hatch, *The Democratization of American Christianity* (New Haven: Yale University Press, 1989), 213.

    4. See Nathan O. Hatch, "The Christian Movement and the Demand for a Theology of the People," *Journal of American History* 67 (1980): 555.

    5. Quoted in Gerald F. De Jong, *The Dutch Reformed Church in the American Colonies* (Grand Rapids: Eerdmans, 1978), 89. In many communities, of course, diversity included both Protestant and Catholic churches. For a thorough discussion of this theme, see Richard W. Pointer, *Protestant Pluralism and the New York Experience: A Study of Eighteenth-Century Religious Diversity* (Bloomington and Indianapolis: Indiana University Press, 1988).

tary."[6] The ideals of democracy, and the economic capitalism that accompanied them, were well on their way to reshaping the structure and experience of the Christian faith. The inevitable result? A long and venerable tradition of interpreting American Christianity in economic terms, with America seen as a vast "religious marketplace," a land where "clerical entrepreneurs" continually compete for "market shares," appealing to prospective "consumers."[7]

The rise of populism and pluralism in American Christianity had their inevitable counterparts in the rhetoric and style of America's religious leaders. The spirit of American democracy had little patience for long-winded sermons, intricate theological arguments, or imposing ecclesiastical hierarchies. Instead, American culture, in matters of both church and state, favored charismatic leadership, relevant plain speech, and decentralized structures of authority. No one better exemplified this spirit than the erstwhile Presbyterian revivalist Charles Grandison Finney, the symbol of both the proliferation and the domestication of the nineteenth-century revival. As Finney advised regarding the gospel ministry, "Do it—the best way you can. . . . [The disciples'] object was to make known the gospel in the most effectual way. . . . It is the preaching of the gospel that stands out prominent there as the great thing. The form is left out of the question."[8] Throughout his colorful career as evangelist, theologian, and college president, it was this unmitigated pragmatism that stood out as a defining feature of Finney's character, a trait held in common with many of America's most loved religious figures.

A final ingredient in the unique recipe of Christianity in the United States came from an unlikely source, the continental Pietists. Peaceable and unassuming, generally uninterested in cultural conquest, the Pietists nevertheless left an indelible mark on American Christianity.[9]

6. See the discussion in Daniel Meeter, *Meeting Each Other in Doctrine, Liturgy, and Government: The Bicentennial of the Celebration of the Constitution of the Reformed Church in America* (Grand Rapids: Eerdmans, 1993), 145–49.

7. Some notable recent examples include R. Laurence Moore, *Selling God: American Religion in the Marketplace of Culture* (New York: Oxford University Press, 1994); and Roger Finke and Rodney Stark, *The Churching of America, 1776–1990: Winners and Losers in Our Religious Economy* (New Brunswick, N.J.: Rutgers University Press, 1992).

8. Charles G. Finney, *Lectures on Revivals of Religion*, ed. William G. McLoughlin (Cambridge: Harvard University Press, 1960), 251. For more on Finney, see Keith Hardman, *Charles Grandison Finney, 1772–1875: Revivalist and Reformer* (Syracuse, N.Y.: University Press, 1987). See also Charles E. Hambrick-Stowe, *Charles G. Finney and the Spirit of American Evangelicalism* (Grand Rapids: Eerdmans, 1996).

9. See Randall Balmer, "Eschewing the 'Routine of Religion': Eighteenth-Century Pietism and the Revival Tradition in America," in *Modern Christian Revivals*, ed. Edith L. Blumhofer and Randall Balmer (Urbana and Chicago: University of Illinois Press, 1993), 1–16. For more, see Randall Balmer, *A Perfect Babel of Confusion: Dutch Religion and English Culture in the Middle Colonies* (New York: Oxford University Press,

Through their small settlements in the American colonies and—more importantly—through their influence on such luminary and significant preachers as Johan Freylinghausen, George Whitefield, Gilbert Tennant, and later, Finney himself, the Pietists modeled a warm-hearted, impassioned, and demonstrative faith that became a hallmark of the emerging pattern of American evangelicalism. They insisted on a religion that could be felt and experienced, on an individual and personal decision to accept baptism, on a dynamic divine presence that could point beyond the hardships of daily life, and on the promise of endless bliss in the life to come. In this new world, where the hardships of the frontier and vigorous individualism went hand in hand, what could be more appealing than a Christian vision that cultivated concern for the individual religious experience of every common person?

Pietist Protestantism was particularly opposed to ritualized liturgical formalism in any and all varieties. Tocqueville, who was himself Roman Catholic, linked this opposition to the cultural milieu of democracy: "I have made it clear that in a time of equality nothing is more repugnant to the human spirit than the idea of submitting to formalities. . . . Ceremonies leave them cold, and their natural tendency is to attach but secondary importance to the details of worship."[10] This comment brings us full circle. Pietistic faith found a natural home in an emerging democratic culture, suggesting again that religious, intellectual, political, and economic realities are always interrelated.[11]

Worship in the Democratic Culture

All of this had a profound effect on Christian worship in North America. To be sure, the traditional patterns of worship inherited from Europe—Anglican, Lutheran, Roman Catholic, Reformed, and Anabaptist—continued in America, especially in ethnically cohesive communities. But alongside these established patterns blossomed what would soon become a dominant and influential pattern variously known as anti-liturgical, free-church, low-church, revivalistic, or frontier worship. Reactions against liturgical formalism were well estab-

---

1989); and Milton J. Coalter Jr., *Gilbert Tennant, Son of Thunder: A Case Study of Continental Pietism's Impact on the First Great Awakening in the Middle Colonies* (Westport, Conn.: Greenwood Press, 1986).

10. Tocqueville, *Democracy in America*, 412.

11. This brief chapter cannot address the complex question of precisely how populism, pluralism, pietism, and pragmatism are interrelated, which historians continue to dispute. At the great risk of overgeneralizing, it can only propose that these traits emerged as distinctive and influential features of North American Christianity.

lished in Protestant Christianity by the time anything distinctively North American emerged. But the freedom and fervor nurtured in North American culture created new and potent forms of free-church worship that persist to this day.

The most obvious examples of this were the revivals themselves, a series of dramatic and quite diverse events that redefined the North American religious landscape. Their liturgical legacy is easy to define: impassioned evangelistic sermons, participatory music, spontaneous outpourings of praise and prayer. All of these elements were focused on one goal: to stimulate and revitalize faith. To be sure, not all revivals looked alike.[12] The frenzy at Cane Ridge in 1801 among grizzled frontier settlers hardly resembled the "reasonable revivalism" among the genteel and elite at a Virginia university or the sustained revival supported by western New York townspeople two decades later.[13] What is certain is that the revivals, in all their manifestations, were a combustion of all the hallmarks of American populist Christianity: exuberant piety, pragmatic leadership, and voluntary assent by common people.

Although they stood apart from weekly worship in most congregations, the revivals left an unmistakable mark on regular corporate worship in many ecclesiastical traditions. Evangelistic preaching, popular music, and spontaneous prayer became the hallmarks of worship in countless American congregations. The most conspicuous liturgical innovations were those related to the process of conversion: the "New Measures" of the "anxious bench," in which prospective Christians could be set apart from the congregation and "preached into conversion," and the altar call, a time for responding to the invitation of the gospel.

This approach to worship was new for most Reformed Christians. Seen from the perspective of the earliest members of the Christian Reformed Church, relative newcomers to the American scene who brought with them cultivated Reformed sensibilities, the liturgical manifestations of American Christianity were an unfortunate departure from tradition. The deviations that stood out included "the replacing of psalms by hymns, the exchanging of solemn choral [congregational] singing with a fast, happy manner of singing, the preaching

12. This is especially important to remember when studying the opponents of revivalism, who are likely not opposing every practice that goes by that name. For Hodge, for example, "Not all revivals were created equal. It was important to distinguish between the proper sort and the wrong kind" (Mark A. Noll, "Introduction," in *Charles Hodge: The Way of Life* [New York: Paulist Press, 1987], 40). The same is true for John Nevin.

13. Arthur Dickens Thomas Jr., "Reasonable Revivalism: Presbyterian Evangelization of Educated Virginians, 1787–1837," *Journal of Presbyterian History* 61 (fall 1983): 316–34.

of shorter sermons, the introduction of choir singing in place of congregational singing, the discontinuation of catechetical instruction, and the indiscriminate looking for something new."[14]

These varied but interrelated factors came together in what James F. White has called "the Frontier worship tradition," which he places alongside Episcopal, Lutheran, Methodist, Reformed, Anabaptist, and Pentecostal worship as a unique Protestant liturgical tradition. In time, White argues, this tradition became "like a liturgical black hole [pulling] many a Lutheran, Reformed, Methodist, Puritan, and even Quaker congregation into its orbit."[15]

The reason for this, I am suggesting, is rooted in the nature of a cultural context that extended far beyond the church itself. North American democracy and capitalism had become a source of images and attitudes that reshaped the Christian experience. Consider Michael Chevalier's 1839 description of camp meetings as "festivals of democracy,"[16] or historian James Bratt's characterization of John Nevin's *Anxious Bench* (a wringing indictment of revivalism) as a "tract of cultural warfare,"[17] or historian William McLoughlin's description of the debate about revivals as the "essence of the quarrel between the Whigs and the Jacksonians."[18] At issue was not just the liturgy of American revivalism but the very social and cultural fabric of the church.

Reformed Worship

But what did this have to do with Reformed worship? After all, Presbyterian and Reformed Christians were hardly the paradigmatic

14. Henry Zwaanstra, *Reformed Thought and Experience in a New World: A Study of the Christian Reformed Church and Its American Environment, 1890–1918* (Kampen: Kok, 1973), 41. See also James D. Bratt, *Dutch Calvinism in Modern America: A History of a Conservative Subculture* (Grand Rapids: Eerdmans, 1984). Although this description was not offered until near the end of the nineteenth century, it is representative of many offered in Northern and Southern Presbyterian and Reformed publications.

15. James F. White, "Liturgical Traditions in the West since 1500," in *Christian Worship in North America* (Collegeville, Minn.: Liturgical Press, 1997), 28.

16. Michael Chevalier, *Society, Manners, and Politics in the United States: Being a Series of Letters on North America* (1839; reprint, New York: Burt Franklin, 1969), 317–21.

17. James D. Bratt, "Nevin and the Antebellum Culture Wars," in *Reformed Confessionalism in Nineteenth Century America: Essays on the Thought of John Williamson Nevin*, ed. Sam Hamstra Jr. and Arie J. Griffioen (Lanham, Md.: American Theological Library Association, 1996), 9.

18. McLoughlin, "Introduction," in Finney, *Lectures on Revivals*, xix. See also Richard Cawardine, "The Second Great Awakening in Comparative Perspective: Revivals and Culture in the United States and Britain," in *Modern Christian Revivals*, ed. Edith L. Blumhofer and Randall Balmer (Urbana, Ill.: University of Illinois Press, 1993).

examples of this democratization process, a distinction that must be left to the Baptists, Disciples of Christ, Methodists, and other "enthusiasts." If anything, it would seem that Reformed and Presbyterian churches—with their insistence on theological training of ministers, their refined intellectualism, and their generally high social standing—would prove to be a counterexample to the democratization thesis.[19] Yet even a quick glance at the accumulated evidence suggests that this view is too simplistic. Reformed and Presbyterian churches were, in fact, significantly influenced by the democratic impulse in American religion.

We can see liturgical resonances of a "people's religion" prior to the nineteenth century among Reformed Christians.[20] For two hundred years, Presbyterian parishioners had gathered both in Scotland and the United States for "Holy Fairs," annual festival-like celebrations of revival preaching and the Lord's Supper.[21] Among Puritans, congregations not only had regular opportunities to participate in Sunday liturgy by critiquing sermons but also exercised unofficial veto power over clerical mandates regarding liturgical music.[22] Both the promotion of Watts's hymns and the rejection of new methods of psalm singing happened because congregations refused to accept the liturgical mandates of ministers.[23] In colonial America, the single most important religious phenomenon may have been the preaching tour of George Whitefield, a rare Calvinist who achieved the status of celebrity. As biographer Harry Stout argues, Whitefield was America's "first inter-colonial hero," whose "greatness lay in integrating religious discourse into [an] emerging language of consumption."[24]

Clearer and more widespread examples emerge from the period of Tocqueville's analysis. In Baltimore, the Third Presbyterian Church

19. It is fascinating to compare this history to the experience among American Lutherans. See Rhoda Schuler, "Worship among American Lutherans: A House Divided," *Studia Liturgica* 25 (1996): 174–91.

20. Populism did not truly come into its own until the period of the revolution. On this point, see Gordon S. Wood, *The Radicalism of the American Revolution* (New York: Knopf, 1992).

21. As described in Leigh Eric Schmidt, *Holy Fairs: Scottish Communions and American Revivals in the Early Modern Period* (Princeton: Princeton University Press, 1989).

22. The matter of critiquing sermons is discussed in Doug Adams, *From Meeting House to Camp Meeting: Toward a History of American Free Church Worship from 1620–1835* (Saratoga, Calif.: Modern Liturgy-Resource Publications, 1981), 28–29.

23. Cyclone Covey, "Puritanism and Music in Colonial America," *William and Mary Quarterly* 8 (1951): 378–88.

24. Harry S. Stout, *The Divine Dramatist: George Whitefield and the Rise of Modern Evangelicalism* (Grand Rapids: Eerdmans, 1991), xiv, xviii.

was founded in 1819, in consultation with proponents of the "New Measures," with the expressed purpose of bringing evangelical zeal to a largely unawakened city. Within a decade, Baltimore Presbyterians—including those of the First and Second Presbyterian Churches— were accustomed to many of the liturgical innovations of the Great Awakening, including fast days, prayer concerts, "methodistic" testimonies, and camp-meeting choruses. The numerical results were modest at best, but the tenor of Presbyterianism in Baltimore had changed.[25]

In Rochester, New York, in 1831, Finney himself preached 350 people into various Presbyterian congregations, applying the full spectrum of revival techniques, including the anxious bench.[26] In Pleasant Valley, Alabama, the annual camp meetings were widely known as a source of spiritual renewal and social cohesion. As one participant commented, "The meetings were delightful and were often followed by an outpouring of the divine Spirit, and an ingathering into the church" (though he hastened to add, "They were conducted with the utmost order and decorum, according to the strictest ideas of Presbyterian worship.").[27] Similar experiences were recounted in Orange Presbytery, North Carolina; Fairfield, New Jersey; and western Pennsylvania.[28]

Then, as now, the usual sign of change was friction over changes in liturgical music. In the Great Awakening of the 1740s, the issue concerned the hymns of Isaac Watts: Could these non-scriptural hymns be sung without violating the Reformed commitment to scriptural worship? In the early 1800s, the issue concerned the use of organs and choirs: Could these appealing "enrichments" truly serve the glory of God? In the middle and late nineteenth century and into the twentieth, the debates raged over gospel hymnody: Could the popular music of Thomas Hastings, Ira Sankey, and Fanny Crosby be a proper addition to a Presbyterian musical diet?

25. Terry D. Bilhartz, *Urban Religion and the Second Great Awakening: Church and Society in Early National Baltimore* (Rutherford, N.J.: Fairleigh Dickinson University Press, 1986), 94–99.

26. This repeated the success Finney had earlier in Rome and Utica, New York. Robert Hastings Nichols, *Presbyterianism in New York State* (Philadelphia: Westminster, 1963), 99–101; and Paul E. Johnson, *A Shopkeeper's Millennium: Society and Revivals in Rochester, New York, 1815–1837* (New York: Hill & Wang, 1978).

27. James Williams Marshall, *The Presbyterian Church in Alabama* (Montogomery: Presbyterian Historical Society of Alabama, 1977), 184.

28. See Robert Hamlin Stone, "Orange Presbytery and the Great Revival," in *A History of Orange Presbytery, 1770–1970* (Greensboro, N.C.: Orange Presbytery, 1970), 36–42; and Fred J. Hood, *Reformed America: The Middle and Southern States, 1738–1837* (University, Ala.: University of Alabama Press, 1980), 169–97.

Confrontations over gospel hymns were especially vexing. While gospel hymns were a source of irritation to establishment Presbyterians, they were the staple of small rural churches and the liturgical lifeblood of Presbyterian missionaries. In 1878, Presbyterian evangelist A. M. Darley held as one of his highest priorities the task of translating a set of Moody-Sankey hymns into Spanish.[29] In contrast, cultured Easterners worked to ferret out the "boisterous, sensational, effervescent style of music" that grew out of revivalist traditions and took root in Presbyterian Sunday schools.[30]

The populist influence was aided and abetted by the reticence of Reformed and Presbyterian churches to be too authoritarian in matters of worship. Still reacting to the perceived liturgical authoritarianism of the Anglican and Roman Catholic traditions, Reformed assemblies consistently refused to endorse set orders of worship or liturgical texts. As a result, pastors found liturgical helps from what Julius Melton termed a "free enterprise system of liturgical provision," as various publishing companies and would-be liturgists produced a variety of hymnals and liturgical handbooks, all of which lacked the imprimatur of official denominational approval.[31] Despite the fact that the authors of these materials included such notable Presbyterians as Charles Baird and A. A. Hodge, they were not the source of greatest influence on Reformed worship. That distinction must go to the legacy of the revival tradition.

Reactions

This is not to say that the history of Reformed and Presbyterian worship in America can be entirely explained as a process of democratization. A more complete picture reveals that Reformed and Presbyterian Christians in America always found these populist impulses to be a source of tension, controversy, and—not unusually—schism. In the 1740s, Old Side and New Side Presbyterians fought over supposed Pietist excesses in the Great Awakening. In the 1800s, ardent evangelists simply left the Presbyterian Church, forming the Cumberland Presbyterian Church, the Christian Church, and the Disciples of Christ. In the 1830s, the Old Side/New Side divide was recapitulated as Old and New School Presbyterians disputed and then split over

29. R. Douglas Brackenridge and Francisco O. García-Treto, *Iglesia Presbiteriana: A History of Presbyterians and Mexican Americans in the Southwest* (San Antonio: Trinity University Press, 1974), 68.

30. From the 1870 Minutes of the General Assembly, quoted in Ernest Rice Thompson, *Presbyterians in the South*, vol. 2 (Richmond: John Knox, 1963), 334.

31. Julius Melton, *Presbyterian Worship in America: Changing Patterns since 1781* (Richmond: John Knox, 1967), 111.

both theological and liturgical departures from traditional Calvinism.[32] While many Methodists, Baptists, and other evangelicals happily embraced the ideals of religious populism, the Reformed often found them to be a source of anxiety. The result, as James F. White concludes, was that "by and large, the history in Scotland and North America among Presbyterians is that of a tradition compromised, becoming vulnerable to both political and cultural pressures as it evolved."[33]

Most of the Reformed and Presbyterian objections to populism and its liturgical correlates were offered in the form of theological critique. For every proponent of popularized worship, there was also a defender of the tradition, someone to uphold "the simple, old-time Presbyterian worship . . . consisting of solemn, earnest prayers led by the minister, plain congregational singing, the impressive reading of Scripture, and the zealous, faithful exposition and application of the Word, followed by an offering for the service of the Lord."[34] Sounding a warning cry against aesthetic and populist innovations alike, one columnist in Virginia's *Central Presbyterian* postulated, "The trouble about these schemes for making the services more attractive is that in proportion as the fancy is tickled, the soul is starved."[35]

The majority of these theological critiques rehearsed the Puritan insistence that liturgical practices be explicitly warranted in Scripture. A small minority, represented by Mercersburg theologian John Nevin, critiqued the revivals in light of John Calvin's rich sacramental theology. Although these two approaches were themselves a source of conflict, together they proved that American populism was setting the agenda. Whereas Presbyterians in early America targeted rhetoric against the formalized liturgies and "set prayers" of the Anglican/Epis-

32. Many significant issues in the Reformed tradition have concerned other issues related more broadly to Americanization. In the 1770s, parties within the Reformed Church in America fought over the strength of ties to the Old World and its structures of authority. And in the 1850s, issues over Americanization kept apart the Dutch cousins, as the Reformed Church in America and the Christian Reformed Church parted ways. See George M. Marsden, *The Evangelical Mind and the New School Presbyterian Experience: A Case Study of Thought and Theology in Nineteenth-Century America* (New Haven: Yale University Press, 1970).

33. James F. White, *Protestant Worship: Traditions in Transition* (Louisville: Westminster John Knox, 1989), 70.

34. George A. Balkburn, ed., *The Life Work of John L. Girardeau, D.D., L.L.D., Late Professor in the Presbyterian Theological Seminary, Columbia, S.C.* (Columbia: State Co., 1916), 141–42, quoted in Erskine Clarke, *Our Southern Zion: A History of Calvinism in the South Carolina Low Country, 1690–1990* (Tuscaloosa and London: University of Alabama Press, 1996), 268.

35. Quoted in Thompson, *Presbyterians in the South*, 426.

copal establishment, later Presbyterians directed theirs toward the infelicities of American revivalism.

Alongside this explicitly theological critique flowed a consistent stream of argumentation that perhaps can best be labeled aesthetic. Presbyterians and the other Reformed churches have generally liked their worship to be reverent, tasteful, even a bit urbane. Populist worship was not only a theological but also an aesthetic affront.

In 1806, the General Assembly of the Presbyterian Church decried the "extravagant and indecent outrages against Christian decorum, which tend to interrupt the devotion of worshiping assemblies."[36] In 1835, Princeton's Samuel Miller produced his *Letters on Clerical Manners and Habits*, which advised clergy against any "coarse, repulsive habits" and lamented "the striking want of dignity" in many Presbyterian services. In 1853, *Presbyterian Magazine* described Cincinnati's new Seventh Presbyterian Church as having a belfry "not surpassed for richness and beauty," an interior "illuminated by a superb chandelier of original design and chaste workmanship," and a gallery of "the most costly and imaginate specimens of its kind." In 1897, the prestigious Church Service Society was founded in part "to promote reverence and beauty in the worship of God in his holy House."[37] And the 1933 Presbyterian Hymnal only grudgingly included popular hymns that "fall below the general standard set for the Hymnal."

Aesthetic concerns led to many liturgical features cherished by American Presbyterians: paid organists, trained choirs, stained glass windows, rhetorically sophisticated sermons, and the like. Robert Dabney, always defending the Puritan ideal of liturgical simplicity, targeted his complaints against "architectural pomps, pictured windows, floral decorations, instrumental and operatic music."[38] To many Presbyterians, Reformed worship could and should provide a dignified and polished alternative to the vagaries of liturgy forged in the American revival tradition.

In truth, it is probably fair to say that most liturgical reforms offered by the Presbyterian and Reformed churches were motivated by a web of spiritual, theological, and aesthetic concerns. From Henry

36. Quoted in Thomas, "Reasonable Revivalism," 325. Likewise, in 1803, the General Assembly issued a pastoral letter lamenting "every species of indecorum in social worship." See Anne C. Loveland, "Presbyterian and Revivalism in the Old South," *Journal of Presbyterian History* 57 (1979): 43. See also Union Seminary (Virginia) Professor John Holt Rice's call for "rule of externam decorum," in "Hints on Revivals of Religion," *Evangelical and Literary Magazine* 6 (January 1823): 7, quoted in Thomas, "Reasonable Revivalism," 316.

37. These examples are drawn from Melton, *Presbyterian Worship in America*, 29–34, 67–68, 122.

38. For these two examples, see Thompson, *Presbyterians in the South*, vol. 3, 345–46.

Van Dyke's leadership in producing the 1906 *Book of Common Worship* to the vast collaborative effort on the 1993 *Book of Common Worship*, from Louis Benson's hymnological scholarship to Clarence Dickinson's contribution as musician, editor, and professor, from the 1873 liturgy of the Reformed Church in America to the 1987 *Psalter Hymnal* of the Christian Reformed Church, from Charles Baird's 1855 compilation of historic Christian liturgies to the histories of Reformed worship authored by James Hastings Nichols and Howard Hageman—indeed, the whole procession of directories of worship, hymnals, books of worship, and books of liturgical scholarship demonstrates for the most part a commitment to *balance* pastoral relevance and theological ideals.[39]

But even these studied attempts to deepen and strengthen Reformed worship rather consistently revealed that American populism was setting the agenda. As these works were proposed, developed, and then defended, adherents clearly had one eye on the prospective influence of whatever American popular culture was offering at the time. Whereas sixteenth-century Reformed worship was forged in mutual opposition to Catholic ritualism and Anabaptist freedom, Reformed worship in America has taken shape in light of an ongoing dialog with various forms of American populist Christianity. What America has contributed to Reformed worship is not a set of particular liturgical practices but rather a consistent engagement with a populist impulse.[40] It may not be an overstatement to suggest that the corporate worship in any given Presbyterian or Reformed congregation in the United States received its identity from the way in which its shapers responded to the pull of American populism.

This thesis also cuts to the heart of the experience of Reformed and Presbyterian Christians outside the mainstream of American culture.

39. On the 1873 liturgy of the RCA, see Howard Hageman, "Liturgical Development in the Reformed Church in America: 1868–1947," *Journal of Presbyterian History* 47 (1969): 262–89. On the procession of Presbyterian sources, see Ronald B. Byars, "Challenging the Ethos: A History of Presbyterian Worship Resources in the Twentieth Century," and Morgan F. Simmons, "Hymnody: Its Place in Twentieth-Century Presbyterianism," both in *The Confessional Mosaic: Presbyterians and Twentieth-Century Theology*, ed. Milton J. Coalter, John M. Mulder, and Louis B. Weeks (Louisville: Westminster John Knox, 1990).

40. It is significant that the two most important histories of Reformed worship— Howard Hageman's *Pulpit and Table: Some Chapters in the History of Worship in the Reformed Churches* (Richmond: John Knox, 1962) and James Hastings Nichols's *Corporate Worship in the Reformed Tradition* (Philadelphia: Westminster, 1968)—are both structured chronologically and thematically rather than geographically. This has the effect of obscuring regional differences but also of pointing to common themes that a chapter such as the present one is bound to overlook. See also Menna Prestwich, ed., *International Calvinism, 1541–1715* (Oxford: Clarendon Press, 1985).

The inevitable Americanization of non-English-speaking immigrants—from the Dutch in the eighteenth and nineteenth centuries to Korean-Americans in the twentieth—has always been much more than a process of learning America's version of the English language. It has involved coming to terms with America's love affair with freedom, democracy, and popular culture. In matters of worship, the true measure of Americanization may be not so much the ease with which such groups speak English but the extent to which they feel compelled to produce worship services with appeal, in forms that are shaped by America's popular culture.

Religious populism and opposition to it also drive to the heart of the African American Presbyterian experience. In early America, Presbyterians had little success in evangelizing black Americans, in part because of a didactic and condescending attitude that demanded decorum and denied freedom of expression in worship.[41] Reformed opposition to the populism of the Methodists and Baptists effectively thwarted efforts to evangelize black Americans. Later chapters in the history of black Reformed Christians center around the tension between the "two worlds" of traditional Reformed theology and worship and a populist orientation that promoted liberation, community, and unique forms of black worship.[42]

Reformed Worship Today

It is no great stretch to posit that the same forces are at work today. Reformed worship today, as much as ever, is shaped by the ongoing tension created by the vast influence of popular culture. The old admixture of features that spawned American revivalism—populism, pluralism, pragmatism, pietism—continue to combine in new and innovative ways. Seeker services, market analyses, popular music, informal preaching—these and many other current practices appear to be the modern-day heirs of the revival tradition. Today's arguments for and against praise choruses recapitulate populist themes heard time and time again in the nineteenth century. Wave after wave of homiletical theory proposes to solve the problem of engaging America's fickle audience.

In 1971, *Presbyterian Life* explored "new ways to worship." In 1991, *Reformed Worship* offered "the issue you thought you'd never see" on the emerging "Praise & Worship Movement."[43] Both are symbols of the persistence of populist themes into the present. Both are symbols

41. See Hatch, *Democratization of American Christianity*, 102–13.
42. See Clarke, *Our Southern Zion*, 122–64; and Gayraud S. Wilmore, *Black and Presbyterian: The Heritage and the Hope* (Philadelphia: Geneva Press, 1983).
43. *Presbyterian Life* (1 July 1971); *Reformed Worship* 20 (June 1990).

of the tension that this orientation continues to generate for Reformed Christians.

Nor has the imagery of capitalism and democracy left us. Acknowledged or not, many of even the church's celebrations are subtly shaped by economic concerns, as Leigh Eric Schmidt perceptively points out in *Consumer Rites*.[44] To this day, church growth theorists—of both mainline and evangelical stripes—invite us to purchase subscriptions to *Net Results* and buy books entitled *Entertainment Evangelism*.

The familiar reactions are also present. Doctrinal and aesthetic critiques of populist worship practices continue to appear at a rapid pace. They are often so interrelated that it is difficult to discern where one stops and the other starts. For every church that eagerly embraces populist innovations, there are others who enjoy an opposite identity, seeking to be known as proprietors of good taste or bastions of orthodox theology.

Meanwhile, most congregations live somewhere in the middle, trying to assimilate invitations to rediscover historic patterns of worship and music from the worldwide church at the same time as they attempt to discern the differences between the baby boomers and Generation Xers.

To be sure, today's situation has led to some strange twists on the old themes. For one, some of the more conservative Presbyterian and Reformed denominations seem to be the most eager to embrace the New Measures of today's church. For another, popular religious culture is now driven by an aggressive multimillion-dollar industry that has reshaped our patterns of thinking, speaking, and personal interaction. But for the most part, our history suggests that as much as things change, today's challenges bear striking resemblance to those of our ancestors.

Americanization as the Inculturation of Christian Worship

All of this can leave us feeling more than a little queasy, for unlike cultural historians, on whose work the preceding analysis is dependent, we liturgical leaders cannot rest with perceptive analysis. We must move beyond historical and cultural description, comfortably offered from the carrel of a university library, to offer liturgical prescriptions in the context of real-world, everyday ministry. This is especially formidable in a world in which many of us are lost somewhere in the fray of the so-called worship wars. Somehow, we must strive to balance concern for the relevance of our ministry in a pervasively popu-

44. Leigh Eric Schmidt, *Consumer Rites: The Buying and Selling of American Holidays* (Princeton: Princeton University Press, 1995).

list, pragmatist culture with theological integrity and stewardly use of God's gifts of music, rhetoric, and the arts.

One of the many contributions of Vatican II to twentieth-century Christian worship was its insistence that liturgical expression reflect the particular cultural patterns of local congregations. This insistence calls to mind Calvin's admonition that "for the upbuilding of the church those things not necessary to salvation ought to be vigorously accommodated to the customs of each nation and age."[45] Since Vatican II, a small cadre of liturgists has attempted to be self-conscious about how this accommodation—variously termed contextualization, indigenization, or inculturation—can best take place. Spurred on in part by postmodern concern for cultural particularity, this project has been approached enthusiastically by many ecclesiastical traditions. The Roman Catholic Church has produced a much discussed "indigenous rite" for Zaire. Protestants have eagerly encouraged the development of indigenous musical repertoires in Africa, South America, and Southeast Asia. And many traditions are exploring the stunning variety of cultural expressions that contribute immeasurably to the liturgies of the world church.[46]

Yet there is one notable exception. What about inculturation for those of us in North America? Indeed, some of the same people who promote vigorous inculturation overseas lament its most aggressive forms on American soil. And what are seeker-sensitive services, market analysis, and popular music if not a radically inculturated form of Christianity?[47]

No doubt this puts the matter too simplistically. But before we hurry either to baptize or reproach the prophets of the new liturgical populism, perhaps we had best consider the lessons of this project of inculturation. If the literature on inculturation has taught us anything, it is that any given culture is an ambiguous phenomenon. Any given cultural feature—populism, pluralism, pragmatism included— carries with it blessings and curses. At its best, populism encourages a vigorous spirituality, concern for the forgotten poor, and participation of the people; at its worst, it leads to excessive pandering, theological

45. John Calvin, *Institutes of the Christian Religion,* ed. John T. McNeill, trans. Ford Lewis Battles, Library of Christian Classics (Philadelphia: Westminster, 1960), 4.10.30.

46. For an overview, see my "Theological and Conceptual Models for Liturgy and Culture," *Liturgy Digest* 3, no. 2 (summer 1996): 5–46. For studies of worship around the world, see Karen B. Westerfield Tucker, ed., *The Sunday Service of the Methodist: Twentieth Century Worship in World-Wide Methodism: Studies in Honor of James F. White* (Nashville: Kingswood Books, 1996); Anita Stauffer, ed., *Worship and Culture in Dialogue* (Geneva: Lutheran World Federation, 1994); and the special 1995 issue of *Reformed Liturgy and Music.* See also the issue, "Worship and Popular Culture," *Reformed Liturgy and Music* 30, no. 2 (1996).

47. This point is suggested by White, *Christian Worship in North America.*

excess, and a willingness to compromise belief and betray tradition. At its best, pluralism teaches us to marvel at the stunning diversity in the created order and in the church, helping us better sense what it is to be a member of the body of Christ; at its worst, it can degenerate into disunity or promote an "anything goes" attitude that transforms a vague openness to religious diversity into ideology. And at its best, pragmatism is an antidote to endless theological speculation and clerical indifference; at its worst, it is willing to sell off the faith, turning the scandal of the gospel into an appealing counterfeit. There can be little doubt that North American Christianity—including American Presbyterianism—has featured some of the best and worst of each.

If cultural analysis involves such huge ambiguities, then so does evaluating strategies for ministry. What seems like a wholesale capitulation to market forces may be for many a breath of spiritual fresh air after years of stagnant routinized Christianity. Conversely, what seems like an antiquarian interest in liturgical history and academic theology may be an avenue for promoting spiritual depth and vitality.

Perhaps the greatest gift we can seek is the gift of discernment. As Lewis Smedes wisely teaches us, with one eye on Philippians 1:10, "Discernment, not sheer intellect, not true grit, but simply being awake and having a nose for what is going on beneath the surfaces, and having a sense for the more fitting response to it—this is what makes for a class act on the moral stage."[48] It also makes for a class act in matters of worship.

Discernment helps us learn to tell the difference between evangelistic zeal and personal aggrandizement, between aesthetic critiques that are spiritually astute and those that are simply pretentious, between theological arguments that truly defend the gospel and those used to protect somebody's turf.

Tocqueville concluded his analysis of American Christianity with the following advice: "By respecting all democratic instincts which are not against it and making use of many favorable ones, religion succeeds in struggling successfully with that spirit of individual independence which is its most dangerous enemy."[49] May God's Spirit give us grace and wisdom for this challenging task.

48. Lewis B. Smedes, *Choices: Making Right Decisions in a Complex World* (San Francisco: Harper & Row, 1986), 97.

49. Tocqueville, *Democracy in America*, 414.

8

Theological Issues
in the Frontier Worship Tradition
in Nineteenth-Century America

It is generally conceded that Charles Grandison Finney is the quintessential figure in nineteenth-century American religious history. He represents at once the demise of orthodox Calvinism, the rise of evangelical revivalism, and the egalitarian spirit of Jacksonian America. Few, if any, American religious leaders have ever duplicated Finney's advantageous admixture of intellectual acumen, pragmatic instinct, and charismatic leadership. More than anything, Finney is known as the symbol of both the proliferation and the domestication of the nineteenth-century revival. And no development in American religious history of this period is as significant as the revival. Whether on the grain fields of Kentucky or in the halls of the prestigious University of Virginia, whether intended as a means for large-scale evangelization or as a mutation of the Scottish sacramental season, the revival was singularly responsible for redefining the religious landscape in nineteenth-century America.

Revivals were hardly new in the nineteenth century. But in the nineteenth century, the revivals engendered their most enduring legacy, spawning a new and distinct tradition of Christian worship. Earlier revivals generally had happened within the contexts of churches with established liturgical traditions. A revival might interrupt a liturgical pattern but generally did not displace it. In the nineteenth century, however, the pattern of revival worship became the basis of regular weekly worship in thousands of evangelical congregations across North America. To this day, thousands of North American Christians worship each week in what might be called a revivalist liturgical pattern.[1]

Revivalism in America

Nineteenth-century revivalism was no monolithic entity.[2] What is often described as one large movement is instead a complex mosaic of various movements isolated by space, time, and cultural context. The frenzy at Cane Ridge in 1801 among grizzled frontier settlers could hardly have resembled the "reasonable revivalism" among the genteel and elite at the University of Virginia or the sustained revival supported by western New York townspeople two decades later. The social fabric of a camp meeting in a cornfield barely resembled that of a revival in a tall-steepled church in upstate New York or in the hallowed halls of Yale University.[3]

Alongside these important issues was a series of disputes that took a distinctly theological turn. In responding to the threat posed by Finney and his New Measures accomplices, orthodox pastors and theologians went deep into their repertoire of theological arguments to refute New Measures practices. Despite the anti-intellectual tenor of much of revivalism, Finney and the promoters of New Measures revivalism also generated an impressively large body of theological prose to justify their means.[4] These theological arguments are the concern of this chapter. More precisely, this chapter attempts to catalog

1. See James F. White, *Protestant Worship: Traditions in Transition* (Louisville: Westminster John Knox, 1989), chap. 10.

2. This is especially important to remember when studying the opponents of revivalism, who are likely not opposing every practice that goes by that name. As Mark Noll observes, for Hodge, "not all revivals were created equal. It was important to distinguish between the proper sort and the wrong kind. Sadly, as he viewed the world, the wrong kind had predominated in America" (Mark A. Noll, "Introduction," in *Charles Hodge: The Way of Life* [New York: Paulist Press, 1987], 40). The same is true for John Williamson Nevin.

3. For accounts of these and other distinct revivals, see Arthur Dicken Thomas Jr., "Reasonable Revivalism: Presbyterian Evangelization of Educated Virginians, 1787–1837," *Journal of Presbyterian History* 61 (fall 1983): 316–34.

4. See George M. Marsden, *The Evangelical Mind and the New School Presbyterian Experience* (New Haven: Yale University Press, 1970), for a sustained argument against the interpretation of nineteenth-century American evangelicalism as anti-intellectual, a view promoted by influential works by Richard Hofstadter, Sidney Mead, and Perry Miller. See Hofstadter, *Anti-Intellectualism in American Life* (New York: Knopf, 1963, 1966); Mead, *The Lively Experiment: The Shaping of Christianity in America* (New York: Harper & Row, 1963); and Miller, *Life of the Mind in America: From the Revolution to the Civil War* (New York: Harcourt, Brace, and World, 1965). Liturgical scholars who assume that the revivals were an anti-intellectual movement perpetuate an interpretation of the nineteenth century that has been largely rethought by Marsden and others.

the range of theological arguments brought to bear in the raging dispute over New Measures revivalism.[5]

One challenge in this effort is to distinguish distinctly theological arguments from those that are more political or aesthetic. One type of accusation that is difficult but necessary to ignore are the frequent aesthetic judgments rendered against New Measures revivalism. Such judgments are omnipresent and colorful, such as Asahel Nettleton's dismissal of Finney as an "ignoble vulgus";[6] the statement of the 1806 General Assembly of the Presbyterian Church that decried the "extravagant and indecent outrages against Christian decorum, which tend to interrupt the devotion of worshiping assemblies";[7] or any of the dozens of calls for decorum by Princeton's Samuel Miller, who advised that parsons mount their pulpit with a "mixture of gravity and gentleness."[8] Also to be ignored is that most persistent argument in the history of the church: "We've never done it that way before" or, in the more circumspect words of one writer, "Many devout people are always annoyed at needless innovations."[9] The arguments of aesthetics and tradition, while hinting at important theological corollaries, are ignored in this chapter in favor of more explicitly theological arguments.

5. But though the two poles are relatively easy to observe, what separated them was a complex web of social, cultural, economic, political, and theological realities. William McLoughlin describes the debate about revivals as the "essence of the quarrel between the Whigs and the Jacksonians," suggesting its political ramifications (William G. McLoughlin, "Introduction," in Charles G. Finney, *Lectures on Revivals of Religion*, ed. William G. McLoughlin [Cambridge: Harvard University Press, 1960], xix). See also Richard Cawardine, "The Second Great Awakening in Comparative Perspective: Revivals and Culture in the United States and Britain," in *Modern Christian Revivals*, ed. Edith L. Blumhofer and Randall Balmer (Urbana, Ill.: University of Illinois Press, 1993). Fred J. Hood observes that which revival a person could support was largely dependent on social class (*Reformed America: The Middle and Southern States, 1783–1847* [University, Ala.: University of Alabama Press, 1980], 172). Further complicating factors include geographic location and ethnic identity. The revivals, thus, are as interesting to social and cultural historians as to intellectual and liturgical historians.

6. Quoted in Nathan O. Hatch, *The Democratization of American Christianity* (New Haven: Yale University Press, 1989), 196–97.

7. Quoted in Thomas, "Reasonable Revivalism," 324–25. Likewise, in 1832, the General Assembly issued a pastoral letter lamenting "every species of indecorum in social worship" (Anne C. Loveland, "Presbyterians and Revivalism in the Old South," *Journal of Presbyterian History* 57 [1979]: 43). See also Union Theological Seminary (Virginia) Professor John Holt Rice's call for a "rule of external decorum," in "Hints on Revivals of Religion," *Evangelical and Literary Magazine* 6 (January 1823): 7, quoted in Thomas, "Reasonable Revivalism," 316.

8. Quoted in Julius Melton, *Presbyterian Worship in America: Changing Patterns since 1787* (Richmond: John Knox, 1967), 32. For a discussion of Miller's career, see Anita Schorch, "Samuel Miller, Renaissance Man: His Legacy of 'True Taste,'" *Journal of Presbyterian History* 66 (1988): 71–88.

9. "On Certain Changes in Forms of Worship," *Presbyterian Magazine* II (September 1852): 404, quoted in Melton, *Presbyterian Worship in America*, 54.

Also to be ignored are the debates regarding church polity. There was widespread fear, for example, that revivalism would lead to the demise of Sunday services.[10] There was persistent debate about the education that should be required of ordained ministers. In addition, there were ongoing disputes regarding ecclesiastical authority and the structure of church government, either arguments that it was too rigid (by Barton Stone) or that it was too loose (by Calvin Colton).[11] Each of these issues hints at the debate over revivals that involved both the particular polity of a given tradition and practical considerations regarding the way in which the church would organize itself in a new geographical environment. Despite the theological issues that come to bear on these polity concerns, this chapter neglects them in favor of more explicitly theological arguments.

Most often, theological debate over New Measures revivalism is described in terms of one basic development: the demise of ortho-dox Calvinism and the rise of evangelical Arminianism. Calvinist or-thodoxy, especially with respect to the relationship between human and divine agency, was amply represented by the Old School revival-ism of William Sprague and Asahel Nettleton in the cultured East and James McGready in the frontier West.[12] The evangelical Armin-ian hybrid of human and divine cooperation was represented by the New School revivalism of Finney and Albert Barnes, as well as the camp meeting theology of Barton Stone. Finney and his cohorts, it is thought, smoothed out the rough edges of Calvinist predetermin-ism, leaving his opponents to defend this seemingly antiquated sys-tem of thought. These two theological positions constitute the two poles around which much of nineteenth-century American Chris-tianity revolved.[13]

No doubt this analysis is largely correct, as far as it goes. But Finney and New Measures revivalism together with their antagonists point to a far more complex theological discussion than can ade-quately be described in terms of a single Calvinist-Arminian contin-uum. This chapter describes and analyzes the full range of theological discussion that was engendered by New Measures revivalism, catalog-

10. Loveland, "Presbyterians and Revivalism," 42.
11. Alfred A. Cave, "Calvin Colton: An Antebellum Disaffection with the Presbyte-rian Church," *Journal of Presbyterian History* 50 (1972): 43; Ben M. Barnes, "Factors In-volved in the Origin of the Cumberland Presbyterian Church," *Journal of Presbyterian History* 45 (1967): 273–89; and 46 (1968): 58–73.
12. John Opie Jr., "James McGready: Theologian of Frontier Revivalism," *Church History* 34 (1965): 451. McGready was well versed in the theology of Edwards.
13. See Hood, *Reformed America,* 170. The fact that Nevin's *Anxious Bench* was writ-ten in defense of true revivals, namely, the old kind, reveals the important distinction between them.

ing four large clusters of theological issues that surface as most important. Its scope is limited to the theological discussion carried on among those who considered themselves a part of the Reformed theological tradition.[14] In carrying out this task, this chapter is guided by a not-so-hidden agenda: to uncover the theological issues at stake in the shaping of a new and radical paradigm for Christian worship. It is hoped that the following analysis can illuminate a relationship often ignored by religious historians and theologians alike, the relationship between belief and worship, creed and cult.

Theological Issues

Human Decision and Divine Prevenience

The first and largest cluster of theological issues that arose in the era of the Second Great Awakening surrounded the age-old controversy about the relationship between God's grace and human action in bringing about salvation. Scholastic Calvinists maintained that God's grace was given without regard for human decision and only to those whom God elected. This line of thought was held by the Puritans and later in a strong if slightly adapted form by Jonathan Edwards. In contrast, Arminian divines maintained to a greater or lesser degree that humans had the power to make a choice for God and so to aid in their own salvation. This line of thought was held by various seventeenth-century Calvinist "heretics" and was given strong expression in the theology of John Wesley, among others.

By the dawn of the nineteenth century, the hard and fast Calvinist system had long been under attack as educated liberal theologians found the doctrines of original sin and election repugnant and revivalists found them inconvenient. In the end, it was the latter who would be the most influential, giving shape to the central theological matrix of what would come to be called the evangelical century. The one who popularized this evangelicalism was Charles Finney. Called by one historian "more Arminian than John Wesley,"[15] Finney began both his revivals and his systematic theology with an essentially anthropocentric view of religion: "Religion is the work of man. . . . It consists of obeying God with and from the heart. It is man's duty."[16] He countered the hyper-Calvinists for theologizing "as though God was to blame for not

14. The Reformed theological tradition here refers rather broadly to anyone in the Reformed, Presbyterian, or Congregational churches. For an analysis of some of these issues in a study of Lutheran worship, see Rhoda Schuler, "Worship among American Lutherans: A House Divided," *Studia Liturgica* 25 (1995): 174–91.

15. Mark A. Noll, *A History of Christianity in the United States and Canada* (Grand Rapids: Eerdmans, 1992), 177.

16. Finney, *Lectures on Revivals of Religion*, 9.

converting them."[17] This outlook shaped his thought to such an extent that his memoirs could bear the following bit of hubris: "When this [revival measures] was faithfully and prayerfully done, we had a right to expect the Holy Spirit to co-operate with us, giving effect to our feeble effort."[18] Human initiative was the heart of the New Measures gospel.

Finney himself was not the source of this modified Calvinism, for Finney and the other prophets of New Measures revivalism were not so much theological innovators as pragmatic popularizers. The source or genius of their theological program was instead the New Divinity School of theology, personified in particular by Nathaniel William Taylor.[19] In the critical eyes of B. B. Warfield, "Finney's thought was not merely [fitted] into the general mold of Pelagianism, but into the special mold of the particular mode of stating Pelagianism which had been worked out by N. W. Taylor."[20] Although Taylor was not himself directly embroiled in controversy over the excesses of New Measures revivalism, his writings—which emphasized the benevolence of God, God's moral government, and human free agency—were widely read by Finney and other leaders of New Measures revivalism.[21]

The demise of traditional Calvinism had implications for other doctrines as well. Particularly vulnerable was the traditional doctrine of original sin, which asserted that all persons are born into sin and guilt through Adam and require God's grace to overcome sin and receive salvation.[22] Particularly important in this discussion was Albert Barnes, whose 1835 treatise on the subject "skirted the doctrine of original sin" at best and helped to precipitate the 1837 split of the Old and New School Presbyterians. Finney also minimized the import of original sin, stressing the psychological inevitability of sin as opposed to its biological necessity.[23]

17. Quoted in Paul E. Johnson, *A Shopkeeper's Millennium: Society and Revivals in Rochester, New York, 1815–1837* (New York: Hill & Wang, 1978), 96.
18. Charles G. Finney, *Memoirs of Rev. Charles G. Finney Written by Himself* (New York: Revell, 1876), 154–55.
19. William R. Sutton, "Benevolent Calvinism and the Moral Government of God: The Influence of Nathaniel W. Taylor on Revivalism in the Second Great Awakening," *Religion and American Culture* 2 (1992): 23–47. For a discussion of Taylor's theology in context, see Robert C. Whittemore, *The Transformation of the New England Theology* (New York: Peter Lang, 1987), 241–88.
20. B. B. Warfield, *Princeton Theological Review* 19 (1921): 17.
21. James E. Johnson, "Charles G. Finney and a Theology of Revivalism," *Church History* 38 (1969): 341, reports that Finney spent at least one night at the home of Taylor. Further, at the same time that Finney was at the height of his success as a revivalist, Taylor's system was much discussed among New England clergy and theologians.
22. See H. Shelton Smith, *Changing Conceptions of Original Sin: A Study in American Theology since 1750* (New York: Charles Scribner's Sons, 1955).
23. Leonard I. Sweet, "The View of Man Inherent in New Measures Revivalism," *Church History* 45 (June 1976): 207.

What is so intriguing about this theological dispute is that it was never confined to theological textbooks; it lived in the lives of people and churches all across the still-young country. In 1825, at the founding of Rochester's Brick Presbyterian Church, its leaders promulgated the following doctrinal statement: "The only reason why men do not embrace the Gospel is a voluntary opposition to God and holiness. And that the nature of this opposition is such, that none will believe in Christ, but as faith is wrought in their hearts by the influence of the Holy Ghost; . . . that God did from Eternity choose some of our sinful race to everlasting life, through the sanctification of the Spirit unto obedience and belief of the truth, so that repentance, faith, and obedience are not the cause but the effect of election." But by 1831, following the Finney revival in Rochester, the same session issued a remarkably revised statement: "We believe God, in infinite goodness, has provided a savior for lost man, who is Jesus Christ and that in consequence of this atonement, righteousness, and intercession, all who will repent of their sins and believe in him, will be saved from hell, and received to eternal glory."[24] Here was a theological change that shaped the work of local church leaders and the lives of individual Christians.

Most significantly, however, this theological shift had dramatic implications for the revival-style worship that Finney and Barnes promoted. For one, it invigorated the evangelistic motivation of the revivalists. Gone with Old School Calvinism was any sense of fatalism that it may have encouraged. The pool of potential converts was limitless, waiting only for the application of the proper techniques. The pool was so large for Barnes that his words even sound with universalist overtones: "It is with particular interest that we are permitted to proclaim that all that will believe, all, not a part, shall infallibly be saved. . . . To all, I say, if you believe the gospel, heaven is yours."[25]

In addition, this Arminian language raised the stakes for techniques of revival. If a human decision for God could play a role in achieving salvation, then any human technique for bringing about that decision was warranted and worth pursuing at all costs. As an 1830 correspondent of the *Charleston Observer* noted, "Though properly accorded to the Spirit of God as their efficient cause, [revivals] depend nevertheless upon human instrumentality."[26]

24. *Brick Church Session Minutes*, December 1825 and June 1831, quoted in Johnson, *Shopkeeper's Millennium*, 187 n. 5.

25. Albert Barnes, *The Way of Salvation* (New York: n.p., 1836), 13–14, quoted in Hood, *Reformed America*, 179.

26. "Communications," in *Charleston Observer*, 17 April 1830, 62, quoted in Loveland, "Presbyterians and Revivalism," 38.

Further, this Arminian theology was the underpinning of specific revival techniques. Most famous of these was the "anxious bench," on which persons ripe for conversion would be seated so that they could be made the object of both intercessory prayers and sermonic exhortations. The doctrinal basis for such practices was clearly operative. Hardly appreciative of the practice, Princeton Seminary's Samuel Miller was nevertheless quick to make this connection:

> When this exciting system of calling to "anxious seats,"—calling out into the aisles to be "prayed for," &c., is connected, as, to my certain knowledge, it often has been, with erroneous doctrines;—for example, with the declaration that nothing is *easier,* than conversion:—that the power of the Holy Spirit is not necessary to enable impenitent sinners to repent and believe;—that if they only resolve to be for God—resolve to be Christians—*that* itself is regeneration—the work is already done:—I say, where the system of "anxious seats," &c., is connected with such doctrinal statements as these, it appears to be adapted to destroy souls wholesale![27]

John Nevin's more famous harangue against the anxious bench makes similar connections to an Arminian theological basis.

Finally, this theological debate had important implications for the rhetoric of revival. Revivals were hardly new at Finney's time, following several generations of sacramental seasons in both the Old and New Worlds, as well as the particularly American revivals of the Great Awakening. But New Measures revivalism proclaimed a different gospel. Whereas traditional Calvinist revivalists, following on the heels of the Great Awakening, motivated their hearers with an appeal to hope for salvation, New Measures revivalists proclaimed that salvation was dependent on personal initiative. The former called their hearers to live in hope, the latter to make a decision, on their own strength, for the Lord.[28] Both strands had a deep appreciation for the depths of human sinfulness.[29] But New Measures revivalists contended that the

27. Samuel Miller, *Letters to Presbyterians* (Philadelphia: Anthony Finley, 1833), quoted in Marsden, *Evangelical Mind,* 78–79.

28. James McGready, for one, was a revivalist who deeply opposed the encroachment of Arminian thinking (Opie, "James McGready," 451). McGready yet sounded traditionally Calvinistic: "The unconverted sinner is as incapable of acting faith or laying hold of Christ, as a man born blind is of opening his eyes and beholding the natural light or as a dead corpse is of performing the works of a living man" (quoted in Keith Watkins, "The Sacramental Character of Camp Meetings," unpublished paper, 26).

29. Sweet, "View of Man," 206–7. See also Jonathan M. Butler, *Softly and Tenderly Jesus Is Calling: Heaven and Hell in American Revivalism, 1870–1920* (Brooklyn: Carlson Publishing, 1991), which notes that sermons on judgment and hell were still used to incite the listener to accept conversion.

first step in overcoming sinfulness was a decision that any person could make.

The case for Finney's Arminianism must not be stated too strongly, however. Finney, too, wrote that without God's Spirit, the whole of the revival will fail: "I want you to have high ideas of the Holy Ghost, and to feel that nothing good will be done without his influences."[30] Later in his life, he admitted, "I have thought that at least in a great many instances stress enough has not been laid upon the necessity of divine influence upon the hearts of Christians and of sinners. I am confident that I have sometimes erred in this respect myself."[31] Finney and New Measures revivalists did not do away with divine agency in the process of conversion; rather, they rewrote the formula by which the relationship between human and divine agency could be understood. And how they rewrote it was certainly less a function of doctrinal positioning than of a pragmatic approach to revival: Whatever theological emphasis would generate a successful revival was deemed superior.[32] As Leonard Sweet has observed, "Finney could sidestep with remarkable agility the doctrinal rigidities of divine agency and human ability because he believed that both were of equal truth, but not of equal usefulness."[33] And this very concern, that of usefulness, is the key to unlocking Finney's theological system.

Conversion and Sanctity

A second cluster of theological issues brought on by the revivals concerns the process by which one becomes a Christian and stays a

30. Finney, *Lectures on Revivals of Religion*, 102.

31. *Oberlin Evangelist*, 12 February 1845, cited in Johnson, "Charles G. Finney," 349–50.

32. See Finney, *Lectures on Revivals of Religion*, 181–82, where Finney notes that ministers must know when to stop using a given revival technique.

33. Sweet, "View of Man," 210. Samuel Hopkins had solved the problem by sharply distinguishing between regeneration (God's work in revivifying human hearts) and conversion (the human response of faith). But Finney simply asserted the autonomy of the human will to bring about conversion. This moderate position, between extreme Calvinism, on the one hand, and extreme Arminianism, on the other, became the most typical theological orientation of nineteenth-century evangelicalism. A fine example of this are the theological statements issued by the new Cumberland Presbyterian Church. Speaking of a revision of the Westminster Confession, Philip Schaff writes, "The Cumberland Confession teaches on the one hand conditional election and unlimited atonement, and on the other, the final perseverance of the saints. It is an eclectic compromise between Calvinism and Arminianism; it is half Calvinistic and half Arminian, and makes no attempt to harmonize these antagonistic elements" (Philip Schaff, *Creeds of Christendom*, 4th ed. [New York: Harper & Brothers, 1919], 1:815 and 3:771–76 for the Cumberland Confession). See also Hubert W. Murrow, "Cumberland Presbyterian Theology: A Nineteenth Century Development in American Presbyterianism," *Journal of Presbyterian History* 48 (1970): 203.

Christian. Regarding the conversion process, a particularly galling feature of New Measures revivalism, according to the Old School Presbyterians, was the excessive dependence on human emotion. Siding with Horace Bushnell, himself no great fan of New Measures revivalism, Charles Hodge wrote:

> No one can fail to remark that this too exclusive dependence on revivals tends to produce a false or unscriptural form of religion. It makes excitement essential to the people, and leads them to think that piety consists in strong exercises of feelings, the nature of which it is difficult to determine. The ordinary means of grace become insipid or distasteful, and a state of things is easily induced in which even professors of religion become utterly remiss as to all social religious duties of an ordinary character.[34]

Hodge's ally William Sprague—himself a revivalist, but of the Old School variety—agreed: "The Holy Spirit employs the truth . . . in the work of conversion; and the truth can never find its way to the heart, *except through the understanding.*"[35]

The revivalists, however, had little sympathy for intellectualism. They sided instead with New Divinity preacher Nathan Strong: "The increase of doctrinal or speculative knowledge, be the degree ever so great, hath no tendency to regenerate a person."[36] In crass terms, it was good for nothing. The lifelong process of learning about God and God's ways was replaced by a single moment's experience of conversion. Whatever would bring about that conversion—emotional exhortation, a tear-jerking anecdote, or histrionic exhibition—was vigorously promoted. Thus, in the words of Fred J. Hood, "The Old School method of social control through religious indoctrination gave way to the New School method of social control through individual conversion."[37]

Finney, for his part, was not a vigorous promoter of intense emotionalism for its own sake. Finney's protracted meetings were not Cane Ridge, with colorful outbursts of emotion. He even questioned the value of emotion, noting that emotion could easily blind human will and reason. But he saw great prospects for the combination of excited emotion and chastened reason as means to conversion: "Where mankind are so reluctant to obey God, they will not until they are ex-

34. Charles Hodge, "Bushnell on Christian Nurture," *Biblical Repertory and Princeton Review* 19 (October 1847): 520–21, quoted in Noll, *Charles Hodge*, 41.

35. William Sprague, *Lectures on Revivals of Religion* (Albany, N.Y.: Webster & Skinner, 1832), 20, quoted in Hood, *Reformed America*, 171, italics added.

36. Nathan Strong, *Sermons on Various Subjects, 1798*, quoted in David W. Kling, *A Field of Divine Wonders: The New Divinity and Village Revivals in Northwestern Connecticut, 1792–1822* (University Park, Pa.: Pennsylvania State University Press, 1993), 97.

37. Hood, *Reformed America*, 169.

cited."[38] Finney, following on the heels of the New Divinity clerics, emphasized the human will and its ability to make the decision that was necessary to bring about salvation and begin the sanctified life. If emotion could stimulate, challenge, and chasten the will, then exploiting the explosiveness of emotion was indeed warranted.

Related to the experience of conversion was a new emphasis on sensing the work of the Holy Spirit. While Calvinists wrangled about the way in which the work of the Holy Spirit related to human work, Finney was concerned that his followers live in the power of the Spirit. He was eager to speak of the role of the Spirit in his own life: "The Holy Spirit descended upon me in a manner that seemed to go through me body and soul."[39] Whereas traditional Calvinists had always given the Spirit a high place in trinitarian doctrinal formulae, Finney emphasized the role of the Spirit in personal religious experience.

New Measures revivalists also raised important issues about the Christian life after conversion. Their emphasis on this point maintained their opposition to cold intellectualism. In Barnes's memorable words, "Knowledge is good, but holiness is better."[40] Their concern for Christian holiness, for living the sanctified life, spawned a century-long movement based on the notion that Christian pilgrims could and should achieve perfection, even in this life.

Like everything else, this theology of perfectionism—the one New Measures doctrine that both Old and New School Presbyterians argued against[41]—had primarily pragmatic origins, for Finney and his allies were faced with the problem of the backsliding of many of those who were converted at a revival. Some who had gladly accepted conversion in the emotionally charged atmosphere of a protracted meeting could not sustain their devotion in the long and arid months that followed. For such folk a new message was needed.

This need was met head-on by Finney in what became one of his most enduring legacies, the doctrine of perfectionism.[42] Intimated at in his 1837 *Lectures to Professing Christians* (note: not to "sanctified" Christians) and fully developed in his 1846 *Lectures on Systematic Theology,* Finney's doctrine of perfectionism asserted without qualms that humans must strive to live perfectly even on this side of the grave. Undoubtedly influenced by John Humphrey Noyes, Finney's notion of the life of sanctification involved "perfect obedience to the law of God,

38. Quoted in Sweet, "View of Man," 214.
39. Finney, *Memoirs,* 20.
40. Albert Barnes, *The Power of Holiness in the Christian Ministry* (Philadelphia: William F. Geddes, 1834), 3, quoted in Hood, *Reformed America,* 181.
41. Marsden, *Evangelical Mind,* 79–82.
42. John Opie Jr., "Charles G. Finney and Oberlin Perfectionism," *Journal of Presbyterian History* 46 (1968): 42ff.

and as the law requires nothing more than the right use of whatever strength we have . . . a state of entire sanctification is attainable in this life, on the ground of natural ability."[43] Soon his ideas spread throughout the territories he had evangelized, leading to various clerical gatherings at which supporters could defend and refine what came to be known as "Oberlin Perfectionism." Participants in an 1841 convention in Rochester generated what may be taken as the credo of the new doctrine: "The advocates of this doctrine affirm that obedience to the moral law, or a state of entire consecration to God in this life, is in such a sense attainable as to be an object of rational pursuit with the expectation of attaining it."[44]

For Finney, a main ingredient in the road to Christian perfection was not only being saved but being eager to save others: "Every truly converted man turns from selfishness to benevolence, and benevolence surely leads him to do all he can to save the souls of his fellowman [sic];"[45] the desire to convert sinners was to be "the leading and main object" of the Christian life.[46] The Christian life, for Finney, was one of disciplined restraint that eschewed frivolity, on the one hand, and dourness, on the other. The question for every believer was the same: "Do you husband your time, your strength, your all in such a way as to make the most of your influence for the promotion of the glory of God?"[47] With such injunctions Finney reflected his essentially optimistic assessment of the potential of the human will to attain perfection.

Thus, it is not surprising that the response to Finney was not entirely favorable. New School critic George Duffield carried out an extended repudiation of Finney's *Lectures on Systematic Theology* in a series of articles written for the *Biblical Repository* in the late 1840s. Amazed that Finney had "departed from the faith he once held," Duffield was particularly incensed at Finney's perfectionism: "The views he slanders are those of the Westminster Confession of Faith, which teaches that 'believers be not under the law as a covenant of works to be justified or condemned.'"[48] Finney's perfectionism was to Duffield nothing more than a new bondage to the law, an unnecessary relin-

43. Charles G. Finney, *Lectures on Systematic Theology*, ed. J. H. Fairchild (Grand Rapids: Eerdmans, 1969), 407.

44. Quoted in David J. Weddle, *The Law as Gospel: Revival and Reform in the Theology of Charles G. Finney* (Metuchen, N.J.: Scarecrow Press, 1985), 247.

45. Charles G. Finney, *Sermons on Gospel Themes* (New York: Revell, 1876), 344.

46. Charles G. Finney, *Lectures to Professing Christians* (New York: Garland Publishing, 1985), 23.

47. Finney, in *Oberlin Evangelist*, 27 March 1839, 60. See discussion in James H. Moorhead, "Charles Finney and the Modernization of America," *Journal of Presbyterian History* 62 (1984): 105.

48. George Duffield, "Review of Finney's *Theology*," *Biblical Repository*, 3rd series, 4 (1848–49), quoted in Marsden, *Evangelical Mind*, 123.

quishing of grace. Much later, B. B. Warfield spoke of the "staring Pelagianism of the whole construction,"[49] undoubtedly echoing the sentiments of his predecessor, Charles Hodge.[50]

Finney managed to respond to such charges, arguing that "the liberty of the gospel does not consist in being freed from doing what the law requires, but in a man's being in such a state of mind that doing it is itself a pleasure instead of a burden."[51] But what was clear is that the theological stakes had been raised. The discussion that had begun over Arminianism now spilled over into ethics.

The Enlightenment God

Revivalism also had implications for the doctrine of God proper, with two themes standing out as especially important. The first, concerning God's transcendence, bordered on mere aesthetic concern, but nevertheless retained theological overtones. The revivals and the theology that accompanied them, it was argued, were simply too irreverent for a sovereign God. In response to early camp meetings, the 1805 General Assembly of the Presbyterian Church countered, "True religion is a most rational and scriptural thing. . . . God is a God of order and not of confusion; and whatever tends to destroy the comely order of his worship, is not from him, for he is consistent with himself," a concern hinted at in 1803 and amplified in 1806.[52] Later, in a manner typical of revivalism's detractors, Gardiner Spring lamented "a familiarity, a boldness, an irreverence in their prayers, which [is not becoming for] worms of the dust in approaching Him before whom angels veil their faces."[53]

Along with this more intimate rhetoric for approaching God came a decreasing emphasis on divine judgment. Back on the frontier, James McGready had been a hellfire preacher who did not shrink from preaching sermons entitled "The Sinner's Guide to Hell."[54] Finney, too, preached the fear of hell, retaining this last vestige of the old revival style of Edwards. He certainly had an exalted view of the human person, but this did not mitigate his terror at the judgment of God, at least not until later in his career. The only difference for Finney was

49. B. B. Warfield, *Studies in Perfectionism*, vol. 2 (New York: University Press, 1931), 208.

50. Charles Hodge, "Finney's Lectures on Theology," *Biblical Repertory and Princeton Review* 19 (April 1847): 237–77; and in Charles Hodge, *Essays and Reviews* (New York: R. Carter, 1879).

51. Finney, *Lectures to Professing Christians*, 206.

52. *Minutes of the General Assembly of the Presbyterian Church in the United States of America, 1789–1820* (Philadelphia: Presbyterian Board of Education, 1847), 334.

53. Quoted in Melton, *Presbyterian Worship in America*, 55.

54. See Butler, *Softly and Tenderly Jesus Is Calling*, 28.

that judgment was something humans brought on themselves: "If you choose the way of sin, you will be damned."[55] But Finney marked the end of an era, for, as Jonathan Butler observes, "Revivalists could not frighten sinners with a God who was no longer angry."[56] The mitigation of Calvinist orthodoxy could not and did not long sustain a sense of terror for the God of judgment.

Second, the revivalist theology of Finney participated in a larger theological movement that redefined the nature of God in Enlightenment terms. As James Turner concludes, Finney "had moved closer to the Deists than he wanted to imagine,"[57] as demonstrated by telling passages from his *Lectures on Revivals of Religion* that described "God as the Creator and Governor of the universe, the God of nature, who works according to the fixed laws of physics and of psychology that he has made known to man." Finney's vision was Newtonian to the core. The "fixed laws of physics" assured both the harvest of a good crop of grain and the success of a properly organized revival. In his words, "It is impossible for us to say that there is not as direct an influence or agency from God, to produce a crop of grain, as there is to produce a revival."[58] And though God established these laws, to be sure, God also was subject to them. This was a moral world, in which natural laws reigned supreme. One could neglect them only to one's peril.

Finney's appropriation of a larger Enlightenment vision did not go unnoticed by Hodge, who observed in his review of *Lectures on Systematic Theology* that "a very slight modification in the form of statement, would bring the doctrine of Mr. Finney, into exact conformity to the doctrine of the modern German school, which makes God but a name for the moral law or order of the universe, or reason in the abstract."[59] The attacks of Hodge were not unfounded, for much of New Divinity theology in general and Finney's theology in particular had rewritten almost every major doctrine according to the Enlightenment vision. Recall Jonathan Edwards Jr.'s theology of the atonement, for example: "By the atonement, it appears that God is determined that his law shall be supported; that it shall not be despised or transgressed with impunity."[60] Later, Warfield would argue that Finney's system, and the New Divinity theology that lay behind it, was "less a theology than a system of morals."[61] While overstated, this

55. Finney, *Lectures on Revivals of Religion*, 244.
56. Butler, *Softly and Tenderly Jesus Is Calling*, 2.
57. James Turner, *Without God, without Creed: The Origins of Unbelief in America* (Baltimore: Johns Hopkins University Press, 1985), 78.
58. Finney, *Lectures on Revivals of Religion*, 13.
59. Hodge, "Finney's Lectures on Theology," 239.
60. Quoted in Kling, *Field of Divine Wonders*, 106.
61. B. B. Warfield, *Perfectionism* (New York: University Press, 1931), 193.

epigram gets at the heart of the larger theological issue of New Measures revivalism.

Perhaps Finney could not escape the stranglehold of the Enlightenment; its influence was far too vast to be avoided. In any case, in adopting the moral universe of the Enlightenment thinkers, Finney forged the alloy of Arminianism and Enlightenment rationalism that would be the foundation of evangelical theology to the present day. Finney's faith in revival techniques was nothing less than faith in a rationally discernible moral order. And again, the stakes had been raised: What seemed like a dispute over Calvinist orthodoxy now had ramifications not just for the living of the Christian life but also for the very cosmology in which it would be lived.

Christ, Church, and Sacraments

Finally, revivalism was accompanied by shifts in Christology, ecclesiology, and sacramental theology. Although the New Measures revivalists were hardly concerned with the technicalities of sacramental theology, their practice shaped the sacramental spirituality (or lack thereof) of thousands of new converts and, indeed, the emerging tradition of frontier worship. Up until the early nineteenth century, sacramental celebration was a close bedfellow of religious revival. Revivals grew, in fact, out of Scottish sacramental seasons.[62] Some of even the more radical camp meeting revivalists contended for a high sacramental theology. James McGready, Presbyterian revivalist in Kentucky, spoke of the sacrament as "one of the nearest approaches to God that can be made on this side of eternity . . . where the Holy One of Israel here confers and sups with pardoned rebels."[63]

But the New Measures revivalists could not maintain such an elevated doctrine. For one, their participation in Enlightenment thinking diminished their capacity to accept such a high view of divine presence at the Lord's Table. For another, camp meetings led to a divorce of the sacraments and the experience of the divine presence, shifting the signs of divine presence from "the objectivity of the sacraments to the objectivity of physical and psychological experience," a divorce that was especially prominent in the Methodist and Presbyterian traditions, though not so prominent in the Disciples.[64] As Leigh Eric Schmidt observes, "The ritual of coming forward to the anxious bench or seat of decision became the sacra-

62. For this history, see Leigh Eric Schmidt, *Holy Fairs: Scottish Communions and American Revivals in the Early Modern Period* (Princeton: Princeton University Press, 1989).

63. Quoted in Watkins, "Sacramental Character," 19.

64. Ibid., 29.

mental focus of the new revivalism and dislodged the Eucharist from its former centrality."[65]

The Reformed response to such developments was twofold. The first came from Old School theologian James W. Alexander, whose argument called into question any use of the Lord's Supper in conjunction with evangelistic efforts. In Britain and in the colonies, the Lord's Supper was an occasion for evangelism, a practice well supported by the theologizing of America's Solomon Stoddard.[66] But Alexander contended that putting baptism and the Lord's Supper together focused more on the individual person than on Christ's death. Alexander's argument applied to Old and New Measures revivalists alike, with special concern for the extremities of the New Measures practices. How could the life of the church, and the sacraments in particular, focus on the acts of Christ if all manner of attention was given to the human act of making a decision for Christ?

A somewhat different response was levied by those who yearned for a higher sacramental doctrine. Foremost among them was Mercersburg theologian John Williamson Nevin. Nevin produced one of the most profound sacramental theologies of the nineteenth century in which he claimed that "as the Eucharist forms the very heart of the whole Christian worship, so it is clear that the entire question of the Church, which all are compelled to acknowledge—the great life problem of the age—centers ultimately in the sacramental question as its inmost heart and core."[67] He found the worship of New Measures revivalists especially lacking in this regard: "The Spirit may work," he wrote, "on men's minds, exciting pious thoughts or feelings of devotion, by the presence of a majestic cataract, or a whirlwind, or a smiling beautiful landscape; and why not then with equal ease through the graphic and affecting representation of the blessed Eucharist?"[68] Nevin believed that by undermining sacramental practice and piety, the New Measures revivalists had threatened the very foundation of the church.

More than anything, however, the issue of the theology and practice of the sacrament hinted at a deeper issue, the understanding of the church by New Measures revivalists. Any organic notion of the nature of the church was suppressed in favor of the important personal decision that individuals need to make to bring about their conversion.

65. Schmidt, *Holy Fairs*, 207.

66. Watkins, "Sacramental Character," 3.

67. John Williamson Nevin, *The Mystical Presence and Other Writings on the Eucharist*, ed. Bard Thompson and George H. Bricker, Lancaster Series on the Mercersburg Theology, vol. 4 (Philadelphia: United Church Press, 1966), 23.

68. John Williamson Nevin, "Doctrine of the Reformed Church on the Lord's Supper," *Mercersburg Review* (1850): 449.

Thus, the individual was emphasized over against the catholic church in what John Boles has called revivalism's "theology of individualism."[69] In this view, the church is, in the words of John Locke, "a voluntary society of men, joining themselves together of their own accord in order to [sic] the public worship of God, in such a manner as they judge acceptable to him, and effectual to the salvation of their souls."[70] Echoing Locke's own influential political theory, this view made the existence of the church more dependent on an individual's decision for Christ than on Christ's ongoing presence in the world.

What this Enlightenment ecclesiology replaced was nothing less than the biblical-theological motif of the church as a covenanted people. As Schmidt has observed, "More than simply eclipsing the old revivalism, the new American revivalism undermined one of the basic assumptions at the heart of the sacramental occasion, that of the Scottish Presbyterians as a covenanted people."[71] This was evidenced as much as anything by the change in rhetoric of the new nineteenth-century revival churches: That parents were no longer identified as "federally holy" in the Directory of Worship of the Cumberland Presbyterian Church had more significance than the loss of a technical phrase.[72] Already in the theology of Edwards were seeds of the demise of covenant theology. By the time of the New Divinity theologians, the notion of covenant was no longer operative in any meaningful sense. As New Divinity preacher Nathan Strong argued, "External covenant relations will prepare no one for heaven."[73] Finney hardly remedied the low view of the church. His *Lectures on Systematic Theology* did not contain a chapter on ecclesiology. While he despised intra-church conflict, he saw the mission of the church as being more important than its unity: "It is evident that many more churches need to be divided. . . . Let them separate, and each work in his own way, and they may both enjoy the blessing."[74] And when it came to church polity, Finney advocated whatever worked.[75]

The most vigorous opponent of New Measures revivalism, Nevin, did not enter the argument until the 1840s, when revivalism began to threaten the structure of the German Reformed Church on behalf of

---

69. John B. Boles, *The Great Revival, 1784–1805* (Lexington: University of Kentucky Press, 1972), 125–42.

70. Ibid., 126. See *The Works of John Locke* (London: Thomas Tegg, 1823), vol. 6, 13.

71. Schmidt, *Holy Fairs*, 208.

72. Stanley R. Hall, "The American Presbyterian Directory for Worship: History of a Liturgical Strategy" (Ph.D. diss., University of Notre Dame, 1990), 177.

73. Nathan Strong, *Consecration of the New Brick Church,* quoted in Kling, *Field of Divine Wonders,* 109.

74. Finney, *Lectures on Systematic Theology*, 222f.

75. Moorhead, "Charles Finney and the Modernization of America," 95–110.

which he labored at Mercersburg. Nevin, in his famous treatise *The Anxious Bench,* decried the unmitigated pragmatism of the revivalists, claiming that "the most dangerous foe with which we are called to contend, is again not the Church of Rome but the sect plague in our own midst."[76] His vision of the church was, in contrast, transcendent and catholic: "Partaking in this way of one and the same life of Christ, Christians are vitally related and joined together as one great spiritual whole; and this whole is the Church. The Church, therefore, is His Body, the fullness of Him that filleth all in all. The union by which it is held together, through all ages, is organic."[77] As James Hastings Nichols argues, this particular theological vision was nothing less than "the polemical response to what its adherents saw as the chaos or arbitrary subjectivism in American church life," a situation largely shaped by New Divinity theology and New Measures revivalism.[78] The Lockean idea of the church was simply too tepid for Nevin's taste.

If New Measures revivalism led to the demise of regular sacramental practice and a redefinition of the nature of the church, then it is inevitable that it led to controversy regarding the person and work of Jesus Christ. Christological questions were not at the center of the debate, to be sure. But, like every major liturgical shift, revivalism led to a new Christology, whether or not this was spelled out in theological treatises. This shift has been interpreted, in the words of David Kling, speaking about New Divinity theology, as a shift in emphasis to "God's work of regeneration" from "Christ's work of redemption."[79] Undoubtedly, this much is true. Christ's work on the cross had less importance than the moral nature of God or human decision, if not in theological systems then certainly in sermonizing and revivals. One specific issue concerning the mediation of Christ is particularly worth observing. Already in 1832, the young Hodge wrote of the revivals:

> The constant exhortation is, to make choice of God as the portion of the soul, to change the governing purpose of the life, to submit to the moral Governor of the universe the specific act to which the sinner is urged as immediately connected with salvation, is an act which has no reference to Christ. The soul is brought immediately in contact with God, the Mediator is left out of view. We maintain that this is another Gospel. . . . We

76. Quoted in Hatch, *Democratization of American Christianity,* 165.

77. John Williamson Nevin, "Catholic Unity," in *The Life and Work of John Williamson Nevin,* ed. Theodore Appel (Philadelphia: Publication Office of the German Reformed Church, 1845), 219. For a helpful discussion of Nevin's ecclesiology, see John B. Payne, "Schaff and Nevin, Colleagues at Mercersburg: The Church Question," *Church History* 61 (1992): 169–90.

78. James Hastings Nichols, *The Mercersburg Theology* (New York: Oxford University Press, 1966), 93.

79. Kling, *Field of Divine Wonders,* 103.

do not intend that the doctrine of the mediation of Christ is rejected, but that it is neglected; that the sinner is led to God directly; that he is not urged, under the pressure of the sense of guilt, to go to Christ for pardon, and through him to God, but the general idea of submission (not the specific idea of submission to the plan of salvation through Jesus Christ) is urged as (the) making a right choice. Conviction of sin is made of little account, Christ and his atonement are kept out of view, so that the matter of salvation is not distinctly presented to the minds of the people.[80]

Here Hodge was especially instructive about the larger theological ramifications of New Measures revivalism, for the new techniques had led to an inevitable shift in emphasis. With all the talk of God's moral government and human personal decision, there was far less room for the central idea of Christ's mediation. Little wonder that sacramental theology and ecclesiology suffered as they did.

In sum, most commentators on New Measures revivalism assert that the central theological issue at stake was the Arminian question, the question of human agency. But this was only one small portion of the theological landscape that New Measures revivalists remade, for in addition to extending the influence of Arminianism, the New Measures revivalists were also prophets of a newly developed perfectionism, an Enlightenment cosmology, and a new, slender approach to questions of church and sacrament. The new paradigm of Christian worship that they birthed was shaped according to each of these theological arguments and since has molded millions of American Christians in a similar faith.

Implications

The theological issues raised in this chapter are about much more than the revivals. Their presence is the result of the deep seismic shifts in the convergence of Enlightenment rationalism and a Newtonian worldview, in the subsequent takeover of American academia by Scottish Common Sense Realism, and in the ongoing struggles between Enlightenment rationalism and romantic idealism, all occurring in the age of Jacksonian democracy, with its exalted view of human progress. The various theological points of view described in this chapter can be understood as mere mirrors of these larger movements. Finney is the quintessential Jacksonian; Nevin, the classic ro-

80. Charles Hodge, "The New Divinity Tried," *Biblical Repertory and Princeton Review* 4 (April 1832): 278–304; and in *Theological Essays: Reprinted from the Princeton Review* (New York: Wiley and Putnam, 1846), 12, quoted in David F. Wells, "Charles Hodge," in *The Princeton Theology* (Grand Rapids: Baker, 1989), 49.

mantic idealist; perfectionism, the ideal of progress stated in theological terms.

The theological issues raised here stand by themselves as ample reflections of new ways of understanding, living, and worshiping as Christians. For better or worse, many of the theological insights, ritual actions, and ways of living that were born in this period, arising out of these particular struggles, have persisted to the present day. This is no more true than with respect to Christian worship, for the revivals of early nineteenth-century America generated a tradition of Christian worship beholden less to denominational or confessional loyalties than to a uniquely American appreciation of both the individual soul and whatever means might turn that soul to the Lord.

In this birthing of a new worship tradition, the theological debate provided much of the impetus for the particular rituals that would endure. For one, the theology of the moment certainly had more weight than the theology prayed and spoken throughout the history of the church. The liturgies of the early church or of Bucer or Calvin held little esteem for these worshipers. For another, the revivalists, however pragmatic they might have been, still labored in the context in which theological discourse had implications for every facet of life. Theology, mediated first by Scripture and then by respected theologians, was the source and standard by which Christians guided their lives and worship. Surely, Kling is correct in stating that the New Divinity theologians believed all religious ritual was an outgrowth of theology.[81] Much the same could be said of Finney.

This important relationship between worship and theology, reforged in the early nineteenth century, is instructive for the careful student of Christian worship and carries with it themes and lessons for the church today. Three such insights seem especially worth mentioning. First, the genesis of the frontier worship tradition introduced and promoted a new norm or standard by which worship could be judged to be effective. Already in 1787, the proposed Presbyterian Directory of Worship suggested that worship should be executed so as to "revive the spirit and appearance of devotion."[82] But now, every liturgical decision was based on what would produce the most conversions. Finney's attitude was especially pronounced.[83] As Leonard Sweet observed, Finney's pragmatism even extended to prayer.[84] And it

81. Kling, *Field of Divine Wonders*, 75.
82. Quoted in Robert Milton Winter, "American Churches and the Holy Communion: A Comparative Study in Sacramental Theology, Practice, and Piety in the Episcopal, Presbyterian, Methodist, and German Reformed Traditions, 1607–1875" (Ph.D. diss., Union Theological Seminary, Virginia, 1988), 418.
83. Finney, *Lectures on Revivals of Religion*, 189–93.
84. Sweet, "View of Man," 213.

certainly extended to theology: Finney disowned traditional Calvinism most simply because it was not conducive to revival.[85] Such pragmatism, founded on the influential legacy of Lockean rationalism, left its own permanent mark on Protestant worship. Since the time of Finney, generations of Christians have evaluated their worship as much by the criteria of success as by the standard of faithfulness. This legacy reached a second climax with Dwight L. Moody, who once declared, "It makes no difference how you get a man to God, provided you get him there,"[86] and seems to be approaching such heights or depths even today.

Second, despite its reputation as an anti-intellectual movement, the revival movement was theologically aware. It may be true that the revivalists were not as interested in theological precision as in results, but in promoting their agenda, they generated an impressive mass of theological prose. Finney's contribution numbers several volumes, and a mere compendium of Alexander Campbell's theology is enough to fill a good-size treatise.[87] Despite the fact that the reputation of the revivalist preachers has long suffered from unwarranted charges of anti-intellectualism,[88] any cursory examination of the sources warrants the evaluation that these revivalists were no theological novices. It is this very point that makes this history seem so removed from today, for while the pragmatism of these revivalists has endured, the theological awareness that attended their pragmatism has often not, a fact that ought to sound a warning among the followers of Finney today.

Third, the theological issues at stake in New Measures revivalism were more far-reaching and complex than simply a watering down of Calvinism. The reigning orthodox position in nearly every loci of systematic theology was called into question by Finney and his allies. Even the brief treatment possible in this chapter has demonstrated that New Measures revivalism put at stake not only the doctrines of election and original sin but also the doctrines of the church and sacraments, the understanding of Christ and the atonement, the conception of the Holy Spirit, and the nature of Christian discipleship and spirituality. The attack on New Measures revivalists was waged by Scottish Common Sense realists and romantic idealists, each of whom raised questions out of their own intellectual orientation and with respect to their own agendas. This complex of theological issues ought to serve as a sufficient reminder that any change in theological or rit-

85. Finney, *Memoirs*, 42–60.

86. Quoted in Johnson, "Charles G. Finney," 357.

87. See Royal Humbert, ed., *A Compend of Alexander Campbell's Theology* (St. Louis: Bethany Press, 1961).

88. See Opie, "James McGready," 445–56, which reveals how theologically sophisticated McGready really was.

ual practice is bound to have implications for much more than the particular issues it first addressed, just as the revivals began with a new theology of conversion but later discovered the need for a new theology of sanctification.

The history of New Measures revivalism warrants the careful attention of the church today. The influence and significance of revivalism are vast and impressive. Revival worship has flourished in America, persisting as the largest tradition of worship to this day.[89] Sunday morning worship ever since has been marked by its definitive shape: preliminaries, sermon, harvest (altar calls). The aesthetic that the revivals generated, however unwittingly, has remained the guiding force in the development of music and art for worship. An entire century of popular religious music, auditorium-style worship spaces, and the industries they support have the revivals to thank for their genesis. Thus, one of the most significant steps that contemporary American Christians can make toward self-understanding is to open this chapter in the history of the church and learn from its pages.

89. White, *Protestant Worship*, 172.

PART

4

Musical Studies

9

The Spirituality
of the Psalter
in Calvin's Geneva

Recent interest in the study of spirituality—or, to use a more Calvinian term, *piety*—has provided scholars with a stimulating vantage point from which to examine topics otherwise relegated to relative obscurity as the domain of highly specialized disciplines.[1] The study of spirituality is invigorating in part because of its attention to the interplay of a complex set of factors—including theology, religious institutions and artifacts, and social and economic conditions—in shaping the piety of both elite and common folk.[2] For the simple reason that religious life inevitably involves the complex interaction of worship, ethics, and doctrine, the study of spirituality relies on interdisciplinary exchange to discern the unique and salient features of the piety of a given group of people. In light of these interests, this chapter explores the shape of spirituality in Calvin's Geneva by examining one of

1. See, for example, Bradley C. Hansen, ed., *Modern Christian Spirituality: Methodological and Historical Essays* (Atlanta: Scholar's Press, 1990); Bernard McGinn, "The Letter and the Spirit: Spirituality as an Academic Discipline," *The Cresset* (June 1993): 13–23; Walter Principe, "Pluralism in Christian Spirituality," *The Way* 32 (1992): 54–61; and Sandra M. Schnieders, "Spirituality in the Academy," *Theological Studies* 50 (1989): 676–97.
2. This resembles many of the interests of social historians, as summarized in Natalie Z. Davis, "From 'Popular Religion' to Religious Cultures," in *Reformation Europe: A Guide to Research*, ed. Steven Ozment (St. Louis: Center for Reformation Research, 1982), 321–41.

its most famous and distinctive artifacts, the metrical psalter. Most studies of the psalter either describe the theological justification for its existence, chronicle its multiple editions, or catalog its many texts and tunes. This chapter seeks to move beyond these tasks to ask about its meaning and significance in the lives of the Genevan faithful.[3]

This task immediately suggests a series of pertinent questions—liturgical, aesthetic, theological, musicological, economic, and cultural questions: How were these psalters used? How did they function in public worship? Who owned them? What rationale was used to promote and defend them? What function did they have in people's daily lives? How did their tunes sound to sixteenth-century ears? How did they contribute to the religious identity of the Genevan people?[4] This chapter cannot fully answer all these questions, but it will attempt a rapid survey of the key features of the psalter in order to discern what it might teach us about the shape of Calvinist spirituality. What will emerge is not a revolutionary view of spirituality in Calvin's Geneva but rather an appreciation for the extent to which the metrical psalter was both an expression of and influence on this particular way of being Christian.[5]

That metrical psalmody was a significant influence can hardly be disputed. The Genevan Psalter of 1562 was the object of what has been called "the most gigantic enterprise ever undertaken in publishing until then."[6] In the first two years alone, over twenty-seven thousand copies of the 1562 Psalter were issued.[7] Even with some of its profits designated for charity, it was enough of a moneymaker to cause a scandal

3. For an example of this type of work, see Tessa Watt, *Cheap Print and Popular Piety, 1550–1640* (Cambridge: Cambridge University Press, 1991).

4. This question was inspired by Natalie Davis's query as to "what new powers of social definition are given to words, songs and voices, which play so important a role in the new liturgy?" ("From 'Popular Religion' to Religious Cultures," 325).

5. Thus, this chapter is, in part, an apologetic for taking the psalter more seriously in social, cultural, and religious histories of the Reformation. This is warranted not only by its economic success but also by its religious significance. In addition, this topic raises larger sociocultural issues related to the growing role of music in European culture. As H. G. Koenigsberger has argued, "It was the very alliance of religion and music which allowed music to play an increasingly important and, eventually, even preponderant role in the European psyche" ("Music and Religion in Early Modern European History," in *Politicians and Virtuosi: Essays in Early Modern History* [London: Hambledon Press, 1986], 180).

6. Lucien Febvre and Henri-Jean Martin, *The Coming of the Book: The Impact of Printing, 1450–1800*, trans. David Gerard (London: NLB, 1976), 318.

7. Pierre Pidoux lists twenty-six editions published by Vincent in 1562 in *Le Psautier Huguenot du XVIe siècle*, vol. 2 (Basel: Edition Baerenreiter, 1962), 93–115. Forty-four editions were issued within three years. Robert Kingdon notes that within two years, 27,400 psalters were issued (*Geneva and the Coming of the Wars of Religion in France, 1555–1563* [Geneva: Droz, 1956], 100). For the economic aspects of the printing of

among Genevan printers.[8] Within just a few years, the number of copies of the Genevan Psalter may well have reached one hundred thousand in over thirty editions, in addition to the thousands of copies printed in translation in nine languages. As Robert Kingdon has observed, the psalter was "an essential for practically every literate member of the Protestant congregations being formed all over Europe."[9]

The importance of the psalter is also underscored by the high priority it had with the Genevan Reformers. The call for sung psalmody in worship was one of Calvin's first acts of liturgical reform and one to which he was dedicated throughout his life. Calvin first heard psalm singing during his first visit to Strasbourg, where Protestant congregations had, by the mid-1530s, a decade of experience in singing psalms in worship.[10] Already in the first paragraph of his 1537 *Articles for Church Organization*, Calvin called for singing psalms "for the edification of the church."[11] Then, in 1539, Calvin released his first psalter, the *Aulcuns pseaulmes et cantiques mys en chant*, for his exile congregation in Strasbourg. It was a collection of twenty-two texts by Clem-

psalters, see E. Droz, "Antoine Vincent et la propagande protestante par le Psautier," in *Aspects de la propagande religieuse* (Geneva: Droz, 1957). Editions of the complete Psalter were also issued from Lyon, Paris, Caen, and Saint-Lo. The languages into which the Psalter was translated include at least German, Dutch, Italian, Spanish, Bohemian, Polish, Latin, Hebrew, and English; see Orentin Douen, *Clément Marot et Le Psautier Huguenot*, vol. 2 (1878; reprint, Neiuwkoop: B. De Graaf, 1967), 610–12. My count of the editions of the completed psalter is taken from Jean-Daniel Candaux, *Le Psautier de Genève, 1562–1865* (Geneva: Bibliothèque publique et universitaire, 1986), 166.

8. Kingdon, *Geneva and the Coming of the Wars of Religion*, 99–100.

9. Robert Kingdon, "Patronage, Piety, and Printing," in *Church and Society in Reformation Europe* (London: Variorum Reprints, 1985), 17:27. The estimate of one hundred thousand copies is Kingdon's.

10. See Patrice Veit, "Le chant, la Réforme et la Bible," in *Le temps des Réformes et la Bible*, ed. Guy Bedouelle and Bernard Roussel (Paris: Beauchesne, 1989), 662–64; and Allen B. Mullinax, "Musical Diversity in Reformation Strasbourg: Martin Bucer's Strasbourg Song Book (1541)," *The Hymn* 45, no. 1 (1994): 9–13.

11. References to Calvin's writings in this chapter will include the citation of the selection from Calvin's edited works, followed by a citation of the English translation. Frequently cited works are identified by the following abbreviations: OS = *Ioannis Calvini Opera Selecta*, ed. Peter Barth, Wilhelm Niesel, and Dora Scheuner, 5 vols. (Munich: C. Kaiser, 1926–62); CO = *Ioannis Calvini Opera quae supersunt omnia*, ed. Wilhelm Baum, Edward Cunitz, and Edward Reuss, 59 vols. (Brunsvigae: A. Swetschke and Son, 1843–48); *Corpus Reformatorum*, vols. 29–87 (Brunsvigae: A. Swetschke and Son, 1843–48). Translations are identified by the following abbreviations: 1536 *Institutes* = John Calvin, *Institutes of the Christian Religion* [1536], trans. Ford Lewis Battles (Grand Rapids: Eerdmans, 1975); 1559 *Institutes* = John Calvin, *Institutes of the Christian Religion* [1559], ed. John T. McNeill, trans. Ford Lewis Battles, Library of Christian Classics, vols. 20–21 (Philadelphia: Westminster, 1960); *Treatises* = John Calvin, *Theological Treatises*, trans. J. K. S. Reid, Library of Christian Classics, vol. 22 (Philadelphia: Westminster, 1954). This citation is from "Articles concernant l'organisation de l'église," OS, 1:369; *Treatises* 48.

ent Marot and Calvin himself that were set to tunes drawn primarily from the earlier German psalters.[12] The first major Genevan edition was issued in 1542 as *La forme des preieres et chantz ecclesiastiques*, a collection of both Calvin's basic liturgical texts and thirty-nine metrical psalms and canticles, mostly by Marot.[13] Several editions of the evolving psalter were printed in Geneva during the next two decades, eventually incorporating the tunes of Louis Bourgeois, who came to Geneva in 1542 as a music educator, and later, the metrical translations of Theodore Beza, who finished where Marot had left off prior to his departure from Geneva.[14] Finally, the complete Genevan Psalter was issued in 1562, a volume with 152 texts—each psalm, the Ten Commandments, and the Song of Simeon— set to 125 different tunes.[15]

Metrical Psalms in Genevan Liturgy

Because the metrical psalter was first and foremost a liturgical book,[16] we must notice the how and where and why of its liturgical

12. For a modern edition, see R. R. Terry, *Calvin's First Psalter* (London: E. Benn, 1932). Texts included Marot's settings of Psalms 1, 2, 3, 15, 19, 32, 51, 103, 104, 114, 130, 137, 143; Calvin's settings of Psalms 25, 36, 41, 138, 113 (unrhymed); the Ten Commandments with Kyrie; the Nunc Dimittis; and the Apostles' Creed. For Calvin's texts and their tunes, see Markus Jenny, *Luther, Zwingli, Calvin in Ihren Liedern* (Zürich: Theologischer Verlag, 1983). For an English translation of these texts, see Ford Lewis Battles and Stanley Tagg, eds., *The Piety of John Calvin* (Grand Rapids: Baker, 1978).

13. See the facsimile edited by Pierre Pidoux (Kassel: Bärenreiter, 1959).

14. The most important were the 1543 *Cinquante pseaumes en francios par Clem. Marot*, which included twenty-five new Marot texts and revised versions of earlier ones without music, and the 1551 *Pseaumes octante trois David*, which included thirty-five Bourgeois tunes and, for the first time, texts by Theodore Beza. The latter volume was reprinted each year until 1554, with six new Beza texts added in the final installment.

15. It was published as *Les pseaumes mis en rime francoise, par Clement Marot, and Theodore de Beze*. A facsimile of this was edited by Pierre Pidoux (Geneva: Droz, 1986). For a popular but well-researched discussion of this volume, see Candaux, *Le Psautier de Genève*. For the music in modern notation, see Waldo Selden Pratt, *The Music of the French Psalter of 1562: A Historical Survey and Analysis* (New York: Columbia University Press, 1939). Eighty-five melodies were taken from the 1551 publication; forty were new, written by a certain "Maitre Pierre," who could be any one of four musicians with that name in Geneva at the time. For the critical edition of Marot's texts, see Samuel Jan Lenselink, *Les psaumes de Clement Marot* (Assen: Van Gorcum, 1969). For the critical edition of Beza's texts, see Pierre Pidoux, *Psaumes mis en vers français* (Geneva: Droz, 1984).

16. Thus, to a student of Renaissance printing, the metrical psalter belongs more to the genus of ecclesiastical books than of musical publications: "The pattern of publishing is quite different from that for other musical matter, involving different printers, different techniques . . . and different approaches to reaching the market, which had itself been defined in a different manner" (Stanley Boorman, "Early Music Printing: Working for a Specialized Market," in *Print and Culture in the Renaissance*, ed. Gerald P. Tyson and Sylvia S. Wagonheim [Newark: University of Delaware Press, 1986], 223).

use. One Antwerp resident who attended Easter worship in Calvin's former congregation in Strasbourg left this record:

> On Sundays . . . we sing a psalm of David or some other prayer taken from the New Testament. The psalm or prayer is sung by everyone together, men as well as women with beautiful unanimity, which is something beautiful to behold. For you must understand that each one has a music book in his hand; that is why they cannot lose touch with one another. Never did I think that it could be as pleasing and delightful as it is. For five or six days at first, as I looked upon this little company, exiled from countries everywhere for having upheld the honor of God and His Gospel, I would begin to weep, not at all from sadness, but from joy at hearing them sing so heartily, and, as they sang, giving thanks to the Lord that He had led them to a place where His name is honored and glorified. No one could believe the joy which one experiences when one is singing the praises and wonders of the Lord in the mother tongue as one sings them here.[17]

Such a description also accords well with what we know of Geneva. Unison singing by the entire congregation was a customary part of weekly worship. More specifically, psalms were sung in conjunction with the confession of sin in the Sunday morning, Sunday afternoon, and Wednesday services,[18] with additional psalms sung at the Lord's Supper.[19] Psalms may also have been sung at Sunday midday cate-

17. Alfred Erichson, *L'Église française de Strasbourg au seizième siècle d'après des documents inédits* (Strasbourg: Librairie C. F. Schmidt, 1886), 21–22, quoted in Charles Garside, "The Origins of Calvin's Theology of Music, 1536–1543," *Transactions of the American Philosophical Society* 4 (1969): 18. We could only hope for such accounts from the Genevan church. Regarding the detail of the people carrying their books to worship, in 1581, the eleventh Synod of the French Reformed Church ordered that metrical psalms be bound with prayers and the catechism; an earlier decision mandated that worshipers bring their psalters with them to worship (John Quick, "The Acts, Decisions, and Decrees of the XI. National Synod of the Reformed Churches of Christ in the Kingdom of France, Held for the Second Time in the City of Rochel, and Year of Our Lord, 1581," in *Synodicon in Gallia Reformata* [London: Parkhurst and Robinson, 1692], chap. III, art. XL, p. 139); see also J. A. Lamb, *The Psalms in Christian Worship* (London: Faith Press, 1962), 14.

18. In the Genevan liturgy of 1542, a psalm was sung following the common confession. In the related 1545 French liturgy for Strasbourg, the confession was followed by absolution and the singing of both tables of the Ten Commandments with Kyrie (OS, 2:19). See the discussion in Hughes Oliphant Old, *The Patristic Roots of Reformed Worship* (Zurich: Theologischer Verlag, 1975), 89; and Bruno Bürki, "La sainte cène selon l'ordre de Jean Calvin 1542," in *Coena Domini I: Die Abendmahlsliturgie der Reformationskirchen im 16./17. Jahrhundert* (Schweiz: Universitätsverlag Freiburg, 1983), 347–67. On 11 November 1541, the council established Wednesday as a day for prayer. See Wulfert de Greef, *The Writings of John Calvin*, trans. Lyle Bierma (Grand Rapids: Baker, 1993), 129 n. 14.

19. The 1542 liturgy called for singing psalms or reading Scripture during the distribution of the bread and cup. The liturgies after 1545 called for the singing of the Song of Simeon after the Supper (OS, 2:49).

chetical services[20] and possibly at other liturgical gatherings.[21] Thus, the spirituality of the psalter is, in part, a *liturgical* spirituality.

The Choice of Psalms for Liturgical Use

The more interesting liturgical question concerns which psalms were sung at what occasions and why. Three types of evidence help us sort this out.

The first and most obvious data are simply the records of which psalms were available and published at a given time. It must be remembered that Geneva did not have a complete psalter until two years before Calvin's death. For most of Calvin's life, printed psalters included metrical settings for less than half of the biblical psalms.

The choice of which psalms were included is revealing. Almost all of the first psalms set in metrical form were either wisdom psalms or psalms of confession. This is perhaps a natural result of the placement of sung psalmody immediately following the prayer of confession in the Genevan liturgy.[22] The other striking pattern in the early metrical psalms is the predominance of psalms that either lament or reflect on trouble caused by the psalmist's enemy. In fact, this tendency is so marked that psalms of praise are strikingly underrepresented. Only three of the twenty-two texts in the 1539 Psalter are psalms of praise.

20. These services were mandated in the 1541 *Draft Ecclesiastical Ordinances* (CO, 10:19, 27; *Treatises* 62, 69). See also Hughes Oliphant Old, *The Shaping of the Reformed Baptismal Rite in the Sixteenth Century* (Grand Rapids: Eerdmans, 1992), 196.

21. In the 1536 edition of the *Institutes*, Calvin wrote, "At sermons there are quiet and silence, appointed places, the singing together of hymns, days set apart for the receiving of the Lord's Supper, the discipline of excommunications, and any others. The days themselves, the hours, the structure of the places of worship, what psalms are to be sung on what day, are matters of no importance" (OS, 1:257; 1536 *Institutes* 206).

22. In 1539, the psalter included the following psalms on the theme of confession and forgiveness: 32, 51, 103, 130 (Marot), 25, 36 (Calvin); these wisdom/law psalms: 1, 15, 19 (Marot); and the Ten Commandments. The only explicit psalms of praise included were those that were linked to the Lord's Supper (113, 138), as well as Psalm 104. Several psalms featured the theme of God's protection as a refuge from enemies: 3, 46, 91, 114, 137, 143. The 1542 *La forme des prieres et chantz ecclesiastiques* contained metrical settings for Psalms 1–15 (all Marot), reflecting a commitment to set the entire psalter in course. Other psalms that were added beyond these included Psalms 22, 24, 37, 38, 115—psalms that either lament the activity of the wicked or call for forgiveness and purity of heart. Notably lacking were songs of praise. Marot's 1543 *Cinquante psaumes en francois* contained nineteen new psalm translations. What is striking about Marot's choice of psalms is the prevalence of the theme of God as a refuge from the enemy. It is featured in nearly every psalm Marot chose (including at least 18, 23, 25, 33, 36, 43, 45, 46, 50, 72, 79, 86, 91, 101, 107, 110, 118, 138). Again, few psalms of praise or thanksgiving were included (only 33, 107, 118, 138). In Perrot's list, Psalms 1, 15, 119, 128, and the Ten Commandments—that is, five of the ten listed—explicitly emphasized divine law (Pidoux, *Le Psautier Huguenot*, 2:3, 15, 25).

Of the nineteen psalms Marot set to meter in 1543, all but one refer to "the enemy," and only four are psalms of praise. Perhaps these choices reflect Calvin's identification with the suffering David and his sense of impending peril, traits that are so amply evidenced in his psalm commentary.[23] In any case, for many years, Genevan spirituality was formed primarily by psalms of penitence and lament.

A second type of data are records of the use of "proper" psalms for certain occasions. For example, Charles Perrot, a rural pastor of the Genevan church and a colleague of Beza, specifically indicated that he sang the Ten Commandments at his catechetical services—one table of the law at the beginning and one at the end—and that he sang the Song of Simeon and Psalm 23 at the Lord's Supper (the banquet reference in the psalm providing the obvious rationale).[24] Likewise, the sung creed, the Ten Commandments, Psalms 103 and 138, and the Song of Simeon were especially linked with the Lord's Supper in at least some of the editions of Calvin's Genevan liturgy.[25] It is significant that the Lord's Supper psalms (103 and 138) are not penitential but psalms of praise and ones that feature the *sursum corda* theme so prominent in Calvin's eucharistic theology.[26] Thus, despite the aban-

23. See Calvin's preface to the *Commentary on the Book of Psalms*, trans. James Anderson (Grand Rapids: Eerdmans, 1949), xxxv–xlix.

24. Charles Perrot, "Managing a Country Parish," in *Calvinism in Europe, 1540–1610: A Collection of Documents*, trans. Alastair Duke, Gillian Lewis, and Andrew Pettegree (Manchester: Manchester University Press, 1992), 49, 51–52. This document was translated from the *Archives d'Etat de Genève, Archives Communales, Etat Civil, Genthod*, 1. For more on Perrot, see G. H. M. Posthumus Meyjes, "Charles Perrot (1541–1608): His Opinion on a Writing of Georg Cassander," in *Humanism and Reform: The Church in Europe, England, and Scotland, 1400–1643*, ed. James Kirk (Oxford: Blackwell, 1991), 221–36, and its notes. Perrot came to Geneva in 1564 and was appointed pastor in 1568.

25. The specific reference to both Psalm 138 and the Song of Simeon disappeared in the 1542 Geneva liturgy, one of many simplifications (or concessions?) Calvin made to Genevan conservatism. In Calvin's 1545 Strasbourg liturgy, Psalm 138 was sung during the distribution of the elements (Bürki, *Coena Domini*, 350). Hughes Oliphant Old, commenting on the 1539 Psalter, writes, "We would suggest that the Song of Simeon, Psalm 113, and Psalm 138 were intended for the Communion and Post-Communion Thanksgiving. Psalm 25 and the Ten Commandments were probably meant to be sung after the Prayer of Confession" (*Patristic Roots of Reformed Worship*, 89). Psalm 138 was specified for use after the sacrament after 1545 in the Strasbourg rite. After 1549, the Genevan Lord's Supper liturgy concluded with the Song of Simeon. Psalm 103 was added in the 1556 liturgy. Lamb also suggests that more psalms may have been sung than were specified (*Psalms in Christian Worship*, 143).

26. The psalm pictures the Lord as high and lifted up but also as one who regards the lowly. *Sursum corda* refers to the opening of the ancient eucharistic liturgies "lift up your heart to the Lord." This phrase aptly summarizes a main theme in Calvin's eucharistic theology, namely, that in the Lord's Supper, we are lifted up into heaven by the power of the Holy Spirit to commune with the ascended Christ.

donment of elaborate Roman lectionaries in Genevan worship, there remained a sense of "liturgical propers," particular texts that were associated with particular liturgical acts.

The third and perhaps the most interesting data regarding the liturgical use of the Psalms are the detailed tables that were printed in every psalter after 1549.[27] Proposed by Bourgeois and authorized by the Genevan council in 1546, these tables, which were framed and hung in the three Genevan churches, specified which psalms would be sung at each Sunday morning, Sunday afternoon, and Wednesday service.[28] In 1549, the entire extant psalter could be sung every seventeen weeks. By 1562, twenty-five weeks were required, with the congregation singing upward of thirty stanzas per week.[29] In this final form of the table, many psalms were divided into two or three sections and sung over the course of both Sunday services or each service in a given week.[30]

Not surprisingly, the tables did not specify any psalms for particular festivals or seasons—with exceptions allowed only for the Lord's Supper.[31] The tables did not allow for the selection of a psalm that was pertinent to the sermon of the day. Nor were the Psalms ordered sequentially as *lectio continua*. Pierre Pidoux does observe that "care was taken to choose [psalms] which stressed praise and thanksgiving for Sundays, and those containing supplications for the service of prayer on Wednesday mornings."[32] Beyond that, the only guiding principle in the formulation of these tables seems to have been the intent of singing approximately the same number of stanzas at each service.

In any case, this liturgical data provides poignant clues regarding the liturgical spirituality of the Genevan church. It tells us that psalm singing was a discipline, a discipline of sung prayer. Apparently, favor-

27. The tables for 1549, 1553, and 1562 are printed in Pidoux, *Le Psautier Huguenot*, 2:45, 63, 135.

28. The authorization was given on 11 May 1546. They were hung at St. Pierre, St. Magdeleine, and St. Gervais (Pidoux, *Le Psautier Huguenot*, 2:32, 55).

29. One fascinating thing these charts tell us is that as the number of psalms in the psalter grew, the more the people sang. By 1562, the congregation sang perhaps six to seven psalms per week. We do not know for certain that the tables were followed, although the fact that they were so carefully revised with each new addition to the psalter certainly suggests that they were used.

30. Some psalms may also have been chosen because they were more singable. In Charles Perrot's rural parish of the Genevan church, Psalms 1, 2, 15, 24, 42, 119 (aleph et beth), 128, 129, 130, and the Ten Commandments were used at the Sunday service, each split into two parts that were sung at the beginning and at the end. Perrot makes this indication despite the fact that the complete Genevan Psalter had long been finished and distributed (*Calvinism in Europe*, 49).

31. At the Lord's Supper, the Ten Commandments replaced the appointed psalm, and the Song of Simeon was sung (Bürki, *Coena Domini*, 350).

32. Pierre Pidoux, "The Fourth Centenary of the French Metrical Psalter,"*Reformed and Presbyterian World* 26 (1960–61): 354.

ite psalms were not sung to the exclusion of others (though we might wonder if this was the reason the charts were adopted). Even those psalms that would later be deemed liturgically questionable (e.g., Psalm 137) were regularly sung.[33] Thus, in one of the ironies of Reformation liturgy, the Genevan church adopted a regimen of psalm singing not entirely unlike that of Benedictine monasticism.

"Performance" Practice of Genevan Psalmody in Worship

The choice of psalms, however, is only one liturgical issue. We must also ask what these sung psalms sounded like. In the medieval Genevan church, music was likely rendered by the select *schola cantorum*.[34] But in the Reformation era, the entire congregation sang—men, women, and children together—an innovation in an era in which women's voices could otherwise be heard in worship only in a convent.[35] The children, for their part, were the leaders of the song. In the 1537 *Articles*, Calvin instructed:

> This manner of proceeding seemed especially good to us, that children, who beforehand have practiced some modest church song, sing in a loud distinct voice, the people listening with all attention and following heartily what is sung with the mouth, till all become accustomed to sing communally.[36]

This practice must have continued, for in 1561, the city council mandated that new psalm tunes not be used until they were taught to the congregation by the school children.[37] Although Calvin argued against a distinction between congregation and choir, he did allow children to serve as the precentors of the people.

33. In the 1562 table, Psalm 137 was sung in conjunction with Psalm 113.

34. The *schola cantorum* refers to the choir of monastic, clerical, or lay singers who provided music during the medieval mass. See Claude Tappolet, "Fragments d'une histoire de la musique à Genève," *Revue Musicale de Suisse* 93 (1953): 15–16; and Robert Homer Leslie Jr., "Music and the Arts in Calvin's Geneva: A Study of the Relation between Calvinistic Theology and Music and the Arts, with Special Reference to the *Cent cinquante pseaumes* (1583) of Pascal de L'Estocart" (Ph.D. diss., McGill University, 1969).

35. See Pidoux, *Le Psautier Huguenot*, 1:xiv; and Susan Lee Youens, "Music in the French Reformation and Counter-Reformation" (Ph.D. diss., Harvard University, 1975), 13. On women's roles in liturgy, see Natalie Davis, *Society and Culture in Early Modern France* (Stanford: Stanford University Press, 1975), 86–87.

36. OS, 1:375; *Treatises* 54. A brief reference to children is also found in the 1541 *Draft Ecclesiastical Ordinances;* CO, 10:26; *Treatises* 67. The most prominent precentors *(chantres)* were Guillaume Franc (1541–45), Louis Bourgeois (1545–52), and a certain "Maitre Pierre" who was mentioned in various Genevan records.

37. Pidoux, *Le Psautier Huguenot*, 2:124, council minutes for 25 December 1561. See also Leslie, "Music and the Arts in Calvin's Geneva," 120–21.

What Calvin did not allow was the accompaniment of song by instruments of any kind. For Calvin, instrumental music in worship properly belonged only to the Old Testament dispensation. As Calvin advised, when the biblical writers spoke of musical instruments, it "was not as if this were in itself necessary." Rather, instrumental music "was useful as an elementary aid to the people of God in these ancient times," an aid that was no longer necessary after Christ.[38] Perhaps it was in part because of this lack of instrumental leadership that psalm singing retained its strong roots as the songs of the people. In any case, we must acknowledge that psalm singing was not a refined art. As Perrot recorded, "I decided that I would not sing at those services where there wasn't another man present to help in the singing, but I did sing with another man even if there were no women or girls to join in. Some people know the Psalms very imperfectly."[39] The sounds reverberating from Geneva were hardly those of the papal court or the Chapel Royal.

Theology of Worship

A final liturgical issue is essentially theological, concerning what Genevan worshipers believed about the nature and purpose of public worship. Unfortunately, we do not have a repository of diaries or journals from Genevan residents that give testimony to their particular liturgical spirituality. We have only Calvin's thoughts on this subject, though we know these thoughts were regularly conveyed from Genevan pulpits and were featured in the written preface of nearly every printed psalter.

For Calvin, the entire liturgical act, including psalm singing, was viewed as an activity of God among his people.[40] In Calvin's words, when the Psalms are sung, "we are certain that God has put the words in our mouths as if they themselves sang in us to exalt his glory."[41] For Calvin, this divine action was construed in trinitarian

38. CO, 32:10–11 (Commentary on Ps. 92:3); see also CO, 24:162 (Commentary on Exod. 15:20).

39. Duke et al., *Calvinism in Europe*, 50.

40. Old, *Patristic Roots of Reformed Worship*, 95, 259; and Hughes Oliphant Old, "The Prophetic Criticism of Worship," in *John Calvin and the Church: A Prism of Reform*, ed. Timothy George (Louisville: Westminster John Knox, 1990), 234. See also Jeffrey T. VanderWilt, "John Calvin's Theology of Liturgical Song," *Christian Scholar's Review* 25 (1995): 63–82.

41. "La forme des prieres et chantz ecclesiastiques"; OS, 2:17; Ford Lewis Battles, "John Calvin: The Form of Prayers and Songs of the Church," *Calvin Theological Journal* 15 (1980): 160–65. Hereafter this translation is identified as "Letter to the Reader." This famous letter is a classic statement on Calvin's views on music. It shows indebtedness to Bucer's preface to the 1541 Strasbourg hymnal (see Lenselink, *Les psaumes de Clement Marot*, 158–62).

terms,[42] in which Christ is "the chief conductor of our hymns," the one who "hallows our lips . . . to sing the praises of God," while the Holy Spirit is the prompter who urges the people to sing.[43] Within this framework, psalm singing, as the act of the people, had the particular role of both praise and prayer. As Calvin said, "As for the public prayers, they are of two sorts: some of them make use of speaking alone, the others are with singing."[44] The Psalms were not sung primarily for didactic purposes but rather for the congregation to extol the glory of God. As Hughes Oliphant Old concludes, "Psalmody is not primarily thematic, decorative, or didactic, but doxological."[45]

Further clues to the shape of this liturgical spirituality are found in Calvin's justification for the inclusion of sung psalmody in worship. In the 1537 *Articles*, he observed:

> There are the psalms which we desire to be sung in the Church, as we have it exemplified in the ancient Church and in the evidence of Paul himself, who says it is good to sing in the congregation with mouth and heart. We are unable to compute the profit and edification which will arise from this except after having experimented. Certainly as things are, the prayers of the faithful are so cold, that we ought to be ashamed and dismayed. The psalms can incite us to lift up our hearts to God and move us to an ardour in invoking and exalting with praises the glory of his Name.[46]

Already here we find the theme that becomes a common refrain in all of Calvin's descriptions of sung psalmody in the liturgy: Sung psalms *incite* the people to praise. In the 1541 *Draft Ecclesiastical Ordinances*, Calvin wrote, "It will be good to introduce ecclesiastical songs,

42. The trinitarian shape of Calvin's liturgical theology is explained in recent works by Philip Walker Butin, "Constructive Iconoclasm: Trinitarian Concern in Reformed Worship," *Studia Liturgica* 19 (1989): 140–42; "Reformed Ecclesiology: Trinitarian Grace according to Calvin," *Studies in Reformed Theology and History* 2, no. 1 (1994): 19–27; and *Revelation, Redemption, and Response: Calvin's Trinitarian Understanding of the Divine-Human Relationship* (New York: Oxford University Press, 1995), 101ff.

43. CO, 55:29, 193; John Calvin, *Commentary on the Epistle to the Hebrews*, trans. William B. Johnston (Grand Rapids: Eerdmans, 1963), 27, 211. See also CO, 37:68 (Commentary on Isa. 42:10).

44. OS, 2:15; "Letter to the Reader," 162–63.

45. Old, *Patristic Roots of Reformed Worship*, 253–54.

46. In the same document, Calvin echoes these sentiments: "Further, it is a thing very expedient for the edification of the Church, to sing some psalms in the form of public devotions by which one may pray to God, or to sing his praise so that the hearts of all be aroused and incited to make like prayers and to render like praises and thanks to God with one accord" ("Articles concernant l'organisation de l'église"; OS, 1:375, 369; *Treatises* 53, 48). In the 1536 *Institutes*, Calvin had remarked, "It is fully evident that unless voice and song, if interposed in prayer, spring from deep feeling of heart, neither has any value or profit in the least with God" (OS, 1:103; 1536 *Institutes* 74).

the better to incite the people to prayer and to praise God."[47] In the Letter to the Reader that prefaced the 1542 liturgy, Calvin echoed, "Singing has great power and vigor to move and inflame men's hearts to call upon and praise God with a more vehement and burning zeal."[48] With ample care taken to avoid romanticizing this rhetoric, we can observe that this is hardly the language of a cold, calculating intellectualism or of a dour, somber ethos that persists in many caricatures of Genevan liturgy.

That the Psalms were chosen to call forth these affections is no surprise, for Calvin understood the Psalms not only as the written Word of God but also as the "anatomy of the soul," a mirror of the religious affections. So many of the grand themes of Calvin's theological vision—the majesty and glory of God, the pattern of divine initiative and human response, the precariousness of the human situation—were so lucidly, so existentially, so prayerfully presented in the Psalms. The Psalms were certainly one of Calvin's most cherished portions of Scripture.[49] His commentary on the Psalms, with its rhapsodic preface, is ample proof of that.[50] And it is no surprise that this commentary was, in the words of James Luther Mays, "shaped by the notion of the congregation" and "determined by his purpose to let the psalms edify the readers in prayer, praise, and conduct."[51] At the very least, the singing of psalms must be considered an important dimension of Calvin's own liturgical spirituality.

The Text and Tunes of the Genevan Psalter

Texts

The aspects of Genevan liturgy already discussed provide a stimulating context for the second broad topic of this chapter, the texts and tunes of the Genevan Psalter. This liturgical context highlights what

47. CO, 10:26; *Treatises* 67. See also CO, 31:324–25 (Commentary on Ps. 33:2).

48. OS, 2:15; "Letter to the Reader," 163. One can also hear in these lines a hint of a Platonist aesthetic, which becomes explicit in Calvin's 1543 addition to the 1542 letter. "For there is scarcely anything in this world more capable of turning or bending hither and thither the customs of men, as Plato has wisely remarked (Rep. 3.12, 401B; Law 2.8, 664B). And actually we know by experience that it has a secret power, almost unbelievable, to move morals in one way or another" (OS, 2:16; "Letter to the Reader," 163–64).

49. Battles and Tagg, *Piety of John Calvin*, 8.

50. CO, 31:13–36. The influence of Bucer is important for understanding this dimension of Calvin. In Strasbourg, Calvin came into contact with both psalm singing and Bucer's 1529 commentary on the Psalms.

51. James Luther Mays, "Calvin's Commentaries on the Psalms: The Preface as Introduction," in *John Calvin and the Church: A Prism of Reform*, ed. Timothy George (Louisville: Westminster John Knox, 1990), 197–98. See also James A. De Jong, "'An Anatomy of All Parts of the Soul': Insights into Calvin's Spirituality from His Psalms Commentary," in *Calvinus Sacrae Scripturae Professor: Calvin as Confessor of Holy Scripture*, ed. Wilhelm H. Neuser (Grand Rapids: Eerdmans, 1994), 1–14.

may be the greatest irony of the Genevan Psalter, the fact that, unlike Roman Catholic psalmody, the texts used were not the actual words of the biblical Psalter but were instead poetic reworkings of the Psalms in metrical form. The reason for this is straightforward enough: The Psalms needed to be rendered in a singable musical form, and metrical psalmody was judged to be the most singable. What is surprising is that nowhere does Calvin, nor any other early Reformer, feel compelled to justify this departure from the text of Scripture, the text believed to be placed upon the lips of the people by God himself.[52] Not until twenty-three years after Calvin's death did Genevan printers alter Calvin's famous preface to defend the use of psalms in verse.[53]

Perhaps this lacuna can be explained by the circumspect attention given to the biblical texts by the Genevan poets, a priority directly linked to humanist interest in the Hebrew text of the Old Testament. Marot's earliest psalm settings were written for the French court, exemplifying a long tradition of setting the biblical psalms to verse by the best poets of the age.[54] Marot was a careful student of the biblical text, working primarily with the French text of the Psalms. His work demonstrates familiarity with Bucer's commentary on the Psalms and an attempt to be sensitive to the form and poetic rhythm of the original.[55] Upon arrival in Geneva, Marot even revised his settings to ren-

52. In his original invitation to Georg Spalatin to provide metrical settings for the Psalms, Luther gives evidence of holding a similar view: "But I would like you to avoid new-fangled, fancied words and to use expressions simple and common enough for the people to understand yet pure and fitting. The meaning should also be clear and close as possible to the psalm. Irrespective of the exact wording, one must freely render the sense by suitable words" (J. Pelikan and H. T. Lehmann, eds., *Luther's Works: American Edition*, vol. 53 [Philadelphia: Fortress, 1965], 221).

53. The added text reads as follows: "And as for the verse translation, to make it more easily sung by the common people, in Church or elsewhere, we hope that it will not be given too much weight, not as if it were word for word the Scriptural text, which we know to be impossible. Nevertheless, since an attempt has been made to get close to the truth of the Hebrew with as little variation as possible, and since several good and learned people give testimony every day to their consolation, we have not created difficulties about changing in several places what can be seen as less correct and acceptable to the majesty of such a sacred work" (Candaux, *Le Psautier de Genève*, 55). This edition includes seventy slight alterations in the Marot and Beza metrical texts, changes likely suggested by the scholarship that produced the 1587 revised French translation of Scripture.

54. M. A. Screech, *Clément Marot: A Renaissance Poet Discovers the Gospel* (Leiden: Brill, 1994). Recent accounts of Marot's life and work continue to appear at a rapid pace. See C. A. Meyer, *Clément Marot et autres études sur la littérature française de la Renaissance* (Paris: Honoré Champion Éditeur, 1993); and Jean-Luc Déjean, *Clément Marot* (Paris: Fayard, 1990). See also H. P. Clive, *Clément Marot: An Annotated Bibliography* (London: Grant and Cutler, 1983).

55. This is developed further in Michel Jeanneret, *Poésie et tradition biblique au XVIe siècle: Recherches stylistiques sur les paraphrases des psaumes de Marot à Malherbe*

der the biblical text more faithfully, incorporating exact scriptural phraseology where possible in the metrical scheme. Such care was only fitting for a repertoire that was often bound together with the Bible and, on occasion, was even printed in canonical order in the middle of the Old Testament.[56]

This concern for the voice of the original text was reflected in the stunning variety of poetic meters used to render the Psalms. Unlike the bland and uniform metrical configurations of English psalmody in the same period, the Genevan Psalter featured 110 different meters, each chosen to capture the unique sense of a given psalm.[57] Thus, despite their willingness to recast the biblical psalms in metrical form, Marot and Beza demonstrated respect for the biblical texts as the written Word of God, which in itself was a chief characteristic of Genevan piety.

Tunes

This respect for the texts of the biblical psalms was also reflected in the Genevan tunes. Calvin argued that the tunes "be moderate, in the manner that we have set it, to bear a gravity and majesty fitting to the subject."[58] This was accomplished by linking the musical expression of the tunes with the meaning and meter of the text. Like nearly every humanist musical theorist of the age (including those who had influence at the Council of Trent), the Genevan composers set out to render the metrical texts as lucidly as possible.[59]

(Paris: Corti, 1969), 51–87. A more critical analysis of the liberties Marot took with the biblical text is offered by A. Muller, *La Poésie religieuse catholique de Marot à Malherbe* (Paris: Foulon, 1950), 37–53. The influence of Bucer's commentary was first explored in depth by P. A. Becker, *Clément Marots Psalmenübersetzung* (Leipzig: Teubern, 1921). Marot's attention to the features of Hebrew poetry is discussed in Screech, *Clément Marot*, 27; and Elizabeth Catherine Wright Coppedge, "The Psalms of Clément Marot and Jean Antoine de Baïf: A Discussion of Translation and Poetry in Sixteenth-Century France" (Ph.D. diss., New York University, 1975). It is significant that Marot identified his metrical settings as "translated into French verse, according to the Hebraic truth" (*Oeuvres complètes*, vol. 2, ed. A. Grenier [Paris: Librairie Garnier Frères, 1921], 310). To place this discussion in a larger Reformation context, see Veit, "Le chant, la Réforme et la Bible," 659–81.

56. Candaux, *Le Psautier de Genève*, 37. For more information, see Bettye Thomas Chambers, *Bibliography of French Bibles, Fifteenth- and Sixteenth-Century* (Geneva: Droz, 1983).

57. Pratt, *Music of the French Psalter*, 26. For a comparison of the Genevan tradition with psalmody in England, see Emily R. Brink, "Metrical Psalmody: A Tale of Two Traditions," *Reformed Liturgy and Music* 31, no. 1 (1989): 3–8.

58. OS, 2:17; "Letter to the Reader," 165.

59. This connection is explored generally by Édith Weber, "L'humanisme musical au XVIe siècle et ses répercussions sur le chant d'Église protestant et catholique," in *Humanisme et foi Chrétienne*, ed. Charles Kannengiesser and Yves Marchasson (Paris:

At the most basic level, this meant reflecting the meter and cadence of the texts in the tunes. One hundred and ten different textual meters required a vast variety of tunes. Not until the publication of Beza's final set of texts was any tune used twice. As a result, texts and tunes were closely identified with one another. A reference to a given psalm could refer just as easily to the tune as to its text. Perhaps this suggests in part why the tunes were so tenaciously guarded. When Bourgeois changed one without permission, his reward was a day in prison.[60]

On a subtler and long unnoticed level, the tunes reflected the content of the text in the musical mode out of which they were constructed.[61] Thus, the tune for Psalm 51 was in the dark phrygian mode, while the tune for Psalm 19 radiated with the brightness of the mixolydian mode.[62] Again, we must not be tempted to romanticize; this music was not full-blown baroque text painting. But neither was it the distanced, ethereal ethos of medieval plainchant.

This discussion of the Genevan tunes brings us to the central issue of twenty-first century musicological study of the Genevan Psalter. This issue concerns the relationship between the Genevan tunes and two contemporaneous musical genres: the secular French chanson and medieval plainchant. This issue also, I might add, has implications for an understanding of Genevan spirituality.

Beauchesne, 1976), 239–54; and more fully in her *La musique mesurée à l'Antique en Allemagne,* 2 vols. (Paris: Klincksieck, 1974). See also V. E. Graham, "Music for Poetry in France (1550–1580)," *Renaissance News* 17 (1964): 307–17; and Don Harrán, *Word-Tone Relations in Musical Thought: From Antiquity to the Seventeenth Century* (Neunhausen-Stuttgart: Hänssler-Verlag, 1986), 76–101. That Calvin had no corner on this insight is evidenced by the works of the famous Venetian music theorist Zarlino, who, in his 1558 *Istituzioni harmoniche,* argued, "[Plato] puts the text as the principal element ahead of the others; and the two remaining parts are subservient to it: for after he has revealed the whole by means of the parts he says that harmony and rhythm must follow the text and not vice versa. And this is as it should be" (trans. in Edward Lowinsky, "Music in Renaissance Culture," *Journal of the History of Ideas* 15 [1954]: 537). To compare Calvin to the Council of Trent, see Édith Weber, *Le Concile de Trente et la Musique: De la Réforme à la contre-Réforme* (Paris: Honoré Champion, 1982), 9–10; see also Edward Patte, "John Calvin and Choral Music," *Choral and Organ Guide* 18 (1965): 6–17.

60. On 3 December 1551. Pidoux, *Le Psautier Huguenot,* 2:52. Bourgeois did not proceed with his innovations without Calvin's approval, and, in fact, Calvin came to Bourgeois's defense and sought his release. The changes remained in subsequent editions of the psalter. See Pidoux, introduction to the facsimile of the 1562 Psalter, 16.

61. See Jan R. Luth, "Where Do Genevan Psalms Come From?" *Reformed Liturgy and Music* 5 (1993): 41–42. See also Piet van Amstel, "The Roots of Genevan Psalm Tunes," *Reformed Music Magazine* 3 (1992): 54. This is not dissimilar from Plato's consideration of the propriety of various modes for certain functions, as discussed in *The Republic.*

62. The contrast between these two modes is comparable, though not identical, to that between the minor and major scale.

For most of the twentieth century, students of the Genevan Psalter believed that its tunes most resembled and, in fact, were based on secular chanson melodies. This theory was pioneered in Orentin Douen's monumental study of these tunes in the 1880s. Douen even proposed direct links between known chanson and Genevan tunes. However, more recent scholarship, most notably that of Pierre Pidoux, has effectively discounted most of these conclusions.[63] Although an idiomatic resemblance between the psalm and chanson melodies cannot be denied, only a few Genevan tunes at most can be traced to previously existing secular tunes.[64]

A more promising, if covert, connection exists between the Genevan tunes and medieval plainchant. A first clue for this thesis comes from Bourgeois himself, who wrote of his use of "some hymns which we in the past misused."[65] A second clue comes from a 1616 Catholic publication that called for a *recovery* of tunes from "the Protestants who have stolen our notes to put beneath their Hugue-

63. The first challenge to Douen's approach was Emmanuel Haein, "Le problème du chant choral dans les Eglises Réformées et le Trésor liturgique de la Cantilène Huguenot" (Ph.D. diss., 1926). Douen's claims were perpetuated throughout much of the twentieth century, including in such notable sources as Gustav Reese, *Music in the Renaissance* (New York: W. W. Norton, 1954), 360.

64. The tune for Psalm 138, for example, is strikingly similar to the tune for Marot's chanson "Quand vous voudrez faire une amie" and "Une pastourelle gentille." See Édith Weber, "Religieuse Chrétienne (Musique)," *Encyclopaedia Universalis* (Paris: Encylopaedia Universalis, 1992), 19:749–50.

65. Bourgeois, from the afterword to the 1551 Genevan Psalter, quoted in Luth, "Where Do Genevan Psalms Come From?" 41; and Pierre Pidoux, "History of the Genevan Psalter II," *Reformed Music Journal* 1 (1989): 34. Further conclusions are explored in his *Vom Ursprung der Genfer Psalmweisen* (Zurich: n.p., 1986). The combined work of Emmanuel Haein and H. Hasper suggests that over fifty psalm tunes may have been based in part on plainchant melodies (H. Hasper, *Calvijns beginsel voor den zang in den eredienst*, 2 vols. ['s-Gravenhage: Martinus Nijhof, 1955 and 1976]). A chart of the most prominent examples is included in Robin A. Leaver, *"Goostly Psalmes and Spirituall Songes": English and Dutch Metrical Psalms from Coverdale to Utenhove, 1535–1566* (Oxford: Clarendon, 1991), 49. Piet van Amstel goes so far as to suggest that "it is possible to discern a certain 'word-play' in the choice of Gregorian melody for a particular psalm text. . . . It is quite possible that the composer in borrowing well-known Gregorian melodies wished to link up with the sentiments that lived among the common people," although he admits this is a matter of conjecture ("Roots of Genevan Psalm Tunes," 51). See also Bernard Smilde, "The Roots of the Melody for Psalm 84," *Reformed Music Magazine* 1 (1989): 88–92. The one case in which this type of connection is most likely is the link between *Victimae paschali laudes* and Psalm 80. This is acknowledged even by Pidoux: "By means of notes—as the Biblia pauperum did by means of pictures—the Christian Easter is connected with the Jewish Passover, an inspiration which can only come to an author who is equally at home in musical composition as in the convolutions of Biblical exegesis" ("The History of the Origin of the Genevan Psalter," *Reformed Music Journal* 1 [1989]: 67).

not heresies."[66] These allusions have been largely confirmed by recent musicological analyses. In fact, the Gregorian roots of several Genevan tunes is now largely assumed. Perhaps the most notable example is the resemblance between the Genevan tune for Psalm 80 and the plainchant melody for the Easter hymn *Victimae pascali laudes*.[67]

But, of course, this approach can also be taken to an extreme, for though short musical motifs or formal structures in the Genevan tunes may signal the appropriation of a medieval inheritance, the overall musical culture was altogether different. The careful attention to textual meter and the dance-like rhythms that prompted Queen Elizabeth to call these "the Genevan jigs" signal precisely that. At the end of musicological analysis, it must be finally admitted that the Genevan tunes are both alike and unlike the two vastly different musical repertories of the chanson and the plainchant. Genevan psalmody was not the otherworldly music that the Gregorian tunes had become, nor was it the simple appropriation of secular tunes from the local pub. Like so much of Reformed piety, the metrical psalter was neither radically identified with nor radically withdrawn from the secular culture of the day. And so, even the otherwise technical research of musicologists provides evidence for building a case about the nature of Genevan spirituality.

Metrical Psalms outside the Liturgy

This blurring of the distinction between sacred and secular is further illuminated by the third and final broad topic, the use of the metrical psalms outside the liturgy. Already in 1539, Marot, echoing Desiderius Erasmus and various patristic sources, had written of "the time approaching when a laborer at his work, a driver in his cart, a craftsman in his shop, lightens his toil with psalm or canticle, when shepherds and shepherdesses make the rock resound with song praising the holy name of their Creator."[68] Calvin himself would soon con-

66. From *Rossignols Sauvages*, quoted in Édith Weber, "Les mélodies du Psautier huguenot des origes à nos jours," in *La controverse interne au protestantisme, XVIe-XXe Siècles, actes du 2ème colloque Jean Boisset* (Montpellier: Université Paul Valéry, 1983), 185–97. See also Luth, "Where Do Genevan Psalms Come From?" 41–42.

67. Adapting plainchant melodies for Protestant vernacular hymns was not uncommon. Early examples include adaptation of plainchant melodies in the 1524 *Chorgesangbuch*, edited by Johann Walter. See W. Blankenburg, "Johann Walters Chorgesangbuch von 1524 in hymnologischer Sicht," *Jahrbuch für Liturgik und Hymnologie* 18 (1973/74): 65–69.

68. Marot, *Oeuvres complètes*, 303–9, quoted in Allen Cabaniss, "The Background of Metrical Psalmody," *Calvin Theological Journal* 20 (1985): 201. The patristic sources were likely mediated to Marot and Calvin through Erasmus; see *The Paraclesis* (1516), in John C. Olin, ed., *Erasmus: Christian Humanism and the Reformation* (New York: Harper Torchbooks, 1965), 97.

tend, "Even in houses and in the fields [singing] would be for us an incitement and as it were an organ to praise God, and to raise our hearts to him for him to console us, as we meditate upon his power, goodness, wisdom, and justice."[69] This ordinary, everyday use of music featured nothing less than the metrical psalms themselves.

There is little doubt that the Genevan psalms found a significant place outside the liturgy because of Calvin's influence. All published music was subject to approval by the Company of Pastors, a body who deferred to Calvin's thinking on the matter. And Calvin's thinking clearly reflected two tendencies. On the one hand, Calvin had a high view of music and its place in the life of the community. For Calvin, music was one of the many gifts lavished by God on his people. Even of instrumental music, Calvin had advised, "It ought not to be thought of as superfluous," for "it may minister to our pleasure, rather than our necessity."[70] On the other hand, Calvin had a relatively restrictive view of what comprised a permissible musical repertory.[71] As Calvin had preached, "All our mirth should always tend to the glorifying of God."[72] Calvin and the Genevan council were quick to ban secular music that they perceived to be base or bawdy.[73] Already in 1538, Calvin and Guillaume Farel's overture to the Synod of Zurich proposed both to promote psalmody and to prohibit "lascivious songs."[74] In the 1547 *Ordinances for the Supervision of Rural Churches*, parishioners were

69. OS, 2:15–16; "Letter to the Reader," 163. This sentence is the beginning of the section of the Letter to the Reader that was added by Calvin in 1543. This sentence creates a striking juxtaposition with the final section of the 1542 version of the letter, which reads, "There is a great difference between the music that one makes to give joy to men at table and in their houses on the one hand and the Psalms, which are sung in the church in the presence of God and his angels" (OS, 2:15; "Letter to the Reader," 163). Regarding this passage, Charles Garside comments, "The antithesis between the secular and the sacred could scarcely be more pointed." Garside explains the juxtaposition by examining the development of Calvin's thought on this matter in the early 1540s ("Origins of Calvin's Theology of Music," 20–24).

70. CO, 23:100; John King, trans., *Commentaries on the First Book of Moses Called Genesis by John Calvin* (Grand Rapids: Eerdmans, 1948), 1:218. This dimension of Calvin's thought has been ignored by a long line of historians, including Douen, who have lamented Calvin's supposed "puritanical" hostility to music.

71. Charles Garside has argued that Calvin's distrust of secular music grew during the early years of his time in Geneva ("Origins of Calvin's Theology of Music," 25).

72. CO, 51:724; John Calvin, *Sermons on Ephesians* (Edinburgh: Banner of Truth Trust, 1973), 553.

73. This was an integral part of the discipline that the Genevan council promoted in decisions regarding every aspect of Genevan life. See Robert M. Kingdon, "The Geneva Consistory in the Time of Calvin," in *Calvinism in Europe*, 22. One incident of notoriety featured a number of youths who were arrested for singing psalms derisively in the Genevan streets. See William G. Naphy, *Calvin and the Consolidation of the Genevan Reformation* (Manchester and New York: Manchester University Press, 1994), 188.

74. Pidoux, *Le Psautier Huguenot*, 2:1.

instructed, "If anyone sings songs that are unworthy, dissolute or out-rageous, or spins wildly round in the dance, or the like, he is to be im-prisoned for three days, and then sent on to the Consistory."[75] Secular songs were not likely prohibited altogether. Instrumental performances continued in Geneva and were even featured at a 1551 council ban-quet, although they were carefully regulated.[76] The proliferation of psalm-related musical genres in Geneva was, no doubt, spurred on by Calvin's distrust of secular music.

The most picturesque evidence for the extra-liturgical use of the psalter comes from Calvin's Roman Catholic detractors, whose argu-ments against singing the Psalms outside liturgy provide ample proof of its existence. This critique would be wielded most eloquently by Michel de Montaigne, whose primary contact with Calvinists was in France:

> It is not without much reason, it seems to me, that the Church forbids the promiscuous, inconsiderate, and indiscreet use of the sacred and di-vine songs which the Holy Spirit dictated to David. We must not bring God into our acts save with reverence and heedfulness full of honour and respect. Those words are too divine to have no other use than to ex-ercise our lungs and please our ears. It is from the inmost thoughts that they should be brought forth, and not from the tongue. It is not right to allow the shop-boy, among his empty and frivolous thoughts, to enter-tain and amuse himself with them. Nor surely is it right to see the holy book of the sacred mysteries of our faith tossed about in the hall and the kitchen. They were formerly mysteries; now they serve for recre-ation and pastime.[77]

In Geneva, Roman devotee Artus Desiré argued against three Prot-estant practices: allowing women to sing in worship, prohibiting all forms of polyphony in worship, and profaning sacred music by allow-ing it to be sung outside the liturgy.[78]

75. "Ordinances for the Supervision of Country Churches"; CO, 10:55; *Treatises* 81. Interestingly, this penalty was worse than the one for drunkenness.

76. Pidoux, *Le Psautier Huguenot*, 2:49, from council minutes for 13 March 1551. See also Leslie, "Music and the Arts in Calvin's Geneva," 114ff., 142–43, 217.

77. "Of Prayers," in George B. Ives, trans., *The Essays of Michel de Montaigne* (New York: Heritage Press, 1946), 426.

78. Youens, "Music in the French Reformation and Counter-Reformation," 9–13, 159–60, 166; and discussion in H. P. Clive, "The Calvinistic Attitude to Music and Its Literary Aspects," *Bibliotheque d'Humanisme et Renaissance* 19 (1957): 311–19. This ar-gument is presented in a mock debate between archetypal Protestant and Catholic fig-ures entitled *Les Combatz du fidelle Chrestien*. Apparently, however, not all Catholics shared this view. One account, recorded in 1610 (notably two generations after Calvin), grudgingly observed that psalms "were received and welcomed by everyone with as much favour as ever any book was, not only by those with Protestant sympathies, but also by Catholics; everyone enjoyed singing them" (Florimund de Raemond, *L'histoire*

But where and when were the Psalms sung outside the liturgy? We know that students at the Genevan academy rehearsed psalms one hour a day.[79] We also know that psalms were likely used in private and family devotion. Euan Cameron even suggests that "the Marot Psalter, perhaps above all else, became the standard vehicle for the devotional life of French-speaking Protestantism."[80] The anecdotal evidence for this is certainly compelling and prevalent. In one especially idyllic account, produced in Cambrai, France, in 1566, a Protestant recounted, "I was led to knowledge of the Gospel by . . . my neighbor, who had a Bible printed at Lyon and who taught me the Psalms by heart. . . . The two of us used to go walking in the fields Sundays and feast days, conversing about the Scriptures and the abuses of priests."[81] More trenchant is the account of Bastille-bound Huguenot Anne de Bourg. Although he was "confined in a cage where he suffered all the discomforts imaginable," nevertheless he "rejoiced always and glorified God, now taking up his lute to sing him psalms, now praising him with his voice."[82] The Genevan evidence for the devotional use of the psalter is not as prevalent, save for one poem, *La maison de solitude*, which pictures a young woman who turns from the bustle of town life to offer prayer and song to God.[83]

Then also there are records of numerous incidents of the Psalms being used as battle hymns for Calvinists all over Europe. Such inci-

---

de la naissance, progrez, et décadence de l'hérésie de ce siècle [Paris, 1610, and Rouen, 1628–1629], quoted in Howard Slenk, "Psalms, Metrical," in *New Grove Dictionary of Music and Musicians*, vol. 15, ed. Stanley Stadie [London: Macmillan, 1980], 349); see also Youens, "Music in the French Reformation and Counter-Reformation," 159–60; and Barbara Sher Tinsley, *History and Polemics in the French Reformation. Florimond de Raemond: Defender of the Church* (Selinsgrove: Susquehanna University Press, 1992). The matter of allowing women to sing in worship was common in Catholic critiques. One Parisian writer lamented, "The fine-voiced maidens let loose their hums and trills . . . so the young men will be sure to listen. How wrong of Calvin to let women sing in Church" (quoted in Davis, *Society and Culture in Early Modern France*, 86).

79. This was mandated by the city council in 1543 and affirmed by the 1559 *L'Ordre de collège de Genève* (Pidoux, *Le Psautier Huguenot*, 2:29, 111). See also Leslie, "Music and the Arts in Calvin's Geneva," 147; and OS, 2:366–67. This was also apparently the pattern in Strasbourg. See Clyde William Young, "School Music in Sixteenth-Century Strasbourg," *Journal of Research in Music Education* 10 (1962): 129. To compare this to the larger Reformation context, see Frederick W. Sternfeld, "Music in the Schools of the Reformation," *Musica Disciplina* 2 (1948): 99–122; and Leslie, "Music and the Arts in Calvin's Geneva," 102, 108, 132ff. The Psalms were not simply taught by rote but by a system of music reading, which was necessary for learning to sing polyphonic settings of the Psalms. Bourgeois wrote a curriculum for teaching the rudiments of music. Such instructional works were often contained in the prefaces to the psalters.

80. Euan Cameron, *The European Reformation* (Oxford: Clarendon, 1991), 256.

81. Davis, *Society and Culture in Early Modern France*, 189.

82. *Histoire ecclésiastique* (1560), a work that was formerly attributed to Beza (quoted in Slenk, "Psalms, Metrical," 352).

83. Clive, "Calvinist Attitude," 299.

dents have been ably chronicled by Stanford Reid, who concluded that "more than all the fine theological reasoning, both the catechism and the psalter entered into the very warp and weft of the humblest members' lives."[84] The most colorful examples have a French provenance. Upon hearing the stirring singing of Psalm 118, one French officer observed, "When the Huguenots do this, they are ready to fight well."[85] To Reid's collection of anecdotes must be added one example of which Calvin himself was aware. In June of 1551, a certain Jean Guerand described an uprising in Lyon that involved

> a large number of people who began to hold meetings and assemblies with two or three hundred men and women, the men carrying swords and other arms, singing, large and small together, the psalms of David translated by Clement Marot . . . to attract to their damnable sect many other people, although there were great and clear laws against singing the said psalms and holding such meetings and assemblies . . . for which a few of them were imprisoned at the King's pleasure.[86]

In this environment, psalm singing was a risky political act.

The Genevan Christians did not face such adversarial conditions as their counterparts in France and the Low Countries, but there is ample proof of their psalm singing outside the liturgy. Evidence from Geneva comes not so much in the form of personal anecdotes as in the presence of musical repertories that derive from the psalter.

Related Genres

The extra-liturgical use of psalms can be tracked in the development of two distinct but related genres.[87] Of particular significance

84. W. Stanford Reid, "The Battle Hymns of the Lord: Calvinist Psalmody of the Sixteenth Century," *Sixteenth Century Essays and Studies* 2 (1971): 37. Also, "the vernacular-metrical psalm . . . became woven into the fabric of sixteenth century Calvinist thought and life—one might say it became part of the Calvinist mystique" (53).

85. Ibid., 47 n. 39. For other examples, see Barbara B. Diefendorf, "The Huguenot Psalter and the Faith of French Protestants in the Sixteenth Century," in *Culture and Identity in Early Modern Europe (1500–1800): Essays in Honor of Natalie Zemon Davis*, ed. Barbara B. Diefendorf and Carla Hesse (Ann Arbor, Mich.: University of Michigan Press, 1993), 41–63; Howard Slenk, "The Huguenot Psalter in the Low Countries" (Ph.D. diss., Ohio State University, 1965), 200ff.; and John Leith, *Introduction to the Reformed Tradition* (Atlanta: John Knox, 1981), 186.

86. Pidoux, *Le Psautier Huguenot*, 2:51; and Frank Dobbins, *Music in Renaissance Lyon* (Oxford: Clarendon, 1992), 12. In 1559, three to four thousand Calvinist demonstrators occupied the left bank of the Seine in Paris and paraded while singing psalms. See also Menna Prestwich, "Calvinism in France, 1555–1629," in *International Calvinism, 1541–1715*, ed. Menna Prestwich (Oxford: Clarendon, 1985); and Davis, *Society and Culture in Early Modern France*, 84, 171–72.

87. An additional genre was the paraphrases of psalm texts composed by humanist poets for their sheer poetic value. See I. D. MacFarlane, "Religious Verse in French Neo-

was the virtual explosion of polyphonic settings of the Genevan tunes. In 1547, Louis Bourgeois printed a collection of four-part settings of the Psalms that was published in Lyon, either because of the inadequacy of Genevan printers or because the Genevan council was as yet opposed to their dissemination.[88] Many of the most famous French-speaking composers—Arcadelt, Certon, Goudimel, Janequin, and Le Jeune—would follow his lead. In Geneva, polyphonic music was printed as early as 1554, with thirteen volumes of polyphonic music printed between 1554 and 1559, and twenty-eight volumes printed by the end of the century.[89] In all, over two thousand settings of the Genevan texts and tunes were produced. It comes as no surprise then that one recent commentator has averred that "the complete polyphonic Calvinist repertory [psalm settings, instrumental arrangements, *chanson spirituelle*, and contrafacta] rivals, in quantity at least, the Parisian chanson, the Italian madrigal, and the polyphonic Lutheran chorale."[90]

It is important to note that these settings were *not* intended for liturgical use.[91] Calvin was clear that they did not belong in the liturgy, where only unison, unaccompanied psalms would suffice. Composers,

Latin Poetry," in *Humanism and Reform: The Church in Europe, England, and Scotland, 1400–1643*, ed. James Kirk (Oxford: Blackwell, 1991); and Rikvah Zim, *English Metrical Psalms: Poetry as Praise and Prayer, 1535–1601* (Cambridge: Cambridge University Press, 1987).

88. The collection was entitled *Cinquante Pseaulmes*. The latter view regarding their publication is most common, although both Leslie ("Music and the Arts in Calvin's Geneva," 192) and Pidoux ("History of the Origin of the Genevan Psalter," 33) have argued for the former view. The latter view is reflected, for example, in Suzanne Selinger, *Calvin against Himself: An Inquiry in Intellectual History* (Hamden, Conn.: Archon Books, 1984), 112.

89. Leslie, "Music and the Arts in Calvin's Geneva," 192. These settings are either simple four-part homophonic settings or melismatic. Typically only the first verse of a psalm is set polyphonically. For a more complete discussion of this genre, see Mildred E. Bisgrove, "Sacred Choral Music in the Calvinistic Tradition of the Protestant Reformation in Switzerland and France, 1541–1600" (Ph.D. diss., New York University, 1969).

90. Slenk, "Psalms, Metrical," 352. This influence may have extended outside Calvinism, as Slenk observes, "Although the Marot-De Bèze texts and their melodies were early associated with the Calvinist movement, they were for a time considered common artistic property. . . . They attracted both Catholic and Protestant composers" ("The Huguenot Psalter in the Low Countries," 237–38); see also Dobbins, *Music in Renaissance Lyon*, 259. Further work could helpfully compare this development in the Low Countries with the use of the Genevan tunes elsewhere.

91. This assertion is contested by Ludwig Finscher, "Psalm," in *Musik in Geschichte und Gegenwart*, vol. 10 (Kassel: Bärenreiter-Verlag, 1962), col. 1706, who, in turn, is soundly countered by Pierre Pidoux, "Polyphonic Settings of the Genevan Psalter: Are They Church Music?" in *Cantors at the Crossroads*, ed. J. Riedel (St. Louis: Concordia, 1967).

it would seem, were ready to comply. As Claude Goudimel penned in the preface of one volume of his polyphonic settings, "We have added three parts to the psalm tunes in this volume: not that they may be sung thus in the church, but that they may be used to rejoice in God particularly in the homes."[92] Similarly, a later preface records, "You have, then, what seems to be sufficient to give honest contentment to the Christians who will help themselves with this book, bringing it to the general assemblies, and singing [the Psalms] according to the customary fashion as well as using it for private enjoyment."[93] This passage suggests that a single publication was used both in liturgical assemblies, where only the melody was sung, and in the home, where a full polyphonic texture could be enjoyed.

The second genre, the contrafacta, consisted of musical examples in which either the text or the tune was borrowed from a previously existing source. By the mid-sixteenth century, such parody techniques already had a long history. In Calvin's Geneva, it is possible that both the texts and the tunes of the psalter had a life of their own independent of each other. The metrical psalm texts were occasionally paired with completely different, often polyphonic, music. Just as Francis I and the members of the French royal family had sung Marot's metrical texts to their own tunes,[94] so now these texts were paired with music other than the official, liturgical tunes. The purpose of this genre was to sanctify the otherwise secular music of notable chanson composers, chief among them Orlando di Lasso.[95] Lasso's music was highly respected, but his choice of texts was not. As one Huguenot printer commented, the texts were "so profane, so dirty and bawdy,

92. Pidoux, "Polyphonic Settings of the Genevan Psalter," 70. As Slenk concludes, "In their prefaces, the composers of the Calvinist repertory stated that they had retained 'the usual melody which is sung in church,' because so many people enjoyed singing the psalms outside of church 'in a more melodious setting,' from the art of music" ("Psalms, Metrical," 351).

93. Pidoux, *Le Psautier Huguenot*, 2:154–55; trans. in Pidoux, "Polyphonic Settings of the Genevan Psalter," 70–71. In one of their more colorful appropriations, these polyphonic settings were also taken up in the Genevan version of the theater. Psalm tunes were used in Joachim Coignac's 1551 *La desconfiture de Goliath*. In 1566, printer Jean Saugrin of Lyon included in the biblical drama *La musique de David* four-part settings of the Ten Commandments, Psalm 55, the *Nunc Dimittis*, and a contrafactum on Psalm 59, with melodies and texts (in all but the latter) straight from the Genevan Psalter. Also, Claude Goudimel likely wrote the music, based on the Psalms, for three dramas by Louis des Masures printed in the same year (see Dobbins, *Music in Renaissance Lyon*, 268–69).

94. See Millar Patrick, *Four Centuries of Scottish Psalmody* (London: Oxford University Press, 1949), 13.

95. Leslie observes that a great deal of music from northern Europe and France was used, but little if any was used from Italy, including none of Palestrina ("Music and the Arts in Calvin's Geneva," 225).

that chaste and Christian ears are horrified by them."[96] So either Lasso's texts were altered, or an entirely new text was imported. Frequently, these texts were psalm texts, and occasionally they were the texts of the Genevan Psalter.[97] In addition, there are examples of new texts being paired with the Genevan psalm tunes.[98] In the preface to one collection issued in Lyon, singers were advised that if they did not understand the printed music, they could simply sing the words to common psalm tunes.[99]

Social Context

The significance of these musical genres is clarified in light of the nature of Genevan society. One remarkable feature of the polyphonic settings of the psalter is their musical sophistication. The more complex settings are a daunting assignment for even the best choirs. As such, they serve as evidence for the growing literate and educated portion of the Genevan populace.[100] Although Geneva began the century, as William Bouwsma has observed, politically and culturally backward, by the 1550s, it was a cultural center.[101] Presumably, the proliferation of these polyphonic psalm settings provides an indication of the ways in which educated Genevan citizens included music as part

96. Quoted in Youens, "Music in the French Reformation and Counter-Reformation," 188. The printer is Pierre Haultin of La Rochelle. This observation is widely shared by recent scholars. Edward Lowinsky referred to these texts as having "an untarnished obscenity such as no other period in the history of music has witnessed" ("Music in Renaissance Culture," 526); see also Leslie, "Music and the Arts in Calvin's Geneva," 204–25.

97. The first five *chansons spirituelles* in Didier Lupi are psalms. See Honegger, *Les Chanson Spirituelles;* Susan Lee Youens, "Huguenot Contrafacta of Secular Chansons: 1555–1597," in "Music in the French Reformation and Counter-Reformation," 173–212; and Hélèn Harvitt, *Eustorg de Beaulieu: A Disciple of Marot* (New York: AMS Press, 1966), 87–114.

98. Youens lists a collection printed in Lyon in 1564 that featured new *chanson spirituelle* texts paired with Genevan tunes.

99. *Cantique chantés au Seigneur* (1564), in Claude Goudimel, *Œuvres complètes* (New York: Institute of Mediaeval Music, 1967–), 14:85–102. See also Dobbins, *Music in Renaissance Lyon*, 265. One *chanson spirituelle*, "Confession de la foy chretienne," used the Genevan tune for Psalm 119 (Laurence Guillo, *Les Éditions musicales de la Renaissance Lyonnaise, 1525–1615* [Paris: Klincksieck, 1991], 58).

100. As Robert Leslie reasons, "The printing of such music in the city during and following the time of Calvin points towards the availability of a musical education of sufficient scope through the Academy as would encourage appreciation for and performance of polyphonic music, as well as a profitable market for the printing of polyphonic music" ("Music and the Arts in Calvin's Geneva," 157). Based on Pidoux's work, Leslie briefly describes the contents of each of these volumes (195–201).

101. William J. Bouwsma, "The Peculiarity of the Reformation in Geneva," in *Religion and Culture in the Renaissance and Reformation*, ed. Steven Ozment (Kirksville, Mo.: Sixteenth Century Journal Publishers, 1989), 70.

of their leisure pursuits. Commenting on the wide range of music publications in Geneva, Robert Leslie has noted, "The fact of their publication in Geneva indicates a musical and religious breadth of mind scarcely associated with the Calvinist reformation."[102]

Nevertheless, there is nothing to give the impression that the tunes and texts of the psalter belonged primarily to the educated elite.[103] In fact, the psalter's largest significance may well have been its influence among the illiterate and uneducated. As Jeannine Olson's research has documented, even the poor and children in care of hospitals were provided with psalters. Indeed, if a poor Genevan citizen had any book, it was just as likely to be a psalter as a Bible or a catechism.[104] If, as Robert Scribner has argued, "the Reformation was made not just by many individuals holding a common belief, but by collective forms of behavior,"[105] then metrical psalm singing was a maker of the Reformation. If, as Steven Ozment has argued, the Reformation was a "lay enlightenment" brought about by vernacular publications and a "bold religious certitude,"[106] then psalm singing was likely both a cause of and evidence for the upsurge of new forms of lay piety. Calvin wrote eloquently of songs "imprinted on our memory," that we may "never to cease singing them."[107] For this, no education or literacy were required. Although conceived and produced by the likes of Calvin, Marot, and

102. This comment is related to the publication of Latin works. Leslie continued, "Such works would not have been printed, much less re-printed, without the approval of Calvin and the Company of Pastors, whose agreement to their appearance and use allowed musically proficient Genevese to stay in contact with musical developments in the rest of Europe" ("Music and the Arts in Calvin's Geneva," 205).

103. In her study of "cheap print" in England, Tessa Watt argues that "the evidence of cheap print questions the rigidity of this 'polarization' of experience between godly and ungodly, elite and poor. In these cheapest of printed wares, Protestant doctrine and conservative piety were integrated" (*Cheap Print and Popular Piety*, 326). See also Roger Chartier, *The Cultural Uses of Print in Early Modern France*, trans. Lydia G. Cochrane (Princeton: Princeton University Press, 1953).

104. Jeannine E. Olson, *Calvin and Social Welfare: Deacons and the Bourse Française* (Selinsgrove: Susquehanna University Press, 1989). A large-print psalter was even given to one poor man (54, 237 n. 14). The hospital provided psalters for children (225 n. 10) along with Bibles. If a poor Genevan citizen had any book, it was likely a psalter, Bible, or catechism (74). This is even more striking when we realize how early this is in the history of printed books. For many, the Bible, psalter, or catechism was likely one of the first printed books they or anyone in their family owned. The distribution of psalters was a primary missionary activity of the Geneva Bourse Française (50ff.).

105. Robert Scribner, "Is There a Social History of the Reformation?" *Social History* 4 (1976): 501, quoted in Heiko A. Oberman, "Die Gelehrten die Verkehrten: Popular Response to Learned Culture in the Renaissance and Reformation," in *Religion and Culture in the Renaissance and Reformation*, 43.

106. Steven E. Ozment, *The Reformation in the Cities* (New Haven: Yale University Press, 1975), 165.

107. OS, 2:17; "Letter to the Reader," 164.

Bourgeois, the psalter was no respecter of class. In the culture of oral-
ity that still pervaded so much of the populace, the psalter joined the
sermon and the catechism as the chief means of spiritual formation.[108]

The Spirituality of the Psalter in Calvin's Geneva

So what does all this say about the shape of piety in Calvin's Geneva?
Neither Geneva nor any other Reformation city could claim to have pioneered a psalm-based spirituality.[109] The Psalms had been ever present
in the medieval period in everything from the Benedictine office to medieval vernacular psalters.[110] Nevertheless, the particular pattern of
singing the Psalms that was given definitive shape in Calvin's Geneva
was a significant development for the typical Genevan citizen. What
was new included the singing of whole or large portions of individual
psalms rather than the versicles used in the medieval mass; the use of
metrical reworkings of the text rather than the Psalms themselves; the
use of the vernacular rather than church Latin; the singing of the
Psalms by the entire congregation, not just the *schola cantorum;* and finally, the prevalent use of the Psalms outside the liturgy.[111] Perhaps
three statements serve to summarize the nature of this piety.

108. I am not suggesting that the mere fact of the psalter's existence automatically
signals the presence of a vibrant lay spirituality, but rather that to the extent that such
piety was present, it was the psalter, sermon, and catechism that were significant in
shaping it. See Ozment, *Reformation in the Cities,* 15ff.; and R. A. Houston, *Literacy in
Early Modern Europe* (London and New York: Longman, 1988), 57, 106. The Psalms,
along with the catechism, Ten Commandments, creed, and Lord's Prayer, were an important part of the growth of European literacy. The use of readings and songs as "propaganda" for the nonliterate is explored in Natalie Davis, "The Protestant Printing
Workers of Lyons in 1551," in *Aspects de la propagande religieuse,* ed. G. Berthaud et al.
(Geneva: Droz, 1957).
109. As Ford Lewis Battles observed in this connection, "One of the mysteries of the
Hebrew-Christian tradition is that so many pieties, so many ways of worship, can derive from the same book" (*Piety of John Calvin,* 10).
110. On the role of the psalter in medieval devotion, see Richard Kieckhefer, "Major
Currents in Late Medieval Devotions," in *Christian Spirituality: High Middle Ages and
the Reformation,* vol. 2, ed. Jill Raitt (New York: Crossroad, 1987). The piety of medieval
Geneva is discussed in Henri Naef, *Les Origines de la Réforme à Genève,* vol. 1 (Geneva:
Droz, 1968), 135–55, 171–79, 192–208. For a convenient summary, see William L. Holla-
day, *The Psalms through Three Thousand Years: Prayerbook of a Cloud of Witnesses* (Minneapolis: Fortress, 1993). Historical precedents for metrical psalmody are traced in Cabaniss, "Background of Metrical Psalmody," 191–206. Medieval metrical psalms are
compiled in *Psalteria rhythmica: Gereimte Psalterien des Mittelalters,* 2 vols. (Leipzig:
Riesland, 1900). Much more could be done to explore the influence of medieval metrical psalmody. On vernacular translations of the Psalms, see, for example, Febvre and
Martin, *The Coming of the Book,* 250. Vernacular psalm singing was also introduced
long before this by the Waldensians and Hussites.
111. As such, it bears close resemblance to Lutheran metrical psalmody. See N.
Müller, "Die frühen Wittenberger Psalmlieder im Evangelischen Kirchengesangbuch.

First, at its root, it was a corporate and liturgical spirituality. Calvin had contended that "the chief use of the tongue is in public prayers, which are offered in the assembly of believers, by which it comes about that with one common voice, and as it were with the same mouth, we all glorify God together, worshiping him with one spirit and the same faith."[112] Whether in the nave of St. Pierre's or in a small rural Genevan parish, the center of this spirituality was in the gathered congregation that sang the prescribed psalms week after week to familiar and sturdy tunes.

Second, it was a spirituality of the Word. In her study of print and culture in Strasbourg, Miriam Chrisman suggests that through congregational psalm singing, "the words of Scripture became an intimate part of [the laity's] thoughts and prayers. Music thus played an important role in opening up the Scriptures to the laity. Through singing they became familiar with the Word."[113] There is no reason that the same assessment cannot be made about Geneva.

Finally, this spirituality blurred the distinction between liturgy and life. Whereas Roman Catholic sensibilities preferred a clear line between liturgy and secular life, the Calvinists freely sang these texts and tunes in their homes and fields. The same impulse that led the Reformers to question medieval monasticism and that drove Calvin to extend the influence of the gospel to every nook and cranny of Genevan life was mirrored in the very way these metrical psalters were used.[114]

Reformatorisches Kirchenlied und biblische Hermeneutik," *Jahrbuch für Liturgik und Hymnologie* 26 (1982): 102–17. The chief differences between the Lutheran and Calvinist metrical psalms consist in the differences between French and German prosody and in the fact that Calvinist churches used exclusively psalms in liturgy, whereas Lutheran congregations developed a large repertoire of vernacular hymns.

112. OS, 1:103; 1536 *Institutes* 74. This point is further developed in Barbara Jo Douglas, "Prayers Made with Song: The Genevan Psalter, 1562–1994," in *Pledges of Jubilee: Essays on the Arts and Culture, in Honor of Calvin G. Seerveld,* ed. Lambert Zuidervaart and Henry Luttikhuizen (Grand Rapids: Eerdmans, 1995), 285–307.

113. Miriam Usher Chrisman, *Lay Culture, Learned Culture: Books and Social Change in Strasbourg, 1480–1599* (New Haven: Yale University Press, 1982), 166.

114. This blurring of the lines is not unique to Calvin's Geneva. Christopher Reynolds has recently argued that the sacred/secular distinction is problematic in any interpretation of fifteenth- and sixteenth-century music ("Sacred Polyphony," in *Performance Practice: Music before 1600,* ed. Howard Mayer Brown and Stanley Stadie [New York: Norton, 1989], 185–200); see also Lewis Lockwood, "Music and Religion in the High Renaissance and the Reformation," in *The Pursuit of Holiness in Late Medieval and Renaissance Religion,* ed. Charles Trinkhaus and Heiko A. Oberman (Leiden: Brill, 1974), 500–501.

10

Soul Food
for the People
of God

Dieticians have taught us to live by the maxim "We are what we eat." Our capability for developing muscle tone and warding off diseases is due, in part, to the nutritional value of the food we eat. The same is true for the soul. What goes into our soul shapes who we are. It sculpts our fundamental identity. It provides resources to build spiritual muscles and to ward off spiritual diseases.

And what more soul-shaping force can we imagine than the songs we sing? Even when we are tired or depressed, old songs well up from within us and dance on our plaintive, whistling lips. When we are old and can remember little else, we are still likely to recall the songs learned in childhood. Music has the uncanny ability to burrow its way into our spiritual bones. When it comes to matters of spirituality and faith, we are what we sing.

There is no need to overstate the case. Music is not all-powerful. Many things shape our souls, including our parents' attitudes, our friends' priorities, and our television consumption. But music is certainly among these potent soul-shaping forces. As Aristotle and many since have claimed, music has formative power. It will either corrupt us, inoculate us, or—to use a Pauline phrase—build us up.[1]

---

1. As in 1 Thess. 5:11.

This is especially true of the music we sing in church, for this music is offered in the name of God. The guardians of our liturgical music have much to say about the music that feeds our souls. Pastoral musicians have the important and terrifying priestly task of placing words of sung prayer on people's lips—and not only words but also the melodies that interpret those words and give them affective shape. This happens every time they choose a song and accompany a hymn. Such musicians also have the holy task of being stewards of God's Word. Choices of which anthem texts and theological themes will be featured in worship represent a degree of control over people's spiritual diets. To say it in a sentence, to be a church musician—and by extension, a music editor, hymnal committee member, or church music professor—is to be a spiritual dietician.

This food metaphor is not uncommon in the world of religion. We speak of liturgical or musical "taste," of liturgical "menus." We even buy books with titles such as *Chicken Soup for the Christian Soul*. But have we paused to learn from this metaphor? Have we considered its implications for the way we live and worship?

Let us consider another aspect of life. Our ability to handle time wisely can be enlightened once we discover how consistently we speak of time in language derived from commerce (we speak of time as money, something to be spent, saved, and invested). We can learn a great deal about our culture's view of an argument when we realize how often we speak of arguments using the language of war (the argument is either won or lost). These and other common metaphors become instructive when we use them self-consciously, with consideration. After all, metaphors, according to Nelson Goodman, consist of "teaching an old word new tricks."[2] Further, extended metaphors, what Max Black calls "sustained and systematic metaphors" or "models," have the potential to open up new meaning for us, to go beyond what we intended when we first used the term.[3] A metaphor, says Colin Gunton, is a "vehicle of discovery." In the words of Vincent Brümmer, metaphors "enable us to see those features of the world which we have been conditioned to overlook." Janet Soskice adds, "A good metaphor may not simply be an oblique reference to a predetermined subject but a new vision, the birth of new understanding, a new referential access. A strong metaphor compels new possibilities of vision." Gail Ramshaw speaks of the "moment of tension" in which "the

2. Nelson Goodman, *Languages of Art* (Indianapolis: Hackett Publishing, 1976), 69, 73.

3. Max Black, *Models and Metaphors: Studies in Language and Philosophy* (Ithaca, N.Y.: Cornell University Press, 1962), 236.

human imagination discovers that the odd word [metaphor] is more profoundly true than factual description."[4]

Happily, recent language theorists have given us permission to analyze the metaphors we use. As Donald Davidson observes, "Many of us need help if we are to see what the author of a metaphor wanted us to see and what a more sensitive or educated reader grasps." Davidson goes on to suggest that "the legitimate function of so-called paraphrase is to make the lazy or ignorant reader have a vision like that of a skilled critic."[5] Davidson's words echo a similar point made by Black. He argues that explaining a metaphor need not weaken its appeal or force: "Explication or elaboration of the metaphor's grounds, if not regarded as an adequate cognitive substitute for the original, may be extremely valuable. A powerful metaphor will not more be harmed by such probing than a musical masterpiece by analysis of its harmonic and melodic structure."[6] I take these words as permission to analyze my metaphor of choice—nearly, but not, I trust, to the point of death.

I want to suggest that our practice and understanding of ritual and liturgical music can be enlightened by considering this fairly pedestrian metaphor (congregational song as food) and developing this metaphor as a model, a comprehensive way of thinking. I suggest that the virtue of this metaphor is not only its aptness but also its accessibility. Philosopher of language Andrew Ortony lauds good metaphors as being able to "achieve a certain communicative compactness, since all the applicable predicates belonging to the metaphorical vehicle are implied succinctly through the vehicle itself."[7] In other words, this food metaphor can generate twenty pages of analysis, with a few dozen footnotes. But at the same time, any parish musician can write a one-page newsletter article about liturgical music as "soul food" and be reasonably assured that most readers will understand the message.[8]

At the start, we should note that food is not the only metaphor that

4. Colin Gunton, *The Actuality of the Atonement: A Study of Metaphor, Rationality, and the Christian Tradition* (Grand Rapids: Eerdmans, 1989), 31; Vincent Brümmer, *Model of Love* (Cambridge: Cambridge University Press, 1993), 10; Janet Soskice, *Metaphor and Religious Language* (Oxford: Clarendon Press, 1985), 57–58; Gail Ramshaw, *Liturgical Language: Keeping It Metaphoric, Making It Inclusive* (Collegeville, Minn.: Liturgical Press, 1996), 7–8.

5. Donald Davidson, "What Metaphors Mean," in *Philosophy of Language*, ed. A. P. Martinich (New York: Oxford University Press, 1990), 440.

6. Black, *Models and Metaphors*, 46. For more on this theme, see my "Metaphor in Liturgical Studies: Lessons from Philosophical and Theological Theories of Language," *Liturgy Digest* 4, no. 1 (1997): 7–45.

7. Andrew Ortony, "Metaphor," in *The Oxford Companion to the Mind*, ed. Richard L. Gregory (New York: Oxford University Press, 1987), 480.

8. In this chapter, read the text as an address to the broad audience and the notes as a guide to the conceptual spine beneath the main argument.

can help us think about ritual and liturgical music. We often think about our ritual music in terms of *communication:* A song or performer expresses an emotion from one person to another,[9] or a song accomplishes communication between God and us.[10] Or we think of music as a *commodity*—something to buy, sell, or copyright, something to attract people to our parish or congregation. These images may be helpful to a point. But notice that they conceptualize music as being external to us. Music as soul food paints a verbal picture of something that once ingested becomes indistinguishable from us. It is something that is identity shaping, soul forming, and spiritually nourishing. Let us consider seven dimensions of this metaphor.

Liturgical Music as Spiritual Nourishment

First, consider the straightforward claim that congregational song is a means of spiritual nourishment. Just as the physical substances in our food become building blocks for our physical bodies, so too the textual and musical substances in our singing become the building blocks for our life of faith.[11]

9. This is also the force of most expressivist aesthetic theories. Leo Tolstoy, for one, believed that the expressive qualities of art allowed it to be a primary form for communicating emotion: "To evoke in oneself a feeling one has once experienced and having evoked it in oneself then by means of movement, lines, colours, sounds, or forms expressed in words, so to transmit that feeling that others experience the same feeling—that is the activity of art. Art is a human activity consisting in this, that one . . . consciously by means of certain external signs, hands on to others feelings he has lived through, and that others are infected by these feelings and also experience them" (Leo Tolstoy, "What Is Art?" in *Art and Philosophy: Readings in Aesthetics,* 2d ed., ed. W. E. Kennick [New York: St. Martin's Press, 1964], 10). Passages such as this have encouraged the use of communication metaphors for understanding the way in which art works. Thus, terms such as *sender* and *receiver* are applied to particular dimensions of aesthetic experience.

10. This fits naturally with one of the most prominent metaphors or models for worship—that of personal encounter. For example, in their textbook on worship, Duncan Forrester, James McDonald, and Gian Tellini define worship as follows: "Worship is therefore both a personal and a corporate encounter with God. . . . We understand worship as being an encounter with God, which can be illumined by analogies with encounters among human beings. An encounter takes place between people; it is inter-subjective. . . . The whole Christian understanding of God and his dealings with people rules out an understanding of worship which is less than a personal meeting. Christian worship is not awe in the face of an irresistible and unresponsive Power, nor is it the attempt to manipulate by magic or placate by offerings remote deities or the forces of nature. Christian worship is an 'I-Thou,' not an 'I-It' relationship" (Duncan Forrester, James I. H. McDonald, and Gian Tellini, *Encounter with God,* 2d ed. [Edinburgh: T & T Clark, 1996], 40, 53). Here the root metaphor for worship is a personal metaphor: Worship is like the interaction or encounter between two personal subjects.

11. For more on the role of music in the fullness of the Christian life, see Don E. Saliers, "Singing Our Lives," in *Practicing Our Faith: A Way of Life for Singing People,* ed. Dorothy C. Bass (San Francisco: Jossey-Bass Publishers, 1997), 179–93.

That this is so is a matter of simple testimony. Any of us could name people in our congregations who have faced the death of a loved one, battled back from disease, or survived an abusive relationship in part because the church's songs lived in their souls. As we sing, we learn the songs that we will hum to ourselves in moments of deep despair. Our songs of lament and hope form us as people of faith and hope. Gospel musician Thomas Dorsey set the poignant words of "Precious Lord, Take My Hand" to music after the death of his infant son and wife. At every step of our encounter with death, music is surely one divine grace that enables us to keep going. In moments when words fail us, music gives us something to say. It gives us a way of expressing our lament and our hope. Death isolates us; it leaves us alone. Singing together is the one act that protests this solitude of suffering. One wise pastoral musician said that every week as she led congregational singing, she was rehearsing the congregation for a future funeral. (This makes me wonder, What if we planned our music with this as a primary goal? "Musician, why did you choose that piece of music?" "Well, it fit the texts of the day, it was well crafted, it challenged us musically—but mostly I picked it because you'll need to know that piece when your family is preparing to bury a loved one.")

Good music can also inoculate us from spiritual disease. Consider the prominent spiritual disease of sentimentality: religious experience as candy-coated happiness and bliss. If we feed our souls a steady diet of musical candy, we will have little spiritual protein to sustain us. This is no more true than at Christmas. Here is a time of year when broken and hurting and grieving people often hurt the most. And yet it is a time of year when we most often serve up rank sentimentality in our music. This can happen as easily with music sung by pop artists as with music sung by English choir boys. Even really good choirs often sing many songs that are lullabies to Jesus or that are about three ships sailing in or about unknown words such as *fum* or about swinging steeple bells or merry gentlemen not being dismayed—all of which prevent us from focusing on the incomprehensible paradox of the incarnation. When the incarnation *does* come through, when we do sing "Hark, the Herald Angels Sing" (one of the most theologically profound of all carols) and actually attend to the meaning of the text, our souls are fed with the protein of deep spiritual life.

But how does this nourishment happen? Our bodies break down food by means of various gastric acids. What is the mechanism by which music turns into spiritual nourishment? Consider three possibilities: the mechanisms of mental imagination, the sheer physicality of singing, and the sculpting of emotional space.[12]

---

12. This point is similar to that of ritual theorists who have begun to probe the biological roots and by-products of ritual action. See, for example, Tom F. Driver, *The*

First, mental imagination: The more our minds are impressed by the pictorial language of the texts we sing, the more the images in these texts shape our souls. My wife does psychophysiology research in which she hooks people up to little electrodes, has them imagine things, and monitors their heart rate, sweat, and blood pressure. As people imagine different scenes, their physiology changes predictably. Our bodies react to vivid narrative and images, bearing witness to the close relationships among cognition, emotion, and physiology.

Her methodology has me imagining testing people in the pew. Imagine that we could produce a printout of our physiological responses to various liturgical images, music, or narratives. Especially vivid and compelling images and especially poignant music would, we might safely conjecture, register a physiological response. Aside from the physiological response, we know by simple testimony that the images, sounds, and narratives of sung prayer have powerful force to shape our souls. Occasionally, a text will name an experience we all know about but have never been able to express. (My gold medal here goes to Fred Pratt Green for "a new dimension in the world of sound" in the hymn "When in Our Music God Is Glorified," and my silver goes to Isaac Watts's "What language shall I borrow to thank thee, dearest friend.") Occasionally, such texts are so forceful that they give us a new way of thinking, praying, or even living.

Second, congregational song becomes nourishing soul food through the physical exertion of singing. Part of music's power derives from its physicality. Music requires breath. One thing that distinguishes song from speech is the sustained breath it requires. At our birth, God breathed into us the breath of life. In our singing, we return that breath to the giver. Athletic skill is a matter of muscle memory. So is singing. Singing is athletic. It depends on physical exertion. Good athletes can shift gears—muscularly speaking. Congregations must too. Try singing your favorite hymn like an operatic soloist. Notice what it demands physically. Now sing it as a lazy and tired parishioner whose spouse dragged him or her to the early service. One expe-

Magic of Ritual (San Francisco: HarperSanFrancisco, 1991), chap. 5; and Rebecca J. Slough, "'Let Every Tongue, by Art Refined, Mingle Its Softest Notes with Mine': An Exploration of Hymn-Singing Events and Dimensions of Knowing," in *Religious and Social Ritual: Interdisciplinary Explorations,* ed. Michael B. Aune and Valerie DeMarinis (Albany, N.Y.: State University of New York Press, 1996), 175–206. As Slough concludes, "Hymn-singing events are an intersection of ritual action, social psychology, art, theology, and spirituality that deserves attention. Explorations of these events could help illuminate the noetic qualities of various types of relationships that are set in motion through ritual and the intersubjective nature of ritual action in general. Knowledge of the ritual participant as a social and interrelated self is needed to understand better how ritual action specifically changes his or her relationships, ideas, affections, and/or faith" (200).

rience will shape the soul for good, the other probably won't. One reason we remember songs we have sung is that our physical exertion is a means of imprinting the memory of a song on our soul. No wonder that John Calvin argued that "singing has great strength and power to move and to set our hearts on fire in order that we may call on God and praise him with a more vehement and more ardent zeal."[13]

Third, music unconsciously sculpts the emotional contours of our religious experience. Aside from the text, music is a significant language in its own right. It is more than a shell for the text. The music we sing shapes the affections of our souls. It gives emotional content to the text. It interprets the text. Each of music's building blocks—melody, rhythm, harmony—has power and force. Poorly chosen music can trivialize a text. Well-crafted music can make even a banal text tolerable. Take the three-word text "Eat this bread." Music can make that single text mysterious, sentimental, celebratory, funereal, or meditative. Whatever systematic theologians have to say about the eucharist, lived sacramental theology (the theology by which most people live each day) more often is written by the mood or ethos the music at our sacramental celebrations evokes. Our better hymnals and anthem collections provide eucharistic music that expresses the full range of emotion, from quiet meditation to exuberant thanksgiving.

Liturgical-Musical Diets

Second, this nourishment comes to us through patterns and habits of reception: We all have a discernible liturgical-musical diet. We also have many options for a liturgical-musical diet. Arguably, no other religion in recorded history features such a dazzling variety of music—everything from elaborate Byzantine chant to exuberant Methodist frontier songs; from the Dionysian ecstasy of the Toronto Laughter to the Apollonian reserve of a Presbyterian metrical psalm; from the trancelike music of Taizé refrains to the precise, classical, rhetorical patterns of Watts and Wesley; from the serene beauty of a Palestrina motet to the rugged earthiness of an Appalachian gospel quartet; from the enforced silence of Quaker corporate mysticism to the sustained exuberance of an African American ring shout sermon. Given this wide range of choices, the patterns our choices make reveal much about the angularities of our spiritual life and the spiritual life of our congregations. In fact, sometimes the more variety a grocery store has, the more conservative our actual shopping choices become—we recoil from the variety.

13. John Calvin, preface to *The Form of Prayers and Ecclesiastical Songs*, in *Ioannis Calvini Opera Selecta*, ed. Peter Barth, Wilhelm Niesel, and Dora Scheuner, vol. 2 (Munich: C. Kaiser, 1952), 15.

238   Musical Studies

Although we have many options, we have a limited number of choices. Our diets are limited. Physically, we consume roughly eleven hundred meals a year—a number that allows for astonishing (but still limited) variety. Musically, in our congregations, we are even more limited. Suppose that your congregation sings five hymns or songs per Sunday service. Suppose that a faithful member of your congregation is present at forty-five of those services per year—allowing for three weeks of vacation, two weeks of visiting family, and two weeks of illness. That worshiper will sing a total of 225 hymns per year. But, of course, some of those hymns will be sung more than once. If fifteen of those hymns are sung three times and twenty-five are sung twice, this parishioner will sing no more than 170 different hymns each year—and that number includes Christmas carols. How many of those hymns does this worshiper really know? Except for a few remarkable and vivid examples, hymns sung just once will probably not become a part of this worshiper's musical makeup (though some hymns are known so well that they are a part of the makeup of a congregation even if they are not sung often).

So for the sake of argument, let us suppose that an average worshiper (musically speaking) really knows 150 hymns, three to four psalm tones or tunes (depending on your tradition), and two settings of the liturgy (probably all generous assumptions). The musical connoisseurs may know more.

If this is the case, then we have a very difficult job. In effect, this means that a working repertoire in a given congregation is about 30 percent of the total number of selections in any respectable hymnal. And this diet needs to include everything that is spiritually healthy. It must include the entire range of Christian affections: thanksgiving, supplication, lament. It must narrate the entire Christian story: creation; fall; Christ's birth, teaching, suffering, death, resurrection, and ascension; the sending of the Spirit; and the coming of the kingdom of God. It must include hymns concerning the entire range of Christian teaching: social justice, evangelistic witness, and prayer. It should include selections from a range of cultural locations and ethnic communities—in both time and space—in order to introduce us to the native prayer language of many parts of the holy, catholic church. It should include songs in a variety of emotional registers, from the contemplative to the exuberant. Further, this diet needs to include songs of ethnic religious identity, whether "Lord, You Have Come to the Lakeshore," "Lift Every Voice and Sing," or "I Am So Glad Each Christmas Eve."

Let us suppose that a healthy diet includes some new selections every year, lest the congregation's diet ossify and die. But, of course, too many new selections will overwhelm a congregation and set members on the difficult journey of endless innovation. So suppose we can effectively add ten selections to this diet every year. (We may do more than ten new things, but only ten will stick and become a part of this diet.) And if this happens, then ten things will drop off the list.

In sum, every congregation has a different musical diet. Some perhaps know 250 or even 300 selections well. Some know no more than 100. Some know a higher percentage of service music or psalm tones or tunes; others know a higher percentage of hymnody. But everyone has an identifiable diet, and that diet says a great deal about the forces that shape our souls. And this little math exercise, however artificial, is instructive in another way. We need to be careful about which ten new things we will learn each year, for a congregation's knowledge is limited.

Feeding as an Event

Third, in our culture and perhaps in most cultures since the dawn of time, food is about a lot more than feeding. Eating is a social act. We eat to cement friendships, to close business deals, or to nurture a romantic relationship. If food were just about feeding, we could attach an automatic feeder to ourselves—a sort of permanent IV—to help us get this task out of the way quickly. That is silly. And so is singing for its own sake, singing for the sake of simply manipulating sound or making various noises. We sing together for a purpose, to accomplish a task.

After a date, we would be frustrated if the person we were seeing said, "The salads were wonderful tonight, thank you" and said nothing about us. The point of a date is the relationship, not the food. The point of a business lunch is the business deal. The point of worship is God. The point of liturgy is to enact the relationship we have with God in Christ through the work of the Holy Spirit. Just as a date is diminished without food, so our worship is impoverished without music. But the date does not exist for food, and worship does not exist for the sake of the music. That is why John Wesley advised, "Above all, sing spiritually. Have an eye to God in every word you sing. Aim at pleasing him more than yourself, or any other creature. In order to do this attend strictly to the sense of what you sing, and see that your heart is not carried away with the sound, but offered to God continually; so shall your singing be such as the Lord will approve here, and reward you when he cometh in the clouds of heaven."[14]

Liturgical music finds its highest purpose in the enactment of the liturgy. A primary criterion for liturgical music is whether it serves or enables liturgical action. Liturgical music is not an end in itself. It is a

14. From *Select Hymns*, 1761, quoted in preface to *The United Methodist Hymnal* (Nashville: United Methodist Publishing House, 1989), vii.

means for enabling corporate prayer. The highest purpose of liturgical music is to enable full, conscious, and active liturgical participation at the deepest level possible for people of all sorts.

If the main point of Christian worship is to engage in a series of personal, relational actions between the gathered community and its Creator (e.g., confessing sin, praising God, interceding for divine intervention), then good congregational song enables these actions to be accomplished. Music is one means of expression, like speech or dance, by which people accomplish certain actions.[15]

While we can easily agree with this, we often fail to choose music to accomplish the particular purposes of the liturgy. We often choose music that is in the ballpark of the texts of the day and declare our liturgical planning good enough. Just as preachers sometimes have a sermon to preach that is in search of a text, we have a hymn or psalm to sing that is in search of a proper liturgical slot. We get the theme right but fail to reach the standard of the liturgical purpose of music.

We also often fail to develop conversational habits that reflect a functional understanding of music in worship. Walking away from a worship service and saying, "That organist played a fabulous introduction to the opening hymn" is like walking away from a dinner party and saying, "The wine was especially fragrant." It may be altogether true—but beside the point. It would be much better to say, "Today that music helped me to pray."

This way of thinking also helps us avoid another temptation: thinking of music as the means of God's revelation. Not long ago I received a call from an ordained pastor asking advice on finding a worship leader. I asked, "What are you looking for?" The answer? "Someone who can make God present in our midst" (a rather loaded expectation). We might call it "musical transubstantiation." No medieval sacramental theologian could have put it in stronger terms. Language like this is increasingly present in want ads for parish musicians. Increasingly, churches are looking for people whose creativity, personal testimony, and charismatic personality can turn an ordinary moment into a holy moment. This tendency is not limited to charismatics.

15. Variations on this theme have been developed by a diverse group of theorists, including Cipriano Vagaggini, Gerardus van der Leeuw, John Foley, and Nicholas Wolterstorff. See, for example, the following statements. Cipriano Vagaggini: "In the same way, it is not because of any value of its own that art is entitled to admission into the liturgy, but in so far as it can serve the liturgy's particular end, in so far as it can help the church express her worship or sanctify the faithful" (*Theological Dimensions of the Liturgy*, trans. Leonard J. Doyle and W. A. Jurgens [Collegeville, Minn.: Liturgical Press, 1976], 32); Gerardus Vander Leeuw: "It is obvious that music used in worship must have its own style, its own character, which is determined by the form of worship and its historical development" (*Sacred and Profane Beauty: The Holy in Art* [London:

Churches with names like Community Church of the Happy Valley and St. Stephen's in the Swamp may well tend to hire musicians who can make holy moments such as these. One does it with a general piston no. 8, and one does it with a microphone and a drum set—but both are striving to make God present in a true if elusive sense.

Certainly this concern for attending to holy moments is important. Yet no one, no matter how charismatic, can make a moment holy by their own creativity, ingenuity, or effort. Scripture records a long line of those who tried: the prophets of Baal at Carmel, the servant who wanted to support the ark as it moved, the magician Simon Magus. I am told that at the dedication of the concert hall and chapel at Luther College, Westin Nobel chose the anthem on the Pauline text "God does not dwell in temples made of human hands," a powerful reminder that God's presence is to be received as a gift. It cannot be engineered or produced. Those of us who are called to be liturgical musicians must understand both the prospects and the limitations of our role.

Weidenfield and Nicolson, 1963], 270); Nicholas Wolterstorff: "Good liturgical art is art that serves effectively the actions of the liturgy . . . enabling the actions to be performed with clarity . . . without tending to distract persons from the performance of the action . . . [and] without undo awkwardness and difficulty," and also, "The Christian liturgy is a sequence of actions: confession, proclamation of forgiveness, praise, and so forth. And works of art—passages of music, for example—can be more or less fitting to these distinct actions. What fits the act of confession well may be quite unfitting to the action of praise." And later, "It is habitual for musicians trained within our institution of high art to approach the music of the liturgy by insisting that it be good music, and to justify that insistence by saying that God wants us to present our very best to Him—all the while judging good music not by reference of the purposes of the liturgy but by reference to the purpose of aesthetic contemplation" (*Art in Action: Toward a Christian Aesthetic* [Grand Rapids: Eerdmans, 1980], 185, 116, 184). John Foley: "We have to understand liturgy itself in order to see how music and the other arts operate within the liturgy, for the purposes of it, rather than outside it for other purposes. . . . Music, dance, homiletics, gesture, and decoration partake of this overarching form, each contributing its own substance to liturgy's semblance. . . . Composers, musicians, choreographers, etc., must be masters first of the liturgy and only then artists of their art form" (*Creativity and the Roots of Liturgy* [Washington, D.C.: Pastoral Press, 1994], 4, 268). "*Appropriateness* is another demand that liturgy rightfully makes upon any art that would serve its action. The work of art must be appropriate in two ways: 1) it must be capable of bearing the weight of mystery, awe, reverence, and wonder which the liturgical action expresses; 2) it must clearly *serve* (and not interrupt) ritual action, which has its own structure, rhythm and movement." And, "If an art form is used in liturgy it must aid and serve the action of liturgy since liturgy has its own structure, rhythm, and pace: a gathering, a building up, a climax, and a descent to dismissal. It alternates between persons and groups of persons, between sound and silence, speech and song, movement and stillness, proclamation and reflection, word and action. The art form must never seem to interrupt, replace, or bring the course of liturgy to a halt" (*Environment and Art in Catholic Worship* [Washington, D.C.: United States Catholic Conference, 1978], no. 21, no. 25). This is a self-conscious repudiation of purist art-for-art's-sake aesthetic theories.

Liturgical-Musical Taste, Liturgical-Musical Etiquette

Fourth, appropriating food well requires skills. It requires cultivating table etiquette and good taste. Parents spend a great deal of time cultivating these skills in their children: a sense of adventure and willingness to try new things, self-control or knowing when to quit, good judgment for understanding what a balanced diet is, discipline to eat according to a healthy diet, the ability to savor food and not to gorge oneself. Then there is a second set of skills that helps us move beyond childhood manners to become genuine connoisseurs: discernment about good and better items, knowledge about the way in which a food functions in its culture, knowledge of ingredients and the ability to discern them while eating.

Similar skills are needed to receive the gift of music well. At the basic level, we need a willingness to try new things, judgment about theological soundness, discipline to avoid simple self-gratification. We need full, conscious, active participation in our liturgical music making. There are also skills that will help us become connoisseurs, but cultivating these skills is a luxury that most of us do not have. We are in congregations that need remedial work.

In a brilliant and winsome chapter in his book *Religious Aesthetics*, Frank Burch Brown identifies four aesthetic sins (identified with four types of people) that apply to food and congregational song equally well. First, there is the aesthete, the person who loves his or her Bach straight and could not care less if that music enables liturgical action. In Burch Brown's words, this is "the person whose chief goal is not glorifying and enjoying God but glorying in the aesthetic delights of creation." Second, there is the philistine, the one who "does not highly value or personally appreciate anything artistic and aesthetic that cannot be translated into practical, moral, or specifically religious terms." This is the sin, Burch Brown notes, that is exposed in Alice Walker's *The Color Purple*, in which Shug says to Celie, "I think it pisses God off if you walk by the color purple in a field somewhere and don't notice it." Third, there is the intolerant, the one who "is keenly aware of aesthetic standards of appraisal, but elevates his or her own standards to the level of absolutes. . . . [It is] the aesthetic equivalent of the sin of pride. . . . It severs human ties and does violence to the freedom, integrity, and self-hood of others." This is a temptation that particularly confronts the intellectual and cultural elite. Fourth, there is the indiscriminate, the one whose "radical aesthetic relativism . . . indiscriminately [embraces] all aesthetic phenomena." Such people "cannot even distinguish between what in their own experience has relatively lasting value and what is just superficially appealing."[16]

16. Frank Burch Brown, *Religious Aesthetics* (Princeton: Princeton University Press, 1989), 152–56.

Let us frankly acknowledge that in this area we have many problems. All of us have a different prayer of confession to offer. Indeed, many in our congregations are like babies who refuse to try a new variety of Gerbers: When confronted with anything interesting, they simply close their mouths. Some are ashamed, some embarrassed. Some are musically free but emotionally constipated. Others are filled with both sophistication and arrogance. Some are sophisticated but indiscriminate: We've never met a hymn we didn't like.

Happily, such vices are not the only story. Moments of liturgical-musical virtue happen too. One week some worshipers express delight in their discovery of a canticle, psalm, or hymn that conveys their prayers better than they could have done themselves. Another time a worshiper with a chest cold is not able to sing and for the first time listens to the sounds of corporate singing around him and is moved by the power of this common expression. Perhaps another worshiper, while singing a text, is struck by the power of the thought expressed and adds it as a quotable quote at the bottom of her email signature. Another time your congregation pulls off the unthinkable: They sing a meditative prayer text softly, without singing weakly.

The question for those in positions of liturgical ministry is how to evoke these experiences, how to develop these aptitudes and tastes, to nurture these virtues and transform the corresponding vices. Here we run into two equal and opposite errors: One is not trying at all, the other is trying to engineer the experience through pedantic playing or pedantic explanations.

In general, our efforts to nurture virtuous manners for liturgical-musical reception have been stymied by the claim that good art must speak for itself. Good art does speak for itself, provided we know the language it speaks. Think of an art form about which you know little, perhaps ballet or architecture. Think of how much a teacher or docent could open up the experience of that art form. At a French restaurant, my experience is immeasurably enriched by a server who can invite me into the experience of the culinary delights of the meal. Those of us who serve as church musicians need to not only play music creatively but also teach people the skills to appreciate and receive this gift. We need to cultivate taste. We need, in the words of Alice Parker, "to project our vision," to communicate our expectations and hopes winsomely.[17] And there are many specific, practical ideas to make this happen:

17. Alice Parker, *Melodious Accord* (Chicago: Liturgical Training Publications, 1991), 3.

- For one hymn a week, print in your order of service a way to sing it: "Sing mysteriously," "sing meditatively," "sing with resolve," "sing with gritted teeth." So much new hymnody has an honesty that demands care lest we trivialize what we are singing.
- Lead singing by singing. Imitate John Bell, Alice Parker, or Mary Oyer. You may feel completely vulnerable in doing so, but there is no better way to evoke vocal singing than by use of the human voice.
- Host a living room sing-along for twenty members of your congregation. Sing hymns old and new. Teach taste in the context of warm hospitality.
- Provide a list of good, available recordings of worship music during the Christmas shopping season to help members of your congregation find good recordings of church music (having good sounds in our ears is the first step in genuine appreciation).
- Teach a sixth-grade Christian education class to write new verses to hymns. Then pick the best of their contributions and sing them at the following week's service.
- Twice a month, print a short note in your Sunday bulletin about the music of the day.
- Provide young children in your congregation who are studying piano with good, simplified accompaniments to hymns so they can learn them while young.

It has been said that church music is more like music education than music performance. There is much truth in that claim. Those of us who serve as worship leaders are like mentors in liturgical prayer. But we need to teach not only the prayers to speak but also the language with which to offer them.

The Eater

Fifth, a good cook needs to be aware of those who are eating. The nature of those we are serving makes all the difference for what and how we cook. For your church youth group, you would serve pizza. For a noon Bible study, you might serve chicken salad.

So too in congregational song. We need to prepare music for a wide range of people: young and old, seeker and saint. To do so, we need music that is both well crafted and vernacular. At its best, liturgical music, and especially congregational song—the song of the primary liturgical choir—needs to be readily embraced by people with little musical, poetic, or aesthetic training. At the same time, it needs to be well crafted enough to provide spiritual protein (not merely the carbohydrates we more easily embrace). Erik Routley once defined hymns as "songs for unmusical people to sing together . . . [and] such poetry as unliterary people can utter together."[18] Nicholas Temperley concluded his massive study of English parish church music by saying that "hymns exist for the singers, not for an audience, still less for a critic. If a hymn tune gives pleasure to a musical connoisseur, this must be a merely incidental benefit."[19] By these definitions, hymns are vernacular, radically inculturated forms of expression.

This immediately calls to mind recent work on liturgical inculturation. One of the many contributions of Vatican II to twentieth-century Christian worship was its insistence that liturgical expression reflects the particular cultural milieu of local congregations.[20] Since Vatican II, a small cadre of liturgists has attempted to be self-conscious about the way in which this accommodation—variously termed contextualization, indigenization, inculturation—can best take place. (The Nairobi Statement of the Lutheran World Federation is one of the better examples, arguing that healthy congregations have worship that is self-consciously transcultural, contextual, countercultural, and cross-cultural—all at the same time.)[21] Spurred on by postmodern concern for cultural particularity, this project has been approached enthusiastically by many ecclesiastical traditions. The Roman Catholic Church has produced a much discussed "indigenous rite" for Zaire. Protestants have eagerly encouraged the development of indigenous musical repertoires in Africa, South America, and Southeast Asia.[22]

Significantly, the recent move toward inculturation has both promoted and limited indigenous forms of expression. It has encouraged indigenous forms only insofar as they complement the historic structure of Christian worship. Generally speaking, proponents have argued that Christian worship should arise naturally out of its cultural environment but should also be designed to resist aspects of the cul-

18. Erik Routley, *Christian Hymns Observed* (Princeton: Prestige Publications, 1982), 1.

19. Nicholas Temperley, *The Music of the English Parish Church*, vol. 1 (Cambridge: Cambridge University Press, 1979), 347.

20. This insistence calls to mind John Calvin's admonition that "the upbuilding of the church ought to be vigorously accommodated to the customs of each nation and age" (John Calvin, *Institutes of the Christian Religion*, ed. John T. McNeill, trans. Ford Lewis Battles, Library of Christian Classics, vol. 2 [Philadelphia: Westminster, 1954], 4.10.30).

21. A summary of this statement is printed in Gordon Lathrop, *Holy People: A Liturgical Ecclesiology* (Minneapolis: Fortress, 1999), appendix 1.

22. For an overview, see my "Theological and Conceptual Models for Liturgy and Culture," *Liturgy Digest* 3, no. 2 (summer 1996): 5–46. Typical examples of this work include S. Anita Stauffer, ed., *Worship and Culture in Dialogue* (Geneva: Lutheran World Federation, 1994); idem, "Worship and Culture: Five Theses," *Studia Liturgica* 26 (1996): 323–32; and Anscar Chupungco, *Liturgical Inculturation: Sacramentals, Religiosity, and Catechesis* (Collegeville, Minn.: Liturgical Press, 1992).

ture that run counter to the central tenets of the Christian faith. They have argued that worship should avoid both "cultural irrelevancy" and "cultural capitulation."[23]

The problem here arises when we force a false choice between excellence and accessibility. On the one hand, we might choose well-crafted but inaccessible music and then present it in a patronizing way. Just as a wine snob can rob the joy associated with wine by shaming me in my ignorance of specific French burgundies, so too liturgical musicians can rob worshipers of the joy of their music making by implying that they do not know enough to be proper worshipers. On the other hand, we err equally when we choose vernacular, accessible, but poorly crafted music. The tough music to find is that which is simple without being simplistic, childlike without being childish.

A Community for Eating

Sixth, food is powerfully uniting. In *Babette's Feast*, the concluding celebratory meal brought a sacramental joy rarely experienced. If your worship committee is divided over worship style or musical practices, do not meet in your church parlor. Meet at a nice restaurant. Shared food creates community.

The same is true for music. Music is powerfully uniting. Whether at a Bobby McFerrin concert, a Columbine memorial service, or a Notre Dame football game, music forges first-person-plural experiences. There is nothing quite as powerful as finding yourself in the middle of fifty, five hundred, or fifty thousand people singing. Recall these powerful words of Dietrich Bonhoeffer:

> It is the voice of the Church that is heard in singing together. It is not you that sings, it is the Church that is singing, and you, as a member of the Church, may share in its song. Thus all singing together . . . serves to widen our spiritual horizon, make us see our little company as a member of the great Christian Church on earth, and help us willingly and gladly to join our singing, be it feeble or good, to the song of the Church.[24]

In this way, congregational song differs from many of the genres and institutions of high art in Western culture. In concert music, we value the proficiency of the solo artist. In the context of the liturgy, profi-

23. Kenneth Smits, "Liturgical Reform in a Cultural Perspective," *Worship* 50 (1976): 98.

24. Quoted in Evangelical Lutheran Church in America, *With One Voice* (Minneapolis: Augsburg Fortress, 1995), 5.

ciency is redefined. Here the highest value is enabling a group of musical amateurs to make music together. As Nicholas Wolterstorff argues:

> Liturgical art is not the artist "doing his own thing," the artist "doing her own thing," with the rest of us standing by as appreciators and critics. Liturgical art is the offering of the artist to the liturgical community for *its* praise and confession and intercession. Liturgical art is art on *our* behalf, art enabling *us* to complete the cosmic circle. In liturgical art, the liturgical community finds *its* artful priestly hands and voice.[25]

In liturgical art, no pride of place is offered to the autonomous, solitary, artistic genius. Instead, the liturgical artist is called to take the role of servant, giving worshipers a voice they never knew they had to sing praise and offer prayer to God.

Service as pastoral musician-liturgists requires not only theological and artistic conviction but also hospitality. If we cannot help people enter into the significance and meaning of what we offer, all the best music in the world will be like a "clanging cymbal." The craft and coordinating and "performance" in the work of the church musician find their ultimate goal and purpose in welcoming the people of God to experience the power and joy of profound and communal liturgical participation.

Whom do we welcome to our musical feasts? Do we actually welcome a community? Do our texts have a breadth of viewpoint? Are our tunes more communal than soloistic (vocal embellishments do not work well)? Do we welcome children? Do we welcome people who speak other musical languages? Do our "eating" habits foster community? (Restaurant menus are okay, but if you want a real community experience, order family style. Our churches have suffered from moving from potluck, family style music to liturgical menus from which everyone simply chooses his or her favorites.)

Liturgical Musician as Spiritual Chef

Seventh and finally, we come to the people who make this happen. Good food requires a cook. Congregational music requires a cantor, a church musician, a chief facilitator, an enlivener. A good cook creates meals that are both adventuresome and accessible. There will be potatoes alongside the new soufflé recipe as a sign of comforting familiarity. So too a good cantor always helps us have good encounters with new things and comfortable experiences with well-loved things. A good cook (and musician) is the master of making complex ingredi-

25. Nicholas Wolterstorff, "What Is This Thing—Liturgical Art," in *Art in Worship—Clay and Fiber* (Grand Rapids: Calvin College Center Art Gallery, 1988), 7.

ents come together into something with a winsome simplicity. Both good cooks and good church musicians have fun experiencing the sheer joy of imagination. A good cook can help people appreciate a new dish by explaining something about it. A good musician is a teacher who can invite people into the experience of music. A good cook has imagination for preparing food with visual and olfactory appeal. A good musician prepares music with a winsome and infectious delight. A good cook has restraint. Too much spice kills a dish. So too a liturgical musician: Too much musical folderol kills a hymn. A good cook makes good judgments about fittingness: You would not serve hot dogs at a wedding reception or shrimp cocktail at a campfire. An experienced cook works by instinct. So does a musician. The right tempo is largely a matter of the feeling you have in your gut. A good cook is appreciated but is not the center of attention. The food event is not about the cook. Nor should the church music event be about the musician. When the musician becomes a celebrity, the entire project is endangered. A good cook is sensitive to the specific situation, the specific time and place. The best diet and food preparations are specific. A resident musician, like a resident chef, provides the best leadership and space to respond to last-minute changes, responding to the human situation of a congregation. A good cook is efficient, working with only three to five dishes per meal and a limited budget. Church musicians get four to five hymns per service, a limited number of organ stops, singers, and support. In both cooking and church music, too many helpers ruin the broth, and even in church music there are often too many cooks in the kitchen.

If we have not already crossed the line of decency, we could press this analogy even further. In church music, there are dieticians—publishers and hymnal committees who choose what will be available to us (like supermarket buyers who determine which products will be sold). There are writers, theorists, and professors who write books about what a good diet looks like. There are recipe books: published organ arrangements, instrumental obligatos, liturgical handbooks. There are chefs: parish musicians who actually serve up the dish each week. And there are master chefs: workshop leaders who travel the liturgical conference circuit to give us new ideas.

In both cooking and music, the key element is always the people involved. What the church needs most is not another hymnal, larger choirs, more technology, a revised prayer book, or another set of published scripts. What the church needs most is discerning, prayerful, joyous *people* who treat their work as worship planners and leaders as a holy, pastoral calling. As Alice Parker reminds us, "There are churches in all denominations in this country where congregations do sing well, and it is always because there is at least one person who is actively expecting it."[26]

Nourishment, diet, meal, manners, eater, chef—song, repertoire, liturgy, participation skills, worshiper, pastoral musician. True, this analogy does reach its limits. It does not work in every way. For one, the metaphor may be too strong. Without food, we die. Without music, we simply find other ingredients to take in to our souls; we are simply shaped by other forces. For another, the metaphor may be too passive. Music is something we not only take in but also send out. When we sing, we do not merely ingest. We also project. We need the communication metaphor too.

Despite these necessary caveats, liturgical music as soul food is a metaphor, a model, that is at once clear, accessible, and instructive. In every shopping mall in America, there are bookstores that stock entire rows of books in the Chicken Soup for the Soul series. Maybe these books are spiritually nourishing, but if you want real nourishment, look for something that will *sing* its way deep down into your soul. Books can be broth, all right. But if you want consommé, buy a hymnal.

26. Parker, *Melodious Accord,* 6. For more on the role of the pastoral musician, see Virgil C. Funk, ed., *Pastoral Music in Practice 5: The Pastoral Musician* (Washington, D.C.: Pastoral Press, 1990); and Paul Westermeyer, *The Church Musician,* rev. ed. (Minneapolis: Augsburg, 1997).

11

The Blessing and Bane
of the North American
Evangelical Megachurch

In 1831, Alexis de Tocqueville made a much heralded tour of the young United States of America. The astute French itinerant, whose observations have long been a staple of American cultural history, was especially intrigued by the phenomenon of American religion. "There is," he wrote, "no country in the world where the Christian religion retains a greater influence over the souls of men than in America."

But Tocqueville was struck not only by the relative prominence of religion in America but also by its distinctive character. "In France," he continued, "I had almost always seen the spirit of religion and the spirit of freedom marching in opposite directions. But in America I found they were intimately united and that they reigned in common over the same country. . . . I cannot better describe it," he concluded, "than by styling it a democratic and republican religion."[1]

While much has changed over time, a good deal has also remained the same. The populist impulse in American religious expression is

---

1. Alexis de Tocqueville, *Democracy in America*, ed. J. P. Mayer and Max Lerner (New York: Harper & Row, 1966), 268, 271–72, 265. In the same passage, Tocqueville concludes, "For the Americans the ideas of Christianity and liberty are so completely mingled that it is almost impossible to get them to conceive of the one without the other" (270).

alive and well. It is especially prominent in the large evangelical mega-churches that are now part of the urban landscape in nearly every major metropolitan area.

The vast influence of these congregations demands analysis and comment. My purpose in this chapter is fourfold: to describe the most salient features of worship in megachurches, to analyze what is at the heart of this movement, to offer a strategy to critique it, and to suggest some future challenges for all who are concerned about congregational song. The title is the thesis: The music of the megachurch is both a bane and a blessing. The key task is discerning which of its dimensions fall in each category.

Description

Suppose we define megachurches in terms of two criteria: their large size and their decidedly populist, evangelistic, even entrepreneurial orientation. York Minster would be large enough to qualify but would not be populist enough. An InterVarsity student fellowship group at Cambridge would be populist and evangelistic enough but not large enough. These two criteria would leave us with a pool of roughly four hundred churches in North America, a relatively small, if influential, number of congregations.[2]

In light of this definition, I offer six statements to describe the most salient features of congregational song in these congregations. These comments are intended to be descriptive, not evaluative, the kind of statements that might be offered by a participant-observer cultural anthropologist rather than by a musical or liturgical critic.[3] These statements, which may seem obvious to some, are intended to introduce the topic to those unfamiliar with the North American megachurch.

First, the music of these churches is typically expressed in two distinct forms or genres: the performance-oriented genre of Christian Contemporary Music (i.e., CCM or, more popularly, Christian Rock)[4] and the participation-oriented genre of what have come to be called

2. The numbers are suggested by John Vaughan, a frequent commentator on large congregations in North America. See John Vaughan, *Megachurches and America's Cities* (Grand Rapids: Baker, 1993).

3. For more on the value and limits of phenomenological and social scientific methodologies in the study of Christian worship, see my "For Our Own Purposes: The Appropriation of the Social Sciences in Liturgical Studies," *Liturgy Digest* 2, no. 2 (1995): 6–35.

4. A good sense for the motivation behind this genre can be found in Steve Miller, *The Contemporary Christian Music Debate: Worldly Compromise or Agent of Renewal* (Wheaton: Tyndale, 1993); and Dan Peters, Steve Peters, and Cher Merrill, *What About Christian Rock?* (Minneapolis: Bethany, 1986).

Scripture or praise choruses.[5] Generally speaking, both genres feature several common musical traits: driving, fast-paced rhythms; simple harmonic structures; significant repetition; use of the major mode; and loud accompaniment. In both cases, music is created to sound like commercial, popular music. In this world, prerecorded background tapes, individual microphones for each lead singer, and multi-thousand-dollar sound systems are as common as organ shoes and choir stalls might be in traditional parishes.

Second, the texts of this music are drawn primarily from two sources: from excerpts of scriptural hymns of praise and from narratives of religious experience. In both genres, one of the highest priorities is that the language be vernacular, even colloquial, in style, diction, and form. These are texts of direct discourse, of conversational speech. The language used avoids complexity and nuance and purposely eschews images that are subtle, elusive, and symbolic in favor of intelligibility and accessibility.[6]

Third, music in these congregations is most often led not by an organist or by a trained or amateur choir but by a team of lay worship leaders often called a worship team. These worship teams are a cross between a rock band and a liturgical cantor at a Catholic folk Mass. Like the Good News Band at the Community Church of Joy in Phoenix, Arizona, these teams both perform contemporary music and lead the assembly in singing. In addition to making music, they also serve as liturgists, offering commentary on the music and the progression of the service.

Fourth, music in these four hundred churches is almost always amplified. Acoustic sounds are a foreign musical language in many North American megachurches. We would be hard-pressed to find a megachurch congregation that ever sings without the aid of an expensive, multi-track sound system. This, in turn, influences musical and textual forms. It demands deliberate harmonic rhythms, textual repetition, and a strong rhythmic presence in order to maintain musical ensemble.

Fifth, this music is rendered on a large scale. My first four statements are true not only of megachurches but also of a wide variety of evangelical and Pentecostal churches, summer camps, and university student fellowship groups all over the world. What makes megachurches different is their large scale: music that is offered before an

5. The best sources of music for these congregations are hymnals or song collections published by individual congregations, such as Handt Hanson, *Spirit Touching Spirit: A Contemporary Hymnal* (Burnsville, Minn.: Prince of Peace Publishing, 1987); or several volumes of music published by Willow Creek Community Church (South Barrington, Ill.).

6. See, for example, G. A. Prichard, *Willow Creek Seeker Services: Evaluating a New Way of Doing Church* (Grand Rapids: Baker, 1996), 193.

assembly of two thousand or more people, with a band of fifteen musicians, amplified through twenty to forty speakers in the space of several thousand square feet.

Sixth, there is a persistent if limited role in these congregations for traditional hymnody. Most of them regularly sing a small, select number of hymns, mostly hymns that have burrowed their way into the larger cultural consciousness: "When I Survey the Wondrous Cross"; "Amazing Grace"; "Crown Him with Many Crowns"; "O for a Thousand Tongues to Sing"; "Holy, Holy, Holy"; in addition to several well-known Christmas carols. These hymns are often "repackaged" with simplified harmonic progressions, shortened texts, and added percussion parts but are recognizably the same hymns that can be found in many traditional hymnals.[7]

Interpretation

Using these descriptive statements as a foundation, we move now into interpretation. What is going on underneath the surface? What are some of the cultural, historical, theological dynamics that give this movement its distinctive shape?

First, many North American megachurches find a sense of identity in their approach to worship and music. These churches are often known not by the creeds they profess or by the programs they offer but by the worship, and especially the music, they celebrate. Consequently, they invest a significant amount of time and energy in their music programs. They spend as much money on music as large cathedrals spend on professional choirs, and many of them require auditions for participation in their music program.[8] Their music is not classical or traditional, but it is professional. The words *quality* and *excellence* are as ubiquitous in the magazines and consulting literature of megachurches that promote contemporary worship as they are in sources such as *The Hymn* that promote traditional worship.

Second, megachurches and the populist impulse they represent are nothing new.[9] These megachurches and their music are today's version

---

7. Consultant Sally Morgenthaler, for example, admits that traditional hymns can be acceptable if they are "repackaged" in the "'90s sound" (*Worship Evangelism: Inviting Unbelievers into the Presence of God* [Grand Rapids: Zondervan, 1995], 211–40).

8. See, for example, Timothy Wright, *A Community of Joy: How to Create Contemporary Worship* (Nashville: Abingdon, 1994), 71.

9. For more on this historical point, see Donald J. Bruggink, "Contemporary Context and the Biblical and Theological Roots of Reformed Worship," *Reformed Review* 48 (1994–95): 77; Rhoda Schuler, "Worship among American Lutherans: A House Divided," *Studia Liturgica* 25 (1996): 174–91; and James White, "Worship and Evangelism from New Lebanon to Nashville," in *Christian Worship in North America: A Retrospective, 1955–1995* (Collegeville, Minn.: Liturgical Press, 1997): 155–72.

of what Toqueville described as "democratic religion." Given the prominent features of North American culture, there is absolutely nothing surprising about the emergence of megachurches and their music. As has been common throughout the history of worship in North America, popular culture, not elite or highbrow culture, drives liturgical and hymnological expression. For this reason, many studies of worship in the last decade have attempted to analyze it in terms of larger sociocultural patterns, in terms of consumerism, MTV, or individualism.

Third, the music in North American megachurches is chosen to complement a discernible liturgical structure. Most megachurches have ignored or dismissed traditional forms of Christian liturgy. Yet nearly all feature a self-conscious pattern, or *Ordo*, for worship. The typical liturgical structure in these congregations features a decisive split between a time for worship and a time for teaching. Music is typically prominent in the first part of the service, which features a sequence of actions that leads the congregation from exuberant praise to contemplative worship.[10]

This sequence is supported by a growing body of popular theological literature that describes the movement of a worshiper from "the outer courts" into "the holy of holies" of God's presence. In this pattern, music is the means for encounter with God. Music is sacramental.[11] The language used to describe it is often as stark and highly charged as medieval eucharistic theology: Sung praise ushers worshipers into God's presence (we might almost add *ex opere operato*, the phrase used to convey the perceived efficacy of the priest's words to effect the transubstantiation of the elements in the medieval mass). Writings speak of a desire for the tangible experience of a direct relationship with God, generally articulated in theological language inherited from the Charismatic movement.[12] Key words in these discussions include *intimacy, authenticity, relationality,* and *warmth.*

Music functions to mediate a sense of God's presence, not through layers of artistic sophistication or through deep-rooted symbolic expression (as in Paul Tillich's notion of meditation on works of high art)[13] but rather through direct speech to God, in which music gener-

10. See, for example, Barry Liesch, "A Structure Runs through It," in *Changing Lives through Preaching and Worship*, ed. Marshall Shelley (Nashville: Moorings, 1995), 244–54.

11. Jack Hayford has asserted that "glorious praise . . . is the very prerequisite to knowing [God's] presence" (foreword in *Songs for Praise and Worship* [Waco: Word Music, 1992], ii).

12. Robert Webber, *Signs of Wonder: The Phenomenon of Convergence in Modern Liturgical and Charismatic Churches* (Nashville: Abbot-Martyn Press, 1992); and any issue of *Worship Leader* or *Psalmist* magazine.

13. See, for example, Paul Tillich, "One Moment of Beauty," in *On Art and Architecture*, ed. John Dillenberger (New York: Crossroad, 1987), 234.

ates a palpable experience that is interpreted as an encounter with God. This theological view has also shaped forms of expression. The ubiquitous medley of songs in many of these churches is intended to move beyond rational, didactic use of language to a time of extended prayer, meditation, and the experience of God's presence.

Fourth, North American megachurches have generated a large, independent industry that supports these forms of artistic expression. This industry is complete with published and recorded music, copyright licensing procedures, magazines, and conferences. It is supported by a vast network of Christian radio stations and has generated a roster of well-known models and heroes—pastors, musicians, and consultants.[14] This industry may well influence the worship of more congregations than the so-called establishment industry of denominational hymnals that is well represented by the book service of the Hymn Society of the United States and Canada. This industry, like every industry, is market-driven. It pays attention to what sells and attempts to react to the market.

Fifth, these churches have had a vast influence on every aspect of church life in many North American congregations. They have drawn the attention of major news media and are already the subject of a bevy of scholarly articles and dissertations. They have shaped patterns of congregational life in nearly every denomination, and their influence is spreading well beyond North America as they export their philosophy to Europe, Asia, and the Pacific Rim.[15] Their influence is especially significant in matters of worship and music.

Megachurches are like liturgical laboratories for free church Protestants.[16] Just as English cathedrals were the laboratories that produced many of the hymns and anthems that are the staple of the musical diet in some parish churches, today the American megachurch has become the laboratory that has produced the musical forms, styles, and genres that have influenced thousands of other congregations.

This influence has changed the most fundamental assumptions and the basic working vocabulary with which many North American Christians approach congregational song. Thousands of North Ameri-

14. Most of the well-known figures have published books—which provide a helpful way of sensing the motivation and rationale behind the movement.

15. Willow Creek Community Church, for example, has a department devoted to international ministries. For a discussion in England that is similar to the one in this chapter, see Robin Sheldon, ed., *In Spirit and in Truth: Exploring New Directions in Music in Worship Today* (London: Hodder & Stoughton, 1989).

16. I make this point in light of the reflections of Michael Perham in "'Liturgical Laboratories of the Church': The Role of English Cathedrals in Anglican Worship Today," in *Like a Two-Edged Sword: The Word of God in Liturgy and History: Essays in Honour of Canon Donald Gray*, ed. Martin R. Dudley (Norwich: Canterbury Press, 1995), 179–94.

can Christians simply assume that music in worship is properly rendered by a guitar-led praise band, not an organ, and that the basic genre of liturgical music is not hymnody but choruses and ballads. Indeed, for these Christians and the hundreds of music and worship leaders in their midst, the idea of a Hymn Society would seem quaint.

In sum, the music that is prominent in North American megachurches today is the product of a complex web of historical, theological, sociological, and cultural forces. It is as complex a phenomenon for study as the medieval mystery plays of York Minster, the Genevan Psalter, or the early hymns of Methodism.

Critique

In light of this complexity, any critique is bound to be a risky, if necessary, undertaking. The tendency among some hymnologists and hymnwriters is to dismiss these congregations and their music as second-rate Christian kitsch. This type of rhetoric is nothing new. In North America, the pages of *The Hymn* have regularly featured rather acerbic rhetoric to protest genres deemed aesthetically deficient. The 1950s featured debates about Victorian hymns; the 1960s, debates about gospel hymns. In the 1970s and 1980s, debates centered around folk music and praise choruses.[17]

Yet this is not the approach I advocate. The problem with this approach is that it effectively cuts off communication with a huge and growing part of the body of Christ and can, at times, abandon the relative objectivity of good scholarship to which those of us in the academy aspire. I argue that we must critique this movement but in a way that proponents of the movement will respect. The challenge is to be neither indiscriminate nor intolerant, neither aesthetes nor philistines.

My interest is neither to defend these megachurches nor to reject them but rather to find a way to structure a meaningful conversation with their musicians and pastors and consultants—in much the same way as various ecumenical forums have allowed Methodists, Roman Catholics, and Lutherans to probe differences in eucharistic theology

---

17. The discussion in the 1950s concerning Victorian tunes is epitomized by Ray Francis Brown, "Appraising 20th Century Hymn Tunes," *The Hymn* 3, no. 2 (April 1952): 37–44, 63. Brown reserves special judgment for Victorian tunes, which he regards as being "uncritically accepted" and "very superficial." Journal editor George Litch Knight concluded in the next issue that "there seems to be no limit to the open season when it comes to condemnation of Victorian hymn tunes" (3, no. 3 [July 1952]: 72). Similar comments on gospel, folk, and rock idioms are evident in articles such as Paul E. Elbin, "Fanny Crosby and William H. Doane Have Had Their Day," *The Hymn* 21, no. 1 (January 1970): 12–16; Emmett R. Sarig, "Ignoring Rock Won't Make It Go Away," *The Hymn* 21, no. 2 (April 1970): 42–45; and H. Myron Braun, "Mod Worship and How It Grows," *The Hymn* 22, no. 2 (April 1971): 48–50.

and practice. I propose to proceed with a critique of this movement on the basis of what might be called a distinctly "hymnological" aesthetic.

The topic of this chapter invariably raises matters related to aesthetic taste. We often call for "better hymnody" that embodies "higher musical quality."[18] Yet we often do not specify what that means. Our inclination may be to import or modify aesthetic theories and sensibilities geared toward other artistic expressions (e.g., concert music) and apply them to congregational song.

This does help us to some extent. For one, it allows us to say that hymns should meet some basic musical and textual criteria—that music should have a sense of tension and resolve, that texts should not feature mixed metaphors. These criteria, while absolutely necessary, are insufficient, failing to account for what is unique to the genre of hymns. Some additional criteria are needed.

For these, let me draw on recent conversations in the small sub-discipline of what might be called liturgical aesthetics.[19] A recent spate of books, offered in conversation with theological and philosophical aesthetics, has attempted to answer the question, What makes for good art in the context of Christian worship? Answers to this question nearly always feature three theses.

First, liturgical art, including hymnody, is functional. Its goal, its raison d'être, is to serve the purposes of the gathered church. If the main point of Christian worship is to engage in a series of personal, relational actions between the gathered community and its Creator (e.g., confessing sin, praising God, asking for divine intervention), then good hymnody enables these actions to be accomplished.

18. See, for example, this early statement of purpose for the Hymn Society: "The object of the society shall be to cultivate the devout use of *better* Christian hymns and hymn tunes; to encourage the writing and publishing of hymns that express the temper of modern Christian life and thought, and also of hymn tunes of *genuine musical merit* and best adapted to congregational singing; to secure the union of hymns and tunes that are closely related in emotional content and worshipful significance; to promote the collection of hymnodic data, new and old, encourage research and stimulate full discussion and the special preparation of addresses, articles and reviews upon subjects hymnodic; to the end that there may be *improvement* and greater inspiration in these hymnodic and musical modes of praise and prayer in the worship of God" (William Watkins Reid, *Sing with Spirit and Understanding: The Story of the Hymn Society of America* [New York: Hymn Society of America, 1962], 2.

19. See my "Toward a Liturgical Aesthetic: An Interdisciplinary Review of Aesthetic Theory," *Liturgy Digest* 3, no. 1 (1996): 4–87; Hermann Reifenberg, "Liturgieästhetik: Feier des 'Heiligen' Im Magnetfeld des 'Schönen': Perspektiven, Ausprägungen, Differenzierungen und Gesamtverständnis Christlicher Kultästhetik," *Archiv Für Liturgiewissenschaft* 26 (1984): 117–46; Don E. Saliers, *Worship as Theology* (Nashville: Abingdon, 1994); idem, *Worship Come to Its Senses* (Nashville: Abingdon, 1996); and idem, "Aesthetics, Liturgical," in *The New Dictionary of Sacramental Worship*, ed. Peter Fink (Collegeville, Minn.: Liturgical Press, 1990), 30–39.

This thesis suggests a criterion for evaluating liturgical arts, including hymnody. It suggests that liturgical art, at its best, embodies the purposes of liturgical action and is meant to carry out, to perform, to enact, to make real the shared actions of the gathered ecclesial community. Good liturgical art, including hymnody, not only excels in the criteria of its own genre but also enables the actions of corporate worship.

Hymns serve the purposes of Christian corporate worship. Though they have value for personal devotional use, for humming on the streets, for serving as the basis for elaborate compositions for choir and organ, their primary purpose is to allow a gathered community to thank God, confess sin, ask for divine intervention, and express hope for the coming kingdom of God. Music is one means of expression, like speech or dance, by which people accomplish certain actions.

Variations on this theme have been developed by a diverse group of theorists, including Cipriano Vagaggini, Gerardus van der Leeuw, John Foley, and Nicholas Wolterstorff.[20] Their work is a self-conscious repudiation of purist art-for-art's-sake aesthetic theories.

Second, liturgical art, including hymnody, is vernacular. At their best, hymns are a musical form that can readily be embraced by people with little musical, poetic, or aesthetic training. In the case of hymnody, the vernacular is an aesthetic virtue, not a vice. (See the discussion in chapter 10.)

Third, the liturgical arts, including hymnody, are communal. In this way, they differ from many of the genres and institutions of high art in Western culture. In concert music, we value the proficiency of the solo artist. In the context of the liturgy, proficiency is redefined: Here the highest value is enabling a group of musical amateurs to make music together. As Nicholas Wolterstorff argues:

> Liturgical art is not the artist "doing his own thing," the artist "doing her own thing," with the rest of us standing by as appreciators and critics. Liturgical art is the offering of the artist to the liturgical community for its praise and confession and intercession. Liturgical art is art on our behalf, art enabling us to complete the cosmic circle. In liturgical art, the liturgical community finds its artful priestly hands and voice.[21]

Gordon Lathrop makes a similar point:

> In current European-American culture, certain kinds of art will be misplaced in the meeting: art that is primarily focused on the self-expression of the alienated artist or performer; art that is a self-contained per-

20. See chapter 10, note 15.
21. Nicholas Wolterstorff, "What Is This Thing—Liturgical Art," in *Art in Worship—Clay and Fiber* (Grand Rapids: Calvin College Center Art Gallery, 1988), 7.

formance; art that cannot open itself to sing around a people hearing the word and holding a meal; art that is merely religious in the sense of dealing with a religious theme or enabling individual and personal meditation but not communal engagement; art that is realistic rather than iconic; art, in other words, that directly and uncritically expresses the values of our current culture.[22]

In liturgical art, no pride of place is offered to the autonomous, solitary, artistic genius. Instead, the liturgical artist is called to take the role of servant, giving worshipers a voice they never knew they had to sing praise and offer prayer to God.

A Hymnological Aesthetic and the Music of North American Megachurches

How do the megachurches, and their music, fare with these three criteria? The results are mixed.

First, does this music support the actions of Christian corporate worship? In some cases, it clearly does not. In some cases, songs and hymns are sung and chosen because of their immediate appeal. They may express a vaguely religious sentiment or theological theme, but their intended effect is to lead people to say, "I enjoyed that music" or "That was a neat song" rather than, "Through that song I confessed my sin to God" or "Through that song I rehearsed God's mighty deeds in history as a way of rendering praise." Just as some parish musicians might choose a given Renaissance anthem simply because it is musically impressive or allows the choir to demonstrate its facility with Renaissance performance practice, so too some musicians at megachurches choose music for reasons that have nothing to do with the purposes of Christian worship.

In other cases, music in megachurches does complement liturgical action. Songs and hymns are chosen to lead worshipers from praise of God's works in salvation history to confession of sin to intercessory prayer. For example, I have witnessed the use of a simple chorus such as "In Our Lives, Lord, Be Glorified" as a refrain during intercessory prayer—much like a spoken refrain from a prayer book (e.g., "Lord, in your mercy, hear our prayer").[23] In this case, everything about the music and the way it was rendered—the text, the posture of the musicians, the introduction of the song—pointed to the way in which it functioned to enable a particular liturgical action. Whatever we might say about the

22. Gordon Lathrop, *Holy Things: A Liturgical Theology* (Minneapolis: Fortress, 1993), 223.

23. Bob Kilpatrick, "In My Life, Lord, Be Glorified," in *Songs for Praise and Worship*, 196.

tune or text of this chorus, it can be used to meet this criterion quite well. In sum, this first criterion commends some of this music, but not all of it.

Second, is this music vernacular? It is difficult to answer anything but yes. The most prominent goal of many musicians at megachurches is to provide music in the musical and textual language of their people, people whose sensibilities are shaped primarily by popular and commercial forms of music. It is on this point that megachurches present their greatest challenge to all churches in the industrialized West. This challenge can helpfully be addressed in terms of lessons learned from recent attempts at inculturation, mentioned above.

On the one hand, recent work on inculturation has taught us that this process is universal and inevitable.[24] The North American megachurch is one more example to confirm this maxim. Just as fourth-century basilicas reflect the age of Constantinian rule, just as the congregational dances of Zairean Roman Catholics reflect the spirit of the culture, the North American megachurch reflects a culture shaped by popular music, television, and a deep-seated populist orientation. Toqueville would not be surprised.

Significantly, there is one notable exception to the recent aggressive drive toward inculturation—inculturation "at home" in the industrialized West. Ironically, some of the same people who promote vigorous inculturation overseas lament its most aggressive forms at home.[25] To avoid or dismiss the megachurch is to avoid one of the most tangible expressions of inculturation at work.

On the other hand, recent work on inculturation has taught us that the process has limits. Inculturation is not an excuse to excise essential elements from the Christian gospel or patterns of worship. And in some cases, this is exactly what happens in megachurches, especially in congregations that have done away with corporate confession of sin, corporate lament, frequent celebrations of the Lord's Supper, and communal celebrations of baptism.[26]

24. As Mark Searle concluded, "So natural . . . and so inevitable is this process [of inculturation] that the issue confronted by Church authorities has usually been not whether enculturation should be undertaken but whether it should be approved or stopped" ("Culture," in *Liturgy: Active Participation in the Divine Life*, Federation of Diocesan Liturgical Commissions [Collegeville, Minn.: Liturgical Press, 1990], 28).

25. As Hugh Montefiore has observed, it is "comparatively easy to ask awkward questions about the suitability of another culture as the vehicle for communicating the Gospel; but it is very difficult to ask them about one's own" (*The Gospel and Contemporary Culture* [London: Mowbray, 1992], 1).

26. Marva Dawn decries the "dumbing down" of worship resulting from consumer-driven church-growth strategies. Dawn has developed a strident critique of "sub-Christian" music that is "theologically correct but shallow." As she argues, "Shallow music forms shallow people" (*Reaching Out without Dumbing Down* [Grand Rapids: Eerdmans, 1995], 172, 175).

Similarly, inculturation is not an excuse for restricting the affective range of hymnody. If anything, local cultural experience should be a resource for enriching and deepening the expression of faith through music, not limiting it. Again, in some cases, megachurches have not fared well on this score, particularly when their music becomes homogenized, when the traits described above (fast-paced rhythms, major mode) come to characterize not just most but nearly all of their music.

Again, this criterion helps us both appreciate and critique the approach of the North American megachurch. An inculturated musical diet may well take in sounds and forms of expression from popular culture, but it must also self-consciously seek to transcend its cultural environment to express the full power, nuance, and affect of the Christian faith.

Third, is this music communal? Some of it is. Indeed, some leaders write articles such as "Helping People Sing Their Hearts Out."[27] At the same time, two factors militate against it. For one, musicians in many megachurches work with models who are primarily performers. While some so-called traditional churches are tempted to look for role models among classical performing artists, some megachurches are tempted to look for role models among popular performing artists.

The problem is that both types of models are performing artists, often solitary figures with enormous talent. As a result, a good deal of this music, while vernacular, is not participatory. It often attempts to be just the opposite—with architecture and acoustics that support presentational but not participatory events.

For another, the large scale of the megachurch dramatically affects the mode of participation in this music. Social psychologists tell us that large spaces and throngs of people tend to have one of two effects. As is the case with a large-scale Welsh hymn festival, megachurches may encourage vigorous mass singing. But as is the case with singing the national anthem before many sporting events, they may allow people to avoid active musical engagement. For whatever reason, worshiping with the average American megachurch is often more like singing at a sporting event than at a Welsh hymn sing. In this case, the large scale allows for anonymity and a lack of participation. This may not be inherent in the music, but it is common.[28]

27. Howard Stevenson, "Helping People Sing Their Hearts Out," in *Changing Lives through Preaching and Worship*, 234–43. Stevenson concludes, "Our most important choir is made up of the men and women with untrained voices who sit in the pews" (235). Similarly, Morgenthaler maintains that "spectator worship has always been and will always be an oxymoron" (*Worship Evangelism*, 49).

28. See, for example, Wright, *Community of Joy*, 58–59; and Ed Dobson, *Starting a Seeker Service: How Traditional Churches Can Reach the Unchurched* (Grand Rapids: Zondervan, 1993), 33.

In sum, if we are opposed in principle to forms of popular culture, then the music of North American megachurches is something to be ignored or wished away. However, if we are willing to engage these churches, then these criteria may help us sort out which music in these churches is a blessing and which is a bane.

These criteria commend accessible texts that complement and enable liturgical actions such as praising, confessing, proclaiming, interceding. They critique performance practices that discourage active singing by the entire community. And they encourage the creation of new texts and tunes that embrace the affective range and nuance of the Christian faith.

Future Directions

I conclude with some brief challenges regarding the future of congregational song and the future of hymnological study. Consider three challenges that emerge from this topic.

First, a general challenge: This topic challenges us to develop a clearer, more precise, and more consensual statement about aesthetic quality in hymnody. A theoretical approach that simply repeats platitudes that hymns should be tasteful or maintain excellence is not specific enough to function well in conversations with megachurches or with other populist forms of religious expression.

Whatever its bane, one blessing of the North American megachurch may be that the entire church will be forced again to articulate clearly the kinds of liturgical practices and patterns of congregational song that cohere most fully and profoundly with the gospel of Christ.

Second, a challenge to scholars, including historians, theologians, social scientists, and hymnologists: If the next century is to feature conversations between those who practice so-called classical forms of hymnody and those who practice more populist forms, then we desperately need more scholarly work to support that conversation.

A significant amount of scholarly work has explored the intellectual, theological, and musical dimensions of hymnody. Hymns have often been studied with methods that are typically developed for the study of concert music or theological treatises. More work is needed on the level of social or cultural history. Work is needed that considers personal diaries to be as valuable a source as critical musical editions. How have hymns functioned in the lives of people who are not trained as musicians, theologians, or pastors? In what ways have previous musicians resolved perceived tensions between aesthetic excellence and accessibility?[29]

29. This kind of work is becoming more common in studies of the sixteenth century. See, for example, Natalie Z. Davis, "From 'Popular Religion' to Religious Cul-

Third, a challenge to hymn writers, poets, editors, and publishers: The North American megachurch challenges us to redouble our efforts to compose and publish music that not only meets poetic, theological, and musical criteria but also respects attempts to embrace vernacular and populist forms of expression. Quality music is a necessity not just for accomplished choirs and classically trained musicians but also for praise teams at North American megachurches. What songs will (realistically) be sung in a North American megachurch?

In an unpublished dissertation proposal, Charles Fromm, the editor of *Worship Leader* magazine and a tireless advocate of populist forms of hymnody, asserts that "the New Song that is being developed today is awaiting the influence of people who will recover the great themes of scripture and express them in poetic and profound lyrics."[30] That is something with which the members of the Hymn Society have some experience.

The compositional process always begins by identifying the constraints of a given project. Why not take as a compositional constraint the task of writing music for a praise team at a North American megachurch? Do we have the creativity to compose music that meets every aesthetic textual and musical criterion and respects the pervasive, permanent, and influential institutional context of the North American megachurch?

The congregational song of North American megachurches, surely a bane to some and a blessing to others, presents all advocates of congregational song with a sturdy challenge. Tocqueville concluded his analysis of North American Christianity with the following advice: "By respecting all democratic instincts which are not against it and making use of many favorable ones, religion succeeds in struggling suc-

tures," in *Reformation Europe: A Guide to Research*, ed. Steven Ozment (St. Louis: Center for Reformation Research, 1982), 321–41; Tessa Watt, *Cheap Print and Popular Piety, 1550–1640* (Cambridge: Cambridge University Press, 1991); H. G. Koenigsberger, "Music and Religion in Early Modern European History," in *Politicians and Virtuosi: Essays in Early Modern History* (London: Hambledon Press, 1986); and Miriam Usher Chrisman, *Lay Culture, Learned Culture: Books and Social Change in Strasbourg, 1480–1599* (New Haven: Yale University Press, 1982). I have attempted to apply the lessons from this literature to the study of the Genevan Psalter in "The Spirituality of the Psalter in Calvin's Geneva." For examples of this approach in the study of music and worship in America, see Nathan O. Hatch, *The Democratization of American Christianity* (New Haven: Yale University Press, 1989), 146–61; and Terry D. Bilhartz, *Urban Religion and the Second Great Awakening: Church and Society in Early National Baltimore* (Rutherford, N.J.: Fairleigh Dickinson University Press, 1986).

30. Charles Earl Fromm, "Training the Barbarians: The Lasting Impact of the Jesus Movement Revival Music on Contemporary Worship" (unpublished manuscript, Fuller Theological Seminary, 1997).

cessfully with that spirit of individual independence which is its most dangerous enemy."[31] This call to discerning engagement is as relevant today as it was then. May God's Spirit give us grace and wisdom for this challenging task.

31. Tocqueville, *Democracy in America*, 414.

PART

5

Pastoral Studies

12

Making Good Choices in an Era of Liturgical Change

Near the opening of the Book of Philippians, Paul records his prayer for the Philippian Christians:

> And this is my prayer, that your love may overflow more and more with knowledge and full insight to help you to determine what is best, so that in the day of Christ you may be pure and blameless, having produced the harvest of righteousness that comes through Jesus Christ for the glory and praise of God.
>
> 1:9–11 NRSV

At the heart of this prayer is Paul's desire that his readers exercise the classical virtue of discernment. He wants them to be able to make good choices, to "determine what is best."[1] In his prayer, Paul gives us the anatomy of this virtue. He points to three necessary building blocks for discernment: love, knowledge, and insight. He also describes the desired result of exercising this virtue: holiness and righteousness that will contribute to the glory and praise of God. In this way, the virtue of discernment energizes and empowers the thoughtful, mature Christian life.

In matters of worship, this is exactly the virtue that Christians need today. We already have passion concerning the subject of worship.

---

1. This chapter is adapted from material presented in "The Virtue of Liturgical Discernment," *Christian Courier* (31 May 1999), and "Spirit-Charged Worship," *Calvin Seminary Forum* (spring 1999).

The charged rhetoric of worship wars shows no signs of abating. In most congregations, there is no lack of opinions about worship matters and no lack of willingness to share them.

We also have voluminous liturgical resources at our fingertips. Our bookstores, magazines, and web sites provide us with more songs, prayer texts, and worship service outlines than have been available at any period in church history. Worship conferences have increased tenfold in the past ten years. And even evangelical seminaries are finally offering courses on this central activity of church life.

But for all this energy and all these resources, we often lack the discernment to make good use of them. In fact, what we may need most is a healthy prayer of confession to admit our lack of discernment.

To help make such a prayer concrete, let me provide some examples of the lack of this virtue, drawn mostly from experiences described by my students at Calvin Theological Seminary, Tyndale Seminary, and Northern Baptist Seminary.

In one congregation, a group protested the use of Scripture choruses because they simply repeat the same line ten times over. The same group went on to ask their choir director to sing Handel's "Hallelujah Chorus." (True, Handel might have a bit more musical nuance and force than Maranatha, but the naive use of this argument is still problematic.)

In another congregation, a worship leader protested the use of written prayers because they were so predictable. When the worship committee reviewed tapes of earlier services, however, it discovered that this worship leader had "spontaneously" spoken the same, identical prayer in four consecutive services.

In another congregation, three church leaders recommended and enforced wholesale liturgical change on the basis of attending one conference on worship and evangelism, without so much as one month's discussion and prayer with the congregation.

In another, a church council refused to adopt a proposal to celebrate communion more frequently because "it would cease to be special," an argument that (curiously) is rarely applied to preaching.

What we have here are situations in which committed Christians have somehow lost their theological and pastoral equilibrium. They may have been advocating important and helpful positions, but they lacked the love, knowledge, or insight to help their congregations discuss them in discerning ways.

The Anatomy of Liturgical Discernment

So what exactly is discernment? Discernment is a classical virtue, a common theme in the Hebrew Scriptures, the New Testament, and classical philosophy. Discernment is what Solomon wanted when he asked for "an understanding mind . . . to discern between good and evil" (1 Kings 3:9 NRSV). It is what Paul discusses in Romans 12:2 when he says that the "renewing of [our] minds" will help us "discern what is the will of God" (NRSV). Discernment or prudence, says Augustine, is "love distinguishing with [wisdom] sagacity between what hinders it and what helps it. . . . Prudence is love making a right distinction between what helps it towards God and what might hinder it."[2] Joseph Pieper identified it as "a studied seriousness . . . a filter of deliberation" and "the perfected ability to make decisions in accordance with reality . . . the quintessence of ethical maturity."[3] Lewis Smedes, more colloquially, says that it is "having a nose for what's going on under the surface."[4] Discernment, then, is nearly synonymous with a slightly larger category—wisdom.

Consider some specific ingredients in the recipe for discernment. For one, discernment implies being open to examine any innovation or new practice. We cannot make discerning choices without knowing the options. Discerning people are always willing to give a person, a movement, or a worship style a fair hearing. Discerning church musicians, for example, might have on their shelf music from Vineyard, Maranatha, Hosanna, as well as Taizé, Iona, and the Hymn Society.

Yet discernment is not the same thing as a blanket endorsement. Indeed, discernment requires at least occasionally saying no—a difficult word to utter in our postmodern age. Discerning worship leaders know, for example, that cultivating a warm, hospitable tone in worship does not require comments that are glib or flippant. Discerning leaders will distinguish "warm" from "flippant" and then sound a resounding no in regard to the latter.

For this to work, as Paul suggests, discernment requires "knowledge and full insight." Worship leadership requires spiritual maturity and a desire to grow in the knowledge and love of the Lord. The New Testament prerequisites for office bearers likely cover liturgical leadership as much as attendance at church council meetings. Indeed, worship leadership requires more than good intentions. As with any other ministry or vocation within the church, it is a calling. The Spirit gifts some for this ministry. It is our challenge to cultivate those gifts and refine them for the building up of the church.

The growth of lay worship leaders has arguably been one of the most sweeping liturgical changes of the past century. This can be very

2. Augustine, *Against the Manichaens* 15, par. 25.
3. Joseph Pieper, *Prudence* (London: Faber and Faber, 1959), 36, 49.
4. Lewis Smedes, *Choices: Making Right Decisions in a Complex World* (San Francisco: Harper & Row, 1986), 97.

good—a way for congregations to take ownership of worship, a way to express the "priesthood of believers." This works best when lay leaders are committed students of Scripture, when they are the kind of people who are eager to attend a worship conference or read a new book on worship. It does not work so well when leaders lack a taste for such things. In fact, many worship leaders cannot name a single book on the theology of worship. Most denominations (admirably) require preachers to pursue rigorous seminary studies before preaching. Yet we require of worship leaders only that they be willing to attend a single rehearsal or committee meeting. We would do well to lovingly challenge our worship leaders to grow in the knowledge and love of God.

Further, as Paul reminds us, discernment requires love—even in matters of worship. John Calvin agreed. When discussing whether Christians should kneel in worship, for example, Calvin observed that some worship practices will inevitably change to accommodate to the culture of the age. He also warned against rash, sudden, and poorly reasoned change and then concluded, "But love will best judge what may hurt or edify; and if we let love be our guide, all will be safe."[5] Here Calvin portrayed love in service of discernment.

Not that we need sentimental love in today's discussions. Today's discussions must begin with tough love as we seek worship practices that lead to the long-term health of the church. They require tender, empathetic love as we take seriously the testimonies of fellow Christians about their own experiences of worship. For example, we must protest all simplistic caricatures of those who promote more frequent celebrations of the Lord's Supper as irrelevant, and those who discuss worship's relevance as irreverent.

Finally, discernment happens best in community. Paul prayed, "To help you [all] determine what is best." Paul loved the second person plural. He prayed for a community that would determine what is best.

Faithful lay Christians are the backbone of church life. Most churches are blessed with wise people who have the kind of spiritual discernment that could help churches make decisions based on something more than personal tastes. These are the voices that must be heard in our worship discussions.

But often they are not. Behind some of the recent liturgical skirmishes lie innovations driven by those who have ignored the community aspect of discernment. Occasionally, church leaders see wise and

5. John Calvin, *Institutes of the Christian Religion* [1559], ed. John T. McNeill, trans. Ford Lewis Battles, Library of Christian Classics, vols. 20–21 (Philadelphia: Westminster, 1960), 4.10.30.

discerning laypeople as simply a hindrance to future growth. Some church growth experts encourage church leaders to see them that way.

True enough, some people express their views without love and without knowledge, in other words, without the necessary ingredients in the recipe for discernment. But when love and knowledge are expressed in community, then the church lives up to its identity as nothing less than the body of Christ.

It may surprise you that I began this chapter on worship not by writing about worship per se but by writing about love, knowledge, and community. I chose this strategy because of my growing conviction that many of today's discussions about worship are less about worship than about power, politics, and personal taste. The antidote to this is a loving, community-oriented search for wisdom. The antidote is praying for, cultivating, and exercising the gift of discernment.

The Theologically Discerning Mind: A Case Study

Many aspects of worship today require a discerning spirit, but few are as theologically significant as the role of the Holy Spirit in worship. Consider this as one case study for applying the gift of discernment. How should a discerning Christian community seek to receive and embrace the gift of the Spirit in worship?

The emphasis on the Holy Spirit's work in Pentecostal and charismatic circles is well known. But you might be surprised to hear that the Reformed tradition is famous for its emphasis on the Holy Spirit in worship. Hughes Oliphant Old, Reformed theologian, historian, and pastor, contends, "If there is one doctrine which is at the heart of Reformed worship it is the doctrine of the Holy Spirit."[6] A number of Calvin scholars, including B. B. Warfield, have called John Calvin nothing less than "a theologian of the Holy Spirit."[7]

Indeed, if you read the sections of Calvin's *Institutes of the Christian Religion* on worship-related topics, you will discover that the Holy Spirit is the grammatical subject of many of the key sentences about worship. The Spirit lifts us up into the presence of Christ at the Lord's Supper. The Spirit illumines our hearts as we hear God's Word proclaimed. The Spirit inspires our praise and prayers. In Calvin's words, "That the Word may not beat your ears in vain, and that the sacraments may not strike your eyes in vain, the Spirit shows us that in them it is God speaking to us, softening the stubbornness of our heart,

6. Hughes Oliphant Old, *The Patristic Roots of Reformed Worship* (Zurich: Theologischer Verlag, 1975), 341.

7. See Benjamin B. Warfield, *Calvin and Augustine* (Philadelphia: Presbyterian & Reformed, 1956), 484–85; and I. John Hesselink, *Calvin's First Catechism: A Commentary* (Louisville: Westminster John Knox, 1997), 177–87.

and composing it to that obedience which it owes the Word of the Lord."[8]

In sum, the Spirit makes possible each broad movement in worship—both the human-Godward movement of praise and prayer, and the God-humanward movement of proclamation and spiritual nourishment. In the drama of worship, the Spirit has the leading role. Worship is charged with divine activity.

Exactly how this happens is, of course, difficult to explain. Any attempt to explicate this fully is likely to be hopelessly inadequate. And perhaps we ought to shrink back from trying to state too precisely how the Spirit works. Yet with Scripture's help we can determine when our way of thinking about the Spirit's role in worship has become distorted. Consider three common problems.

A first problem occurs when we ignore or downplay the Spirit's role in worship. Not long ago, a worship conference attendee remarked that she was quite content not to hear talk of "all that Holy Spirit stuff." This remarkable comment gave the impression that she had distaste for the Third Person of the Trinity. The Holy Spirit is Jesus' gift to the church. Should we not embrace this gift?

A second problem is limiting our view of the Spirit's role to only the spontaneous or ecstatic elements of worship. We confess that the Spirit worked through the authors of Scripture to produce the highly refined poetry of the Psalms as well as the spontaneous sermons of Peter and Paul. While the Spirit led early Christians to speak in tongues, the Spirit of God also brought order out of chaos at creation. If the Spirit works through both order and spontaneity, why do we sometimes confine the Spirit to only the spontaneous (as when we casually say, "Well, we didn't have time to plan worship this week; I guess we will have to let the Spirit lead today" or "Let's get away from our planned service so the Spirit can lead")?

As *Authentic Worship in a Changing Culture,* a synodical study report of the Christian Reformed Church in North America, makes clear:

> We shouldn't link the Holy Spirit with less planning or less formality. The Holy Spirit can be powerfully present in a very highly structured service and can be absent in a service with little structure. Beyond questions of style and formality, the question always before us is this: does this act of worship bring praise to God through Jesus Christ in the Holy Spirit?[9]

8. Calvin, *Institutes* 4.14.10.
9. *Authentic Worship in a Changing Culture* (Grand Rapids: CRC Publications, 1997).

Indeed, the Spirit may well work through both the careful preparations of a preacher and a sentence the preacher had not planned on saying. The Spirit may work through both the diligent planning of a worship committee and the spontaneous prayer request or testimony of a worshiper.

A third problem is the temptation of thinking that we can bring about an experience of the Spirit, that we can somehow engineer the Spirit's work. This is no different from thinking that we can manipulate divine action by "pulling the right lever" with certain words, sounds, or movements. (Acts 8:18ff. has a thing or two to say about that.) This leads to the age-old trap of thinking that we are the primary agents who make worship what it is, that powerful pulpit rhetoric or musical excellence can, by themselves, make worship into an encounter with God. Scripture is clear: The Spirit's presence is always a gift. It can never be engineered or produced.

When we fall into one of these three temptations, we alternate between quenching the Spirit (1 Thess. 5:19) and grieving the Spirit (Eph. 4:30). In contrast, we need to both welcome and honor the Spirit.

The theological insistence that the Spirit makes worship what it is—like most key theological points—has direct liturgical implications. One of them has to do with how we pray for the Spirit. Throughout the history of the church, prayers for the Spirit's active presence in worship have been a fundamental element of Christian worship. These prayers are sometimes called "invocations" or "epiclesis" (from *epicleo*, "to call upon").

This type of prayer is beautifully preserved in nearly every classic form of liturgy for baptism and the Lord's Supper at least as far back as the fourth century. The classic example of this type of prayer in the Reformed tradition is the prayer of illumination before the reading of Scripture and the sermon. An invocation or epicletic prayer is essentially saying, "Lord God, the power of what we are about to experience is not the result of our creativity, imagination, or insight. It is purely a gift. May your Spirit work powerfully through this reading of Scripture, this sermon, this celebration of the sacrament. And because of the Spirit's work, may we be given the grace to see Jesus Christ more clearly through what we are about to do."

In recent years, some churches—occasionally in the name of making sacramental celebrations more "spirited"—have abandoned the use of classical liturgical prayer forms and have subsequently failed in their improvisations to include prayer for the Spirit's action. Others rely exclusively on classical forms but have no idea of the power, beauty, genius, and gospel-proclaiming truth of such epicletic prayer. Each approach can miss one of worship's main ingredients.

Here is an example of why we need to think theologically about how and why we do what we do in worship. Thoughtful prayers for the Spirit's active presence place us in a posture of expectation and hope. They both invite us to expect the Spirit's work in our midst and comfort us with a reminder that worship's divine encounter—like faith and salvation—is more like a gift we receive than an accomplishment we achieve.

How do we know if the Spirit has been active in worship? Ecstasy or solemnity by itself does not tell us. The Spirit can use both. One hint may be our response to a service. Consider the difference between the following post-service comments: "My, what impressive music today" versus "Thank you, musician, for helping me pray more deeply today." And, "Wasn't that a brilliant sermon?" versus "In this service, I encountered the risen Lord." One of the Spirit's main character traits is that of always pointing toward Christ. The Spirit is a witness and an advocate for the person of Jesus. If we leave a worship service comforted and challenged by a faith-filled encounter with Jesus Christ, then we can be grateful for the Spirit's work in our hearts. Such is the insight of those who "discern the spirits."

Discernment at Work: Examples from Congregational Life

But what about other examples of discernment at work? Consider the following examples of recent developments in several congregations. None of the following paragraphs can do justice to the complexity of these situations, but I hope they can suggest the importance of going deeper than our normal default positions on these topics.

One discerning leader openly studied the growth of seeker services and concluded that these public, evangelistic events have much to teach us about evangelism but also that they are poor substitutes for services of Word and sacrament. The result was a church that held weekly services of Word and sacrament and also regular evangelistic events that were not simply a lighter version of a service but a powerful and deeply committed attempt to present the gospel to those who do not know the joy of the Christian faith.

One worship leader, fresh from a seminary course on worship, wanted to reinstate the observance of the Christian year in her congregation. Rather than starting by introducing the more obscure elements of the Christian year, such as Epiphany, she presented the calendar, in the language of her people, as a "year-long spiritual journey with Jesus" and thereby focused on the theological significance of the Christian calendar.

One discerning church musician bought three volumes of recently published praise choruses as a sign of openness to this growing movement and then carefully studied them to find the best 10 percent, in much the same way as a hymnal committee carefully selects only the best 10 percent of extant hymns for inclusion in a hymnal.

Another congregation wanted to celebrate the Lord's Supper more frequently and decided to add celebrations of the Lord's Supper to all the main Christ-centered celebrations of the year (Christmas, Easter, ascension, and Pentecost) rather than to days suggested by the calendar (as on the second Sunday evening of every month). This led the congregation to see this change not primarily as the advancement of a sacramental agenda but as an attempt to respond in the most fitting, deeply biblical way to these key events in salvation history.

One congregation sent representatives to two different conferences on church growth and worship. When they came back with a list of dozens of proposed changes, the congregation—rather than simply adopting all the proposed innovations wholesale—began a process of prayer and discussion that led the entire congregation to become excited about some of the ideas and to set others aside.

One congregation wanted to expand its musical repertoire—and its awareness of the holy, catholic church—by incorporating songs from Africa, Southeast Asia, and South America. Rather than singing these songs as musical adornments in a special worship service, they incorporated one or two of these songs into nearly every service as liturgical responses.

One congregation wanted to incorporate youth more fully into worship. Rather than adding a youth service once a year, they made a commitment to involve at least one youth as an usher, worship team member, or Scripture reader each Sunday and to provide regular training for the youth in regard to those roles.

One congregation wanted to add lay worship leaders but decided to start not by adding a potentially divisive (in their context) worship team but by forming a group of lay Scripture readers who met each week to rehearse the Scripture readings for the following Sunday. The result was thoughtful, appropriately dramatic rendering of the Scripture readings in ways that led everyone in the congregation to look forward to that moment in the service.

One congregation added three teams of worship leaders but wisely provided opportunities for training on the theology and practice of worship.

Here, then, are several congregations blessed with wise, pastoral leaders who are cultivating the gift of discernment. Here are people pursuing the love, knowledge, and community that will create an environment for making good decisions about worship.

The people in these examples, and I in writing this chapter, may be accused of trying to please everyone by choosing a benign middle ground on all sorts of thorny issues. This was not my point at all. Rather, I hoped to reveal what is really at stake in these discussions, to focus on the major points, and to offer models of the virtue at the heart of Paul's prayer.

These examples teach one other important lesson. In each, the gift of discernment prevented congregations from confusing liturgical agendas with worship itself.

One danger in all our discussions about worship style is that we will become so focused on talking about worship that we will actually fail to do it. Worship is about joyful and open listening to the proclamation of God's Word. It is about feeding on the spiritual nourishment we receive from God in the Lord's Supper. It is about offering honest and exuberant praise to a holy, righteous, and loving God. It is about honest confession and—often—lament. When our discussions about worship leave us with something less—when they leave us preoccupied with questions about worship style—we need discerning leaders to call us back to the heartfelt worship of a holy God.

In the end, the activity of discernment is a tool, a means to a higher end, a way of helping us become, through the Spirit's power, "pure and blameless, having produced the harvest of righteousness that comes through Jesus Christ for the glory and praise of God" (Phil. 1:10–11 NRSV). May we yearn for and cultivate this gift and then see it bear fruit in worship that is God-honoring, Christ-centered, and Spirit-inspired. *Soli Deo Gloria.*

13

Planning and Leading Worship as a Pastoral Task

Most of us who plan and lead worship regularly are in constant search for good resources, songs, texts, scripts, and images that we can use in our congregations—preferably by next week.

But perhaps we also are looking for something deeper, something more than techniques. Perhaps we need a perspective, a way of conceptualizing our role as worship leader that will sustain us in our day-to-day work in our congregations.

This is especially true for battle-weary leaders. Many of us are burned out, worn to a frazzle from producing a full menu of services for weeks on end. Others are weary of working in congregations in which "worship war" rhetoric takes the joy out of the job. Still others work tirelessly in congregations that do not seem to appreciate our efforts at all or in congregations in which worshipers come to church with impossibly high expectations of us and amazingly few expectations of themselves. In these situations, we need more than techniques; we need a vision to encourage, sustain, and inspire us.

The Changing Role of Worship Leaders

Over the past several years, a host of publications have featured articles on the changing role of the pastor in Christian congregations. They have attempted to describe the central image that pastors and their congregations have of the pastor's role. Are pastors primarily resident theologians? Skilled orators? Spiritual therapists? Ecclesiastical CEOs?

How a church and its pastor answer the question of identity makes a world of difference. It changes everything about how a pastor prioritizes competing goals, how a church thinks of its mission, how it searches for a new pastor, and how a seminary curriculum is planned.

As worship planners and leaders, we also operate with certain images of our role. These images subtly shape how we go about our work—what conferences we attend, what journals we subscribe to, what we do at committee meetings, how we organize our time.

During the past ten years, I have been privileged to speak with worship leaders in a number of denominations from around the country. I have asked them how they think of their role. Almost always, their comments have fallen into one of the categories described below.

Four Self-Images

Craftspeople

Perhaps we write and deliver sermons, making words come to life with persuasive narratives and apt metaphors. Perhaps we sculpt communion ware or sew banners, finding exactly the right materials, images, and colors. Perhaps we make music, attending to the nuances of phrasing, to memorable melodies, and to convincing harmonies. Or perhaps we labor over writing a prayer or a script for a drama or a new hymn or song. Like the artist Perugino, the musician Palestrina, the preacher John Donne, the hymn poet Isaac Watts, and a host of other Christians throughout the centuries, we are craftspeople.

Directors and Coordinators

We may have job titles such as Director of Music or Worship Coordinator. We spend a great deal of our time recruiting people. We run rehearsals. We have a reserved seat at nearly every meeting. We proofread printed orders of service. We evaluate and buy material. We make countless phone calls to find Scripture readers and flute players and sound people. As one person said to me recently, "This worship stuff is a lot more complicated than it used to be."

Performers

However reluctantly, some of us see ourselves as performers. Whether we play the organ or participate in drama or preach a sermon, there is a performance aspect to our work. And no matter how much we or our congregations protest this label, we are still expected to play chords in tune, to tell interesting stories, or to produce elegant banners. After a service we often hear comments such as "impressive music" or "good job in that drama" or "powerful sermon."

And whether we admit it or not, we do spend energy producing services to generate such comments.

Spiritual Engineers

Some of us see ourselves as what I will call—for lack of a better term—"spiritual engineers." Our primary goal is to inspire people. We want to create moments that are packed with spiritual power. Not long ago, I received a call from a pastor asking advice on finding a worship leader. I asked, "What are you looking for?" The answer: "Someone who can make God present in our midst." Language like this is becoming quite common in want ads for worship leaders. Increasingly, churches are looking for people whose creativity, personal testimony, and charismatic personality can turn an ordinary moment into a holy moment.

A Better Image

These four images are common. But none of them is sufficient for the task.

Our craft is important. But the church does not exist for the sake of drama, poetry, or music.

Our coordinating is necessary. But it is not enough. Martin Luther knew this. He once chided worship leaders by arguing, "We have stuck to founding, building, singing, ringing, to vestments, incense burning, and to all the additional preparations for divine worship up to the point that we consider this preparation the real, main divine worship and do not know how to speak of any other. And we are acting as wisely as the man who wants to build a house and spends all his goods on the scaffolding and never, as long as he lives, gets far enough along to lay one stone of his house."[1]

Our performance is perhaps inevitable. But it too is insufficient. This self-image does nothing to distinguish us from concert-hall entertainment, whether it be the Chicago Symphony or Amy Grant. It is one thing when worshipers greet us with "neat piece" or "fancy playing" or "impressive sermon." It is something entirely different when they simply say, "I am at a loss for words to say thanks. Today you helped me pray."

While these three images of craftsperson, director, and performer are incomplete because they do not shoot high enough, the fourth—that of spiritual engineer—is problematic because it overshoots. Our concern for attending to holy moments is important. Yet none of us, no matter how charismatic we might be, can—by our own creativity

1. E. Plass, ed., *What Luther Says, an Anthology*, vol. 1 (St. Louis: Concordia, 1959), 302.

or ingenuity or effort—make a moment holy. Scripture records a long line of those who tried. Think of the prophets of Baal at Carmel or the servant who wanted to support the ark of the covenant as it was transported. At the dedication of the concert hall and chapel at Luther College, Westin Nobel chose the anthem on the Pauline text "God does not dwell in temples made by human hands"—a powerful reminder that God's presence is to be received as a gift. It cannot be engineered or produced.

These four pictures of our role are incomplete.

Toward a Pastoral Image

We need another, richer image to give us our identity—not to displace these others but to put them all in context, to correct their overstatements. We need to see planning and leading worship as pastoral tasks.

Though only some of us have the word *pastor* in our job title, all of us have shepherd-like roles. We need to take the advice of the fourth-century document *Constitutions of the Holy Apostles:* "Be a builder up, a converter, apt to teach, forbearing of evil, of a gentle mind, meek, long-suffering, ready to exhort, ready to comfort, as one of God." Only after this advice does the ancient church order go on to speak of skill: "When you call together an assembly of the Church, it is as if you were the commander of a great ship. Set up the enterprise to be accomplished with all possible skill, charging the deacons as mariners to prepare places for the congregation as for passengers, with all due care and decency."[2] The craft and coordinating and "performance" in our work find their ultimate goal and purpose if we approach them with a pastoral heart. They find their purpose in acts of hospitality.

As worship leaders, we have the important and terrifying task of placing words of prayer on people's lips. It happens every time we choose a song and write a prayer. We also have the holy task of being stewards of God's Word. Our choices of Scripture and themes for worship represent a degree of control over people's spiritual diets, over how they feed on the bread of life. For holy tasks such as these, the church needs more than craftspeople, coordinators, and performers, and none with the hubris to be spiritual engineers. The church needs pastoral people to plan and lead its worship.

Certainly, our role as shepherd does not displace aspects of the other roles. We still cultivate gifts as clear and articulate speakers, technically proficient musicians, ingenious artists. We are still coordinators, calling meetings, running rehearsals, proofreading copy. While

---

2. Cleveland A. Coxe and Ernest Cushing Richardson, eds., *Ante-Nicene Fathers,* vol. 7 (Grand Rapids: Eerdmans, 1979), 421.

we are not spiritual engineers, we do—with fear and trembling—take the part of priests, placing words of prayer on people's lips that may well resonate deep within their souls and draw them, by the Spirit's power, closer to God.

Profile of a Pastoral Worship Leader

Part of my own growth has come from learning from mentors who have developed ideas like these. I have tried to think hard about their approaches and to figure out what makes them tick. My reflections are incomplete. But at least three things are true about these kinds of people.

A Love of Learning

First, they are people who cultivate the gift of a discerning mind, who have a deep and growing knowledge of Scripture, who love the truth of the Christian gospel and are eager to probe its deepest questions. They are people who love to learn. They know that leading worship requires more than good intentions, so they read books and journals, take courses, and attend conferences to hone their pastoral sensibilities. They know that the quickest way to make worship relevant is to make it a profoundly true portrayal of the Christian gospel.

Pastoral leaders constantly ask whether the psalms, hymns, and spiritual songs of the church's worship are sung so that the Word of Christ may dwell in us richly (the forgotten purpose clause of Col. 3:16). They worry about the link between theology and worship—whether worship in their church depicts God as indifferent and far removed; whether it gives the impression that prayer is simply an act of cognition or, conversely, an act of pure emotion; whether worship in their congregation makes it clear that the Bible is central to the life and faith of the church. They know that worship expresses the deepest theological convictions of the community, that it reveals as much about the belief of the community as do catechisms and confessions. In short, they know what Dutch theologian Gerardus van der Leeuw knew when he quipped that "one can't tap the finger of liturgy without immediately getting the whole hand of theology."[3]

Because of this theological bent, they are always making self-conscious choices between good and bad, better and worse. They are willing to say no to a text or narrative or image or song that is inaccurate, simplistic, or sentimental. They have an instinctive way of telling the difference between evangelistic zeal and personal aggrandizement, between aesthetic critiques that are spiritually astute and those that are simply pretentious, between changes in worship that are wholesale capitulation to market forces and those that are a breath of spiritual

3. Gerardus van der Leeuw, *Liturgiek*, 2d ed. (Nijkerk: Callenbach, 1946), 9.

fresh air after years of stagnant, routine Christianity. Such is the nature of their discerning minds.

A Pastoral Heart

Second, they are people with a pastoral heart. They know the names, faces, and stories of people in the congregation. They can spot visitors and welcome them to the assembly. They know whom to ask to serve as Scripture reader or flute player or sound person—because they know both who has the necessary skills and for whom that participation would be a meaningful act of service.

This is possible because they are people of prayer. They are able to shepherd others because they constantly pray for them. One choir director I know prays for each member of her choir prior to rehearsal. Rehearsals are transformed from a joyless exercise in note learning to a profound opportunity for pastoral care. Perhaps because of this, these people know how to lead others in prayer. They choose texts and songs that lead people not to say, "I enjoyed that music" or "That was a neat song" but instead, "Through that song I confessed my sin to God" or "Through that song I was able to praise God more truly."

A Spirit of Joy

Third, pastoral worship leaders have a spirit of infectious joy. Romano Guardini, a twentieth-century German theologian, once observed, worship "has one thing in common with the play of the child and the life of art—it has no purpose, but it is full of profound meaning. It is not work, but play. . . . From this is derived its sublime mingling of profound earnestness and divine joyfulness."[4] Serving as a congregation's worship leader and planner is like entering a playground. There are all sorts of joyful discoveries awaiting you. There are mentors to learn from, new ideas to explore, creative gifts to develop.

What the church needs most is not another hymnal, a new sound system, a revised prayer book, or another set of published scripts. What the church needs most are discerning, prayerful, joyous people who treat their work as worship planners and leaders as a holy, pastoral calling.

---

4. Romano Guardini, *The Spirit of the Liturgy*, trans. Ada Lane (New York: Sheed & Ward, 1935), 181.

14

Celebrating the Christian Passover in Easter Worship

On April 24, 387 A.D., Augustine of Hippo, whom even Protestants call a saint, was baptized on Easter eve by Ambrose, the famous bishop of Milan, Italy. It must have been a dramatic moment. The baptismal font was a sunken octagonal pool twenty feet in diameter, built to look like a big tomb. Ambrose led the thirty-three-year-old Augustine down two steps into the water and asked, "Do you renounce Satan and all his works?" Augustine said that he did.

"Do you believe in God the Father?" Ambrose asked. Augustine replied, "I believe in God the Father Almighty, maker of heaven and earth."

Ambrose continued, "Do you believe in Jesus Christ?" Augustine answered, "I believe in Jesus Christ, his only begotten Son," continuing with the words of the Apostle's Creed, which was then a mere sixty-two years old but was already well established as an ideal summary of the Christian faith for new believers.

Then Ambrose immersed Augustine in the water, and Augustine quite literally "rose up" out of the tomb-like font, ready to participate in the Lord's Supper for the first time and to live his world-changing Christian life.

Dying and Rising with Christ

In Augustine's time, Easter was the single most important event of the year, far surpassing even Christmas, which appeared comparatively late on the church calendar. Part of the reason for this was that Easter was about more than a historical commemoration of an event in Jesus' life.

Easter worship not only recounted the resurrection story but also explored the world-changing personal and cosmic consequences of the resurrection. Early Christians celebrated Easter with a lot more than bonnets and bunnies, new clothes, and egg hunts. They celebrated by "drowning" and "resurrecting" groups of new Christians, who needed to die and rise in imitation of Christ.

The scriptural source for this baptismal practice is the mysterious but appealing pronouncement of the apostle Paul: "We have been buried with him by baptism into death, so that, just as Christ was raised from the dead by the glory of the Father, so we too might walk in newness of life" (Rom. 6:3–4 NRSV; see also Col. 2:11–12; 3:1–4).

With imaginations considerably flattened out by a data-centered, realistic worldview, we have a difficult time envisioning how we could have died and been buried nearly two thousand years before we were born. But this kind of time warp was a common part of Jewish worship. Especially at Passover, participants recounted, "In every generation each one of us should regard himself *as though he himself* had gone forth from Egypt." Likewise, in Exodus 13:8, Moses commanded, "On that day tell your son, 'I do this because of what the LORD did for me when *I came out* of Egypt.'" For generations after the exodus, the people were to celebrate the Passover as if they had been there.

Actually, we all have experienced this time warp, whether or not we have thought about it. Have you ever wondered about the accuracy of singing "Christ the Lord is risen *today*" or wondered why we bother to sing "Were you there when God raised him from the tomb?" This practice of placing ourselves in the same time zone as biblical events has a long history.

We do not understand Romans 6 to mean that we were physically and literally buried with Christ. Rather, the text helps us to see how Christ's history becomes our history—just as surely as the exodus was the source of identity for the Jewish people. Baptism gives us Jesus' death and resurrection as our primary identity. It makes those events the most important ones in our own spiritual biographies.

Indeed, the waters of baptism symbolize not only the washing of our sins (Acts 22:16) but also our dying and rising with Christ. Water both washes and drowns! That is why some early baptismal fonts looked liked bathtubs while others looked like tombs. The only requirement for each was that it had to contain enough water in which to drown. New learning about this history has led many recent Roman Catholic (and a few Reformed) theologians to conclude that the Baptists are on to something in their use of immersion.

The practice of Easter baptism also gave rise to Lent. Lent got its start not as an extended and somber meditation on the cross but rather as a time of year for a rigorous church membership or discipleship class called the "catechumenate." Candidates for baptism studied Scripture, the Apostles' Creed, the Lord's Prayer, and the Ten Commandments—the very kinds of things that the Heidelberg Catechism and other sixteenth-century catechisms would explain more than a millennium later.

The Christian Passover

So on Easter, early Christians celebrated Jesus' resurrection by baptizing new Christians and remembering their own death and resurrection with Christ. As they did so, one striking feature of their celebrations was the prominence of the Old Testament. In fact, some early worship handbooks recommend up to a dozen Old Testament readings for Easter worship.

The reason for this is that the New Testament uses Old Testament images and themes to explain the significance of Jesus' death and resurrection. Central among those images is the Passover.

Jesus' death and resurrection not only coincided with the Passover but also were interpreted in terms of the Passover. Scripture calls Jesus the "Lamb of God" (John 1:36) and even "the Passover lamb" (1 Cor. 5:7). And just as the Passover celebrated the deliverance of Israel from slavery to freedom, so Easter celebrates deliverance from sin to salvation, from death to life.

The link between Passover and Easter is so strong that many early Christians simply called Easter "the Christian Passover." That is why, in one of his Easter sermons, Augustine could simply announce, "This is our annual festival, our Paschal feast . . . as fulfilled for the people of the New Law by the sacrifice of our savior."[1]

Actually, it is not in any way surprising that they used the name "Christian Passover." Even today most languages use a derivative of the term *Passover*, such as the Italian *pasques*, French *pâcques*, Dutch *paasch*, and Spanish *pascua*. What is odd is that we use the term *Easter*, a term with secular or even pagan roots.

Easter Vigil

The highlight of the Christian Passover celebration in the early church was an extended Easter evening worship service that was in-

1. Philip T. Weller, *Selected Easter Sermons of Saint Augustine* (St. Louis: B. Herder, 1959), 82.

fluenced by themes and images of the Jewish Passover. The service was called Easter vigil.

Easter vigil began with a festive hymn of praise and the lighting of a candle that symbolized Christ as the light of the world. The service continued (often for many hours right into Easter morning!) with a long series of Old Testament Scripture readings and responses. The readings included some of the most theologically rich texts in the Old Testament, including the creation story, the exodus, the sacrifice of Isaac, and the valley of dry bones narrative. The texts were chosen to open up people's imaginations to wonder at the power and glory and saving purposes of God.

The service continued with the dramatic celebration of baptism, like Augustine's, and concluded with a majestic celebration of the Lord's Supper.

To many of us who are used to celebrating the Lord's Supper on Maundy Thursday or Good Friday, it may seem strange to celebrate the Lord's Supper on Easter. Isn't the Lord's Supper supposed to proclaim Jesus' death?

Many early Christians thought so, but they also noticed that the Supper was to be done "in remembrance of me," which they wisely interpreted as referring to Jesus' entire life—his birth, teaching, suffering, death, resurrection, and ascension. In their way of thinking, the Lord's Supper belonged both to Passion Week and to Easter. (If you have never sung both "When I Survey the Wondrous Cross" and "Christ the Lord Is Risen Today" during communion, you have something wonderful to look forward to!)

In the early church, this elaborate service summed up the whole Good Friday–Easter gospel. At first, most churches did not hold separate Good Friday and Easter services. Just as baptism celebrated a dying and rising, so too a single Easter service held together the themes of death and resurrection, sacrifice and deliverance, the image of Jesus as both lamb and shepherd, both servant and prince.

In holding these themes together, early Christians resisted the temptation to overemphasize either the cross or the resurrection at the expense of the other, which so easily leads to an imbalanced view of God and a skewed view of the Christian life. This is the kind of imbalance that many of us North American worshipers experience if we skip from the happy palm branches on Palm Sunday to the triumphant praise of Easter, without remembering the suffering and death of Christ (and acknowledging that we are called to suffer).

Later in his life, Augustine preached at many Easter baptism services. In one sermon, he advised, "Regard yourselves as delivered out of Egypt from a harsh servitude, where iniquity ruled over you, and as having passed through the Red Sea by baptism, in which you received the seal of Christ's bloody cross."[2]

Later, Martin Luther would write a stirring Easter hymn with the words "See, his blood now marks our door; faith points to it, death passes o'er, and Satan cannot harm us. Alleluia!"[3] Now, that is cause for rejoicing!

A Fifty-Day Celebration

Very quickly, early Christians discovered that such a momentous celebration could not and should not be confined to a single service. The Easter vigil itself spilled over into a congregational fellowship celebration. One ancient church order advised its congregations to conclude its long Easter vigil service with a church party: "Thereafter eat and make good cheer and rejoice and be glad, because the earnest of our resurrection, Christ, is risen"[4]—yes, a historical precedent for Easter pancake breakfasts and church potluck suppers.

Many early Christians, in fact, kept on celebrating for an entire season, fifty days in all, leading right up to Pentecost. Augustine himself described Eastertide as "a period, not of labor, but of peace and joy." He noted that in his church in North Africa they prayed standing—even during the "long prayer"—as a "sign of the resurrection." Throughout the season they also sang a deeply moving praise anthem, the "Alleluia," probably right after the Scripture reading, "to indicate that our future occupation is to be no other than the praise of God."[5] They did not tire of singing Easter hymns by the second Sunday after Easter!

By this approach, Easter was more than a daylong party to celebrate the end of Lent or the coming of spring. It was an extended church festival designed to anticipate the coming of the new kingdom. By some it was even viewed as more important than spring gardening, graduations, vacation, and whatever the ancients did while they waited for baseball to be invented.

Our Historical Treasure Chest

The early church was no golden age of Christianity; it was filled with just as many heresies, scoundrels, controversies, and supersti-

2. Ibid., 124.

3. Martin Luther, "Christ lag in Todesbanden," in *Psalter Hymnal* (Grand Rapids: CRC Publications, 1987), hymn no. 398.

4. *Didascalia Apostolorum*, trans. R. Hugh Connolly (Oxford: Clarendon Press, 1969), 190.

5. Augustine, "Letter 55 to Januarius," trans. Wilfrid Parson, in *Fathers of the Church*, vol. 12 (Washington, D.C.: Catholic University of America Press, 1951), 284–85.

tions as the churches of our own era. Still, the practical life of these Christians is a rich treasure chest that we can draw from as we try to grow in the grace and knowledge of our Lord Jesus Christ.

The witness of these Christians challenges us to go deeper in our experience of Easter, to go deeper than thinking of Easter as merely a celebration of the return of spring (a greater temptation to those of us in the Northern Hemisphere than to Christians in the southern half of the world), to go deeper than eggs and bunnies.

Recover the transforming news that Jesus' past resurrection dramatically transforms present and future reality. Delight in the knowledge that Jesus' death and resurrection are stamped on your personal spiritual biography. Relish the time warp when you sing, "Christ the Lord is risen today." Christ, our Passover Lamb, has been sacrificed. Therefore, let us keep the festival!

15

How Common Worship Forms Us for Our Encounter with Death

Facing Death Christianly

Death is humanity's ultimate riddle. We all live under a death sentence. Death is something we cannot elude. Yet unlike any other species, we can actually ponder our own death. We can choose how we will approach it.

And how we approach death is ultimately a deeply religious matter. Death awakens our hopes and fears for our ultimate destiny. Death challenges us to confront religious questions that we may never confront in the hustle and bustle of everyday life. The reality of death opens us up to wonder about the meaning and purpose of life, about reality itself, and ultimately about God.

Christianity is nothing if not a way of thinking about death. At the heart of the Christian religion is the history of a Jewish prophet from Nazareth who died and then, by the power of God's Spirit, conquered death. Everything in the Christian Scriptures either leads up to the account of this death and resurrection or reflects back on it. A good portion of the Christian Scriptures concerns the mystery that the death and resurrection of this Jewish prophet have everything to do with our own dying and living. The Christian tradition provides rich resources for facing death, for coming to understand what it might mean to "die well."

But dying well is not something that modern Christians easily discuss. We have quarantined death from our casual conversations. We do not speak of it easily at a dinner party (or even in church, for that matter). It is difficult to imagine waking up one morning and setting a goal of trying to do better at approaching our own death.

Even if we were to consider death more intentionally, few of us by our own resources or experiences could begin to know what it is to die well. But by listening to the voices of wise saints and the writers of Scripture, we can come to at least an approximate answer to this question. These voices suggest that our encounter with death is best when marked by candor, hope, and solidarity.

Dying well requires frank candor, with honest lament. Honesty demands that we acknowledge that death may be painful, fearsome, even violent, that it brings searing emotional pain. When life has been good, death brings a profound sense of loss. When life has been bad, death brings regret and remorse. Even when it seems a welcome end to months of suffering, death is still a decisive silence. Death is terrible business.

In its finality, death threatens to make life seem vain. "Vanity of vanities! All is vanity," says the ancient preacher (Eccles. 1:2 NRSV). The psalmist echoes, "Our years come to an end like a sigh" (Ps. 90:9 NRSV). Such finality tempts us to shrink back from this deep reality. We are inclined to deny it, euphemize it, or approach it with a resolute and heroic stoicism that pushes away its finality. We are inclined to rationalize our progress through the "stages of grief" rather than confront the finality of death itself.

In contrast, dying well involves lament—honest acknowledgment of the pain, fear, and broken relationships that death brings. In a gripping sermon offered just after he had completed an initial round of chemotherapy treatment for terminal cancer, Rev. James Van Tholen returned to the pulpit to speak these poignant words to his hushed congregation: "We can't ignore what has happened. We can rise above it; we can live through it; but we can't ignore it. If we ignore the threat of death as too terrible to talk about, then the threat wins. Then we are overwhelmed by it, and our faith doesn't apply to it. And if that happens, we lose hope."[1] Here is sober honesty in the face of death.

If honest lament is the first dimension in dying well, the second is its apparent opposite: resilient hope. Dying well, says Amy Plantinga Pauw, is dying with the assurance that death is not the final word.[2]

1. James Van Tholen, "Surprised by Death," *Christianity Today* (24 May 1999): 57–59.
2. Amy Plantinga Pauw, "Dying Well," in *Practicing Our Faith: A Way of Life for a Searching People,* ed. Dorothy Bass (San Francisco: Jossey-Bass, 1997), 163.

The whole of the Christian religion turns on the decisive Easter claim that Jesus Christ conquered death. Dying well means dealing with death redemptively, knowing that we follow the One who has conquered death. For Jesus and for us, the journey through death is still a way of Life, even a way of life abundant.

Christians throughout the centuries have testified to the power of this conquest. The apostle Paul taunted death: "Where, O death, is your victory? Where, O death, is your sting?" (1 Cor. 15:55). Third-century Christian leader Cyprian proclaimed, "Our brethren who have been freed from the world by the summons of the Lord should not be mourned, since we know that they are not lost but sent before; that in departing they lead the way."[3] Aleksandr Solzhenitsyn, when asked if he feared death, replied, "Absolutely not. . . . It will just be a peaceful transition. As a Christian, I believe that there is life after death, and so I understand that this is not the end of life. The soul has a continuation, the soul lives on. Death is only a stage, some would even say a liberation. In any case, I have no fear of death."[4] Likewise, while on his way to the gallows, Dietrich Bonhoeffer testified, "This is the end—for me the beginning of life."[5] These are testimonies that the day of death is also a day of birth, a *dies natalis,* the day of birth to new life. Dying well, then, is realizing that death is more like a door than a wall. To die well is to claim that in life and in death, we belong to God.

This message is a difficult one for our modern world to understand. Dying well confronts the suspicions of our age about the improbability of life hereafter. Yet as Dallas Willard reminds us, "Those who think it is unrealistic or impossible are more short on imagination than long on logic. They should have a close look at the universe God has *already* brought into being before they decide he could not arrange for the future life of which the Bible speaks."[6] Dying well is possible when we cultivate the imagination to sense the beauty and mystery of God's future. Dying well happens when a community faces death with hope—that combination of imagination and faith that turns our attention toward the future.[7]

Yet as with death's horror, so too with redemption's glory, we are tempted to pull back or turn away. Genuine hope, like the shining sun,

3. Cyprian, "Treatises: Mortality," in *The Fathers of the Church,* vol. 36 (New York: Fathers of the Church, 1958), 215.

4. Quoted in David Remnick, "The Exile Returns," *New Yorker* (14 February 1994): 83.

5. Dietrich Bonhoeffer, *Letter and Papers from Prison,* ed. Eberhard Bethge (New York: Macmillan, 1967), 225.

6. Dallas Willard, *Divine Conspiracy* (San Francisco: Harper, 1988), 85.

7. This theme is especially prominent in Lewis B. Smedes, *Keeping Hope Alive* (Nashville: Nelson, 2000).

may cause us to turn away, to shield ourselves from its luminous beauty and power. We prefer to focus instead on the trivialities of everyday life. Our lives remain centered on the mundane, the frivolous, the trifling. (And perhaps in some occasions, this is all that is possible.) Approaching death well, in contrast, involves focusing squarely on the ultimate reality of life beyond death.

So dying well is, in part, a matter of achieving an elusive alloy of sober honesty and resilient hope. The pairing of these virtues is lodged deep in the Scriptures of the Christian tradition. Psalm 103 reminds us that "as for mortals, their days are like grass; they flourish like a flower of the field; for the wind passes over it, and it is gone, and its place knows it no more" (vv. 15–16 NRSV) but then goes on to proclaim that "the steadfast love of the LORD is from everlasting to everlasting on those who fear him" (v. 17 NRSV). In Romans 8, Paul quotes an ancient proverb: "For your sake we face death all day long; we are considered as sheep to be slaughtered" (v. 36; cf. Ps. 44:22), but he nevertheless professes, "I am convinced that neither death nor life . . . will be able to separate us from the love of God that is in Christ Jesus our Lord" (vv. 38–39).

Remarkably, this alloy of honesty and hope is the source of great moral courage for many dying people. Dying well delivers us from insignificant worries, from cultivating peeves, and from nursing grudges. A vivid awareness of impending death leads moral people to confess their sin, forgive their enemies, and seek forgiveness from those whom they have wronged. Dying well heightens our sense of what is most important; it helps us distinguish the important from the trivial. It carries with it a deep awareness, a profound knowing of both human failing and divine grace. It gives us wisdom "to count our days" (Psalm 90). A dying person can help us sort out what is really important. Knowing that *we* will die helps with this too. In the words of Anne Lamott, "My deepest belief is that to live as if we're dying can set us free. Dying people teach you to pay attention and to forgive and not to sweat the small things."[8] And Willard suggests, "Jesus shows his apprentices how to live in the light of the fact that they will *never* stop living."[9]

Yet all of this may seem far too high-minded. How could anyone, even the best saint, achieve this moral triumph? Is dying well simply another massive moral achievement to which we must aspire?

Such questions bring us to the third necessary ingredient in the recipe for facing death well: solidarity. Dying well is not possible alone. "Dying well" is a verb that requires a plural subject. Dying is a social

8. Anne Lamott, *Bird by Bird* (New York: Pantheon Books, 1994), 125.
9. Willard, *Divine Conspiracy*, 86.

act. In the Christian community, one never dies alone (or at least the Christian community should not let this happen). The Christian community together faces death. Only the Christian *community*, with the strength and encouragement of God's Spirit, can ever be said to have faced death well.

Not that community is easily achieved in the face of death. Death isolates us. As Nicholas Wolterstorff points out, "Even shared grief isolates the sharers from each other. Though united in that we are grieving, we grieve differently."[10] Still, we grieve in isolation together. We learn that there is something far deeper that binds us together as a community. We are bound together as the sinews of the body of Christ.

In sum, the recipe for approaching death well includes three necessary ingredients: honest realism, resilient hope, stubborn solidarity. According to the Christian tradition, these three virtues have their ultimate source in the image of our solidarity or union with Jesus Christ. Among the richest of resources in the Christian tradition is the image that Christ's death and resurrection are intimately related to our own. Paul unfolds this mystery as he writes, "When you were buried with him in baptism, you were also raised with him through faith in the power of God, who raised him from the dead. And when you were dead in trespasses and the uncircumcision of your flesh, God made you alive together with him" (Col. 2:12–13 NRSV) and again, "For since death came through a human being, the resurrection of the dead has also come through a human being; for as all die in Adam, so all will be made alive in Christ" (1 Cor. 15:21–22 NRSV). Dying well (or to say it another way, "dying Christianly") is to frame our death in terms of a going down and a coming up, a dying and a rising, just like Jesus' dying and rising. Like Christ, we will all die. But in Christ we will one day rise again.

Mysteriously, the moment we sense our union with Christ, we sense that we are *already* dying and rising. We are dying to sin and rising to new life, dying to anger and fear, rising to hope and deep joy. Long before we encounter death, we have experiences that are analogous to death. Thus, this is a pattern of behavior that is not new at the time of death. It describes the entire Christian life.

Dying well is difficult business in contemporary North American culture. We isolate death from life in the institutional hallways of hospitals. We mark our journey with grief in neatly defined stages that measure our progress. We often approach our deathbed surrounded by more medical machinery than by family and close friends. We leave our death-marking rituals to entrepreneurs of the funeral indus-

---

10. Nicholas Wolterstorff, *Lament for a Son* (Grand Rapids: Eerdmans, 1987), 56.

try rather than to spiritual shepherds. Before we can bury our loved ones and attend to our grieving, we need to make hundreds of choices as consumers to an aggressive funeral industry.

For all the negative things we might say about our culture, it does provide resources that help us: the ability to travel to faraway places to be with those we love in time of death, medical palliative care measures that help us minimize human suffering, and hospice care, which can re-humanize how we respond to death. What we yet lack, and what we must recover, are the deep resources of the Christian tradition that can help us see death for what it is: an end to life on this earth and the day of birth to a new life with Christ.

Weekly Worship as a Matter of Life and Death

Especially in modern North American culture, this alloy of honesty, hope, and solidarity requires an adjustment in our thinking about death. It requires that we cultivate habits that will support us when death takes away our ability to think straight.

Gathering with other believers for common worship is a central source for cultivating and nurturing the practice of dying well. Common worship provides both the message and the motivation to explore the richness of the practices of the Christian life. Public worship—gathering in Jesus' name for prayer, proclamation, and sacramental celebration—shapes us into the kind of people who (together) can face death well. Whether a church is quiet or noisy, formal or informal, old or young, it is important that its worship teaches the skills to face death Christianly. Consider the connections between worship and dying in some common ways of practicing the daily, weekly, and annual rhythms of worship in many Christian communities.

In daily prayer, we acknowledge the gift of life and the possibility of death. In both ancient and contemporary patterns for daily prayer, morning is a time of thanksgiving for the gift of a new day of life. As morning breaks, our prayers thank the Giver of life for the new day. At night, we acknowledge our mortality; we declare that our help and hope is in the name of the Lord. Think of children who pray, "If I die before I wake, I pray the Lord my soul to take," or generations of Christians who have sung, "Teach me to live, that I may dread the grave as little as my bed; teach me to die, that so I may rise glorious at the judgment day."

Weekly Practices

The same life and death message is central in our weekly patterns of worship. In weekly liturgies or services of Word and sacrament, we bear witness to the gospel that sustains us in dealing with death.

In public worship, we gather as the people of God, the body of Christ. Worship begins when we leave our individual residences and "process"—whether by foot or by car—to a common meeting place. By coming together we testify to the world that we stand together to face its strongest assaults. Christian worship forges the community that makes dying well possible. Corporate worship is a weekly testimony to our common calling in community.

In public worship, we offer praise and thanksgiving. In our praise, we testify that God's love is stronger than death. We praise the Lord, who has both endured and conquered death. We express gratitude for the gift of life itself.

In public worship, we celebrate baptism. In baptism, we celebrate that Jesus' death and resurrection make a difference for our living and dying. We celebrate that we, as baptized people, share in Christ's death and resurrection. We acknowledge that, according to St. Paul, "We were therefore buried with him through baptism into death in order that, just as Christ was raised from the dead through the glory of the Father, we too may live a new life. If we have been united with him like this in his death, we will certainly also be united with him in his resurrection" (Rom. 6:4–5). We rehearse the truth that, in words frequently attributed to St. Francis of Assisi, "in baptism we have died the only death that matters."

In worship, we confess sin and hear words of divine grace. As we confess sin, we remind ourselves of our brokenness, our fallenness, our inevitable journey toward death. In honest penitence, we not only confess personal and corporate culpability but also lament brokenness in the world. We cultivate honest prayer before God's face in times of crisis. Then, as we hear divine words of grace or absolution, we are reminded of God's transformation of our journey toward death. We hear again the gospel news that grounds our hope. Confession of sin and words of divine grace, taken together, are a weekly way of cultivating both honesty and hope.

In worship, we hear God's Word read and proclaimed. We cultivate a habit that we will need on our deathbed—the habit of listening in faith to God's Word. A balanced diet of biblical readings offers us both honest assessments of life's limitations and thrilling and imaginative glimpses of God's grace. The biblical Psalms, which have long been at the heart of worship practices, volley between deep thanksgiving and bold and honest lament and provide for us a pattern that will sustain us as we deal with death. Gospel preaching cultivates our imagination to frame our own death in terms of Jesus' dying and rising.

In worship, we offer heartfelt intercessions. We pray for those facing death. We pray in thanksgiving for the lives of those who have gone before. We learn to pray familiar words, "Our Father in heaven, hallowed be thy name," words that will help us pray in those days in the valley of the shadow of death when words fail us.

In worship, we celebrate the Lord's meal, a proclamation of the Lord's death and a foretaste of the heavenly feasting. This meal—which is so physical and tangible—is a sign that the spiritual food of the gospel is meant for embodied people. Proclaiming the Lord's death forms us to know and believe that his death conquered death. Yearning for that heavenly feast helps us face death with hope.

In public worship, we accomplish many of these actions by singing. We sing to praise, to offer thanks, to confess sin, to speak our petitions. As we sing, we learn the songs that we will hum to ourselves in moments of deep despair. One wise pastoral musician said that every week as she leads congregational singing, she is rehearsing the congregation for a future funeral. Our songs of lament and hope form us as people of faith and hope.

Annual Practices

In addition to these weekly patterns, our annual and occasional celebrations drive the point home all the more. The annual pattern of the Christian year provides moments that transform our weekly worship and surprise us with facets of the gospel we might be inclined to forget or ignore.

Our worship during Advent looks forward with anticipation to the day of Jesus' coming. In Advent, we identify with the ancient people of Israel who longed for the Messiah, and we express our longing for the coming of the fullness of God's kingdom, a day when death shall be no more.

At Christmas and Epiphany—at precisely the most difficult time of the year for families who have lost loved ones—we declare the good news of the birth of the Christ child in Bethlehem. We sing praise to the One who is "risen with healing in his wings," the One "born that we no more may die."

Ash Wednesday liturgies remind us that we are made of dust and will return to dust. Ash Wednesday is a bold, honest confrontation with human mortality. To outsiders, Ash Wednesday is the least comprehensible of Christian celebrations. Why have a service that centers on this depressing message? Yet Ash Wednesday is an observance with deep biblical wisdom. It is a day when we live out the injunction of the psalmist: "Teach us to count our days" (Ps. 90:12 NRSV). It is a day that reminds us that God is with us when our lives turn to ashes.

On Good Friday, we continue the theme, remembering and commemorating the death of Jesus Christ. On Good Friday, we enter into the terror of death, hearing Jesus' words, "My God, my God, why have you forsaken me?" On Good Friday, we see that God does not sit back in splendid and distant isolation from death but enters into it, showing that dying will never have to be godless. In this commemoration of death, we sense the power and glory of life and sing, "What wondrous love is this, O my soul."

The annual cycle comes to a grand climax on Easter Sunday, the festival of resurrection. On that day we trumpet the good news that death has been conquered. Easter celebrations portray the life that invigorates all Christian living. We celebrate that we, like Jesus before us, will rise.

On Ascension Day, nearly forgotten in our culture, we celebrate that heaven is the place that can receive a human body, both Christ's and eventually ours. On this day, we celebrate that Jesus "goes to prepare a place for us" so that we will never again have to think of death as the last word.

On Pentecost, we recall the gift of God's Spirit, not only to the followers of Jesus but also to us. The same Spirit that breathed life into Jesus and raised him from the dead now breathes in us the breath of a life that will not end with physical death.

Then, in the darkening days of fall, All Saints' Day reminds us of those in the faith who have gone before us. We acknowledge that we stand united in one community, in the one body of Christ, with those who have died.

In these ways, our daily, weekly, and annual patterns bear witness to this blend of realism, hope, and solidarity that will help us face death. Occasionally, the routines of these patterns are broken open by experiences of life that are so spine-tingling, so extraordinary, so unforgettable that we are shocked or inspired into new and deeper ways of thinking Christianly about death. In one congregation, such a moment occurred when its pastor returned to preach after being stricken by inoperable cancer. In another, it occurred when a young child who was born with heart problems and who was expected to live for only a few months was presented for baptism. In another, it occurred when a very ill member of the congregation finally agreed to allow her priest to pray for her in public as one who was about to die.

Whether in these spine-tingling, once-in-a-lifetime moments of inspiration or in week-in, week-out liturgical routine, worship is a matter of life and death. It is a weekly rehearsal of honest realism and heavenly hope. Weekly worship is a disciplined and patterned piety that forms us as people of faith. Worship orients us to God. It straightens out our world again. It puts us in touch with God's redemptive activity. It connects us with Jesus Christ—his healing, his transforming power, his teaching, his guidance. Worship gives us an outlook, an attitude, a vantage point, a perspective, a lens through which to view the world that is rooted in Jesus' death and resurrection. Worship is an arena in which something is done to us, a place where God's Spirit is at work. The weekly pattern of common worship has the power to shape us into people with the gift or charism of approaching death well. Christian worship holds the Christlike pattern of dying and rising before us. It trains us to be always dying and rising. Christian worship is all about putting death in its place.

Barriers

But perhaps this high-minded rhetoric makes you skeptical. Can you remember when worship did something like that? Why is this power so rarely present in worship? Isn't this all saying too much for the power of worship? Doesn't the routine of worship dull us to its power? Even if worship is so powerful, how many worshipers are attentive to this death-defying message in worship's patterns?

These questions hint at two barriers that Christian communities must identify and combat. First, often worship services do not live up to their rich potential. We water them down. We make worship appealing or fun rather than an honest, hopeful approach to matters of death and life. For worship to have a life-changing message, that message has to be clear and apparent. The words spoken and sung, the gestures, and the space in which we gather actually have to make this possible.

This news that worship can prepare a community for approaching death well comes as a stern, prophetic warning to those who aspire to be priests and prophets in the Christian community. Plan and lead the liturgy in your community as if your life and death depended on it. The services you plan and lead have, by the Spirit's power, the ability to form in people the kind of realism, hope, and solidarity necessary to approach death well. We give our people the most satisfying spiritual food not when we withhold the depth of the gospel but when we deliver it. No saccharine substitute will suffice. The practice of dying well is corrupted and inhibited by sentimental worship that fails to be honest about life.

Second, even when worship is sufficiently honest, deep, and full of hope, worshipers often shrink back from its power. Our habit of shrinking back from both lament and hope is perpetuated by our pulling back from deep participation in worship. When honest words, gestures, and space are all in place, when they actually do set out to put death in its place, then participants must enter into their depth and power. We need to participate fully, consciously, actively. The power of worship to shape us into people who die well depends on our deep participation in worship. If singing hymns of praise about divine grace is to shape us, then we need to experience those songs not simply as nice songs but as luminous hymns of praise for the divine conquest of death. We can have perfect liturgy and imperfect worship. We can get the mechanics of worship right but miss its deep meaning and purpose. Worshipers need to be called not simply to participate in the mechanics of worship but to enter deeply into its purposes and meaning.

For this to happen, worship-oriented reflection and training need to be an enriching part of congregational life. In fact, one of the primary goals of a church education program should be to prepare us for honest and deep participation in worship. Without it, our worship can often become mundane or ritualistic. We need a language to awaken our imaginations so that we can enter into worship more fully.

When congregations do combat these tendencies—when our liturgies *are* honest and filled with Christ-centered hope and when we *do* participate in them fully, consciously, actively—then worship is a tremendous resource for enabling and inspiring us to approach death well. Dying well requires a vivid, biblically shaped imagination about the coming kingdom of God. Worship inspires and shapes that imagination. Dying well requires a community to nourish and sustain it. Worship forms that community. Dying well requires song to comfort and sustain it. Worship rehearses those songs. Dying well requires hope. Worship inspires it. Dying well requires honesty. Worship demands it. If we allow ourselves to slip into hyperbole, we might say that weekly worship is worthwhile if for no other reason than to help us prepare for death. Worship teaches us the rhythms of prayer that will help us to know what to do at the time of our death.

The Valley of the Shadow of Death

All of this happens in the ebb and flow of normal life. But what about our up close experience with death itself? What is worship's role in the valley of the shadow of death?

Here, too, Christian worship is a rich resource for forming us more deeply as people of faith, for helping us to experience the abundant life that is in Christ. Common worship can be the spiritual anchor that expresses our lament and hope during days of crisis, trauma, and our direct encounter with death.

Worship will inevitably have a different role in nearly every death, for no two deaths are alike. Some die after an extended battle with cancer, others after a sudden heart attack, senseless murder, or tragic accident. Some die as prominent members of a community, others in complete anonymity. Some die when another takes their life, others because they take their own. Some die as victims of warfare or terrorism, others at the hands of the death penalty. Some die in ripe old age, others in birth or infancy. Some die as strong Christian believers, others with great doubts and fears. Some die in families and communities of strong belief, others in families or communities with none. Some die in communities with rich and strong worship habits, some in communities with only weak worship habits.

In many and varied circumstances, both contemporary Christian communities and ancient Christian traditions provide beautiful examples of a host of practices that reflect and shape the faith of those facing death. These examples suggest the rich diversity of ways in which worship sustains and nurtures our faith in our encounter with death.

***

> I felt I couldn't pray. My ability to pray left me that day I heard my diagnosis. Yet I knew that my community of faith was praying for me. When my prayers failed, theirs came through. I listened to recordings of worship services in our congregation. As I heard the Psalms being sung, as I heard my name mentioned in the intercessions, I became profoundly grateful for the privilege of being a part of the Christian community.[11]

Dying well does not mean that we rely on the strength of our own prayers. Many fear dying more than death—the uncertainty, the suffering, the loss of control, the fear of being a burden to others, the loneliness. Christian worship, done together, is an act of protest against the loneliness that inhabits the chemotherapy room, the radiation chamber, the AIDs care facility. Those who bring comfort and encouragement and become a community of prayer are Christ's hands, Christ's feet, and Christ's heart made present to those who grieve. This ministry of encouragement and prayer happens in myriad ways, in pastoral visits by ordained clergy, in informal times of prayer with fellow Christians, in formal prayers in public worship for those who are facing death, and in quiet conversations with hospital chaplains. In each case, it is prayer and worship, offered together, that provide strength and encouragement for the sick and dying and for their families and friends.

***

> For our family, the grace to face death came from an unexpected gift. The doorbell rang. When we answered, we found no one there—only a gift basket, a gift given for dying and mourning people. Mom was dying of cancer, and the stranger who came left a gift whose simplicity would have blinded the unsuspecting to its power. The gift was a simple loaf of bread and a bottle of wine. The stranger was our pastor. And the gift was the bearer of God's grace. Our eating and drinking of that gift was not a sacrament in the strict sense. There was no formal liturgy, no large gathered community, no solemn words. But we ate and drank with a

---

11. This example is adapted from a response to a class discussion about this topic.

deep sacramental imagination. We tasted those gifts while sitting around the fireplace late one evening. Stories poured forth about our life with Mom. The piano resounded with hymns—old and new—that sang Mom's faith. Our feasting in this moment of life and death was an echo of the same songs, the same eating and drinking that we shared in our congregation—even as the church's feasting is an echo of another heavenly feast (Revelation 19). Without knowing it, regular participation in the church's sacrament prepared us for this evening of sacramental sharing. Our pastor was a wise caregiver.[12]

Not every mourning family would find such meaning in everyday bread and wine, of course. But many families of faithful Christian people would. They have been prepared for their encounter with death through faithful participation in communities of worship. If such meaning is not found in the form of bread and wine, then perhaps it is found in the regular use of the Lord's Prayer, a hymn of faith, a Scripture reading, or one of worship's symbols. These tangible human cultural products, made holy by their use in worship, shape our imaginations in our encounter with death. They help us see death through the lens of the Christian faith. They anchor us in a tradition of faith that is stronger than any individual, sturdier than any individual congregation.

***

A few years ago I stood with my wife and her family at the bedside of her dying father in a nursing home. He had suffered a massive stroke and was now slowly sinking toward death. While his labored breathing grew shallower and more infrequent, we waited, almost silent, for death to come. As is usually the case in such situations, death arrived on silent feet, with no fanfare. One moment there was a barely alive person, the next, a lifeless body. The moment was not less awesome for its near imperceptibility. After a few moments of silence, tears and hugs, and a prayer, we notified the nurse and began to make some preliminary preparations. We were informed that the funeral director would not arrive for an hour or two. As we waited, our brother-in-law, who is Russian Orthodox, suggested that we follow his tradition, which prescribes that at the moment of death a continuous reading of the Psalms commence. So someone picked up Dad's tattered Bible and began to read Psalm 1. And we continued to read one psalm after another, passing the Bible around the group. At first I assumed that this was merely a pious way of passing time. But very soon we were all powerfully drawn into the words of the psalms as they began to reflect on Dad's life, his faith, his struggles, his destiny. It was almost uncanny how each new psalm led us through the memories and emotions that we needed to explore as we began that long process of grieving. I think we made it to Psalm 40 or so by the

12. Ibid.

time the funeral director finally arrived, and we left off the reading with
some reluctance.[13]

For all the resources in Christian prayer books and devotional
guides, much of what happens in the face of death is improvised. Perhaps the improvised rituals will include prayer, perhaps the singing of
hymns, perhaps the reading of Scripture, perhaps informal eulogies
and remembrances. Perhaps the service will be a death vigil in a hospice care facility, a hospital, or a rest home—an action that will hu-
manize and warm these institutions of care. Perhaps the ritual will be
a time of prayer in a funeral home prior to a time of visitation with
family and friends. Perhaps it will come in the workplace, at home, at
a school. Perhaps it will occur with the full awareness (or even participation) of the one who is dying. Perhaps it will occur several hours after death has visited. In these times, we together claim God's promises
on behalf of both the dying and the mourning—even if the dying or
many of the grieving cannot express these prayers or accept the peace
that comes with praying them.

Such improvised practices have a long history in the Christian tradition. In the early church, liturgical handbooks and church orders
called for common prayer in the hours that led to death and in the
time that intervened between death and burial, as well as at the
burial itself. Christians today who long for rich and honest patterns
of prayer can find deep resources in the practices of the earliest
Christians.

These improvised rituals may well be the occasions of rich experiences of God's grace. Perhaps formerly estranged family members will
reconcile. Perhaps a parent or grandparent will comfort a young
child. Perhaps family members will find deep meaning in helping to
plan the improvised liturgy or to choose hymns for the funeral. Perhaps the occasion will evoke memories that help everyone sense the
giftedness of life, the ways in which the dying one was, however imperfectly, an image bearer of God.

But not every death will present opportunities for such prayer. For
many, there is neither the pain nor the opportunity of these last moments. Deaths that are premature, sudden, or accidental deprive us of
opportunities to say good-bye and also deprive the living and the dying of the opportunity to worship together. In these circumstances,
worship's role is more dramatic.

***

13. Leonard VanderZee, *In Life and in Death* (Grand Rapids: CRC Publications,
1992), 11.

> I dreaded the prospect, but the funeral gave rest to my soul. It did not console me for Eric's absence. Instead it sank deep into me the realization that my son's death is not all there is. . . . It was a liturgy which both thanked God for the presence of Eric among us and expressed our grief upon his no longer being present. It sang of the hope of resurrection. . . . It was a liturgy in which not only words, but also actions and symbols, spoke. . . . We celebrated the Eucharist, that sacrament of God's participation in our brokenness.[14]

Funerals help us, even force us, to mark death *together*. Even for those who are inclined to grieve in solitary silence, the funeral is a social act. In one large city, a quiet and retiring convenience store worker died unexpectedly. Her coworkers came to her funeral, fearing that they would be the only ones there. They were surprised when dozens of people arrived, all members of her church community. They had never imagined that people from so many different walks of life would love one another enough to interrupt their busy schedules to attend a funeral. In this urban world of individual survival, this expression of Christian solidarity was a bold witness to the power of the gospel. For Christian congregations, this sense of solidarity is even stronger when services are held in the normal place for worship rather than in a funeral home or care facility.

At their best, funerals create space for honest lament. They refuse to allow us to deny or neglect death. They refuse to allow us to quell our grief in favor of stoic indifference. They name death as the alien enemy it is. At their best, funerals do not pretend to quiet grief—only the death of those who mourn will end the grieving.[15] But funerals can begin the long process of offering this grief to God. They reinforce the important pattern of bringing all our needs, hopes, and fears to God in prayer.

Funerals also solemnize death—or rather, they solemnize *life*, the life of an image bearer of God. Funerals are events that signal the gravity and significance of the life that was lived. Eulogies provide opportunities to remember the deceased with honesty and thanksgiving. Liturgical planning by the family offers ways of taking ownership of and personalizing the service, giving it a strong sense of identity.

Funerals also give occasion for expressing deep Christian joy and hope. Rites that are sober can still be joyful. The best funerals are not obsessed with divine judgment (as were so many rites in the Middle Ages) or saccharine sentimentality (as are many contemporary North American funerals). Rather, funerals help us tell the difference between surface happiness and deep joy—proving that one can be simul-

14. Wolterstorff, *Lament for a Son*, 38.
15. Ibid., 15.

taneously full of sorrow and full of deep joy. At their best, funerals live up to their name in many recent prayer books as a "service of witness to the resurrection." They are central occasions for proclaiming the heart of the Christian gospel and for offering that good news to all who are present.

Several Christian practices—each practiced by some though not all Christian communities—bear witness to the resurrection. A baptismal pall (cloth covering of the casket) reminds the community that the one who has died lies in union with Christ in baptism. The Lord's Supper may be celebrated as a witness to the resurrection. Scripture is prominent. Sermons or spoken meditations center on the promises of the gospel of Jesus Christ. A candle may be lit as a sign of Christ's light in a world without light. The music may include not only psalms of lament but also hymns of Easter praise. In these ways, funerals draw on resources from deep within the Christian tradition. The earliest Christians announced the hope of the resurrection with every detail of their observance. The deceased was dressed in white, not black. The funeral processions were held during the day, not at night. Music included not only dour lamentations but also joyful alleluias.

In sum, funerals are the place where we can be most intentional about re-framing death, about naming death as dying and rising with Christ. To accomplish this, funerals involve multiple tasks. As we gather, we thank God for life, we remember the life of the one who has died, we remember and proclaim the gospel of Christ—the foundation of our hope—we pray for the grieving, we begin to heal the broken spirits of those who have gathered, we announce the good news of the gospel and invite all who have gathered to drink from the living water of Christ, and we experience the profound solidarity of being united as members of Christ's body. Just as a woven tapestry is enriched by the presence of multiple strands, so too a funeral is enriched when each of these tasks is highlighted and experienced.

Here again, these observations challenge all who plan and lead funeral services to attend to the rich opportunities for pastoral care in their work. Pastors, chaplains, musicians, artists, and other leaders give the Christian community their greatest gifts when they help us pray honestly and hopefully in the face of death. The Christian community has the duty to insist, "Do not give us sentimental words. Do not obscure the gospel of Jesus Christ. Do not simplify the gospel message. Do not minimize the life of this image bearer of God. Do not carry out your work without care." Worship in the face of death cannot transform us if it shrinks back from honesty—or from honest hope. Wise pastoral leaders might also provide death education in the midst of normal congregational life, suggesting guidelines for funeral services that will help families enhance rather than obscure the gospel-proclaiming character of Christian funerals as they make the many decisions necessary in times of death. No doubt, this is formidable work. What comforts some may unnerve or unsettle others. Yet without thoughtful leadership, it is quite possible for a given Christian community to cultivate, by neglect, an uncaring, callous approach that denies the gospel.

This important pastoral work is an opportunity to strengthen not just the family and close friends of those who grieve but also the entire Christian community. If a community prays thoughtfully at the occasion of death, all of its members are given resources for living with honesty and hope in their own confrontation with death. These occasions build up the spiritual muscle that communities will need to face death again. For the living, there is no better antidote to arrogant, sloppy living than intentional visits to a funeral home, a walk through a cemetery, or attendance at a funeral. Rule number one for thoughtful living: Do not miss a funeral.

***

> For me, the strength to carry on came from the strength of week-in, week-out worship services in the months following the funeral. Every week, I came into worship with death on my mind. Worship showed me the larger picture. In quiet moments over the next year, worship surprised me with new ways of approaching my deep, deep grief. I saw the Lord's Supper as a feast shared with all God's children both now and those who have gone before.[16]

The funeral does not mark the end of grieving. Nor does it mark the end of the relationship between public worship and the practice of dying well. Worship remains crucial for sustaining the life of those who grieve. Soon after the funeral, liturgies are filed away, and the community returns to its routine patterns of worship. Those who grieve may experience in this routine—in the gathering, confessing, hearing, eating, dispersing—new and powerful signs of grace. For some, it may be the singing of a favorite hymn. For others, it may be hearing a text that was read at a funeral service of a loved one. For another, it may be the tasting of the cup and bread, signs of Christ's brokenness and divine grace. Thoughtful worship leaders enhance this potential by regularly praying for those who mourn and by deliberately looking for ways to link worship practices with the experience of mourning and the ministry of consolation.

Special practices may enhance this. In one congregation, it may be naming and remembering during an All Saints' Day service or a ser-

16. This example is adapted from a student's response to a class discussion about this topic.

vice based on Hebrews 11–12 those who have died. In another, it may be remembering the anniversaries of death with prayer. In another, it may be prayer during the holiday season for those who are grieving. In another, it may be "Homecoming Sunday," in which a community gathers to renew friendships and remember those in the community who have died. Each of these small practices cultivates the gift of remembrance that dignifies the lives of those who have gone before us and expresses our gratitude for their presence among us.

In contrast, others who grieve may experience worship as arid and empty—perhaps for a season, perhaps for years. This is especially true if worship fails to address matters of life and death, if it fails to express honest lament, if it fails to give rise to genuine Christ-centered hope. But if worship faces squarely the truth and joy of the gospel, if it rehearses the life-changing events of God's history of the world revealed in Christ, if it assumes that the ultimate power of worship is not in the creativity or genius of the worship leaders but rather in the Spirit of God, then God's people may rest assured that worship is an arena in which God's Spirit moves to draw people closer, to lift their hearts, to provide comfort and encouragement.

In all these ways and in all these varied circumstances, common worship provides resources to enable people to approach death Christianly. At its best, worship is immersed in the death and resurrection of Jesus Christ and in our union with Christ in that death and resurrection. Left to our own devices, we are inclined to experience death as the final word, to set our sights on the immediate challenges of living in the wake of death. Public worship in the face of death "sets our sights on things above." It puts us in touch with the divine pattern of dying and rising.

In this age of self-improvement, we may be tempted to ask, "How can I die well?" Dying well, after all, could be depicted as the ultimate human achievement. It is true that dying well requires every ounce of emotional, physical, and spiritual strength we can muster. But finally, it requires more than we can offer. Even the most saintly people can cower in the face of death. Dying well requires divine grace. We praise God that this task of dying well has already been done for us—when Jesus died our death. Dying well is less an accomplishment we achieve than a gift we receive. It is a Pentecost virtue, a gift of the Spirit, and so, something for which we should pray. And one way in which the Spirit helps us prepare (together) to die well is by gracing us with power and beauty in common worship. If our liturgical patterns constantly remind us of dying and rising with Christ, then when we come to the day of death, we will know what to do; we will be well rehearsed. That is, in part, how death loses its sting.

Other Worship-Related Writings by John D. Witvliet

Academic Writings

"The Anaphora of St. James." In *Essays on Early Eastern Eucharistic Prayers*, edited by Paul Bradshaw, 153–72. Collegeville, Minn.: Liturgical Press, 1997.

"At Play in the House of the Lord: Why Worship Matters." *Books & Culture* (November/December 1998): 22–25.

"Beyond Style: Rethinking the Role of Music in Worship." In *The Conviction of Things Not Seen: Worship and Ministry in the Twenty-First Century*, edited by Todd E. Johnson, 67–81. Grand Rapids: Brazos Press, 2002.

"The Contemporary Church, Reformed Theology, and the Practice of Public Worship." *Pro Rege* 25, no. 3 (April 1997): 1–14.

"The Doctrine of the Trinity and the Theology and Practice of Christian Worship in the Reformed Tradition." Ph.D. diss., University of Notre Dame, 1997.

"For Our Own Purposes: The Use of the Social Sciences in Liturgical Studies." *Liturgy Digest* 2, no. 2 (spring/summer 1995): 6–35.

"Liturgical Music in the Reformed Tradition Worldwide," with Emily Brink. In *Christian Worship in Reformed Churches Past and Present*, edited by Lukas Vischer, 324–47. Grand Rapids: Eerdmans, 2003.

"Metaphor in Liturgical Studies: Lessons from Philosophical and Theological Theories of Language." *Liturgy Digest* 4, no. 1 (1997): 7–45.

"Toward a Liturgical Aesthetic: An Interdisciplinary Review of Aesthetic Theory." *Liturgy Digest* 3, no. 1 (winter 1996): 4–86.

"Training Church Musicians as Pastoral Musicians." In *Musicians for the Churches: Reflections on Vocation and Formation*, edited by Margot E. Fassler, 17–22. Yale Studies in Sacred Music. New Haven: Yale Institute of Sacred Music, 2001.

Worship in Medieval and Early Modern Europe: Change and Continuity in Religious Practice, edited with Karin Maag. Notre Dame: University of Notre Dame Press, forthcoming.

Pastoral Writings

"Beyond Style: Asking Deeper Questions about Worship." *Congregations* (July/August 2001): 19–21, 35.

"A Child Shall Lead: Catch the Vision for Children as Full Participants in Worship." *The Chorister* 50, no. 8 (February 1999): 16–17.

A Child Shall Lead: Children in Worship. A Sourcebook for Christian Educators, Musicians, and Clergy. Garland, Tex.: Choristers Guild, 1999.

"Contemporary Worship Comes of Age." *Reformed Worship* 39 (March 1996): 45–46.

"Hymns for December, January, and February." *Reformed Worship* 25 (September 1992): 23–28.

"A Journey with Worshiping Communities around the World: Prayers and Songs for World Communion Sunday." *Reformed Worship* 48 (June 1998): 45–46.

"The Joy of Singing in Canon: Turning the Congregation into the Choir." *Reformed Worship* 30 (December 1993): 40–44.

"Looking Back, Looking Ahead at Changes in Worship." *Reformed Worship* 38 (January 1996): 4–6.

"Planning Primer: A Checklist for Worship Planners." *Reformed Worship* 51 (March 1999): 28–29.

"Series for the Season: Worship—Taking a Closer Look." *Reformed Worship* 56 (June 2000): 30–44.

"Singing Scripture: Suggestions for Singing the Readings for Advent and Christmas." *Reformed Worship* 25 (September 1992): 29–33.

So You've Been Asked . . . to Lead a Worship Service. Worship Leader Pamphlet Series. Grand Rapids: CRC Publications, 1999.

So You've Been Asked . . . to Plan a Worship Service. Worship Leader Pamphlet Series. Grand Rapids: CRC Publications, 1999.

So You've Been Asked . . . to Sing a Solo. Worship Leader Pamphlet Series. Grand Rapids: CRC Publications, 1996.

"A Survey of Recent Changes in Christian Worship in North America." *The Chorister* 49, no. 2 (August 1997): 12–14.

"Table Blessings." *Assembly* 22, no. 2 (May 1996): 714–15.

"Talk before You Call: Questions about Worship for Search Committees and Pastors." *Reformed Worship* 29 (September 1993): 40–42.

"The Virtue of Liturgical Discernment." *Christian Courier* (31 May 1999): 12–13.

"Waiting the Coming Day: The Easter Vigil Service." *Reformed Worship* 22 (December 1991): 22–28.

"Worship Services for the Christian Year." In *Complete Library of Christian Worship*, vol. 5, edited by Robert E. Webber, 137–45, 201–5, 253–55, 261–66, 297–301, 318–22, 349–51, 383–90, 397–401, 427–32. Nashville: Abbot-Martyn Press, 1994.

"Worship Transformed: A Time of Change for Choral Musicians in Christian Churches." *Choral Journal* 38, no. 8 (March 1998): 55–62.

Index